# The Making of International Environmental Treaties

# The Making of International Environmental Treaties

## Neoliberal and Constructivist Analyses of Normative Evolution

Gerry Nagtzaam

*Lecturer, Faculty of Law, Monash University, Australia*

**Edward Elgar**

Cheltenham, UK • Northampton, MA, USA

Published by
Edward Elgar Publishing Limited
The Lypiatts
15 Lansdown Road
Cheltenham
Glos GL50 2JA
UK

Edward Elgar Publishing, Inc.
William Pratt House
9 Dewey Court
Northampton
Massachusetts 01060
USA

A catalogue record for this book is available from the British Library

Library of Congress Control Number: 2009936764

Mixed Sources
Product group from well-managed forests and other controlled sources
www.fsc.org Cert no. SA-COC-1565
© 1996 Forest Stewardship Council
FSC

ISBN 978 1 84844 422 5

Typeset by Cambrian Typesetters, Camberley, Surrey
Printed and bound by MPG Books Group, UK

# Contents

# Foreword

Since the end of the Cold War, neoliberal institutionalist scholarship on global environmental regimes has mushroomed. So too has constructivist scholarship on the role of norms in international politics. However, until this book arrived on the scene, no one has sought to set these interest-based and norm-based approaches against each other in order to test their ability to illuminate why and how different environmental norms take hold in some regimes and not others. Why do some regimes seek to preserve and protect some parts of nature *from* development, while others seek to wisely manage certain parts of nature *for* development? Why do other regimes allow the reckless exploitation of nature without accounting for the consequences? In this book, Gerald Nagtzaam seeks to track the fate of the three over-arching norms of environmental politics – preservation, conservation and exploitation. He shows how the international political battles to shape the international regimes on whales, mining in Antarctica and tropical timber all involved a tussle between these competing environmental norms. They also provide excellent case studies through which to assess rationalist and constructivist approaches to understanding international environmental regimes. In the course of providing a meticulous and detailed history of each of these regimes, Nagtzaam poses some hard questions for both neoliberal institutionalists and constructivists. In the end, he gives two cheers for constructivism (for the whaling and Antarctic regimes) and one cheer for neoliberalism (for the tropical forest regime). He also shows that it is not possible to give 'three cheers' for an integrated rationalist/constructivist explanation, given the incommensurability of each approach in terms of their unit of analysis, epistemology and method, but that working with both approaches, rather than just one, does shed more light on the complex interplay between norms and interests. This book is essential reading for anyone interested in whales, Antarctica, tropical forests or regime theory.

Robyn Eckersley
March 2009
Melbourne

# Acknowledgements

The publishers wish to thank the following who have kindly given permission for the use of copyright material:

Greenhouse Press for Introduction: 'Environmental Exploitation: An Analysis and Taxonomy', *Ecopolitics Online Journal*, **1** (2), Autumn/Winter 2008, pp. 32–42;
The William and Mary Law School for Chapter 4: 'The International Whaling Commission and the Elusive Great White Whale of Preservationism', *William and Mary Environmental Law and Policy Review*, **3** (2), 2009, pp. 375–447.
The *Journal of South Pacific Law* for Chapter 5: 'The International Tropical Timber Organisation and Conservationist Forestry Norms: A bridge too far', *Journal of South Pacific Law*, **13** (2) 2009.

Every effort has been made to trace all the copyright holders but if any have been inadvertently overlooked the publishers will be pleased to make the necessary arrangements at the first opportunity.

This book could not have been written without the help of three special women. For Monica who lit the way, for Robyn who guided me along the path and for Iva who supported me every step.

# List of abbreviations

| | |
|---|---|
| AAC | Annual Allowable Cut |
| ACF | Australian Conservation Foundation |
| ASOC | Antarctic and Southern Ocean Coalition |
| ATCM | Antarctic Treaty Consultative Meeting |
| ATCP | Antarctic Treaty Contracting (or Consultative) Parties |
| ATS | Antarctic Treaty System |
| BWU | Blue Whale Unit |
| CCAMLR | Commission for the Conservation of Antarctic Marine Living Resources |
| CCAMLR | Convention on the Conservation of Antarctic Marine Living Resources |
| CCAS | Convention on the Conservation of Antarctic Seals |
| CEC | Commission of the European Communities |
| CEP | Committee of Environmental Protection |
| CLASP | Centre for Law and Social Policy |
| COMNAP | Committee of Managers of National Antarctic Programmes |
| CRAMRA | Convention on the Regulation of Antarctic Mineral Resource Activities |
| EAMREA | Environmental Impact Assessment of Mineral Exploration/Exploitation in Antarctica |
| ECOSOC | Economic and Social Council of the United Nations |
| EEZ | Exclusive Economic Zone |
| EIA | Environmental Investigation Agency |
| ENGO | Environmental Non-governmental Organization |
| FAO | Food and Agriculture Organization |
| FoE | Friends of the Earth |
| FSC | Forest Stewardship Council |
| GATT | General Agreement on Tariffs and Trade |
| GWG | Guidelines Working Group |
| HST | Hegemonic Stability Theory |
| IBRD | International Bank for Reconstruction and Development |
| ICES | International Council for the Exploration of the Seas |
| ICJ | International Court of Justice |
| ICRW | International Convention for the Regulation of Whaling |
| ICSU | International Council of Scientific Unions |

| | |
|---|---|
| IFAW | International Fund for Animal Welfare |
| IFF | Intergovernmental Forum on Forests |
| IGY | International Geophysical Year |
| IIED | International Institute for Environment and Development |
| IMF | International Monetary Fund |
| IO | International Organization |
| IOC | Intergovernmental Oceanographic Commission |
| IPC | Integrated Program for Commodities |
| IR | International Relations |
| ITC | International Trade Centre |
| ITTA | International Tropical Timber Agreement |
| ITTC | International Tropical Timber Council |
| ITTO | International Tropical Timber Organization |
| IUCN | International Union for the Conservation of Nature (World Conservation Union) |
| IWC | International Whaling Commission |
| LDC | Lesser Developed Country |
| MEA | Multilateral Environmental Agreement |
| MMPA | Marine Mammal Protection Act |
| MSY | Maximum Sustainable Yield |
| NAMMCO | North Atlantic Marine Mammals Commission |
| NATO | North Atlantic Treaty Organization |
| NGO | Non-governmental Organization |
| NMP | New Management Procedure |
| OFI | Oxford Forestry Institute |
| OPEC | Organization of the Petroleum Exporting Countries |
| PEPAT | Protocol on Environmental Protection to the Antarctic Treaty (Madrid Protocol) |
| RMP | Revised Management Procedure |
| RMS | Revised Management Scheme |
| SCAR | Scientific Committee for Antarctic Research |
| SFM | Sustainable Forest Management |
| SI | Survival International |
| TFAP | Tropical Forestry Action Plan |
| TNC | Transnational Corporation |
| TRADA | Timber Research and Development Association |
| UN | United Nations |
| UNCED | United Nations Conference on Environment and Development |
| UNCLOS | United Nations Convention on the Law of the Sea |
| UNCTAD | United Nations Conference on Trade and Development |
| UNDP | United Nations Development Programme |
| UNEP | United Nations Environmental Programme |

| | |
|---|---|
| UNFF | United Nations Forum on Forests |
| UNGA | United Nations General Assembly |
| WCW | World Council of Whalers |
| WILPF | Women's International League for Peace and Freedom |
| WMO | World Meteorological Organization |
| WRI | World Resources Institute |
| WRM | World Rainforest Movement |
| WTO | World Trade Organization |
| WWF | World Wildlife Fund/World Wide Fund for Nature |

# Introduction*

> Is there not the Earth itself, its forests and waters, above and below the surface? These are the inheritance of the human race . . . What rights, and under what conditions, a person shall be allowed to exercise over any portion of this common inheritance cannot be left undecided. No function of government is less optimal than the regulation of these things, or more completely involved in a civilized society. (John Stuart Mill, *On Liberty* (1859))

Norms or '. . . shared expectations about appropriate behaviour held by a collectivity of actors . . .' have been central to the study of domestic politics for over two millennia.[1] Describing and explaining how these norms set societal standards (for example, order and justice) have occupied the minds of countless political analysts, and understanding their role is considered basic to developing robust domestic political theories. The antecedents of the term 'norm' derive from sociological literature and are defined in the sociological domain as 'rules and expectations by which a society guides the behaviour of its members'.[2] Such norms were generally considered to be of two types – either prescriptive, telling us what we can do; or proscriptive, telling us what we cannot.[3]

In the political sphere, there is a legacy of theorizing about norms in global politics dating from Christian theology, Immanuel Kant and the scholars from the English School of International Relations.[4] However, the study of international or global norms[5] has traditionally been relegated to the periphery of

* An earlier version of this chapter appeared as 'Environmental Exploitation: An Analysis and Taxonomy', *Ecopolitics Online Journal* 1, no. 2, Autumn/Winter (2008): 32–42, Greenhouse Press.

1 J.T. Checkel, 'Norms, Institutions and National Identity in Contemporary Europe', *International Studies Quarterly* 43 (1999): 83.

2 Moshe Hirsch, 'Compliance with International Norms in the Age of Globalization: Two Theoretical Perspectives', in *The Impact of International Law on International Cooperation*, ed. Eyal Benvenisti and Moshe Hirsch (Cambridge: Cambridge University Press, 2004), 171 n. 21.

3 Ibid.

4 R. Price, 'Moral Norms in World Politics', *Pacifica Review* 9, no. 1 (1997): 45.

5 International or global norms can be defined as 'those expectations of appropriate behavior which are shared within international society or within a particular

study undertaken by International Relations (IR) theorists.[6] The few theorists who studied norms dismissed them as mere shadows cast by interests, or convenient rationalizations utilized by statesmen.[7] Today, however, across a range of theoretical and methodological approaches, scholars of all persuasions are interested in how norms emerge, evolve and decline (Axelrod and O'Keohane, 1985; Bernstein, 2001; Finnemore and Sikkink, 1998).[8] The once controversial idea, that norms 'matter', is now accepted as a matter of course by all global theorists except the most recalcitrant of neorealists.[9]

At the global level, norms can be found operating in international regimes of all persuasions and the development of a more nuanced understanding of their functions has provided a clearer picture of how regimes evolve.[10]

Robert Keohane, building on the earlier work of John Ruggie and Ernst Haas, has argued that within a regime:

> Norms contain somewhat clearer injunctions to members about legitimate and illegitimate behaviour, still defining responsibilities and obligations in relatively

---

subsystem of international society by states, its constituent entities'. Henning Boekle, Volker Rittberger and Wolfgang Wagner, 'Norms and Foreign Policy: Constructivist Foreign Policy Theory', *Tubingen Working Papers* 34a (1999): 13.

6 For the purposes of this book, I distinguish between ethics which traditionally has been analysed as an individual phenomenon, and instead focus on examining the 'sociology of norms'. H. Shue, 'Ethics, the Environment and the Changing International Order', *International Affairs* 71, no. 3 (1995): 453.

7 Werner Levi, 'The Relative Irrelevance of Moral Norms in International Politics', *Social Forces* 44, no. 2 (1965): 233.

8 J.W. Legro, 'Which Norms Matter? Revisiting the "Failure" of Internationalism', *International Organization* 51, no. 1 (1997): 33.

9 J.T. Checkel, 'International Norms and Domestic Politics: Bridging the Rationalist–Constructivist Divide', *European Journal of International Relations* 3, no. 4 (1997): 473.

10 Stephen Krasner has defined regimes as 'sets of implicit or explicit principles, norms, rules and decision-making procedures around which actors' expectations converge in a given area of international relations'. Stephen D. Krasner, *International Regimes*, Cornell Studies in Political Economy (Ithaca, NY: Cornell University Press, 1983), 2. The regime definition promulgated by Krasner is not without its detractors. O'Riordan and Jordan (1995) are critical of the distinction in that it '. . . is rather broad and ambiguous in delimiting whether phenomena fall under the rubric of international regimes in empirical research. It includes both formal governmental organizations (such as the various United Nation agencies) and regularized forms of policy coordination on a specific issue.' Ian H. Rowlands, 'Classical Theories of International Relations', in *International Relations and Global Climate Change*, ed. U. Luterbacher and D.F. Sprinz (Cambridge, MA: MIT Press, 2001), 55. However, despite its antecedents in neoliberal institutionalism theory, it has been chosen to be used here because it is the term preferred by the majority of global environmental theorists whether neoliberal or constructivist.

general terms. The rules of a regime are difficult to distinguish from a norm; at the margins, they merge into one another. Rules are, however, more specific: they indicate in more detail the specific rights and obligations of members.[11]

In regimes, norms provide a basis for social learning (internalizing moral behaviour[12]) or to pressure and shame moral agents.[13] As R. Charli Carpenter has argued, 'Norms provide an intersubjective context in which discourse and behaviour are interpreted and either condoned or condemned by third parties. As general standards, norms are codified and (sometimes) implemented in the form of specific rules, which actors can choose to obey, break, or re-define.'[14] Norms contribute to choice-making,[15] without being, except in rare cases, the primary determinant of behaviour. The strength of a norm can often be gauged by public response to its transgression.[16]

When states make agreements, the benefits that accrue from normative compliance may not necessarily be material, but may include the need for legitimacy, status or credibility (a good global citizen).[17] As norms become codified within international laws, these laws also add to the pressure to comply and become in turn good indicators of the existence and strength of their underlying norms.[18]

Within the International Relations (IR) discipline, most academic writing on the global environment and regimes has been based on neoliberal institutionalism (hereafter named 'neoliberalism'), which focuses on intergovernmental

---

11 Robert O. Keohane, *After Hegemony: Cooperation and Discord in the World Political Economy* (Princeton, NJ: Princeton University Press, 1984), 59.

12 Radoslav S. Dimitrov, 'Hostage to Norms: States, Institutions and Global Forest Politics', *Global Environmental Politics* 5, no. 4 (2005): 12.

13 Checkel, 'International Norms and Domestic Politics: Bridging the Rationalist–Constructivist Divide', 474–5.

14 R. Charli Carpenter, '"Women and Children First": Gender, Norms, and Humanitarian Evacuation in the Balkans 1991–95', *International Organization* 57 (2003): 670.

15 Friedrich V. Kratochwil, 'Thrasymmachos Revisited: On the Relevance of Norms and the Study of Law for International Relations', *Journal of International Affairs* 37, no. 2 (1984): 356.

16 Dimitrov, 'Hostage to Norms: States, Institutions and Global Forest Politics', 12.

17 R.J. Flowers, 'International Norms and Domestic Policies in Japan: Identity, Legitimacy and Civilization' (Ph.D., University of Minnesota, 2002), 4.

18 Within international law, we can speak of a hierarchy of norms when it comes to examining the efficacy and durability of a norm: international treaties; customary international law; general principles of law recognized by civilized nations; judicial decisions and, lastly, teachings of the most highly qualified proponents of the various states. Boekle, Rittberger and Wagner, 'Norms and Foreign Policy: Constructivist Foreign Policy Theory', 19.

negotiations, institution building and regime effectiveness (Haas et al., 1993; Vogler, 2000; Young, 1998).[19] The challenge of protecting the global environment is often conceptualized by those working within this research programme as 'the management of inter-dependence in a system of sovereign states lacking the kind of central authorities assumed to be capable of providing order and regulation within domestic societies'.[20] Solutions favoured are cooperation and collective action approaches that privilege the concepts of economic growth, market economies and a liberal international system.[21]

Such writings can be considered *neo* as they go beyond the inter-war liberal idealist approach and the pre- and post-war institutionalists' research agenda, to postulate that different institutional frameworks can motivate states to co-operate, especially when facing collective ecological problems. In fact, in the field of environmental multilateralism, the vast bulk of analysis is now conducted within a neoliberal framework (DeSombre, 2002; Hurrell, 1993; Porter et al., 2000).[22]

Since the end of the Cold War, however, another research framework has emerged to challenge the dominance of neoliberalism as the preferred IR analytical approach. A renewed interest in the role of norms, ideas and interests in forming and transforming state structures led some analysts to find in constructivism a superior model for unlocking 'the black box of interest and identity formation'. Proponents claimed that 'state interests emerge from and are endogenous to interaction with structures'.[23]

---

19 Checkel, 'Norms, Institutions and National Identity in Contemporary Europe', 84. As a theory, the roots of neoliberal institutionalism can be traced back to the work of functionalists such as Ernst Haas in the 1950s, which led to the study of the concept of interdependence by those such as Keohane and Nye in the 1970s. This set in place the foundations for the development of what became regime theory in the 1980s. Rowlands, 'Classical Theories of International Relations', 54.

20 S. Jakobsen, 'International Relations and Global Environmental Change: Review of the Burgeoning Literature on the Environment', *Cooperation and Conflict* 34, no. 2 (1999): 207.

21 Steven F. Bernstein, *The Compromise of Liberal Environmentalism* (New York: Columbia University Press, 2001), 3.

22 This is not to say that approaches such as realism and neo-Marxism cannot 'value add' to any analysis on global environmental issues. However, due to both size constraints, and the fact that realists and neo-Marxists are highly sceptical of the idea of morality in global society, it has been decided not to utilize their approaches in this book. Both realists and neo-Marxists are 'masters of suspicion' when it comes to questions of morality, reducing all moral arguments to hidden interests, so any critique of rationalism (neoliberalism) can also be applied to them. Rather, this book will focus on the two approaches which have the most to say on environmental norms, those of neoliberalism and constructivism.

23 J.T. Checkel, 'The Constructivist Turn in International Relations Theory', *World Politics* 50, no. 2 (1998): 326.

With the arrival of constructivism, the old trichotomy of neorealism, neoliberalism and interpretivist approaches was replaced by a dichotomy, with constructivism at one axis and rationalism at the other. (Rationalism, as used here, encapsulates neo-utilitarianism, neoliberal institutionalism and neorealism.)[24]

In the USA, this dichotomy (constructivism versus rationalism) can be characterized as a debate between two lenses through which politics can be observed.[25] One lens is constructivist and may be called the logic of appropriateness. The other is rationalist and may be called the logic of consequences.[26]

Those who ascribe to the logic of consequences imagine that actors evaluate alternative strategies according to the likely consequences, based on their individual or collective objectives. They perceive society as an aggregate of individuals seeking individual ends. Consequently, the only societal obligations they recognize are those granted by consent or contract, always within the framework of each individual's calculated advantage. Questions of identity, rules and institutions are considered peripheral.[27]

However, those who ascribe to the logic of appropriateness perceive action as rule based. Individuals act according to rules and practices within social constructs which are publicly known, foreseen and accepted.[28] March and Olsen consider such rule-guided behaviour to be a conscious process where actors work through a particular situation trying to establish how to act, how and when to apply a particular norm, or how to choose among conflicting rules. The more the norms are contested, the less the logic of the case can be captured by the statement 'good people do X'. Rather the question becomes 'what is "good" in this scenario?' or 'what is the right thing to do?' The question then becomes, 'how do social actors choose what is the appropriate norm to apply in a given case?'[29]

There is, of course, a significant overlap between these two logics. They are not mutually exclusive. The skill resides in determining where and how

---

24 John M. Hobson, *The State and International Relations*, Themes in International Relations (Cambridge: Cambridge University Press, 2000), 145; Antje Wiener, 'Constructivism: The Limits of Bridging Gaps', *Journal of International Relations and Development* 6, no. 3 (2003): 252.

25 Kjell Goldmann, 'Appropriateness and Consequences: The Logic of Neo-institutionalism', *Governance: An International Journal of Policy, Administration and Institutions* 18, no. 1 (2005): 37.

26 Thomas Risse, '"Lets Argue!": Communicative Action in World Politics', *International Organization* 54, no. 1 (2000): 1.

27 James G. March and Johan P. Olsen, 'The Institutional Dynamics of International Political Orders', *International Organization* 52, no. 4 (1998): 949–51.

28 Ibid.: 949–52.

29 Risse, '"Let's Argue!": Communicative Action in World Politics', 6.

each should be applied and whether they can complement or subsume each other.[30]

This book seeks to explore these two methodologies in a systematic way. It asks when and under what conditions constructivism can provide a richer account than neoliberalism of the formation and evolution of the central norms in global environmental regimes.[31] To this end, two questions will be asked:

1. Which approach has the greater explanatory power with regard to the formation and evolution of core environmental norms in environmental regimes?
2. Are the two frameworks rivals or can they be seen as complementary explanations that may be synthesized? Alternatively, is one able to subsume the other within its analysis or are they domain specific?

The focus of this inquiry will be question one, which assumes that neoliberalism and constructivism are rival approaches. Question two will be examined at the end, when the strengths and weaknesses of each methodology have been fully evaluated.

I will examine three global environmental norms in international agreements and how they become accepted by the global community. The norms chosen are:

- environmental exploitation (use and sometimes overuse of a resource);
- conservation (sustainable use of a resource);
- preservation (non-use of a resource).

And they will be examined within three case studies:

- Antarctic minerals;
- whaling regime;
- tropical timber.

These will offer an opportunity to examine the processes of normative contestation and to determine when and why certain environmental norms matter more than others.

---

30 Goldmann, 'Appropriateness and Consequences: The Logic of Neo-institutionalism', 35.

31 J.T. Checkel, 'Why Comply? Constructivism, Social Norms and the Study of International Institutions' (paper presented at the Annual Meeting, American Political Science Association, Atlanta, Georgia, 1999), 30.

The tropical timber regime has been selected as a 'hard case' for constructivists because the core environmental norm of this regime has not 'progressed' beyond exploitation to conservation and/or preservation.[32] A constructivist must show that the norm of exploitation is not entirely reducible to state interests or that it is constitutive of their identities and interests. Neoliberals, on the other hand, can provide a more parsimonious explanation, as they do not privilege learned norms above intrinsic interests. Both methodologies, however, will be tested for their respective accounts of why conservation or preservation, which were strongly promoted by certain non-state actors, failed to become the dominant norm within this regime.

The other two case studies of whaling and Antarctic minerals are more explicit examples of 'progressive' moral normative evolution from an environmental point of view and therefore present rationalists, with their privileging of interests above moral considerations, with a challenge.[33] In the Antarctica case, historically there had been no norm relating to mineral exploitation because it was neither technologically feasible nor economically desirable until the mid-1970s. In a sense, there was a 'normative void' operating since the question of mining had yet to become an issue within the Antarctic regime. The example of Antarctic mineral exploitation has been chosen because it allows for an examination of actors' 'contested positions' and the process of how one particular normative position can defeat rivals to become a dominant norm within a regime. Once mining was considered likely to occur, the fact that a conservationist regime had not been put in place to regulate exploitation allowed a preservationist norm to becoming firmly entrenched for at least the foreseeable future.

On the other hand, the case study of whaling reveals a less clear-cut normative change. Initially, the exploitation of whaling species to the brink of extinction led to a push by whaling states and companies for a conservationist regime, under the International Whaling Commission (IWC). The failure of

---

32 A project's validity can be increased by including a 'hard case' where the value of the controlling variables is unfavourable to the validity of the book tested. R.B. Mitchell and T. Bernauer, 'Empirical Research on International Environmental Policy: Designing Qualitative Case Studies', *Journal of Environment and Development* 7, no. 1 (1998): 17. From a methodological perspective, it is important to assess counterfactual examples, as they can help to sharpen proposed arguments and enable both neoliberals and constructivists to better delimit the scope of their explanations, hopefully stimulating a theoretical dialogue with each other. Checkel, 'Why Comply? Constructivism, Social Norms and the Study of International Institutions', 21.

33 This is not to say that the neoliberal approach is devoid of morality. Rather it privileges a particular form of rationalist/calculative morality that decrees, at the individual level, self-interest and its pursuit as being 'good'. At the global level, it privileges the morality of interstate cooperation as a goal.

whalers to adhere to a conservationist approach opened the door for anti-whaling states and Environmental Non-governmental Organizations (ENGOs) to propose and promote a preservationist approach that still underpins the IWC today, despite a fierce backlash from whaling states.

In these two case studies, we would expect constructivism, with its privileging of discourse, to have greater explanatory power than its rival, as in each case moral arguments were successful and preservationist norms were incorporated. However, it is also necessary to explore how far constructivists are able to rebut or address interest-driven explanations in these cases.

The analysis proposed will contribute to the substantive literature on norm origin, development and replacement of competing norms in the following ways:

- It will show the value of examining both effective and ineffective norms (that is, norms that were not taken up).
- It will examine the competing neoliberal and constructivist approaches to determine which one is superior or if there is potential for complementarity or synthesis.
- It will highlight the need to consider alternative explanations that can potentially advance both the positivist and interpretivist normative research agendas.
- Lastly, it will help stakeholders understand norm change and the strategies and tactics necessary to bring about successful environmental change.

Although descriptions and evaluations of norms in environmental literature proliferate, studies as to why people adhere to particular norms are rare. Even in strategic studies of norms, little analysis has been carried out on the dynamics of norm articulation and internalization and '. . . how [norms] can get started, how a partial norm can be sustained and become well established and how one norm can displace another'.[34] Both neoliberalism and constructivism have examined the crucial role of norms within environmental regimes, but as Jeffrey Legro argues:

> The literature on norms has generally mis-specified their impact because of several conceptual and methodological biases . . . by concentrating on showing that norms

---

34 Robert M. Axelrod, *The Complexity of Cooperation: Agent-based Models of Competition and Collaboration*, Princeton Studies in Complexity (Princeton, NJ: Princeton University Press, 1997), 65.

> 'matter' analysts have given short shrift to the critical issues of which norms matter, the ways they matter, and how much they matter relative to other factors.[35]

Richard Price notes that constructivism research has been limited by being mostly concerned with analysing 'good' norms that are perceived as successful.[36] Cynthia Weber challenges constructivists to explain 'why one set of knowledge claims "wins" and why others are left behind'.[37] Neoliberal analysis to date is also lacking in providing a complete explanation as to why certain norms are successful and why others fail.

Legro posits that analysts, whatever their theoretical persuasion, have two biases relevant to the study undertaken here, which has rendered their analyses flawed. The first bias is an inability to perceive 'norm robustness' as separate from the effects attributed to the norm.[38] There is such a plethora of norms competing in the international arena that one can always 'discover' a norm to explain an effect cited. It is crucial, therefore, to be able to understand why some norms are *more* influential than others *in a particular forum*. The second bias is that most analysis to date focuses on norms perceived to have 'worked' rather than examining case studies where norms have failed or become out-of-date. As Legro correctly argues, '[w]hy norms did not emerge or were not consequential is as important as why they did or were'.[39]

This book responds to these criticisms by Legro, Price and Weber by seeking to discover which of the environmental norms of exploitation, conservation and preservation 'won' (or at least predominated) in a given situation of normative contestation and why. This entails exploring how *much* rival norms have played a critical role within negotiations to create environmental regimes and when and how normative transformation was brought about. It will ask how much the successful norm has mattered relative to other norms and material factors and will also examine cases of norm failure, where 'progressive' environmental norms such as conservation and preservation were unsuccessful (such as the case of tropical timber where conservation has failed to supplant exploitation).

---

35 Legro, 'Which Norms Matter? Revisiting the "Failure" of Internationalism', 31. Price and Checkel support Legro's position, arguing that the current normative debate is now, not that norms matter, but which norms matter in which regimes. Checkel, 'International Norms and Domestic Politics: Bridging the Rationalist–Constructivist Divide', 473; Richard Price, 'Moral Limit and Possibility in World Politics', *International Organization* 62 (2008): 193.

36 Price, 'Moral Limit and Possibility in World Politics', 193.

37 Cynthia Weber, *International Relations Theory: A Critical Introduction* (London: Routledge, 2001), 240.

38 Legro, 'Which Norms Matter? Revisiting the "Failure" of Internationalism', 33.

39 Ibid.: 34.

Unlike much of the research into norm behaviour, this book is primarily concerned then with analysing *competing* norms. Before engaging with the research questions posed, it is necessary to gain an understanding of the philosophical and practical distinctions between the three norms under scrutiny: exploitation, conservation and preservation.

## THE NORMS OF EXPLOITATION, CONSERVATION AND PRESERVATION

All three norms examined in this book started as domestic norms but became global due to the increasingly international character of environmental problems and the transnational activism of ENGOs. It is easier to understand this norm diffusion using a constructivist framework that allows us to unpack multiple and differing meanings of social terms and explore their intersubjective meaning or meanings.[40] For constructivists, such global norms are social and arise from '. . . moral debate and dialogue between states' and other global actors involved in regime negotiations.[41] Thus norms have histories that '. . . emerge out of complex processes of communicative action' involving many stakeholders engaged in a dialogue and contest.[42] The global environmental norms examined here are not categorical; rather they have evolved over time, using the language favoured by various norm advocates to advance their cause.[43] Such practices have then determined the legitimacy of global actors within social contexts.[44]

It is useful to begin with an examination of the norms of exploitation, conservation and preservation from a philosophical viewpoint before embarking on an analysis of how such norms compete within environmental regimes. This is not to say that there is one correct definition of the terms examined. Advocates, as will be seen in the case studies, use differing and sometimes multiple definitions of norms to advance their cause. Many proponents mistak-

---

40 The constructivist understanding of intersubjectivity posits that the more humans interact and communicate, the better they may understand each other and '. . . common meanings may emerge'. Anthony Clark Arend, 'Do Legal Rules Matter? International Law and International Politics', *Virginia Journal of International Law* 38 (1998): 137.

41 Christian Reus-Smit, 'Constructivism', in *Theories of International Relations*, 2nd edition, ed. S. Burchill et al. (New York: Palgrave, 2001), 526.

42 Ibid.

43 Robyn Eckersley, 'Soft Law, Hard Politics, and the Climate Change Treaty', in *The Politics of International Law*, ed. Christian Reus-Smit (Cambridge: Cambridge University Press, 2004), 35.

44 Ibid.

enly conflate the terms when defining their positions and some advocates hide their real position within the rhetorical definitions of another.[45] However, offering conceptual distinctions, based on a long history of environmental philosophical engagement, will help to shed light on the varieties of ways in which the norms are deployed and/or understood by social agents.

The concept of 'exploitation' has received scant conceptual analysis compared to the concepts of conservation and preservation.[46] One of the few authors to explore the meaning of the general concept in any depth is Alan Wertheimer, who has argued that, at the most general level, exploitation occurs when 'A takes unfair advantage of B', thus connoting a wrongful action.[47] However, Wertheimer does not consider the exploitation of nature by humans.[48] Taylor, rather than defining exploitation per se, speaks in terms of an exploitative attitude, which he defines as occurring 'whenever nature is thought of as nothing more than a vast repository of resources, both physical or biological, to be developed, used and consumed by humans for human ends'.[49]

Even in the ecophilosophical literature the concept of exploitation has been only cursorily explored as part of an over-arching Western narrative of the domination of nature. Most ecophilosophical attention has been devoted to the new environmental norms that have challenged exploitation, namely conservation or preservation.[50] Taylor has argued that, for some, the advancement of Western civilization is intricately bound up with the domination of nature in pursuit of the goal of ensuring a better life for the bulk of humanity.[51] Alternatively, some ecophilosophers have made the point that there is a conceptual link between the exploitation of nature and the exploitation of

---

45 For an example of conflation, see Birnie and Boyle, who define conservation in preservationist terms as: '. . . to keep in safety or from harm, decay or loss; to preserve in being; to keep alive'. Patricia W. Birnie and Alan E. Boyle, *International Law and the Environment*, 2nd edition (Oxford: Oxford University Press, 2002), 550. While conservationist rhetoric about the need to save the environment is standard, it would be a brave state or company that would argue in this day and age for reckless exploitation of a resource to occur. Rather the position is put that global resources needs careful conserving or 'wise use' to ensure there are resources available for future generations of humans.

46 Alan Wertheimer, *Exploitation* (Princeton, NJ: Princeton University Press, 1996), 5.

47 Ibid.: 5, 10.

48 Ibid.: 10–12.

49 Paul W. Taylor, *Respect for Nature: A Theory of Environmental Ethics* (Princeton, NJ: Princeton University Press, 1989), 95.

50 Warwick Fox, *Toward a Transpersonal Ecology: Developing New Foundations for Environmentalism*, 1st edition (Boston, MA: Shambhala, 1990), 152–3.

51 Taylor, *Respect for Nature: A Theory of Environmental Ethics*, 95.

disadvantaged groups within society, such as women or indigenous peoples, but again the term is not spelt out but rather left undefined and generally understood as 'bad'.[52]

Humankind has traditionally attempted to portray and justify its environmentally exploitative practices as beneficial to itself. For example, Francis Bacon argued that the dominion of the planet by humans gave them the right to utilize nature for their own exclusive benefit.[53] Such exploitation has been described as springing from the human belief that there is an 'inherent right to take and plunder' natural resources, a belief that has often been justified by referring to the biblical passage that God gave dominion of the planet to humanity for its own uses.[54]

However, it is possible to perceive exploitation as good, if it is in the service of a higher moral goal, for example, the provision of a better quality of life for the citizens of a state. Taylor has argued that within a human ecology, there is nothing morally wrong with choosing an exploitative attitude towards nature, since from a human-centred ethical standpoint, the environment is 'rightly controlled, transformed and consumed in the service of human interests alone' and '. . . [A]side from their actual or potential usefulness to humans, they lack all worth'.[55]

States have historically viewed their exploitation of natural resources, both domestic and global, as a right and in some cases as a good.[56] Principle 21 of the Stockholm Declaration (1972) has enshrined this internationally recognized right to the effect that 'States have the sovereign right to exploit their own resources pursuant to their own environmental policies . . .'.[57] Exploitation of resources such as those examined in this book – minerals, whales or timber – has long been accepted as a corollary of state sovereignty.

---

52 Robyn Eckersley, 'Politics', in *A Companion to Environmental Philosophy*, ed. Dale Jamieson (Oxford: Blackwell Publishing, 2003), 321. For research on the link between nature, feminism and indigenous peoples, see Val Plumwood, *Feminism and the Mastery of Nature* (London: Routledge, 1990).

53 Robin Attfield, 'Christianity', in *A Companion to Environmental Philosophy*, ed. Dale Jamieson (Oxford: Blackwell Publishing, 2003), 105.

54 Peter Brown, *Ethics, Economics and International Relations: Transparent Sovereignty in the Commonwealth of Life* (Edinburgh: Edinburgh University Press, 2000), 44.

55 Taylor, *Respect for Nature: A Theory of Environmental Ethics*, 51–2.

56 S. Sucharitikul, 'State Responsibility and International Liability under International Law', *Loyola of Los Angeles International and Comparative Law Journal* 18, no. 3 (1996): 837.

57 http://www.unep.org/Documents.multilingual/Default.asp?DocumentID=97&ArticleID=1503, accessed 30/01/06.

For the purposes of this book, it will be necessary to advance a working definition of 'exploitation' as it applies to nature. The definition will need to encapsulate both a pejorative application of the word as well as a non-pejorative one (descriptive merely of the unrestrained use of natural resources). Consequently, the term will be understood, drawing on the work of Taylor, as referring to a situation where humanity treats resources as merely instrumental, to be developed and consumed, without consideration for the survivability of the resource, the overall ecosystem or the rights of future generations of humans. This definition incorporates the idea that such resource usage is unsustainable with no consideration for resource replenishment or for the integrity of the overall ecosystem from which it is drawn.

A major problem in analysing the norm of exploitation, then, is that in contemporary times, given its commonly accepted pejorative meaning, arguments for the unrestrained or minimally restrained utilization of a resource are rarely couched in the language of exploitation by its proponents, who prefer to use the language of sustainable utilization or conservation. It is ultimately an empirical question whether the argument proposed by a stakeholder is a conservationist one or whether it is exploitationist under the 'cover' of the language of conservation. For example, we shall see that in the case of whaling, many whaling states such as Japan and the Soviet Union, despite a stated commitment to conservationist principles, continued to engage in exploitative whaling practices, leading to the near extinction of certain whale types. However, the choice not to use the explicit language of exploitation also provides a revealing indication that support for the norm has waned.

In contrast to the norm of exploitation, the norms of conservation and preservation have enjoyed prominence and influence within global environmental regimes.[58] In the nineteenth and early twentieth centuries, the domestic debate between those advocating conservationism and those promoting preservationism led to the creation of the first wave of domestic ENGOs.[59] That domestic debate is now being played out on a global scale[60] and the role played by the transnational successors of these domestic ENGOs will form a key part of this book.

Human understanding of the need to conserve resources is an ancient one. The ancient idea of conservation can be found in such early texts as the

---

58 A. Kellow, 'Norms, Interests and Environmental NGOs: The Limits of Cosmopolitanism', *Environmental Politics* 9, no. 9 (2000): 17.

59 Neil Carter, *The Politics of the Environment: Ideas, Activism, Policy* (New York: Cambridge University Press, 2001), 27.

60 Mark J. Smith, *Ecologism: Towards Ecological Citizenship*, Concepts in the Social Sciences (Buckingham: Open University Press, 1998), 12–13.

Hebrew and Christian Bibles and the writings of Plato and Cicero.[61] Conservationism as a concept:

> concedes that nature is not inexhaustible: accordingly, that there are limits to material growth and that husbandry must therefore be practiced because it becomes necessary to consider the interests of human generations as yet unborn when determining courses of action.[62]

The conservationist approach is bound up with the production process and regards the non-human world merely in terms of its utility.[63] Therefore a conservationist perspective treats the biosphere as a potential resource for human consumption.[64] Such conservation can be of renewable or non-renewable resources, providing there is a husbanding of the resource for use.[65]

This norm can be seen as a breaking away from the exploitative practices of the past and accepting a more rational, cautious approach to the husbanding of potentially scarce resources. Mark Smith has argued that the idea of conservationism has tended to act as a brake '. . . to moderate the pressures for an *exploitative* [my italics] "free for all" inherent in the drives which propel actions in economic markets', thus ameliorating damaging practices of the past.[66] Rodman argues that resource conservation as a norm replaced 'the reckless exploitation of forests, wildlife, soils etc.' with an 'ethical and legal requirement that "natural resources" be used "wisely", in the interests of humanity at large rather than in the interests of a mere few, and considered over the "long run" rather than the short term'.[67] Robyn Eckersley supports this position and argues further that resource conservation can be seen as the first step away from unrestrained development.[68]

---

61 Robyn Eckersley, *Environmentalism and Political Theory: Toward an Ecocentric Approach* (London: UCL Press, 1992), 35.

62 Peter Hay, *Main Currents in Western Environmental Thought* (Sydney: UNSW Press, 2002), 33.

63 Eckersley, *Environmentalism and Political Theory: Toward an Ecocentric Approach*, 36.

64 This approach '. . . mirrors Judeo-Christian traditions, especially in its anthropocentric outlook. Nature and natural entities are not sacred, have no end or justification in and of themselves, and exist solely as means in terms of which human ends might be fulfilled.' Max Oelschlager, *Idea of Wilderness: From Prehistory to the Age of Ecology*, new edition (New Haven, CN: Yale University Press, 1993), 287.

65 Taylor, *Respect for Nature: A Theory of Environmental Ethics*, 298.

66 Smith, *Ecologism: Towards Ecological Citizenship*, 11.

67 Hay, *Main Currents in Western Environmental Thought*, 31.

68 Eckersley, *Environmentalism and Political Theory: Toward an Ecocentric Approach*, 35.

Conservation is in many ways the least controversial environmental norm since it has at its heart a utilitarian, human-centred perspective that seeks the greatest good for the greatest number of humans, a perspective that resonates deeply with many cultures and stakeholders. It embodies a rhetoric of restraint which suits the interests of states seeking better economic returns from their resources. Scientists have often been the transmitters for conservationist norms, since the approach that resources should be wisely used and husbanded for future generations has been central to agriculture and forestry.

If the saving of a resource is *from* utilization rather than *for* utilization, however, we are generally speaking of 'preservation'. John Passmore defines preservation as: '. . . the attempt to maintain in their present condition such areas of the earth's surface as do not yet bear the obvious marks of man's handiwork and to protect from the risk of extinction those species of living beings which man has not yet destroyed'.[69] Max Oelschlager expands on this by arguing that preservationists reject the notion that nature is merely a resource, instead prizing wilderness values, species rarity and diversity.[70] Anne and Paul Erlich are typical of those who espouse a preservationist viewpoint in that they argue that the biosphere has a right to exist.[71] Thus, at its heart, preservationism accords an *intrinsic* or non-instrumental value to the world, even if it conflicts with human interests.[72]

The preservationist argument often has spiritual overtones. According to Neil Carter, it 'represents an attitude of reverence towards nature'.[73] However, resource preservation can be argued on both intrinsic and instrumental grounds. An instrumental approach maintains that humans derive value from the non-human world if the resources enjoyed by humans are allowed to exist unaltered.[74] Such utilization includes using nature psychogenetically (psychological health and maturity), for recreation (gymnasium), for worship

---

69 John Passmore, *Man's Responsibility for Nature: Ecological Problems and Western Traditions* (London: Duckworth, 1980), 101.

70 R.C. Paehlke, 'Environmental Values and Public Policy', in *Environmental Policy in the 1990s: Reform or Reaction*, ed. N.J. Vig and M.E. Kraft (Washington: Congressional Quarterly Inc., 1997), 78.

71 George Sessions, 'Ecocentrism, Wilderness, and Global Ecosystem Protection', in *The Wilderness Condition: Essays on Environment and Civilization*, ed. Max Oelschlager (San Francisco: Island Press, 1992), 102.

72 W. Godfrey-Smith, 'The Rights of Non-Humans and Intrinsic Values', in *Environmental Philosophy*, ed. D.S. Mannison, M.A. McRobbie and R. Routley (Canberra: Department of Philosophy, Research School of Social Science, Australian National University, 1980), 31.

73 Carter, *The Politics of the Environment: Ideas, Activism, Policy*, 27.

74 Hay, *Main Currents in Western Environmental Thought*, 33.

(cathedral), as a retreat (asylum), a laboratory, an art gallery, a silo of genetic diversity,[75] a monument or simply as a place to marvel and wonder at.[76]

Passmore, however, takes it as axiomatic that 'true' preservationist arguments *must* rely on the concept of intrinsic value. This position is at odds with many preservationist theorists, who also include instrumental arguments to support the preservation of nature.[77] However, while it is possible to argue preservationist positions from an instrumental perspective, doing so does a disservice to the intentions of many global actors advocating preservation, who argue that whales or other creatures deserve not to be culled because they intrinsically have a right to exist.[78] At the global level, ENGOs have been primary advocates (with some success) for the position that this intrinsic strand of preservationism should underpin global environmental regimes concerned with the management of species and wilderness areas.

---

[75] The most politically influential arguments for preserving biodiversity appeal to their potential instrumental value to humans for example, medicines, as opposed to an argument based on the intrinsic value of nature. Sessions, 'Ecocentrism, Wilderness, and Global Ecosystem Protection', 96. Therefore, humanity '... should preserve as wide as possible a range of genetic diversity because there is no way of anticipating what our *future* needs might happen to be'. Godfrey-Smith, 'The Rights of Non-Humans and Intrinsic Values', 31. For many environmentalists, however, this instrumental approach to preservation is morally bankrupt because '... to categorize and quantify the benefits of what they take ... is a flawed approach to ... preservation ...'. M.P. Nelson, 'An Amalgamation of Wilderness Preservation Arguments', in *Environmental Ethics: An Anthology*, ed. A. Light and H. Rolston III (Malden, MA: Blackwell Publishing, 2003), 432.

[76] Sessions, 'Ecocentrism, Wilderness, and Global Ecosystem Protection', 97. Nelson further expands on those categories and argues that preservation can be argued (and possibly) justified on the following instrumental grounds: its use as a classroom; on ontogeny grounds (we are what we are because of our environment); cultural diversity (diversity of cultures depends on a variety of ecosystems); national character (designated wilderness areas symbolically enshrine national character); such areas allow self-realization as per the tenets of deep ecology; disease sequestration (viruses in a damaged ecosystem are under extreme selective pressure). When humans enter such a region they bring out potentially deadly epidemics; salvation of freedom (potential sanctuaries from oppressive governments) and that it is 'mythopoetic' (serves as a perfect location for viewing the history of myth) amongst other arguments. Nelson, 'An Amalgamation of Wilderness Preservation Arguments', 423–8. Sessions further proposes that preservation as an argument can be justified in terms of 'the minding animals argument', whereby humanity needs wild animals in a pristine ecosystem so humans can prosper, because human intelligence is 'bound to the presence of animals'. Sessions, 'Ecocentrism, Wilderness, and Global Ecosystem Protection', 98.

[77] W. Godfrey-Smith, 'The Value of Wilderness', *Environmental Ethics* 1 (1979): 310; B.G. Norton, 'Conservation and Preservation: A Conceptual Rehabilitation', *Environmental Ethics* 8 (1986): 196.

[78] Eckersley, 'Soft Law, Hard Politics, and the Climate Change Treaty', 32.

Bryan Norton argues, at least in the short term, that there is little difference between advocating conservationism and preservationism, since both views are dedicated to saving ecosystems and species.[79] However, the two views often diverge at critical moments and may be traced to differing philosophical belief systems. A conservationist may only save a resource for use at a future time, whilst a preservationist desires to keep it forever untrammelled and protected. Thus, sooner or later, they will find themselves at loggerheads. The case studies examined in this book bear this out, since conservationists and preservationists seek goals and advocate practices which are, at times, totally disparate.

## NORMS AND STAKEHOLDERS

Norms do not come out of the ground like dragon's teeth nor do they spring out of the ether. They emerge through the complex interaction of stakeholders arguing new precepts or designing and implementing new strategies within normative and policy debates.[80] The three norms of exploitation, conservation and preservation are constantly being proposed, challenged or supplanted by stakeholders, as the dominant moral norm underpinning global environmental regimes. An understanding of how such norms interact, transform or replace each other is vital to better comprehend how global environmental regimes are created and maintained.

Karen Litfin points out that 'the knowledge-based nature of environmental problems has opened up the playing field to a profusion of unconventional players' whose roles and motivations must be examined to understand how global environmental regimes are created and evolve.[81] Further, researchers must also be aware that norms are not advanced in a vacuum and all advocates confront 'highly contested' arenas where their norms 'must compete with other norms and perceptions of interests'.[82] This book will examine this contestation to determine how norms originate and transform over time to

---

[79] Bryan G. Norton, 'The Cultural Approach to Conservation Biology', in *Environmental Ethics: An Introduction with Readings*, ed. John Benson (London: Routledge, 2000), 146.

[80] M.J. Hoffmann, 'Entrepreneurs and Norm Dynamics: An Agent-based Model on the Norm Life Cycle', University of Delaware, http://www.psych.upenn.edu/sacsec/abir/_private/Pamla/Hoffmann_norms.doc.

[81] K. Litfin, 'Eco-regimes: Playing Tug of War with the Nation State', in *The State and Social Power in Global Environmental Politics*, ed. Ronnie D. Lipschutz and Ken Conca (New York: Columbia University Press, 1993), 111.

[82] Martha Finnemore and Kathryn Sikkink, 'International Norm Dynamics and Political Change', *International Organization* 52, no. 4 (1998): 897.

become dominant within a global environmental regime. Neoliberal analysis of global environmental regimes has traditionally tended to confine itself to states and their interests, but constructivism has opened the door to a host of non-state actors such as ENGOs, scientists, corporations and international organizations. These state and non-state 'normative stakeholders' all play a role in creating and transforming global environmental regimes and their norms.[83]

For decades, IR theorists privileged the state as the central locus of study.[84] Since the end of World War II, '. . . the international world has been formally levelled into one and only one constitutional category: sovereign states'.[85] IR theorists consider states to be the most important global actor because individual states can domestically alter the behaviour of their citizens through the twin means of coercion or persuasion, with repercussions for the global sphere.[86] Paul Wapner argues trenchantly, '. . . even those who focus on the role of norms, values and shared ideas understand them in terms of interstate behaviour. They acknowledge and study them only to the degree that these ideas are involved in the formulation of state interests.'[87]

One cannot examine normative interaction without considering the role of states, because states enter into the bargaining that produces the global environmental regimes and their norms.[88] Neoliberals, therefore, place the state at the centre of their analysis of regimes, by focusing on the state interests that shape the bargaining. They also emphasize inter-state activities, such as the creation of international organizations that further states' interests. In the environmental regimes examined in this book, states are the main actors involved in shaping new norms and challenging or defending old norms. As we shall see, particular states have, in certain circumstances, been staunch proponents of global environmental protection. For example, the support of both the United States of America and Australia was critical to the strengthening of the

---

83 Michael Mason, 'The Governance of Transnational Environmental Harm: Addressing New Modes of Accountability/Responsibility', *Global Environmental Politics* 8, no. 3 (2008): 9.

84 Paul Kevin Wapner, 'Horizontal Politics: Transnational Environmental Activism and Global Cultural Change', *Global Environmental Politics* 2, no. 2 (2002): 37.

85 Robert H. Jackson, *Quasi-States: Sovereignty, International Relations, and the Third World*, Cambridge Studies in International Relations 12 (Cambridge: Cambridge University Press, 1990), 17.

86 Wapner, 'Horizontal Politics: Transnational Environmental Activism and Global Cultural Change', 40.

87 Paul Kevin Wapner, *Environmental Activism and World Civic Politics* (Albany, NY: State University of New York Press, 1996), 67.

88 Jakobsen, 'International Relations and Global Environmental Change: Review of the Burgeoning Literature on the Environment', 209.

regime to ban commercial whaling. However, states have also been active exploiters of resources leading to global environmental degradation. As Eckersley describes it, '. . . there is no shortage of detailed historical accounts of the various ways in which particular states (whether communist or capitalist, developed or undeveloped) have acted as resource plunderers . . .', so an understanding of their role as both protector and despoiler is critical.[89]

However, constructivists studying global issues are increasingly discounting traditional statist frameworks, instead regarding states as one among a plethora of actors on the global scene.[90] This allows constructivist researchers to include an analysis of the advocacy role of non-state actors and their impact on a regime's normative structure. The ideas and norms that shape international environmental regimes usually arise from globalizing networks of concerned citizens, leading NGOs and/or scientists, arguing for models of environmental change from one forum or bureaucracy to another, until they capture a powerful bureaucracy, state or coalition of states to champion their model.

The development of norms within global environmental regimes cannot be adequately explained without regard to NGOs and their campaigns to influence global environmental regimes. In the nineteenth and early-twentieth centuries, the first wave of environmentalists focused on wildlife protection and preserving national resources. The second wave (1960s and 1970s) saw ENGOs mount campaigns on global environmental problems and quality of life issues in technologically advanced societies.[91] The 1980s saw ENGOs at the zenith of their power, developing from being primarily domestic, small and underresourced organizations into global entities with vast resources.[92] While precise information is unavailable, it is estimated that by the 1990s there were over 100,000 ENGOs operating globally, with millions of members.[93]

---

89 Robyn Eckersley, 'Greening the Nation-state from Exclusive to Inclusive Sovereignty, Economy and Ecology' (paper presented at the European Consortium for Political Research Annual Joint Sessions, Grenoble, France, 6–11 April 2001), 4.

90 Wapner, *Environmental Activism and World Civic Politics*, 42; Eckersley, 'Greening the Nation-state from Exclusive to Inclusive Sovereignty, Economy and Ecology', 1–2.

91 S. Kamieniecki, *Environmental Politics in the International Arena: Movements, Parties, Organizations, and Policy* (New York: State University of New York Press, 1993), 6.

92 P.J. Sands, 'The Role of Non-governmental Organizations in Enforcing International Law', in *Control over Compliance with International Law*, ed. W.E. Butler (Norwell, MA: Kluwer Academic Publishing, 1991), 62.

93 Wapner, *Environmental Activism and World Civic Politics*, 2.

ENGO members share a common concern about environmental degradation.[94] ENGOs aim to inculcate in people an 'ecological sensibility', with the aim of moving people to act more responsibly towards the environment.[95] Wapner argues that the ENGOs' mission is to 'identify and manipulate cultural frames of reference to persuade ordinary citizens throughout the world to adopt environmental values'.[96] This approach has often enabled ENGOs to be in the vanguard in promoting new global environmental norms.[97]

Like all NGOs, ENGOs can operate at multiple levels, including local, national and global levels. This book is concerned primarily with those ENGOs that operate at the global level and focus on regional or global environmental protection, such as Greenpeace,[98] WWF[99] and Friends of the Earth.[100] The ENGOs' impact on the global scene is linked to their ability to

---

94 Wapner, 'Horizontal Politics: Transnational Environmental Activism and Global Cultural Change', 39.

95 Ibid.: 46.

96 Ibid.: 49.

97 Lorraine Elliott, *International Environmental Politics: Protecting the Antarctic* (New York: St Martin's Press, 1994), 19.

98 Greenpeace was created in 1969 under the name, Don't Make Waves Committee, a splinter group of Sierra Club members and peace activists. Jacqueline Vaughn Switzer, *Environmental Politics: Domestic and Global Dimensions*, 4th edition (Belmont, CA: Thomson/Wadsworth, 2004), 41. In 1972, it formally took the name Greenpeace, with the aim of being a transnational environmental activist group. Paul Kevin Wapner, 'Politics Beyond the State: Environmental Activism and World Civic Politics', *World Politics* 47, no. 3 (April) (1995): 320. Greenpeace seeks to replace traditional interpretations of exploitationist practices with new frameworks of understanding. Wapner, 'Politics Beyond the State: Environmental Activism and World Civic Politics', 321. In Wapner's words, Greenpeace: 'targets the global cultural realm. It clues into internationally shared modes of discourse, such as moral norms, symbols, and scientific argument, and it manipulates them to induce people to pursue, what Greenpeace assumes are, environmentally sound practices.' Wapner, *Environmental Activism and World Civic Politics*, 14–15.

99 The WWF was founded in 1961 and established a global headquarters in 1962 in Gland, Switzerland. Since then it has funded or been involved in 4000 projects in over 140 states. It involves itself in primarily conservationist projects in differing geographic areas, for example, the Pacific, Africa. Originally, the WWF interpreted conservation as merely saving species. Over time, it realized that this approach was not working and it shifted to attempting to preserve ecosystems. It prefers to work closely with local peoples to create tailored indigenous conservationist solutions. Wapner, *Environmental Activism and World Civic Politics*, 77–83.

100 Friends of the Earth (FoE) was created in 1969 as a splinter group of the Sierra Club. Since that time, it has grown to have chapters in over 50 states with up to a million members. Friends of the Earth aims to alter global economic, social and cultural processes to better reflect environmental sensibilities. In particular, it seeks to influence states to commit to environmental protection by direct lobbying or embar-

exert political influence over states and other actors by direct action campaigns, publicity campaigns, conferences and the use of celebrities to raise public awareness of global environmental issues.[101] ENGOs raise public awareness of environmental issues, lobby decision-makers, organize boycotts and monitor and implement global agreements.[102] ENGOs have also been crucial for regime maintenance by monitoring potential and actual transgression of global environmental treaties.[103]

ENGOs influence global environmental negotiations by putting forth information, ideas and frameworks that would not otherwise have been available to delegates.[104] As Thomas Princen has noted, '[i]n negotiations that have few precedents, little predetermined structure, an ill-defined agenda, and fuzzy outcome expectations, simply sitting at the table confers influence', which can be critical in achieving normative transformation.[105] There are two basic models of NGO action relating to global environmental regimes. One is the 'network model' (for example, the Antarctic and Southern Ocean Coalition) and the other is the 'NGO leader model', where one wealthy global NGO leads the way (for example, Greenpeace with its 3.3 million members worldwide in the case of whaling). The lead NGO model is best suited to lobbying that requires concentrated resources (for example, ships to monitor and publicize the practice of whaling) and the network model is ideal for environmental problems that are diffuse and variable across different regions (for example, pesticides).[106]

On the global scene, Greenpeace and other ENGOs have been crucial in promoting a preservationist ethic within the regimes of whaling and Antarctica. Both regimes have, to some extent, adopted the preservationist ideal as their central norm. Their success has depended largely on their ability to enter negotiations as a full participant, either directly or through agents acting as ventriloquists for small states.

---

rassing states to implement environmental treaties. Wapner, *Environmental Activism and World Civic Politics*, 121–7.

[101] Raymond L. Bryant and Sinead Bailey, *Third World Political Ecology: An Introduction* (New York: Routledge, 1996), 133; Switzer, *Environmental Politics: Domestic and Global Dimensions*.

[102] Michele M. Betsill and Elisabeth Corell, 'NGO Influence in International Environmental Negotiations: A Framework for Analysis', *Global Environmental Politics* 1, no. 4 (2001): 67.

[103] Wapner, 'Horizontal Politics: Transnational Environmental Activism and Global Cultural Change': 42.

[104] Betsill and Corell, 'NGO Influence in International Environmental Negotiations: A Framework for Analysis', 66.

[105] Kellow, 'Norms, Interests and Environmental NGOs: The Limits of Cosmopolitanism', 619.

[106] J. Braithwaite and P. Drahos, *Global Business Regulation* (Cambridge: Cambridge University Press, 2000), 274.

In the case of tropical timber, however, ENGOs have been unable to negotiate as full participants or through proxy states and this is one reason the campaign to prevent exploitation of tropical forests has been unsuccessful to date.

The assessment of the global political role of NGOs, particularly that of ENGOs, has to date been incomplete. Helmut Breitmeier and Volker Rittberger are critical of current NGO scholarship, arguing that despite the plethora of material written on NGOs, there is still 'little systematic knowledge about which actions of which types of NGOs have the greatest impact on international political processes'.[107]

Another group of global actors that has become increasingly important within global environmental regimes are scientists, who provide the technical knowledge and language, as well as encouraging debate and calling on states to act responsibly and comply with existing agreements.[108] This expert knowledge converts readily into political influence in a number of environmental regimes, such as Antarctica and whaling. For many regimes, one of the initial key steps to environmentally protecting a regime is the building of a global scientific consensus that agrees on the issue boundaries and narrows any uncertainties, allowing negotiation to take place.[109] As stated above, many scientists (for example, cetologists) argue from conservationist positions that reflect their scientific beliefs and training.

Transnational Corporations (TNCs) have also become involved in global environmental regime creation and propagation, particularly in the cases of whaling and tropical timber. A TNC can be defined as a 'business that undertake[s] production, sales, and investment within multiple countries and across national boundaries'.[110] What differentiates them from other companies is their quasi-detachment from any one state and their ability to function outside of state control.[111] The sheer scale of these companies means they have a

---

[107] Helmut Breitmeier and Volker Rittberger, 'Environmental NGOs in an Emerging Global Civil Society', in *The Global Environment in the Twenty-first Century: Prospects for International Cooperation*, ed. Pamela S. Chasek (New York: United Nations University Press, 2000), 142.

[108] Braithwaite and Drahos, *Global Business Regulation*, 502; Lorraine M. Elliott, *The Global Politics of the Environment* (Basingstoke: Macmillan, 1998), 120–21.

[109] Pamela S. Chasek, *Earth Negotiations: Analyzing Thirty Years of Environmental Diplomacy* (Tokyo and New York: United Nations University Press, 2001), 28.

[110] Paul Kevin Wapner, 'The Normative Promise of Nonstate Actors: A Theoretical Account of Global Civil Society', in *Principled World Politics: The Challenge of Normative International Relations*, ed. Paul Kevin Wapner and Lester Edwin J. Ruiz (Oxford: Rowman & Littlefield Publishers Inc., 2000), 268.

[111] Ibid.

greater impact on global resource extraction and utilization than many states, since they control assets greater than the gross national product of some nations.[112] Such power has not always been wielded ethically and TNCs have traditionally been considered as organizations that have opposed or reduced the spread of environmental causes to ensure their continuing access to raw materials as well as being a source of pollution.[113]

A study by David Humphreys, Kelly Lee and Michael Pugh has revealed four main routes whereby TNCs have exerted influence:

- They have acquired official representation as members of, or expert advisors to, government delegations negotiating regimes.
- They have organized themselves into associations which are then granted NGO observer status at UN-sponsored negotiations.
- Individual representatives from TNCs have been elected as chairs of committees. For example, in the case of the International Tropical Timber Organization (ITTO), a prominent international timber trader, Ernesto Sanvictores (owner of Armitico and chairman of the Philippines Wood Products Association), was elected chair of the International Tropical Timber Council (ITTC).
- TNCs have provided development assistance to members of various international bodies, such as the ITTO.[114]

In the last few decades, corporations have come to be recognized as major actors on the global scene. With this recognition has come greater awareness of both the environmental damage such entities can do and their potential to act as agents of moral change. Since many corporations cannot exist without access to global resources, they tend not to advocate preservationist ideals but rather positions on a spectrum from outright exploitation to conservation.

TNCs have been responsible for some of the worst cases of exploitation, such as the destruction of tropical forests in Sarawak. On the other hand, other

---

112 Marian A.L. Miller, *The Third World in Global Environmental Politics*, Issues in Third World Politics (Boulder, CO: Lynne Rienner Publishers, 1995), 35; Wapner, 'Politics Beyond the State: Environmental Activism and World Civic Politics', 317.

113 Peter Dauvergne, *Loggers and Degradation in the Asia-Pacific: Corporations and Environmental Management* (Cambridge: Cambridge University Press, 2001), 54; Elliott, *The Global Politics of the Environment*, 123; Gareth Porter and Janet Welsh Brown, *Global Environmental Politics* (Boulder, CO: Westview Press, 1996), 59.

114 David Humphreys, 'Environmental Accountability and Transnational Corporations' (paper presented at the International Academic Conference on Environmental Justice: Global Ethics for the 21st Century, University of Melbourne, Australia, 1–3 October 1997), 4–5.

TNCs have advocated a conservationist position similar to those of certain ENGOs. Where corporate power is strong, particularly in influencing state policy, we can expect to see an exploitative or conservationist norm underpinning a global environmental regime, as in the case of tropical timber.

International Organizations (IOs) are '. . . the bureaucracies that often result from governments working together to solve their problems'.[115] They are often overlooked in regime analyses. The International Whaling Commission (IWC) and the International Tropical Timber Organization (ITTO) are examples. IOs can resolve disputes, manage conflicts, shape international discourse incentives and elaborate norms. Thus they are 'actors' in the regime sense.[116] They may not overtly advocate a particular normative position, but their structure and character can ensure whether a norm becomes dominant or not. In the case of the Scientific Committee on Antarctic Research (SCAR), which considers itself an IO as opposed to an ENGO, its scientific advice has been crucial in providing evidence to support a preservationist position to protect Antarctica's fragile ecosystem.

All of these state and non-state actors seek to establish their preferred norm as dominant within the relevant global environmental regimes. Actors seeking to justify a new norm '. . . try to associate their prescriptions with values that are already accepted as normative within the relevant speech community'.[117] The constructivist Kathryn Sikkink notes that new ideas or norms are likely to be successful if they mesh with pre-existing ideas and philosophies. The best way to 'graft' a moral idea or norm at the global level is when it is '. . . consistent with intersubjective beliefs about the behavior and goals of ideal states'.[118] In the cases studied here, states' own conception of themselves as 'good environmental citizens' can create conducive conditions for the acceptance of moral norms.

## AIM AND STRUCTURE

To recapitulate, this book proposes to unpack the notion of normative transformation within global environmental regimes and explore the following questions:

---

[115] M.G. Schecter, *Historical Dictionary of International Organizations* (London: The Scarecrow Press Inc., 1998), 1.

[116] K.W. Abbott and D. Snidal, 'Why States Act through Formal International Organisations', *Journal of Conflict Resolution* 42, no. 1 (1998): 5.

[117] Reus-Smit, 'Constructivism', 526.

[118] Ibid.: 527.

- Which of the two international relations paradigms used here to investigate global environmental regimes, neoliberal institutionalism and constructivist analyses, has the most explanatory power when it comes to normative transformation within the three case studies examined?
- How can we explain the ascendancy of some environmental norms over others? In particular, how can we explain the rise of, and resistance to, conservation and preservation norms over exploitation norms in environmental regimes?
- Can the two approaches of neoliberalism and constructivism be melded to offer a more robust or rounded analysis of normative transformation or are they incompatible and specific to particular conditions and circumstance?

For decades, the competing schools of neoliberalism and constructivism have both been guilty of exchanging little information, focusing inward on their own theoretical understandings and choosing case studies that suit their own analyses.[119] To bridge this apparent chasm, this book aims to pose to each of the two theories of neoliberalism and constructivism a set of 'hard questions' via an examination of the same three case studies. In the cases of both whaling and Antarctica, can neoliberals explain the dominance of the norm of preservation since it cannot obviously be explained in terms of states' 'interests'? Can constructivism account for normative transformation in these two cases without resorting to an explanation of the use of material levers by actors? In the case of tropical timber, can constructivists explain the role of norms where there are obvious material interests at stake? Answering these questions will enable a more nuanced understanding of the relative strengths and weaknesses of the two theoretical approaches.

To answer the proposed questions, this text will investigate the discursive fora and contexts through which the examined norms were negotiated. This includes examining the proffered arguments put forward by actors and the ideational frameworks utilized to defend positions. The strategies and tactics employed to persuade and manipulate other actors are also analysed, along with a critical reading of the way the normative preferences of the parties are transformed through social interaction. This allows a contrast to be made between norm-driven explanations and interest-driven explanations concerning regime negotiation and normative transformation.

The remainder of this book is organized as follows:

---

119 Marie-Claude Smouts, *Tropical Forests, International Jungle: The Underside of Global Ecopolitics* (New York: Palgrave Macmillan, 2003), 24.

Chapter 1 provides a critical examination of neoliberal institutionalism, focusing on key proponents, its privileging of state interests and how it conceives and analyses norms versus interests, within the three case studies. It sets out a methodology useful to analyse normative transformation and asks how rationalists can account for moral behaviour in norm change.

Chapter 2 undertakes a similar exploration of constructivism, focusing on how norms become accepted or rejected within the global community and the constructivist claim that norms are not merely regulatory but constitutive. Their concept of 'persuasion' is also examined and the willingness of constructivists to analyse stakeholders other than states. It tests a methodological framework developed by Martha Finnemore and Kathryn Sikkink.

Chapter 3 is the case study of Antarctica. It begins with the history of the exploration of the continent and early attempts to exploit the region. It lays out the creation of the Antarctic Treaty system and the various treaty negotiations within that system to protect the region. It uses both a rationalist and a constructivist perspective to analyse treaty negotiations within the Antarctic Treaty Committee Meetings (ATCMs), in particular discussions concerning the designation of Antarctica as a 'world park'. It also examines normative positions as propounded by various parties involved in the negotiations, both state and non-state, to determine which approach has the most influence.

Chapter 4 is the case study of whaling. It outlines a history of whaling exploitation over the centuries and the various attempts, both within and without the IWC (International Whaling Commission), to impose a conservationist regime. This is set against the backdrop of increasing hunting of whales using efficient whale-hunting techniques by fewer states. Paradoxically, as the exploitation of whales accelerated, many states stopped whaling on economic grounds and this chapter explores to what extent this was a significant contributory factor in preservationism becoming dominant in the IWC. Using rationalist and constructivist research techniques, the chapter analyses campaigns by states and NGOs to promote an understanding of the uniqueness and intelligence of whales. It considers whether strategic efforts or moral persuasion have been more successful in creating a whaling moratorium and what has occurred subsequent to the imposition of that ban.

Chapter 5 is the case study of logging, particularly the over-logging and subsequent environmental degradation in the Asia-Pacific. It applies both neoliberal and constructivist perspectives to examine why attempts by members of the ITTC and ENGOs to limit over-logging have been so unsuccessful.

The Conclusion sets out the tentative lessons we can draw from the origin and evolution of environmental norms, the interaction of the actors involved and the potential impact such normative change can have on actors' interests and their effects on global environmental institutions. It offers some tentative suggestions about the implications of this research for the promotion of moral norms applicable to other global environmental problems and expresses the hope that neoliberalism and constructivism may be combined to produce a more rounded analysis that is greater than the sum of its parts.[120]

[120] Oran R. Young, 'Hitting the Mark: Why Are Some International Environmental Agreements More Successful than Others?', *Environment* 41, no. 8 (1999): 28.

# 1. Putting the cart before the horse: neoliberalism, interests and norms

## INTRODUCTION

This chapter sets out to complete three tasks.

- First, to interrogate the theoretical structure and underpinnings of the neoliberal institutionalist research agenda, its conception and treatment of norms.
- Secondly, to provide a robust, representative theoretical model for use in evaluating the three case studies.
- Thirdly, to establish which are the hardest questions challenging the efficacy of the neoliberal approach.

Neoliberal institutionalism has traditionally dominated the study of international environmental agreements (understood as environmental regimes), but is now under challenge from other methodologies, particularly from constructivism. To date, neoliberals have been unwilling to test their results empirically through case studies, preferring to focus instead on developing theoretical viewpoints about global politics.[1]

Central to neoliberal analysis is the premise that principles and norms are the bedrock components of a regime and prescribe orthodox behaviour and proscribe what constitutes deviant behaviour.[2] Norms, according to this analysis, shape states' behaviour by 'matching (exogenously determined) actor's interests and therefore by serving as a "resource" with which to assert their interests'.[3] Thus

---

1 Duncan Snidal, 'Rational Choice and International Relations', in *Handbook of International Relations*, ed. Walter Carlsnaes, Thomas Risse and Beth Simmons (New York: Sage, 2002), 73–4.

2 D. Puchala and R. Hopkins, 'International Regimes: Lessons from Inductive Analysis', in *International Regimes*, ed. Stephen D. Krasner (Ithaca, NY: Cornell University Press, 1983), 86.

3 Henning Boekle, Volker Rittberger, and Wolfgang Wagner, 'Norms and Foreign Policy: Constructivist Foreign Policy Theory', *Tubingen Working Papers* 34a (1999): 7.

the independent variable is *interests* not norms, which are treated as merely '*post-hoc* rationalizations of self-interest'.[4]

Norms have historically been accorded merely a peripheral role within regime analysis. This book will reverse this perspective, focusing on norms as critical to any comprehensive analysis.

## A HISTORY OF NEOLIBERAL INSTITUTIONALISM THEORY

In the late 1970s and early 1980s, neoliberal institutionalist scholars began investigating the impact of economic modernization and increased global economic interdependence, focusing on the norm of cooperation. Their work went beyond the traditional neorealist idea that states were the *only* actors that counted. Robert Keohane, one of the leading writers on neoliberal theory, argued that states are the *principal* actors in global politics.[5]

There is nothing inherent in such an approach that prevents neoliberals from examining the impact and behaviour of other agents besides states. However, doing so makes modelling – the preferred approach of neoliberals – more complex. Given their penchant for theoretical parsimony, neoliberals prefer to ignore this and other outliers, preferring to maintain the state[6] as their primary unit of analysis.[7] However, if we are to understand, for example, how states like France and Australia have changed their conception of their interests in the case of negotiations over the future of Antarctica, we need to 'open the box' and examine endogenous domestic preference formation.

Neoliberal institutionalists have traditionally maintained that the international analogue of a domestic democratic society, in which there are a free market and civil liberties, is a peaceful global order.[8] Steven Krasner argues

---

4 Ibid. While some rationalist proponents, such as Robert Axelrod in *The Complexity of Cooperation: Agent-based Models of Competition and Collaboration* (Princeton, NJ: Princeton University Press, 1997), acknowledge that norms can play a part in establishing and maintaining cooperation, neoliberals tend to treat norms as merely an intervening variable.

5 John Gerard Ruggie, *Constructing the World Polity: Essays on International Institutionalization, The New International Relations* (London and New York: Routledge, 1998) 8.

6 J.T. Checkel, 'Norms, Institutions and National Identity in Contemporary Europe', *International Studies Quarterly* 43 (1999): 84; Robert O. Keohane and Joseph S. Nye, *International Institutions and State Power: Essays in International Relations Theory* (Boulder, CO: Westview Press, 1989), 8.

7 Snidal, 'Rational Choice and International Relations', 83.

8 S. Burchill, 'Liberalism', in *Theories of International Relations*, 2nd edition, ed. S. Burchill et al. (New York: Palgrave, 2001), 63.

that the central tenet of neoliberal theory is that '. . . states are interested in getting to the "Pareto Frontier," the point at which all states maximize their gain through cooperation'.[9] John Hobson makes this analysis more specific when he defines neoliberalism as an approach that understands sovereign states as rational actors that seek to maximize their own long-term interests by creating 'relatively autonomous' international regimes which enhance global state power, thereby enabling states to avoid the sub-optimal anarchy implicit in the international system.[10] Thus neoliberal theory postulates that the conception of international society is necessarily a 'thin one', in that the concept of 'common good' arising from mutually agreed bargains is merely an aggregate of the satisfactions of utility-maximizing states.

Robert Keohane, in his germinal text of 1984, *After Hegemony*, sought to advance beyond traditional liberalism by developing a neoliberal theory of cooperation in global politics. Keohane appropriated three basic assumptions on the nature of the state from neorealist thought and built them into his model. These assumptions were that:

1. States are 'rational egoists', who generally wish to maximize their gains from any transaction, while minimizing costs.
2. Discord prevails as often as harmony in global politics. As Keohane puts it, 'Without the spectre of conflict, there is no need to cooperate'.[11]
3. The state is a 'black box'. Non-state and intra-state (that is, domestic) actors are treated as exogenous since such entities 'continue to be subordinate to the state'.[12]

For Keohane, the state system was one of *possibility*, in that states can thwart the neorealist logic of the system as one of necessity and reform and reshape the global system in order to suit states' interests 'without being punished by the system'.[13] Keohane set the neoliberal framework by arguing that, like neorealists, neoliberals accept that states exist within an anarchical system, that sovereignty is held paramount by states and that these entities

---

[9] Stephen D. Krasner, 'Global Communications and National Power: Life on the Pareto Frontier', in *Neorealism and Neoliberalism: The Contemporary Debate*, ed. D. Baldwin (New York: Columbia University Press, 1993), 237–8.

[10] John M. Hobson, *The State and International Relations*, Themes in International Relations (Cambridge: Cambridge University Press, 2000), 104.

[11] Robert O. Keohane, *After Hegemony: Cooperation and Discord in the World Political Economy* (Princeton, NJ: Princeton University Press, 1984), 54.

[12] Keohane and Nye, *International Institutions and State Power: Essays in International Relations Theory*, 8.

[13] Hobson, *The State and International Relations*, 102.

'pursue self interested goals, which are defined at least partially in terms of relative power and autonomy'.[14]

Building on and refining elements of the neorealist perspective, neoliberals challenge the neorealists' pessimism about human nature and their scepticism about international institutions and regimes. They show that power, understood as relative material capabilities, is the most significant factor (and the only concept) worth studying.[15]

However, for Keohane the difference is that neoliberalism has an interest-based focus. Thus the key research question for him becomes: which parties are benefiting and to what extent?

Keohane and his adherents limit 'which parties' to states only, a point we will return to later in this chapter. In *After Hegemony* (1984), Keohane argues that regimes are only *relatively* autonomous from the states that create them.[16] States create regimes to overcome the 'Gordian knot' of collective action implicit in an anarchic system.[17] Neoliberal analysis can conclusively show that 'cooperation under anarchy' is achievable and that state actors, as rational egoists, can forge homeostatic cooperative regimes that overcome collective action dilemmas.[18]

Neoliberals ascribe, therefore, to the 'logic of consequences', which dictates that state actors evaluate alternative strategies according to the likely consequences for their individual or collective ends. Their view of society is one of a grouping of individuals seeking to satisfy their own individual ends

---

[14] Robert O. Keohane, Joseph S. Nye, and Stanley Hoffmann, *After the Cold War: International Institutions and State Strategies in Europe, 1989–1991* (Cambridge, MA: Harvard University Press, 1993), 5. Neoliberalism postulates that states can think in absolute gains terms, as opposed to neorealists, who argue states should only calculate decisions in terms of relative gains. Neoliberalists like Robert Keohane have argued that in reality '. . . neoliberal institutionalism is not simply an alternative to neorealism, but, in fact, claims to subsume it' and improve upon it. Keohane and Nye, *International Institutions and State Power: Essays in International Relations Theory*, 15.

[15] Andreas Hasenclever, Peter Mayer and Volker Rittberger, *Theories of International Regimes*, Cambridge Studies in International Relations 55 (New York: Cambridge University Press, 1997), 30.

[16] Hobson, *The State and International Relations*, 98.

[17] This enabled Keohane to explain the endurance of regimes after US hegemony. By de-linking regimes from hegemony and embedding them in state power, neoliberal analysts are able to argue that such regimes are more 'resilient' or 'robust' than neorealists suggest. It is important to note that regime autonomy is only relative '. . . since it is states that intentionally create regimes in order to avoid conforming to the logic of short term gains (associated with anarchy), so that they can enhance their long-term absolute gains'. Ibid.

[18] Thomas Risse, '"Lets Argue!": Communicative Action in World Politics', *International Organization* 54, no. 1 (2000): 1–39 at 4–5.

by calculative means. For neoliberals, societal obligations are only granted by consent or contract and always within the scope of calculated self-interest. Neoliberal researchers generally dismiss the question of identity.[19]

Neoliberals draw heavily on economic theories of information and transaction costs and on game theory.[20] Game theory is a subset of rational choice theory that social scientists apply to 'interactive' situations where the outcome is determined by both a player's own behaviour and the strategic moves of other players. It enables analysts to formalize social structures and evaluate the impact of structure on individual decisions.[21] Critics charge that such games simply reproduce 'already known' information or use technical language to hide the paucity of their analysis. However, while the mathematics can be daunting to the neophyte, game theory can provide novel insights into coordination problems and the social world.[22]

For example, neoliberals use the Prisoner's Dilemma (a type of game theory) to demonstrate when actors can be expected to cooperate or defect. In a single game, a neorealist would argue, it is better to defect and avoid cooperation. Keohane argues that in repeated games, that is, if the players expect to meet again in the future, such a course of action invites retaliation and it is better for players to cooperate.[23] Proponents of this approach, like Robert Keohane, argue that such scenarios are common in international politics and are valuable in working out when actors may choose to cooperate.[24] For

---

19 James G. March and Johan P. Olsen, 'The Institutional Dynamics of International Political Orders', *International Organization* 52, no. 4 (1998): 949–51.

20 Neoliberalism as a rationalist theory is conducive to the choice-theoretic assumptions of microeconomic theory. This theory assumes all actors are '. . . atomistic, self interested and rational'. Christian Reus-Smit, 'Constructivism', in *Theories of International Relations*, 2nd edition, ed. S. Burchill et al. (New York: Palgrave, 2001), 213. These actors are pre-social since their identities and interests are *autogenous*, and they are concerned primarily with rationally achieving their own self-interests within the environmental constraints of the world. Secondly, and following from the above, these actors' interests are assumed to be already formed (*exogenous*). Consequently, international society is envisaged as a strategic realm in which actors come together to pursue their pre-defined interests. Actors are not inherently social, but atomistic rational beings who tolerate social relations to optimize their interests. Reus-Smit, 'Constructivism', 213.

21 Moshe Hirsch, 'Compliance with International Norms in the Age of Globalization: Two Theoretical Perspectives', in *The Impact of International Law on International Cooperation*, ed. Eyal Benvenisti and Moshe Hirsch (Cambridge: Cambridge University Press, 2004), 173.

22 Snidal, 'Rational Choice and International Relations', 73.

23 Keohane, *After Hegemony: Cooperation and Discord in the World Political Economy*, 75.

24 Hasenclever, Mayer, and Rittberger, *Theories of International Regimes*, 30–32.

Keohane, the social world is best captured by repeated Prisoner's Dilemma games, since over time states come into reciprocal contact with each other and can learn to cooperate for mutual benefit.[25] Using this model, neoliberals argue that the main impediment to cooperation is cheating and that this should be borne in mind when creating regimes.[26]

Other gaming variants include the Assurance Game, where all parties must comply with an agreed rule. Gaining information about other participants' plans is crucial to compliance. The Coordination Game is similar, but with multiple Pareto equilibria, over which participants have divergent goals. The Game of Chicken examines situations where the best result may be either unilateral action or mutual cooperation. Non-cooperative behaviour can be avoided if both parties realize that mutual defection yields the worst outcome for both parties.[27] The Asymmetric Deadlock game models a situation where one party has no intention to seek agreement. The deadlock can be broken if the anti-agreement party can be made to see the value of agreement.[28]

Theoretical modelling in the form of the Prisoner's Dilemma, Assurance, Chicken and other games has advanced the neoliberal research agenda considerably and has become a standard metaphor amongst neoliberal theorists for global anarchy.[29]

Some critics have charged that game theory is too theoretical to use in real-life case studies. To some extent, Robert Putnam's gaming theories have attempted to address this flaw and to delve into an analysis of real world situations. Putnam utilizes a theory of 'two-level games' to analyse reciprocal causation between national and global politics.[30] Putnam in his 1988 study

---

[25] Hobson, *The State and International Relations*, 98.

[26] R.J. Flowers, 'International Norms and Domestic Policies in Japan: Identity, Legitimacy and Civilization' (Ph.D., University of Minnesota, 2002), 3.

[27] Hirsch, 'Compliance with International Norms in the Age of Globalization: Two Theoretical Perspectives', 175–8.

[28] Deborah S. Davenport, 'An Alternative Explanation for the Failure of the UNCED Forest Negotiations', *Global Environmental Politics* 5, no. 1 (2005): 108–9. The gaming approach utilized by neoliberals is not without its critics. Ian Rowlands, himself a neoliberal, is critical of neoliberalism's emphasis on game theory, arguing that it leads to unrealistic isolation of the game from its international context. Ian H. Rowlands, *The Politics of Global Atmospheric Change: Issues in Environmental Politics* (Manchester: Manchester University Press, 1995), 22–4. Such an approach tends to oversimplify problems, leading to merely binary conceptions of cooperation rather than nuanced answers to the reality of negotiating outcomes. J.K. Sebenius, 'Challenging Conventional Explanations of International Cooperation: Negotiation Analysis and the Case of Epistemic Communities', *International Organization* 46, no. 1 (1992): 324.

[29] Snidal, 'Rational Choice and International Relations', 77.

[30] Robert D. Putnam, 'Diplomacy and Domestic Politics: The Logic of Two-level Games', *International Organization* 42, no. 3, Summer (1988): 459.

identifies two types of non-compliance which he labelled voluntary and involuntary. Voluntary defection occurs in cases where a 'rational egoist' chooses to renege in the absence of enforceable contracts. Involuntary defection occurs when a state is unable to back up its initial promise because of a failed domestic ratification.[31] With the Putnam two-level analysis, the defining image is one of state leaders negotiating on two separate 'chessboards' – domestic and international.[32] This overcomes the neoliberal tendency to ignore domestic considerations.

He is unusual amongst neoliberals in that, while focusing on the traditional representatives of states such as executive officials, he allows a role for domestic political parties and NGOs.[33] However, his approach is that of an outlier and is not consistent with the major tenets of neoliberal thought. For Putnam, cooperation by states is fundamental to the long-term utility-maximizing interests of states.[34] However, as a theoretical construct, neoliberal institutionalism seeks '. . . to explain why states eschew independent decision making'[35] and 'bind themselves to mutually beneficial courses of action'.[36] His theory echoes constructivist approaches when he postulates that states 'learn' over time to interact to advance their mutual interests, particularly in policy areas like welfare and the promotion of human rights.[37] Putnam also allows for what he call 'suasive elements' in his approach, stressing that they should not be discounted.[38] He does not examine the concept in depth, but such a concept if implemented would appear to go beyond instrumentalism and into constructivist territory, which may open up new linkages with constructivist research.

For neoliberals, the concept of 'cooperation' between states operating in an anarchic global system for mutually beneficial gains is paramount to their

---

31 Ibid.: 438.

32 Sonia Cardenas, 'Norm Collision: Explaining the Effects of International Human Rights Pressure on State Behavior', *International Studies Review* 6 (2004): 219.

33 Putnam, 'Diplomacy and Domestic Politics: The Logic of Two-level Games', 459.

34 Hobson, *The State and International Relations*, 98.

35 Arthur A. Stein, *Why Nations Cooperate: Circumstance and Choice in International Relations* (Ithaca, NY: Cornell University Press, 1990), 28

36 K. Oye, 'Explaining Cooperation under Anarchy: Hypotheses and Strategies', in *Cooperation under Anarchy*, ed. K. Oye (New Jersey: Princeton University Press, 1986), 2.

37 E. Adler, B. Crawford and J. Donnelly, 'Defining and Conceptualising Progress in International Relations', in *Progress in Postwar International Relations*, ed. Emanuel Adler and Beverly Crawford (New York: Columbia University Press, 1991).

38 Putnam, 'Diplomacy and Domestic Politics: The Logic of Two-level Games', 455.

research agenda.[39] This concept of cooperation is understood to be a '. . . set of relationships that are not based on coercion or compellence'.[40] States elect to cooperate to reduce uncertainty and minimize risks, otherwise chaotic anarchy would be the dominant international principle. They can cooperate, because they are calculating, and see their interests on a given issue as converging, or the gains of cooperation being greater than the costs involved in sustaining a regime, or all of the above.[41] State cooperation is not the opposite of conflict, but is envisaged as a process that is able to manage any potential conflict before it occurs.[42] However, cooperation between states should not be confused with a harmony of interests.[43]

## NEOLIBERALISM AND REGIMES

Neoliberal institutionalists have traditionally approached environmental issues through the study of environmental regimes.[44] The study of international regimes originated within the neorealist approach of Hegemonic Stability Theory (HST) in the 1970s and early 1980s.[45] IR theories such as neorealism

---

39 Christopher C. Joyner, *Governing the Frozen Commons: The Antarctic Regime and Environmental Protection* (Columbia, SC: University of South Carolina Press, 1998), 84.

40 James E. Dougherty and Robert L. Pfaltzgraff, *Contending Theories of International Relations: A Comprehensive Survey*, 4th edition (New York: Longman, 1997), 418.

41 Joyner, *Governing the Frozen Commons: The Antarctic Regime and Environmental Protection*, 84. As put succinctly by Chris Reus-Smit, 'The existence of mutual interests is a prerequisite for international cooperation, but neoliberals insist that the existence of such interests does not itself explain the extent and nature of cooperative relations between states – international cooperation remains difficult to achieve'. Reus-Smit, 'Constructivism', 212. Rather, even if states have mutual interests, the absence of a global authority means states are unwilling to enter into reciprocal arrangements for fear of other states cheating. Reus-Smit, 'Constructivism', 212.

42 Keohane, Nye, and Hoffmann, *After the Cold War: International Institutions and State Strategies in Europe, 1989–1991*, 4–5.

43 Lorraine Elliott, *International Environmental Politics: Protecting the Antarctic* (New York: St Martin's Press, 1994), 7.

44 Eivend Hovden, 'As If Nature Doesn't Matter: Ecology, Regime Theory and International Relations', *Environmental Politics* 8, no. 2 (1999): 50.

45 Hegemonic Stability Theory (HST) argued that a hegemony existing within the international system such as the United States and the actions of such a hegemon facilitated cooperation. The decline in US power in the 1970s saw the theory discredited and discarded by the international relations community. Peter M. Haas, *Saving the Mediterranean: The Politics of International Environmental Cooperation*, *The Political Economy of International Change* (New York: Columbia University Press, 1990), 42–3.

emphasize that hegemons are often initiators of multilateral policies and are prepared to underwrite the sunk costs associated with cooperation.[46] The theory was originally developed with the aim of undermining liberalism and interdependence theory but failed in its objective due to its failure as a predictive theory.[47]

Researchers studying regimes initially focused on the need for a hegemon to impose their will for a regime to coalesce around a given issue area. Once the regime has been created there is an assumption by regime theorists that the hegemon will inevitably be able to influence regime negotiations for the lifespan of the regime.[48] The idea of a hegemon-imposed systemic stability has been comprehensively refuted by regime analysts and an ever-expanding series of case studies has demonstrated that the environmental regimes that have come into being have done so without hegemonic support.[49] Interest-based analyses of regimes have displaced HST and have been extremely influential in the last decade, to the point of emerging as the dominant approach to analysing international regimes. Though not entirely disregarding power differentials, proponents emphasize the role international regimes play in allowing states to realize common interests.[50]

What constitutes a regime is the subject of much debate by IR theorists. It is generally acknowledged that the concept of a 'regime' was invented 'to meet the need for something looser and less rigid than (even) international law or an international organization'.[51]

However, the term has come to mean different things to different theorists and actors. Martin List and Volker Rittberger define a regime broadly as 'a

---

46 Audie Klotz, *Norms in International Relations: The Struggle against Apartheid*, Cornell Studies in Political Economy (Ithaca, NY: Cornell University Press, 1995), 93.

47 Krasner argues that the most glaring problem with HST was its prediction that the free trade agreement of the 1980s would not come into existence because of opposition by the hegemon of that period, the United States. Hobson, *The State and International Relations*, 95.

48 Donald R. Rothwell, *The Polar Regions and the Development of International Law*, Cambridge Studies in International and Comparative Law 3 (New York: Cambridge University Press, 1996), 16.

49 As Porter et al. point out: 'The environmental regimes that have been successfully negotiated have depended on wide consensus among a number of states, not on imposition by the United States.' Gareth Porter, Janet Welsh Brown and Pamela S. Chasek, *Global Environmental Politics*, 3rd edition, Dilemmas in World Politics (Boulder, CO: Westview Press, 2000), 17.

50 Hasenclever, Mayer and Rittberger, *Theories of International Regimes*, 45.

51 I. William Zartman, 'Negotiation, Governance, and Regime Building', in *International Governance on Environmental Issues*, ed. Mats Rolen, Helen Sjoberg and Uno Svedin (Dordrecht: Kluwer Academic Publishers, 1997), 65.

social institution wherein stable patterns of behavior result from compliance with certain norms and rules, whether these are laid down in a legally binding instrument or not'.[52] Porter and Brown argue that this system of norms and rules must be outlined in a multilateral legal instrument enacted by states and designed to regulate their actions in a specific issue area.[53] This narrower definition has tended to be dominant within regime studies and thus regime analysis is usually confined to the study of conventions and treaties in a given area (Jakobsen, 1999) and their creation (for example, Vogler, 2000, on global commons regimes). All three case studies under consideration here are governed by multilateral legal agreements: the International Convention on Regulation of Whaling 1946; the Antarctic Treaty 1959; and the International Tropical Timber Agreement 1983.

As defined in the introduction, Stephen Krasner's influential definition of a regime places norms at the front and centre, yet neoliberals to date have tended to adopt a utilitarian approach to norms that de-emphasizes a regime's social or symbolic components.[54] Vogler argues that regime analysts have lost their way with their focus on positivistic models and their privileging of rationally negotiated intergovernmental agreements. In doing so, regime analysts have moved away from an original understanding of regimes as *social institutions*. He maintains that the key is to understand 'the framework within which actors perform their rational calculus' and the challenge 'is not to reconstruct that calculus but to explain how the underlying rules are shaped and legitimated'.[55] This understanding repositions neoliberalism as not that far apart from current constructivist approaches and may become a way of reconciling the two.

Similarly, Oran Young argues that regimes should be seen as constituting the 'rules of the game' under which transnational actors seek their aims, a

---

[52] M. List and V. Rittberger, 'Regime Theory and International Environmental Management: Actors, Interests and Institutions', in *The International Politics of the Environment*, ed. Andrew Hurrell and Benedict Kingsbury (Oxford: Oxford University Press, 1992), 89–90.

[53] Gareth Porter and Janet Welsh Brown, *Global Environmental Politics* (Boulder, CO: Westview Press, 1991), 20. Thus, regimes are always created and operate in the context of multilateral negotiations. These negotiations occur when states believe the current situation is untenable and that the state may suffer adversely if existing trends continue. This conception of a state's interests argues that, while it is important to agree as to how to manage a particular problem, it is critical to negotiate away as little as possible while obtaining as much benefit as possible. Porter, Brown and Chasek, *Global Environmental Politics*, 13.

[54] Stephen D. Krasner, *International Regimes*, Cornell Studies in Political Economy (Ithaca, NY: Cornell University Press, 1983) 2.

[55] John Vogler, 'Taking Institutions Seriously: How Regime Analysis Can Be Relevant to Multilateral Environmental Governance', *Global Environmental Politics* 3, no. 2 (2003): 38.

position not dissimilar from constructivism.[56] A regime's objective is to create a particular order that benefits all those subject to its constraints.[57] The task of the theorist is to research how regimes mould the behaviour of its transnational actors, concerned to determine how and under what conditions a regime will be effective.[58] The regime literature to date has been mostly confined to *describing* cooperative interaction, exploring and explaining the formation of regimes and specifying the conditions under which institutions *function* effectively.[59] State compliance with a regime is considered a game of 'strategic exchange among egoistic, self-interested actors', with agents leaving a regime the same as when they entered it (in terms of their identities and interests).[60]

Regimes are created in relation to an 'issue area' around which state and other global actors converge.[61] The scope of a regime is usually defined as the boundary of a given issue area since states create regimes to deal with problems that are so closely aligned that they should be dealt with together. These issue areas are understood as:

> sets of issues that are in fact dealt with in common negotiations and by the same, or closely coordinated bureaucracies, as opposed to issues that are dealt with separately and in uncoordinated fashion. Since issue areas depend on the actor's perceptions and behaviour rather than on inherent qualities of the subject-matters, their boundaries change gradually over time.[62]

For example, the Antarctic Treaty deals with a range of issues relating to a clearly defined geographic area: that of Antarctica and its surrounding seas. Whaling and tropical timber regimes focus on a particular 'material resource',

---

[56] Oran R. Young, 'Hitting the Mark: Why Are Some International Environmental Agreements More Successful than Others?', *Environment* 41, no. 8 (1999): 1.

[57] Marian A.L. Miller, *The Third World in Global Environmental Politics*, Issues in Third World Politics (Boulder, CO: Lynne Rienner Publishers, 1995), 53.

[58] Young, 'Hitting the Mark: Why Are Some International Environmental Agreements More Successful than Others?', 1.

[59] Effectiveness in this context means bringing about a change in an actor's behaviour which in the absence of a regime would not have not been possible. Oran R. Young, 'The Effectiveness of International Institutions: Hard Cases and Critical Variables', in *Governance without Governance: Change and Order in World Politics*, ed. J.N. Rosenau and E. Czempiel (New York: Cambridge University Press, 1992), 161.

[60] J.T. Checkel, 'Why Comply? Constructivism, Social Norms and the Study of International Institutions' (paper presented at the Annual Meeting, American Political Science Association, Atlanta, Georgia, 1999), 4.

[61] Rothwell, *The Polar Regions and the Development of International Law*, 14.

[62] Keohane, *After Hegemony: Cooperation and Discord in the World Political Economy*, 61.

since they are found in multiple geographic locations (whales in the oceans and tropical forests over multiple states). However, all three can be understand as issue areas, since states and non-state actors have treated each one as an issue needing a regime to regulate it.

Faced with material incentives, agents choose whether to comply, based on the cost/benefit calculations they make.[63] The decision-makers are 'utility maximizers' in neoliberalist terms, in that they have goals (preferences) that they strive to realize through their actions.[64] Decision-makers seek to optimize these preferences via collaboration with other actors.[65] Neoliberals treat preferences as *exogenous*. They explore how preferences are formed and/or change over time.[66] Focusing on fixed preferences has the advantage of allowing neoliberals to focus tightly on an issue in an empirically falsifiable way.[67] However, in the search for theoretical parsimony, they are unable to accommodate change in the character of the actors and the global system.[68]

State actors often try to change their own national preferences through, for example, joint scientific research (which proved vital to creating the Antarctic regime) or cultural and political exchanges with other actors. In doing so, actors not only change their own information 'but also their shared beliefs with respect to equilibrium behaviour, they change their preferences over courses of actions even if their underlying preferences are stable'.[69]

Adherence to, or violation of, a particular global norm depends on a cost/benefit analysis of the existing positive and negative incentives and the time frame in which they are expected to accrue.[70] Thus regimes are seen as

---

63 Checkel, 'Why Comply? Constructivism, Social Norms and the Study of International Institutions', 4.

64 Hirsch, 'Compliance with International Norms in the Age of Globalization: Two Theoretical Perspectives', 172.

65 Nicole Dietelhoff and Harald Muller, 'Theoretical Paradise – Empirically Lost? Arguing with Habermas', *Review of International Studies* 31 (2005): 167.

66 Kjell Goldmann, 'Appropriateness and Consequences: The Logic of Neo-institutionalism', *Governance: An International Journal of Policy, Administration and Institutions* 18, no. 1 (2005): 44.

67 Snidal, 'Rational Choice and International Relations', 84.

68 Ibid.: 80.

69 Ibid.: 85. By 'equilibrium' neoliberals mean 'a statement of consistency among specified elements, that there is no pressure on any of the elements to change given the values of the other elements. It is thus an evaluation of a whole state of affairs and claims only that the elements can co-exist with one another while stipulating nothing about their sequence or causal relationship.' Snidal, 'Rational Choice and International Relations', 76. Ironically, this formulation is understood as more *constitutive* than causal. Snidal, 'Rational Choice and International Relations', 76.

70 Hirsch, 'Compliance with International Norms in the Age of Globalization: Two Theoretical Perspectives', 171. Within regime analysis, the work of Ernst Haas,

altering the structure of incentives facing states and as leading to a consequent altering of a state's behaviour. The Antarctic regime is widely regarded as an example of successful global cooperation between those nations with a historical interest in scientific exploration in Antarctica and a mutual desire to see the area remain peaceful, nuclear-free and unblighted. It was these nations that came together to form the regime.[71] According to neoliberal analysis, fear of open access mining, and a desire to appease a more environmentally conscious domestic electorate, led to a key group of states calculating that it was better to preserve Antarctica. Other states, fearing that an acrimonious debate would endanger the regime by opening up old grievances and that some parties would benefit more than others, were willing to preserve the region for a fixed period of time.

In the case of whaling, several unsuccessful attempts (in the first half of the twentieth century) to create a whaling regime that states would not cheat on culminated in the USA using its new post-World War II status as a global superpower to host a conference where a global whaling regime was created to conserve whaling stocks. However, once again cheating and defections occurred and the exploitation of whales actually increased in the 1950s and the 1960s. Such exploitation was carried out by fewer states as the economic benefits for many states from whaling declined and other goods were substituted. The lack of economic benefit derived from whaling and the realization that whales were close to extinction, coupled with the desire of mainly Western states to appease domestic concerns over the loss of whales as a species, led to the imposition of a global moratorium on whaling. Most states currently accede to the ban since there is no longer any economic incentive to hunt whales, but a few rogue states, in a coalition led by Japan (and other traditional whaling nations, which still have an economic stake in the pursuit of whales), are attempting to bring the regime back to an ostensibly conservationist position.

The tropical timber regime is considered a failure by many ENGOs because states have considered that their economic interests are better served by allowing the harvesting of tropical timbers to continue. The regime was originally created as a cartel to ensure an efficient supply of timber to consumer states.

---

Ruggie and Adler and others has tried to escape this dominant approach with references within their body of work to learning, internalization and persuasion where compliance can be achieved through a process of interest/identity redefinition, but this approach has never really threatened to displace the dominant analyses of material interest calculation. However, it may provide a bridge between neoliberal and constructivist approaches. Checkel, 'Why Comply? Constructivism, Social Norms and the Study of International Institutions', 4–5.

[71] Young, 'Hitting the Mark: Why Are Some International Environmental Agreements More Successful than Others?', 1.

While attempts have been made to strengthen the conservationist aims of the regime, a particularly effective veto coalition, compromising both producer and consumer states, has stymied the development of such a norm.

Such regimes can work at both the individual and collective level. At the individual level, they can 'provide information about potential joint gains from cooperation, reassuring actors that others also intend to join in the cooperative equilibrium and provide timely information about behaviour to diminish incentives to cheat'.[72] But there is also a collective level, where norms of behaviour and shared beliefs are forged. Such common knowledge moves approaches such as neoliberalism away from their individualist roots towards a more collective outlook, which can parallel constructivist research.[73]

While an understanding of the individual and collective behaviour of regimes is reasonably well understood, Oran Young argues that individual *leadership* is not.[74] A critical examination of key states and individuals would help to breach the neoliberal black box of preference formation. Interestingly, such an analysis is consistent with constructivists like Martha Finnemore and Kathryn Sikkink, who consider norm entrepreneurs as important to norm development.

Researchers such as Young argue that well-constructed regimes reduce the incentive for actors to cheat,[75] specifically through recognition that other states can retaliate. This provides a disincentive to defect, while reciprocal behaviour provides an incentive to cooperate.[76] This leads states to conceive of their future in terms of absolute cooperative gains rather than defecting for short-term relative gains. The issue of 'issue linkage' can also prevent states from defecting. States resist particular actions, such as domestic rent-seeking, for fear they will be considered 'rogue' by other states.[77] On the other, some states, such as Japan, press for changes in international regimes (for example, whaling), despite the damage this does to their international reputation. Why is this?

According to neoliberals, regimes are said to transform or evolve in a number of different ways. Internal contradictions within the regime itself can prompt change. Such contradictions can be part of the initial regime or they may emerge over time. In other cases, change is brought about via external

---

72 Snidal, 'Rational Choice and International Relations', 83.

73 Ibid.

74 Oran R. Young and Gail Osherenko, *Polar Politics: Creating International Environmental Regimes*, Cornell Studies in Political Economy (Ithaca, NY: Cornell University Press, 1993), 253.

75 Ibid.: 237.

76 Ibid.

77 Hobson, *The State and International Relations*, 98–9.

factors such as a shift in the relative power between adherent states. Regimes may also be threatened when states redefine their interests following a change in government or when there has been a paradigm shift in uses of technology or patterns of economic interaction.[78] Regime change may be prompted as a strategic response to pressures extraneous to the regime, such as the appearance of new actors with new demands and different expectations of behaviour.[79]

Zartman describes such regime transformation almost poetically in terms of regimes as:

> watercourses flowing through time and space. Neither just the source nor the surface, they involve the entire body of water from its upper manifestations as international agreements to its benthic effects on local politics (and local and national politics' effects on the regime). Regimes are quite different from many other types of agreements in that they are not simply negotiation outcomes, processed and filed, but are living ongoing agreements moving through time.[80]

This changing nature through time is critical to an understanding of regimes and the norms that underpin them. As the norms alter or are supplanted by other norms, regimes are transformed in an ongoing process of negotiation, implementation, loopholes being closed, new members being added or current members leaving and obligations being strengthened or lessened.[81] Young points out that:

> Much of the effort in processes of regime formation goes into discussions of the pros and cons of different ways to frame the problem in contrast to extracting concessions from other participants. It makes a big difference in terms of the discourse of problem solving, for instance, whether an issue is discussed in the language of environmental protection or in the language of sustainable development.[82]

The same lesson holds true for regime transformation and for whether the debate is cast by various stakeholders in terms of exploitation, conservation or preservation.

Such regime change does not tend to occur lightly due to the 'sunk costs', that is, investment in past efforts.[83] Whilst international regimes are constantly evolving, actors generally prefer to obey a regime's rules rather than see the

---

78 Miller, *The Third World in Global Environmental Politics*, 55–6.

79 Elliott, *International Environmental Politics: Protecting the Antarctic*, 22.

80 Zartman, 'Negotiation, Governance, and Regime Building', 57–8.

81 Ibid.: 58.

82 Oran R. Young, 'Fairness Matters: The Role of Equity in International Regimes' (paper presented at the Environmental Justice: Global Ethics for the 21st Century, University of Melbourne, 1–3 October 1997), 5.

83 Elliott, *International Environmental Politics: Protecting the Antarctic*, 20.

regime collapse (for example, the whaling regime). Conversely, if the 'cost' of the behaviour imposed by the regime is considered too high by an actor, they will not abide by the regime's norms. If too many actors regard the regime as being against their material interests, then the regime will collapse.

There are invariably some agents who prefer the status quo. Work done by Gareth Porter and Janet Welsh Brown on 'veto coalitions' is critical to an understanding of norm evolution within regimes from a neoliberal perspective. They postulate that within every issue-specific regime '. . . there is one state or a group of states whose cooperation is so essential to a successful agreement for coping with the problem that it has the potential to block strong international action'.[84] States that oppose or attempt to lessen an agreement are referred to as veto states, or when there is a bloc of them, veto coalitions. This veto coalition's strength is determined by how essential is the need for cooperation of this faction, and their ability to block global action.[85] Veto states often, by their intransigence, reduce agreement to its lowest common denominators, thus weakening an agreement. The case studies will be used to determine if and when this occurs.[86]

Analysing the actions of various states active in preventing (or trying to prevent) normative change will be critical to a 'thick' understanding of norm evolution. An understanding of the actions of the USA, in attempting to prevent the adoption of the Madrid Protocol preserving Antarctica for 50 years from any mining activities, is vital to understanding contested norm transformation. Similarly, the Japanese tactic of lavishing large sums of developmental aid on certain developing nations, to buy support for their campaign to roll back the whaling moratorium, needs to be explored for its impact on regime development.[87] Thus this book will seek to identify veto states and coalitions, what motivates their behaviour and what impact their actions have on norm evolution.

Neoliberalism subsumes norms within its theoretical approach. At the individual actor level, it poses the question of how people should behave. It asks the question what is the best (as in most calculated and hence 'rational') choice in a particular scenario, given the actors' preferences, and based on their interests? At the collective level, the theory analyses how groups can do better

---

[84] Gareth Porter and Janet Welsh Brown, *Global Environmental Politics*, 2nd edition (Boulder, CO: Westview Press, 1996), 14.

[85] Ibid.

[86] Radoslav S. Dimitrov, 'Hostage to Norms: States, Institutions and Global Forest Politics', *Global Environmental Politics* 5, no. 4 (2005): 20.

[87] Alexander Gillespie, *Whaling Diplomacy: Defining Issues in International Environmental Law* (Cheltenham, UK and Northampton, MA, USA: Edward Elgar, 2005) 433–4.

through cooperation.[88] Yet when examining norms within regimes, and attempting to account for regime change, neoliberals have assigned norms a lesser value, holding that norms are primarily regulatory (not constitutive) and are subservient to actors' interests.

Neoliberal institutionalists, when examining regimes, argue that norms are an essential part of what constitutes a regime, but the study of norms by the advocates of neoliberalism remains mostly under-theorized and unexamined. As Hurrell puts it:

> Clearly there are many international norms that derive their compliance pull from a shared sense of justice: human rights most notably, but also, for example, norms against armed conquest and the annexation of territory. Rules and norms of this kind do not develop as a result of the direct interplay of state interests or because of the functional benefits which they provide. Rather than depend on common moral awareness that works directly, if still in fragile and uneven ways, on the minds and emotions of individuals within states.[89]

While neoliberalism is comfortable analysing norms of cooperation, treating such norms as a causative element in explaining why some cooperative ventures work and others fail, it is less clear how well neoliberals can incorporate norms such as justice or appropriateness into their environmental considerations. However, neoliberalism can certainly analyse the impact of norms on regimes, particularly if norms are treated as the actor's objectives.[90]

Moral norms such as conservation and preservation, if accepted by a significant proportion of the global community, can compel states to alter their behaviour. However, neoliberals have rarely chosen to examine such effects. They prefer to assign norms an extremely limited role, one that merely influences the choice of the object of study.[91] Hobson argues that, for neoliberals: 'At most, norms are conceived in rationalism as intervening variables that lie between the basic causal variables (i.e. power actors) and international outcomes'.[92]

More generally, the neoliberal analysis of ideas and norms tends to be conducted in an ad hoc fashion, and comes from outside the neoliberal framework. It is done when the usual suspects of power and interest cannot totally

---

88 Snidal, 'Rational Choice and International Relations', 85.

89 Andrew Hurrell, 'International Society and the Study of Regimes: A Reflective Approach', in *Regime Theory and International Relations*, ed. V. Rittberger (Oxford: Clarendon Press, 1993), 65–6.

90 Snidal, 'Rational Choice and International Relations', 85–6.

91 Matthew Paterson, *Understanding Global Environmental Politics: Domination, Accumulation, Resistance* (New York: St Martin's Press, 2000), 15.

92 Hobson, *The State and International Relations*, 147.

account for state behaviour. This does not challenge the basic neoliberal understanding of regimes as primarily a functional approach to collective action problems. As Wendt argues, an approach that treats the concept of ideas and norms as merely 'intervening or superstructural variables will always be vulnerable to the charge that they are derived from theories that emphasise the base variables of power and interest, merely mopping up unexplained variance'.[93]

A few neoliberals have conceded that the '. . . norms of regimes may be internalised by important groups and thus become part of the belief systems which filter information' and that this in turn '. . . alters the way key participants in the state see cause and effect relationships'.[94] However, Checkel disputes that neoliberals actually apply this insight, arguing that on the whole, for neoliberals, a norm is not internalized by elites, it merely functions as a constraint on behaviour. Such norms are only empowered when elites, facing internal pressure, recalculate their strategies. Their interests (for example, political survival) remain the same, however.[95]

The neoliberal theoretical model assumes that states necessarily gain *material* benefit from the act of cooperation, though even reputational benefits are seen as just a means to some material end. Thus international regimes may impose normative obligations that do not marry with a state's material interests, the benefits that accrue being such intangible gains as increased international legitimacy and a good relationship within the community of states. Although these factors are less tangible and hard to quantify, they are no less important, and the material consequences are deemed no less significant.[96]

Andrew Hurrell argues, contrary to the mainstream neoliberal approach, that the theoretical and empirical task of a regime theorist is to show '. . . that laws and *norms* [my italics] exercise a compliance pull of their own, at least partially independent of the power and interests that underpinned them and which were often responsible for their creation'.[97] Hurrell is rightly critical of the neoliberal approach to norms, arguing that because of their rationalist, positivist underpinnings, neoliberals are incapable of explaining why states

---

93 Alexander Wendt, *Social Theory of International Politics* (Cambridge: Cambridge University Press, 1999), 93.

94 Keohane and Nye, *International Institutions and State Power: Essays in International Relations Theory*, 266.

95 J.T. Checkel, 'International Norms and Domestic Politics: Bridging the Rationalist–Constructivist Divide', *European Journal of International Relations* 3, no. 4 (1997): 477.

96 Flowers, 'International Norms and Domestic Policies in Japan: Identity, Legitimacy and Civilization', 4.

97 Hurrell, 'International Society and the Study of Regimes: A Reflective Approach', 53.

should cooperate on *moral* or *ethical* grounds.[98] Regime theory rarely examines the moral content of the regime. Rather the focus is on whether regimes alter states' behaviour.[99]

Neoliberalism also downplays the alteration in a state's interests following normative change and assigns secondary importance to altruistic motives compared to political and economic interests.[100] Neoliberals such as Porter and Brown emphasize both the political and economic weight powerful states can wield if so inclined.[101] However, as will be demonstrated, the case studies of Antarctica and whaling show that altruistic moral values need not be secondary. They can be a critical factor in normative change.

While regimes are products of strategic bargaining, neoliberals seem unable to appreciate that such negotiations take place within a broader moral context than the self-interest one, especially in the case of environmental regimes.[102]

Thus moral arguments, such as the whale's right to exist, would seem to play no part unless they mesh with the material interest of the state. Further, neoliberal theory, because of its emphasis on material interests, appears to have no explanation for global environmental regimes that reflect a preservationist norm, such as whaling and Antarctic minerals, and that on the face of it are contrary to various states' interests. Vogler agrees that a neoliberal approach which privileges:

> rational choice assumptions cannot encompass the whole range of human motivations and values and particularly those prominent in environmental politics. Politically significant ideas of environmental justice or wilderness values are largely inaccessible to rational choice analysis.[103]

Politics is typically a combination of self-interest and altruism and focusing on one to the detriment of the other impoverishes any analysis. The emphasis on strategic/material interests makes an examination of altruistic behaviour difficult using neoliberal analytical tools. Given that the environmental norms under examination have an altruistic component, one of the

---

98 Ibid.: 65–6.

99 Hovden, 'As If Nature Doesn't Matter: Ecology, Regime Theory and International Relations', 54.

100 Elliott, *International Environmental Politics: Protecting the Antarctic*, 22.

101 Porter and Brown, *Global Environmental Politics*, 14–15.

102 Robyn Eckersley, 'Soft Law, Hard Politics, and the Climate Change Treaty', in *The Politics of International Law*, ed. Christian Reus-Smit (Cambridge: Cambridge University Press, 2004), 32.

103 Vogler, 'Taking Institutions Seriously: How Regime Analysis Can Be Relevant to Multilateral Environmental Governance', 27.

questions neoliberals will have to answer is how they account for altruistic behaviour and normative change within the three case studies, especially when such behaviour is contrary to state material interests. For their 'rational choice' approach to hold up, they need to show that altruistic behaviour is not in fact influential in producing behavioural change, that the only real (and possibly concealed) motivation is a state's strategic interests.

Recently, some regime theorists have begun using the concept of 'social learning' to supplement their interest-based analyses. Thus norms are credited by neoliberals, in some circumstances, as having influence beyond that of material interests. But the explanatory power of norms is only argued in an ad hoc manner, and admitted only when the usual explanations of power and interest in regard to state behaviour are considered insufficient.[104] Such social learning theoretical constructs are at odds with mainstream neoliberalist methodology that utilizes an atomistic individualistic analysis. Such an approach cannot successfully 'model the interaction context during which agents' interests may change'.[105]

Indeed, the neoliberal use of the terminology 'social interactions' is neither social nor an interaction in any real sense. While neoliberals allow that simple learning can occur and agents may thus acquire new information via interaction, such information can only alter future strategies, not the preferences that inform them, since those remain fixed.[106] More sophisticated regime theories must be developed which incorporate a deeper understanding of the crucial role norms play, including that of reflexive learning. While the work of authors like Vogler (2000) and Young (2002) is a positive start, to date there has been only a cursory use of the intersubjective dimensions to regimes by neoliberal researchers.

The fact that there are few neoliberal studies that make explicit the role of global norms in international environmental regimes makes it a difficult, but not impossible, task for the researcher to explore the way altruism changes regimes using a neoliberal perspective. The methodological approach utilized by neoliberals has been mostly shaped by the positivist approach. This same approach underpins that of neorealists who explicitly endorse a Lakatosian model of theory construction, whereby progress is measured by a process of hypothesizing, refutation and proof.[107] This positivist methodology emphasizes that social

---

104 Eckersley, 'Soft Law, Hard Politics, and the Climate Change Treaty', 31.

105 Checkel, 'Why Comply? Constructivism, Social Norms and the Study of International Institutions', 9.

106 Ibid.

107 Reus-Smit, 'Constructivism', 210. However, it should be acknowledged that the positive methodology utilized by neoliberals is often difficult to apply to the social realm. As Peter Haas and Ernst Haas have pointed out: 'Scholars in the natural sciences

phenomena can be understood in the same way as the natural world and that facts and values must be kept separate and will be striven for in this book.[108]

The essence of neoliberal analysis is its emphasis on strategic bargains between *states* that bring about cooperation to solve mutual problems. Normative transformation is only brought about in this view when states' self-interested behaviour is changed by the matrix of strategic bargaining. For states, such institutional bargaining is generally an 'interest-based activity in which participants drive hard bargains designed to promote their own causes'.[109] Consistent with this position, this book will explore how a neoliberal would answer the following standard questions in each case study under consideration:

- Which states have generated which environmental norms and taken which position regarding norm transformation?
- If normative change has occurred, what change to the actor's cost/benefits calculus has occurred and what strategic bargaining prompted such evolution?
- How has domestic preference formation affected particular critical states' interests?
- What incentives/factors have required states to comply with the normative position accepted within a regime?
- What impact, if any, have veto states or coalitions had on norm evolution?
- Have norms become institutionalized within the actor's long-term interest calculations?

Neoliberalists also have to answer the hard question of whether they can account for altruistic behaviour within the three case studies. Lastly, the neoliberal framing of a research agenda is generally understood as highlighting 'given actors' interests (and institutional and other) constraints, what will be the outcome?'[110] A more interesting and potentially far-reaching research question, however, and the one asked here, is 'given actors' interests, how

---

do not face the problem of reconciling competing protean principles. Their units of analysis lack free will.' Peter M. Haas and Ernst Haas, 'Pragmatic Constructivism and the Study of International Institutions', *Millennium: Journal of International Studies* 31, no. 3 (2002): 583.

108 Maja Zehfuss, 'Constructivisms in International Relations: Wendt, Onuf, and Kratochwil', in *Constructing International Relations: The Next Generation*, ed. Karin M. Fierke and Knud Erik Jorgensen (London: M.E. Sharpe, 2001), 3.

109 Young, 'Fairness Matters: The Role of Equity in International Regimes', 6.

110 Snidal, 'Rational Choice and International Relations', 86.

should we rearrange institutional constraints to achieve our normatively desired outcome?'[111] This question offers the possibility of taking neoliberal research into uncharted waters and potentially to thicken the under-theorized neoliberal analysis of norms other than those of 'calculative' rationalism.

---

111 Ibid.

# 2. The gentle art of persuasion: constructivism and norms

## INTRODUCTION

This chapter has three objectives. First, it seeks to investigate critically the constructivist research agenda, with particular emphasis on its (re)conception and treatment of norms. Secondly, it endeavours to establish a robust, representative model of the role of norms that can be tested empirically in the three case studies chosen. Thirdly, it seeks to identify some hard questions that constructivists need to answer if their research project is to progress.

All constructivists, with the possible exception of the postmodern branch of radical constructivism, cleave to two basic understandings of the human world: it is *social* and it is a *construct*.[1] That is, the material world cannot be considered 'objectively knowable' because 'the objects of our knowledge are not independent of our interpretations and our language'.[2]

Consequently, the constructivist research agenda is underpinned by two assumptions. First, the world is both social and material. Secondly, it is their social setting which provides agents with an understanding of their interests (indeed, it constitutes them). For constructivists, the agency/structure question is answered by an ontology of interaction or mutual constitution where neither agents or structures are reducible to the other and neither is made 'ontologically primitive'. Such an approach opens up questions of interest and identity formation not answered by neoliberals, allowing an examination of agents' interests that 'emerge from and are endogenous to interaction with institutional structures'.[3]

---

1 Stefano Guzzini, 'A Reconstruction of Constructivism in International Relations', *European Journal of International Relations* 6, no. 2 (2000): 149.

2 Emanuel Adler, 'Constructivism and International Relations', in *Handbook of International Relations*, ed. Walter Carlsnaes, Thomas Risse and Beth Simmons (New York: Sage, 2002), 95.

3 Joseph Jupille, James A. Caporaso, and Jeffrey T. Checkel, 'Integrating Institutions: Rationalism, Constructivism, and the Study of the European Union', *Comparative Political Studies* 36, nos. 1/2 (2003): 14.

Constructivism as a general theoretical approach is uniquely suited to an investigation of the role of norms in regimes because, in privileging the concept of 'intersubjectivity', it allows the researcher a more contextualized understanding of the social world.[4] Constructivists argue that to understand a given act we must not only examine the actor's perspective but the intersubjective understandings that reveal to us the social meaning of the act in question. For example, kicking the ball into a net and scoring a goal in soccer is only explicable if one understands the background, rules and mores of soccer.[5] At the global level of analysis:

> Constructivism considers intersubjective *knowledge* and ideas to have constitutive effects on social reality and its evolution. When drawn upon by individuals, the rules, norms and cause-effect understandings that make material objects meaningful become the source of people's reasons, interests and intentional acts; when institutionalised they become the source of international practices.[6]

For constructivists, any norm presupposes intersubjective agreement because they are collective expectations.[7] When one group of agents accepts a new principle of appropriate behaviour, this decision can alter the social dynamic for other agents, bringing about change as the others attempt to accommodate the change.[8] Thus, constructivists consider the social world to be one of *becoming* rather than *being*. The constructivist approach is distinguishable from idealism, post-structuralism and postmodernism because it 'accepts that not all statements have the same epistemic value and there is

---

[4] The concept of 'intersubjectivity' is arguably crucial to the constructivist project. Adler's conception of constructivism's value '. . . lie[s] mainly in its emphasis on the ontological reality of intersubjective knowledge and on the epistemological and methodological implications of this reality'. Maja Zehfuss, *Constructivism in International Relations: The Politics of Reality* (Cambridge: Cambridge University Press, 2002), 251.

[5] Friedrich V. Kratochwil, 'Constructivism as an Approach to Interdisciplinary Study', in *Constructing International Relations: The Next Generation*, ed. Karin M. Fierke and Knud Erik Jorgensen (London: M.E. Sharpe, 2001), 30.

[6] Adler, 'Constructivism and International Relations', 102.

[7] Sebastian Maslow and Ayako Nakamura, 'Constructivism and Ecological Thought: A Critical Discussion on the Prospects for a "Greening" of IR Theory', *Interdisciplinary Information Sciences* 14, no. 2 (2008): 136; Thomas Risse and Kathryn Sikkink, 'The Socialization of International Human Rights Norms into Domestic Practices: Introduction', in *The Power of Human Rights: International Norms and Domestic Change*, ed. T. Risse, S.C. Ropp and K. Sikkink (Cambridge: Cambridge University Press, 1999), 7.

[8] M.J. Hoffmann, 'Entrepreneurs and Norm Dynamics: An Agent-based Model on the Norm Life Cycle', University of Delaware, http://www.psych.upenn.edu/sacsec/abir/_private/Pamla/Hoffmann_norms.doc, accessed 31/07/06.

consequently some foundation for knowledge'.[9] Chris Reus-Smit argues correctly that constructivism is best understood as '. . . not a theory but rather an analytical framework' through which to examine the material world and, in this specific case, the origin and transformation of norms.[10]

All constructivist research seeks to ascertain how certain ideas are taken for granted, become dominant or are discarded.[11] Its emphasis on ideas, human interaction and social communication allows the concept of norms to be studied overtly rather than as an afterthought. For constructivists, norms are 'collective expectations about proper behaviour for a given identity'.[12] Such norms constitute actors' social identities, including the identities and interests of states, by providing their content and meaning. Such an approach grounds normative research in mental acts and encompasses the notion that how actors apply norms to classify the world helps us to better understand global politics.[13]

Collectively, norms help define the basic 'rules of the game'. Norms can be violated or altered without undermining their significance or impact. Environmental norms such as conservation and preservation have been violated by actors in all the case studies under review, but still remain significant standards of behaviour to be met by the overall global community. Of course, the strength of a norm at any given time is an empirical question (a point taken up later in this chapter in an examination of Jeffrey Legro's test of the strength of a norm). Norms enable actors to understand the standard of behaviour expected of them by other global actors but actors can still chose to ignore that standard.[14]

9 Adler, 'Constructivism and International Relations', 95. Many scholars describe constructivism mistakenly as 'idealism' or 'ideationalism'. However, constructivists focus on 'norms' rather than 'ideology', arguing that normative behaviour arises out of a legitimated and shared understanding. John M. Hobson, *The State and International Relations*, Themes in International Relations (Cambridge: Cambridge University Press, 2000), 146.

10 Christian Reus-Smit, 'Constructivism', in *Theories of International Relations*, 2nd edition, ed. S. Burchill et al. (New York: Palgrave, 2001), 222.

11 Audie Klotz, 'Can We Speak a Common Constructivist Language', in *Constructing International Relations: The Next Generation*, ed. Karin M. Fierke and Knud Erik Jorgensen (London: M.E. Sharpe, 2001), 232.

12 Ronald Jepperson, Alexander Wendt, and Peter Katzenstein, 'Norms, Identity, and Culture in National Security', in *The Culture of National Security: Norms and Identity in World Politics*, ed. Peter Katzenstein (New York: Columbia University Press, 1996), 54.

13 Adler, 'Constructivism and International Relations', 103; Hoffmann, 'Entrepreneurs and Norm Dynamics: An Agent-based Model on the Norm Life Cycle'.

14 Thomas Risse, '"Let's Argue!": Communicative Action in World Politics', *International Organization* 54, no. 1 (2000): 5.

For constructivists, identity is 'at the core of national and transnational interests'.[15] Thus constructivists argue that states' interests and identities are far more fluid than neoliberalist theory provides.[16] The constructivist conception of interests is that they are always changing and responding to normative structural changes.[17] This fluidity means for constructivism '. . . that identities and interests in international politics are not stable – they have no pre-given nature . . . The important thing is to look at how identities and interests are constructed – how they are made or produced in and through specific interactions'.[18] Critics charge that identity is not as fluid a concept as constructivists maintain, hence identity should be assumed to be fixed for reasons of theoretical parsimony. However, there are many examples where states' identities have altered, such as Germany coming to accept Europe as part of its state identity in the post-World War II period.[19]

At its core, however, constructivism is concerned with socialization and 'reasons for action'.[20] Such reasons can be an individual or group motive and a justificatory claim. Reus-Smit argues that such reasons can:

> have internal and external dimensions, or private and public aspects. Both normative and ideational structures are constitutive of actors' reasons in both dimensions: through processes of socialization they shape actors' definitions of who they are and what they want; and through processes of public justification they frame logics of argument.[21]

The constructivist turn in IR has led to the framing of new and critical questions pertaining to 'the role of identities, norms and causal understandings in the constitution of national interests, about institutionalisation and international governance, and about the social construction of new territorial and non-territorial transnational regions'.[22] However, its success has come at a price, with criticisms from both within constructivist ranks and beyond

15 Adler, 'Constructivism and International Relations', 103.

16 See Seeng Tan, 'Rescuing Constructivism from the Constructivists: A Critical Reading of Constructivist Interventions in Southeast Asian Security', *The Pacific Review* 19, no. 2 (2006): 243.

17 Hobson, *The State and International Relations*, 146.

18 Cynthia Weber, *International Relations Theory: A Critical Introduction* (London: Routledge, 2001), 60.

19 Adler, 'Constructivism and International Relations', 104.

20 Michael Jeffrey Griesdorf, 'Norms as a Rhetorical Competition: Soviet–American Confrontations over Cuba, 1970–85', *Cold War History* 8, no. 3 (2008): 302.

21 Christian Reus-Smit, 'The Politics of International Law', in *The Politics of International Law*, ed. Christian Reus-Smit (Cambridge: Cambridge University Press, 2004), 22.

22 Adler, 'Constructivism and International Relations', 96.

(Goldmann 2005; Legro, 1997) as to the proper way for the constructivist research project to proceed, and particularly as to how norms should be studied.

## THE RISE OF CONSTRUCTIVISM IN INTERNATIONAL RELATIONS

Constructivism became an influential theory in international relations in the 1980s and 1990s. A significant reason for this was that the end of the Cold War was unforeseen by neoliberalists, leading to criticism of this approach as one lacking explanatory and predictive power.[23] A new generation of international relations scholars, heavily influenced by critical theory, saw this as an opportunity to demonstrate the validity of non-rationalist perspectives.[24] At the same time leading rationalists challenged critical theorists to take their research focus beyond a mere theoretical critique and produce a more robust empirical analysis of international relations issues. Constructivists responded to this criticism. They argued that their project was an attempt to marry '. . . critical theoretical insights with empirical evidence' and one that would open up new vistas and approaches.[25]

However, constructivism to date has been less concerned with theory building than with providing another analytical language. In the eyes of critics to the constructivist approach, it does not reveal any insights into global events or phenomena but rather has focused on creating a 'metanarrative'. While some constructivists such as Martha Finnemore are motivated to correct this perceived deficit, constructivism as a general approach has still not corrected this egregious oversight and is limited because of it.[26] This criticism is well founded and this book will focus on testing constructivist theory by applying it empirically to the three case studies, with the aim of advancing the constructivist research agenda.

The social world observed by constructivists is 'broader, more contingent, more unexpected, more surprising and endowed with more possibilities' than is generally admitted by neoliberals.[27] Constructivists, with their more sociological orientation, emerged in the 1990s to offer a general theoretical orien-

23 Ibid.: 98.

24 Reus-Smit, 'Constructivism', 216. Critical theorists, building on the insights of the neo-Marxists, challenged the rationalist project with its positivist assumptions, calling instead for an interpretive approach. Reus-Smit, 'Constructivism', 214.

25 Ibid.

26 Knud Erik Jorgensen, 'Four Levels and a Discipline', in *Constructing International Relations: The Next Generation*, ed. Karin M. Fierke and Knud Erik Jorgensen (London: M.E. Sharpe, 2001), 43.

27 Adler, 'Constructivism and International Relations', 100.

tation and research programme that rivals neoliberal approaches. Its adherents argue that such studies have come about, in part, as a rebellion '. . . against the economistic reasoning that has come to dominate the field over the last decade'.[28] Importantly, constructivists do not dismiss the rationalist project but are critical of the neoliberal approach that characterizes rationality as only *instrumental*. They are concerned to expand the theoretical understanding of rationality to include 'communicative rationality' and to emphasize communication and persuasive logic.[29]

Constructivism was founded on a rejection of the neoliberal construction of rationalism that had come to dominate the field of IR. Significant numbers of IR proponents were utilizing economic modelling as an approach, arguing that such rationalist tools could be applied to a wide range of case studies in international relations. However, constructivists argued that this *homo economicus* approach was to the detriment of the discipline as an explanatory tool, being devoid of cultural content. It led theorists to embrace '. . . *homo sociologicus* and images of society that are cultural and thickly constituted'.[30] *Homo sociologicus* bases his/her actions on a 'logic of appropriateness' which 'takes socially shared, value-based expectations of behavior as its point of reference'.[31] Actors are conceived as following rules that convey particular identities to particular situations, and 'approaching individual opportunities for action by assessing similarities between current identities and choice dilemmas and more general concepts of self and situations'.[32]

This 'logic of appropriateness' formulation has encapsulated within it two different modes of social action and interaction where:

> In many social situations, actors regularly comply with norms that have been thoroughly internalized and that, therefore, 'are taken for granted'. Whereas strategic behaviour is explicitly goal-oriented, the 'taken for grantedness' of norm-regulated behaviour implies that enacting the norm need not be a conscious process, even though norms that are no longer believed will probably disappear or change soon.[33]

---

28 M. Barnett, 'Historical Sociology and Constructivism: An Estranged Past, a Federated Future?', in *Historical Sociology of International Relations*, ed. John M. Hobson and Stephen Hobden (Cambridge: Cambridge University Press, 2002), 99–100.

29 Adler, 'Constructivism and International Relations', 102.

30 Barnett, 'Historical Sociology and Constructivism: An Estranged Past, a Federated Future?', 100.

31 Henning Boekle, Volker Rittberger, and Wolfgang Wagner, 'Norms and Foreign Policy: Constructivist Foreign Policy Theory', *Tubingen Working Papers* 34a (1999): 4.

32 James G. March and Johan P. Olsen, 'The Institutional Dynamics of International Political Orders', *International Organization* 52, no. 4 (1998): 951.

33 Risse, '"Let's Argue!": Communicative Action in World Politics', 6.

The logic of appropriateness allows for a far more complex analysis of human interaction because it also leaves room for a consideration of consequences and embraces questions of identities.[34] James March and Johan Olsen clearly consider the logic of appropriateness superior to the logic of consequences since it preaches inclusiveness and emphasizes complexity and variation. However, its inclusiveness does make for a certain theoretical fuzziness and its fixation on complexity and variation are seen by critics as theory avoidance.[35]

It also dictates that actors choose from a menu of actions 'based upon institutional, moral, or normative standards – preferences and interests themselves are shaped by what is considered appropriate'.[36] This conception of a 'logic of appropriateness' is further understood as being:

> behaviours (beliefs as well as actions) [that] are intentional but not willful. They involve fulfilling the obligations of a role in a situation and so trying to determine the imperatives of holding a position. [. . .] Within a logic of appropriateness, a sane person is one who is 'in touch with identity' in the sense of maintaining consistency between behavior and a conception of self in a social role.[37]

However, the constructivist quest to ascertain reasons for actions leads them to focus not only on the idea of the logic of appropriateness (conformity of action with behavioural standards) but also on the 'logic of argumentation' or the way norms provide the framework in which actors are able to communicate with each other on legitimate questions of agency, purpose and strategy.[38] The emphasis on mutually accepted obligations is why sometimes the framework of constructivism is referred to as one of *obligation* rather than of 'necessity' (neorealism) or 'possibility' (neoliberalism).[39]

Constructivists maintain that neoliberal approaches do not fully capture the depths of contemporary global politics, including the role of agent identity and the way social learning by agents can transform the current global system.[40]

---

[34] Kjell Goldmann, 'Appropriateness and Consequences: The Logic of Neo-institutionalism', *Governance: An International Journal of Policy, Administration and Institutions* 18, no. 1 (2005): 44.

[35] Ibid.: 49.

[36] Hoffmann, 'Entrepreneurs and Norm Dynamics: An Agent-based Model on the Norm Life Cycle'.

[37] Boekle, Rittberger, and Wagner, 'Norms and Foreign Policy: Constructivist Foreign Policy Theory', 4.

[38] Reus-Smit, 'The Politics of International Law', 23.

[39] Hobson, *The State and International Relations*, 148.

[40] Peter M. Haas and Ernst Haas, 'Pragmatic Constructivism and the Study of International Institutions', *Millennium: Journal of International Studies* 31, no. 3 (2002): 576.

For constructivists, politics is not merely a case where actors with fixed preferences interact via a continuum of strategic exchange. Rather constructivist theorists endeavour to explain 'both the content of actor identities/preferences and the modes of social interaction – so evident in everyday life – where something else aside from strategic exchange is taking place'.[41]

The constructivist approach, despite the criticisms of it, accepts the importance of material power and interest calculations, but argues that there are other factors at play.[42] They maintain in the social world there are often factors, particularly ideational factors, that cannot be reduced to a mere strategic exchange between self-interested actors.[43] In the case studies examined here, it is observable that ENGOs attempted to argue ideational positions that in some cases directly contradict certain states' interests, for example, the United States' position on Antarctic mining. It is an empirical test to determine whether, and to what extent, such considerations are able to sway environmental norm development. Constructivists postulate that '... material resources only acquire meaning for human action through the structure of shared knowledge in which they are embedded'.[44] Consequently, actors' interests evolve as identities change and normative structures alter.[45]

For constructivists, what matters are not an individual's value preferences, but rather 'the inter-subjectively shared, value-based expectations of appropriate behavior' that they, and consequently society, share.[46] As such, actors are 'deeply embedded in and affected by the social institutions in which they act'.[47] A social actor is not a *tabula rasa*. When confronted by a problem or an option to act, such an actor draws on 'pre-existing and usually stable schemata, beliefs and ideas about the external world and deeply ingrained norms about appropriate behaviour', such as the idea that preserving whales is a moral 'good'.[48]

---

41 J.T. Checkel, 'The Constructivist Turn in International Relations Theory', *World Politics* 50, no. 2 (1998): 9.

42 Sonia Cardenas, 'Norm Collision: Explaining the Effects of International Human Rights Pressure on State Behavior', *International Studies Review* 6 (2004): 217.

43 J.T. Checkel, 'Social Construction and Integration', *ARENA Working Papers* WP 98/14 (1998): 22.

44 Alexander Wendt, 'Constructing International Politics', *International Security* 20, no. 1 (1995): 73.

45 Hobson, *The State and International Relations*, 146.

46 Boekle, Rittberger, and Wagner, 'Norms and Foreign Policy: Constructivist Foreign Policy Theory', 4.

47 Thomas Risse and Cornelia Ulbert, 'Deliberately Changing the Discourse: What Does Make Arguing Effective?', *Acta Politica* 40, no. 3 (2005): 5.

48 Christoph O. Meyer, 'Convergence Towards a European Strategic Culture? A Constructivist Framework for Explaining Changing Norms', *European Journal of International Relations* 11, no. 4 (2005): 527.

The *raison d'être* of the constructivist project, as perceived by Emanuel Adler, is that '. . . constructivism opens up the "objective facts of world politics, which are facts only by human agreement", as new areas for empirical investigation'.[49] Such an approach attempts to research '. . . the conditions which make the construction of certain representations of reality possible'.[50] Thus for constructivists, norms are 'social facts' that can be studied by the researcher via the case-study method.[51]

Constructivists maintain that social norms are constitutive in that they not only regulate behaviour but also help constitute the identity of actors by defining who are the members of a given social community.[52] The critical point:

> is that social constructivists insist on the mutual constitutiveness of (social) structures and agents. Constructivists claim against individualism that human agents do not exist independently from their social environment and its collectively shared systems of meaning ('culture' in a broad sense). At the same time, social constructivists maintain that human agency creates, reproduces, and changes culture by way of daily practices.[53]

Constructivists maintain that such a constitutive approach to researching the social world can be more than merely descriptive. It can and should also be explanatory of the social world.[54]

They have tended to focus their field of inquiry '. . . on such distinctive processes as socialisation, education, persuasion, discourse and norm inculcation'.[55] Analysing the effects of these types of social communication, for

---

49 Maja Zehfuss, 'Constructivisms in International Relations: Wendt, Onuf, and Kratochwil', in *Constructing International Relations: The Next Generation*, ed. Karin M. Fierke and Knud Erik Jorgensen (London: M.E. Sharpe, 2001), 250.

50 Ulf Hjelmar, *The Political Practice of Environmental Organizations* (Brookfield, VT.: Ashgate Publishing Company, 1996), 32.

51 Adler, 'Constructivism and International Relations', 100. Constructivists distinguish between social and material facts, in that social facts '. . . are facts only by human agreement and which account for the majority of the facts studied in IR, differ from rocks and flowers, because, unlike the latter, their existence depends on human consciousness and language'. Adler, 'Constructivism and International Relations', 100.

52 Risse and Ulbert, 'Deliberately Changing the Discourse: What Does Make Arguing Effective', 5.

53 Risse, '"Let's Argue!": Communicative Action in World Politics', 5.

54 Alexander Wendt, *Social Theory of International Politics* (Cambridge: Cambridge University Press, 1999), 86.

55 Haas and Haas, 'Pragmatic Constructivism and the Study of International Institutions', 577. Persuasion can be conceived of as a process which 'involves changing people's choices of alternatives independently of their calculations about the strategies of other players'. Robert O. Keohane, 'Governance in a Partially Globalized World', *American Political Science Review* 95, no. 1 (2001): 10. For constructivists,

example, while analysing how debate and persuasion reframe issues and promote shared understanding, helps us reconceive the social world as one thickly wired with social rules and standards of acceptable behaviours.[56] This focus suits a project investigating the transformation of environmental norms because as Adler et al. observe, 'the view that *the manner in which the material world shapes and is shaped by human action and interaction depends on dynamic normative and epistemic interpretations of the material world*' (emphasis in original).[57] Constructivist analysis is singularly suitable, therefore, for studying *change*. Rey Kozlowki and Friedrich Kratochwil argue that constructivists attach paramount importance to 'the way individuals adopt changed practices arising from new conceptions of identity and political community, thereby altering interactions among states, or, conversely, the way changed interactions among states alter practices among individuals'.[58]

## A TOPOGRAPHIC MAP OF CONSTRUCTIVIST RESEARCH

Constructivism as a research framework can be encapsulated in three propositions:

1. Actors' social identities and motives for interaction are largely ideational.
2. Their identities affect their interests and goal-seeking.
3. Their actions reflect mutually constitutive relationships developed within social structures.[59]

Reus-Smit proposes that currently constructivism has 'three key axes of debate: between sociological institutionalists, Habermasian communicative action theorists, and Foucauldian genealogists; between unit-level, systemic,

---

the function of debate is to ensure compliance with 'identity related obligations'. Goldmann, 'Appropriateness and Consequences: The Logic of Neo-institutionalism', 47.

56 Adler, 'Constructivism and International Relations', 102.

57 E. Adler, B. Crawford, and J. Donnelly, 'Defining and Conceptualising Progress in International Relations', in *Progress in Postwar International Relations*, ed. Emanuel Adler and Beverly Crawford (New York: Columbia University Press, 1991), 32.

58 Rey Kozlowski and Friedrich V. Kratochwil, 'Understanding Change in International Politics: The Soviet Empire's Demise and the International System', in *International Relations Theory and the End of the Cold War*, ed. Richard Ned Lebow and Thomas Risse-Kappen (New York: Columbia University Press, 1995), 136.

59 Reus-Smit, 'Constructivism', 217–18.

and holistic theorists; and between interpretivists and positivists'.[60] The first debate is between constructivists influenced by sociological institutionalism, by Habermasian communicative action theory and by Foucault's work on knowledge and power. Much of American constructivist thought has developed out of sociological institutionalism represented by John Meyer and the 'Stanford school' of sociology. This approach emphasizes the way 'world culture' constitutes social agents, and actors' identities and interests.[61]

Martha Finnemore argues that, for constructivism '. . . the social structure is ontologically primary. It is the starting point for analysis. Its rules and values create all actors we might consider relevant in international politics, including states, firms, organizations, and even individuals.'[62] Thus, there is a critical place for international non-state actors and international organizations insofar as they help shape global social structures. Consequently those bodies '. . . are effectively the agents that transmit or diffuse the norms of the deep structure, principally by teaching states how to behave' and can be considered to be 'pro-active norm carriers'.[63] Tracking and understanding the role played by these norm transmitters will be critical to understanding the case studies in this inquiry and the methodology to do so will be laid out later in this chapter.

The second variation of constructivist dialect emphasizes the Habermasian approach, which focuses on the 'logics of argument', for instance, the place of communicative action in mediating between agents and intersubjective values (Kratochwil, 1989; Onuf, 1989; Risse, 2000 are all proponents of this approach). Here actors are up against multiple (possibly contradictory) norms of behaviour, which have many possible interpretations. Realists argue that in

---

60 Christian Reus-Smit, 'Imagining Society: Constructivism and the English School', *British Journal of Politics and International Relations* 4, no. 3 (2002): 488. The splintering of constructivist thought is not easily defined for the serious scholar let alone the casual observer. Ted Hopf argues that there are both critical and conventional constructivists; Price and Reus-Smit postulate that there is modern and postmodern constructivism while Immanuel Adler, building on the insights of Lynch and Klotz, distinguishes between modern, legal, narrative and genealogical constructivist approaches. Reus-Smit, 'Imagining Society: Constructivism and the English School', 493.

61 Reus-Smit, 'Imagining Society: Constructivism and the English School', 493. There is an assumption within constructivism that states do not always know what they want and thus how are state interests to be defined? Finnemore and Sikkink argue that 'peer pressure' can bring about the acceptance of a new norm because a state's identity is shaped 'by the cultural-institutional context within which states act'. Martha Finnemore and Kathryn Sikkink, 'International Norm Dynamics and Political Change', *International Organization* 52, no. 4 (1998): 902.

62 Martha Finnemore, 'Culture and World Politics: Insights from Sociology's Institutionalism', *International Organization* 50, no. 2 (1996): 333.

63 Hobson, *The State and International Relations*, 149–50.

such a situation actors will merely go back to self-interested and power-aggrandizing methods, but Habermasian constructivists say that actors will argue with the goal of establishing mutually agreed rules of conduct for the regime. As Agnes Heller puts it:

> Contestants enter the discourse with different values and they all try to justify their values (as right and true). They do this by resorting to values higher than those which they want to justify, by proving that the latter are but an interpretation of the higher values, or that they can be related to these values without logical contradiction.[64]

This is particularly true in the case studies examined in this book where norm advocates, such as ENGOs, use moral arguments that appeal to 'higher values' (for example, the need to conserve regions for future generations), to convince the listener of the rightness of their cause. However, the efficacy of appealing to higher order values is again an empirical question that will need to be evaluated.

The third branch of constructivism is grounded in Foucault's insights on knowledge and power. Richard Price argues that, for Foucault,

> the production of discourses is a form of power, as it constructs categories that themselves make a cluster of practices and understandings seem illegitimate or even inconceivable. This disciplinary power defines what is normal and natural and what is unthinkable and reprehensible.[65]

This approach holds that the origin of norms and their meanings at a point in time and within a particular context are decided discursively and thus are politically contingent. Consequentially, advocates of this approach utilize a 'genealogical' method which 'is strategically aimed at that which looks unproblematic and is held to be timeless; its task is to explain how these present traits, in all their vigour and truth, were formed out of the past'.[66]

The second great cleavage amongst constructivist theorists is over the level at which one conducts analysis. Alexander Wendt's approach is to focus only on the systemic level and to argue that the domestic level is theoretically irrelevant.[67] Wendt's decision to focus on the state as the unit of study has been

---

64 Agnes Heller, *Beyond Justice* (Oxford: Blackwell, 1987), 239.

65 R. Price, 'Moral Norms in World Politics', *Pacifica Review* 9, no. 1 (1997): 9.

66 Jens Bartelson, *A Genealogy of Sovereignty*, Cambridge Studies in International Relations (Cambridge: Cambridge University Press, 1995), 73.

67 Alexander Wendt, 'Anarchy Is What States Make of It: The Social Construction of Power Politics', *International Organization* 46, no. 2 (1992): 393. Wendt's analysis derives two principles for constructivism. The first utilizes the concept of *subjectivity* and holds that people act towards other people and things on the basis of the meaning those people and things have for them. That is why states act

heavily criticized by other constructivists as reifying the state and not enabling the study of other important actors such as transnational communities or NGOs. Limiting constructivism to only studying inter-state relations is not necessary and may in fact be contrary to the constructivist research project that ultimately examines constructing the entire world.[68]

In contrast to Wendt's approach, unit-level constructivists such as Checkel focus on the relationship between domestic social and legal norms and the identities and interests of states in a global system.[69] There is a need for constructivists to be open to examining 'domestic determinants of change . . . since this is the place where national preferences are born, and international practices are produced, reproduced and transformed'.[70] An understanding of how domestic environmental norms become important at the global level and how domestic preference formation influenced norm transformation is critical to the research project undertaken here. The environmental norms of conservation and preservation were borne at the domestic level and their impact is still felt within states, particularly in the case of the tropical timber that is harvested in many states. Further, how preferences are formed domestically is key to understanding how states' representatives are influenced by domestic considerations such as public pressure and voting patterns in the case of issues like exploiting minerals in Antarctica and whaling.

Constructivists who focus on the systemic level have been given the appellation 'transnational constructivists'. This branch of constructivism originated in the 'sociological institutionalism' research stream and over the past decade has created an impressive body of work. It is transnational in that it focuses its research at the international level and is constructivist in that it accepts as a fundamental assumption that reality is socially constructed.[71] Transnational

---

differently to other states as to whether they are perceived as friend or foe, but the logic of anarchy cannot distinguish between the two states of being. Wendt, 'Anarchy Is What States Make of It: The Social Construction of Power Politics', 396–7. Further international politics is not an autonomous sphere in that states are not paradigmatically 'black boxes'. In reality, they are 'an assembly of normatively constituted practices by which a group of individuals form a special type of political association'. Kozlowski and Kratochwil, 'Understanding Change in International Politics: The Soviet Empire's Demise and the International System', 135.

68 Adler, 'Constructivism and International Relations', 108.

69 Peter Katzenstein takes a different approach in his book *Cultural Norms and National Security* (1996) and argues that '[g]enerally speaking social norms in the international society of states are less dense and weaker than those in domestic society'. Hobson, *The State and International Relations*, 165. He argues that 'states differ internally in their make-up and, crucially, that this impacts upon their behaviour in the international system'. Hobson, *The State and International Relations*, 165.

70 Adler, 'Constructivism and International Relations', 110.

71 Boekle, Rittberger, and Wagner, 'Norms and Foreign Policy: Constructivist Foreign Policy Theory', 11–12.

constructivism argues that immaterial structures (institutions, norms) alter states' behaviours and that the neorealist model of an anarchical international system should be displaced by the concept of an international society which 'as a social system, both constitutes the identities and interests of its members and is reproduced by their practices'.[72]

Transnational constructivists, such as Finnemore and Christoph Meyer, argue that state actors within the global arena exhibit a remarkable level of similarity (isomorphism) and that this is due to the pervasiveness of global norms.[73] Finnemore postulates that:

> Conventional theories treat preferences as inherent qualities of actors. Their proponents would expect different actors with different preferences to act differently. Similar action by dissimilar actors in the absence of constraint is anomalous under these theories. Such behaviour is to be expected, however, within a social structural frame. International norms of behaviour and shared values may make similar behavioural claims on dissimilar actors.[74]

Finnemore argues that while domestic politics can influence states' interests, such domestic pressure cannot wholly explain all of a state's interests and that domestic political choices can, in some cases, contradict states' interests.[75] While this may be true in some cases, a tracing and understanding of domestic considerations may unpack a state's interests and allow a more contextual analysis. Similar to neoliberals, transnational constructivists' analyses at the state level treat states as 'black boxed' so as to yield a theoretically parsimonious and sharper framework through which to investigate the material world.

A third group of constructivists has been given the sobriquet of 'holistic', in that its members argue for a unified analytical approach that marries the domestic and international approach and treats them as two sides of the same coin (Hall, 1999; Koslowski and Kratochwil, 1995; Ruggie, 1998). To fulfil the aims of this book, a holistic approach has been chosen so as to move beyond a 'thin version of constructivism' to a constructivism able to 'explain fundamental changes in state identities and social structures'.[76] Holistic

---

72 Ibid.: 12.

73 Ibid. Neorealism attributes this to the necessity of states securing their survival through the mechanism of self-help. But if survival was the motive for such similarities, we would only see such behaviour in regimes directly relevant to the issue of states' survival.

74 M. Finnemore, *National Interests in International Society* (Ithaca, NY: Cornell University Press, 1996), 30.

75 Finnemore, 'Culture and World Politics: Insights from Sociology's Institutionalism', 2.

76 Price and Reus-Smit, 'Dangerous Liaisons? Critical International Theory and Constructivism', 268.

constructivism, which examines both domestic and global social phenomena, is better placed to trace the emergence and development of norms from whatever sources and therefore has the potential to provide a more compelling and richly textured explanation of how, why and where change occurs in the world system. A holistic approach necessarily calls for not just a two-level analysis, as in Putnam, but rather a multi-level analysis that looks not simply at the domestic and foreign policies of states but also at international organizations, corporations and NGOs.

The final debate amongst constructivists is over methodology. As Reus-Smit points out, initially constructivists insisted that the studying of ideas and norms needed an interpretive methodology.[77] This point has been forgotten by those constructivists who defend 'methodological conventionalism' and emphasize a positivist approach. They argue that their explanations do not necessarily need a unique, stand-alone interpretivist methodology.[78] This approach is justified by the observation that constructivism has been caught up for too long in methodological disputes. Secondly, the work of some constructivist authors, such as Kratochwil and Ruggie, is not dissimilar methodologically from that of neoliberalist authors and provides a potential point of intersection between the competing approaches.[79] This approach, Reus-Smit argues, is due to theorists wishing to go beyond mere meta-theoretical debate to undertake empirical analysis.[80] If constructivism is to develop theoretical coherence, it needs to respond to the criticism that it is obsessed with the meta-level and that it is time that it tested its analytical framework empirically to observe what insights and predictions it can glean.

Price observes that, like neorealism and neoliberalism, some strands of constructivist research, building on Wendt's approach, still focus primarily on the state as an actor. However, while such analysis can yield interesting insights, it runs the risk of ignoring other sources of agency and socialization that are crucial to the generation of norms.[81] Other constructivist writers, particularly of the holistic school, argue that there is a need to examine the role

---

77 Reus-Smit, 'Constructivism', 223.

78 Jepperson, Wendt, and Katzenstein, 'Norms, Identity, and Culture in National Security', 67.

79 Reus-Smit, 'Constructivism', 223.

80 Reus-Smit, 'Imagining Society: Constructivism and the English School', 496.

81 R. Price, 'Reversing the Gun Sights: Transnational Civil Society Targets Land Mines', *International Organization* 52, no. 3 (1998): 614. Weber argues that by reifying the state in making it the key decision-maker about the nature of international anarchy (encapsulated in the phrase 'anarchy is what states make of it'), constructivist analysts contradict their own argument that identities and interests are constantly changing. Weber, *International Relations Theory: A Critical Introduction*, 60.

of all global actors involved in creating and maintaining global environmental regimes. Despite constructivism's preoccupation with state analysis to date, there is nothing inherent in the theoretical model that indicates one must focus on a particular level of analysis.[82]

Many recent constructivist studies of the role of norms examine the part played by non-state actors in transmitting and adopting global norms (for example, Finnemore, 1996; Keck and Sikkink, 1998; Klotz, 1995). Given the nature of the research undertaken here, which aims to understand how normative transformation occurs, it is vital to examine the role played by all parties to global regime negotiations. A holistic constructivist approach allows the researcher to go behind the state and allows us to examine the role played by non-state actors such as ENGOs, scientists and corporations.

## CONSTRUCTIVISM AND THE EXAMINATION OF NORMS

Since constructivism is not a unified theory as such, one cannot give *the* constructivist reading of norms. Rather one must present an analysis of the variety of ways constructivism-inspired theorists posit the global system and the role norms play within that structure. Early constructivist research focused primarily on trying to show simply that norms *mattered*, by demonstrating their existence and effect empirically (Finnemore, 1996; Klotz, 1995 and Price, 1997).[83] With that debate effectively settled, recent constructivist research has focused on exploring and explaining *why* particular ideas 'win' when pitted against others in normative debates.[84]

Okereke maintains that the constructivist research agenda, contrary to the assumptions of rationalist theorists, is to demonstrate that global cooperation is not merely a function of states' rational self-interest but has other, superior explanations.[85] Payne notes that constructivist scholars like Finnemore and Sikkink (1999) and Checkel (1999) are interested in '... identifying and explaining the persuasion that ostensibly makes it possible for resonant

---

[82] Checkel, 'The Constructivist Turn in International Relations Theory', 11.

[83] R.J. Flowers, 'International Norms and Domestic Policies in Japan: Identity, Legitimacy and Civilization' (Ph.D., University of Minnesota, 2002), 11.

[84] R.A. Payne, 'Habermas, Discourse, Norms, and the Prospect for Global Deliberation: Paper Prepared for Panel on Transparency and International Politics' (paper presented at the International Studies Association, Los Angeles, California, 15–18 March 2000), 4.

[85] Chukwumerije Okereke, 'Equity Norms in Global Environmental Governance', *Global Environmental Politics* 8, no. 3 (2008): 26.

normative ideas to become shared understandings' noting that such research is invaluable to the constructivist project.[86]

The constructivist approach to international relations clearly has a wider view of the importance of norms than the neoliberal approach. The constructivist model, as distinct from the neoliberal approach that treats norms as primarily reflecting an actor's interests, argues that norms can precede an actor's interests. Norms are not merely regulatory (that is, functioning as constraints or as incentives), rather they are constitutive in that they '. . . legitimise goals and thus define actors' interests'.[87] Such norms consequently act as motives in that they determine the goals states may legitimately strive for, which may include being a 'good' global citizen.[88] Thus a state's interests are arrived at in concordance with the preceding legitimate goals.[89]

Finnemore and Sikkink's definition of a norm draws on general constructivist literature. In short, a norm prescribes 'appropriate behaviour for actors with a given identity'.[90] In a similar vein, Wendt defines norms as collective expectations about behaviour.[91] Conceiving of norms in such a manner imputes to them a causal significance in that they constitute agents' behaviours. Thus constructivists treat norms as 'ongoing social constructions rather than perennial givens' which can be altered or replaced over time.[92] Constructivism argues that agents/states comply with norms through a 'social

---

86 Payne, 'Habermas, Discourse, Norms, and the Prospect for Global Deliberation: Paper Prepared for Panel on Transparency and International Politics', 5.

87 Audie Klotz, *Norms in International Relations: The Struggle against Apartheid*, Cornell Studies in Political Economy (Ithaca, NY: Cornell University Press, 1995), 26. Constructivism argues that global norms carry social content and can be independent of power and constitute (provide states with understandings of interests) states' interests rather than merely constrain. J.T. Checkel, 'Norms, Institutions and National Identity in Contemporary Europe', *International Studies Quarterly* 43 (1999): 84.

88 Charlotte Epstein, 'The Making of Global Environmental Norms: Endangered Species Protection', *Global Environmental Politics* 6, no. 2 (2006): 33.

89 Boekle, Rittberger, and Wagner, 'Norms and Foreign Policy: Constructivist Foreign Policy Theory', 8. There need not be a 'conscious belief in the intrinsic value of an action . . . as a necessary condition of norm-guided behavior', since within a social system what is considered appropriate behaviour may be internalized and not consciously thought about by individual actors. Boekle, 'Norms and Foreign Policy: Constructivist Foreign Policy Theory', 4.

90 Finnemore and Sikkink, 'International Norm Dynamics and Political Change', 891.

91 Zehfuss, 'Constructivisms in International Relations: Wendt, Onuf, and Kratochwil', 72.

92 Ben Rosamond, 'Constructing Globalization', in *Constructing International Relations: The Next Generation*, ed. Karin M. Fierke and Knud Erik Jorgensen (London: M.E. Sharpe, 2001), 202.

learning mechanism' rather than via instrumental calculation or political pressure of a material or other nature.[93] Accordingly, it is not political pressure that brings about normative change, but learning by social agents that leads to compliance with normative prescriptions, a position that will be tested here to see if social learning can explain environmental norm transformation in the case studies.[94]

A constructivist analysis of norms argues that norms diffuse when this process of learning leads actors, usually elite decision-makers, to adopt international norms. Such norms are then said to be internalized and to form a set of '. . . shared intersubjective understandings that make behavioural claims'.[95] Thus this approach presupposes that actors, facing new information and values, adopt new preferences and interests.[96]

Constructivism also maintains that norms are always promoted, contested and resisted by various competing actors within the global system, state or non-state.[97] Their analysis acknowledges that actors employ not only persuasive but also strategic and/or coercive means to achieve their goals.[98] However, Payne argues convincingly that current constructivist research is lacking when it comes to the question of persuasion. As he perceives the problem, '. . . [T]he empirical constructivist work does not tend to show how persuasive processes undergird norm construction'. Rather it mostly demonstrates how norm advocates employ material levers to 'mobilize and coerce decisionmakers to change state policy'.[99] For instance, actors can make threats of imposing sanctions or adverse publicity if practices do not meet certain standards.[100]

Indeed, a significant number of constructivist case studies to date show that norm advocates frequently utilize material levers to 'mobilize and coerce decision-makers to change state policy'.[101] However, constructivists have yet

---

93 J.T. Checkel, 'Why Comply? Constructivism, Social Norms and the Study of International Institutions' (paper presented at the Annual Meeting, American Political Science Association, Atlanta, Georgia, 1999), 8.

94 Ibid.

95 J.T. Checkel, 'International Norms and Domestic Politics: Bridging the Rationalist–Constructivist Divide', *European Journal of International Relations* 3, no. 4 (1997): 475.

96 Ibid.

97 Hobson, *The State and International Relations*, 148.

98 Robyn Eckersley, *The Green State: Rethinking Democracy and Sovereignty* (Cambridge, MA.: MIT Press, 2004), 35.

99 Payne, 'Habermas, Discourse, Norms, and the Prospect for Global Deliberation: Paper Prepared for Panel on Transparency and International Politics', 5.

100 R.A. Payne, 'Persuasion, Frames and Norm Construction', *European Journal of International Relations* 7, no. 1 (2001): 41.

101 Checkel, 'International Norms and Domestic Politics: Bridging the Rationalist–Constructivist Divide', 476–7.

to satisfactorily shed light on the interrelationship between persuasion and material levels. This book seeks to explore this criticism further to determine whether a constructivist analysis can demonstrate whether actors, particularly non-state actors, used persuasion techniques successfully or needed to resort to utilizing materialist/coercive levers. However, it is not strictly necessary for the constructivist analyst to demonstrate that moral norms 'matter to the exclusion of power and interest, in the sense that they must be shown to be untainted by these more "base" material interests in order to have any explanatory power'.[102]

Interests and moral positions are always entwined in global environmental regimes and one does not exist without the other. However, it can be shown that persuasive techniques, as opposed to material interest calculations, do have some independent sway for constructivism to be distinguishable from rationalism.[103] This book uses the case studies to shed further light on the tangled relationship between the resort to persuasion and the use of material levers on the part of different norm advocates.

## THE CONSTRUCTIVIST READING OF THE ORIGIN OF NORMS

Constructivists fall into two broad schools as regards the origin of norms. Those from the transnational socialization school (Finnemore, Keck, Sikkink) argue that international norms can determine state behaviour, while those espousing a societal socialization approach (Checkel) argue that international norms are first generated at the domestic level.[104] This approach argues that since states are the constitutive units of the global system, they are the most important socializing agent when it comes to standards of appropriate behaviour. States as the creators of international organizations work towards the goals of those organizations and comply with norms endemic to founding charters and legal acts. Such international organizations act as socializing agents or 'norm teachers', expressing values to the global community, and comprise both states and non-state actors.[105]

However, while such organizations are created by states, they have been known to develop separate distinct 'personalities' and goals distinct from the intentions of their state creators, for example, the International Whaling

---

102 Eckersley, *The Green State: Rethinking Democracy and Sovereignty*, 37–8.

103 Ibid.: 38.

104 Boekle, Rittberger and Wagner, 'Norms and Foreign Policy: Constructivist Foreign Policy Theory', 8–9.

105 Ibid.

Commission, which has changed from a 'whalers' club' to an organization dedicated to preserving whales. States acknowledge norms created by international organizations because they see themselves as part of the valued community of member states and wish to be recognized as an equal and valuable member of that community. According to constructivists of the transnational socialization school, such as Finnemore, Sikkink and Keck, transnational advocacy coalitions (such as ENGOs), acting as normative entrepreneurs, also play a part in creating and disseminating new norms, as well as demanding the verification of and compliance with existing norms.[106]

For those constructivists advocating a societal socialization perspective, society and its sub-groups, particularly societal 'advocacy coalitions', are seen as the primary socializing agencies. Societal expectations impact upon foreign policy setters in three ways. First, decision-makers may have adopted their societies' expectations of appropriate behaviour through the political socialization that all citizens have inculcated in them. Secondly, before becoming state representatives, politicians have usually had domestic political careers where they have internalized certain values and behavioural repertoires. Lastly, such state delegates behave consistently with regard to norms because that is the way they see the role they are playing as a representative of their state. State representatives are subject to both types of processes. Within global society they are met with expectations addressed to them by members of that society. However, the domestic society of a state expects its national delegates to satisfy their shared standards of behaviour at the international level too.[107]

If both the domestic and the international expectations match, then constructivists say they reinforce each other and such an explanation is particularly powerful. If there are contrary expectations, at least to a medium level of commonality/specificity, then a constructivist prediction is not possible. In the case where the domestic and international levels are not congruent, no prediction is possible either. Henning Boekle, Volker Rittberger and Wolfgang Wagner argue that if there are conflicting domestic societal and international norms, then state foreign policy decision-makers are able to choose the norm which best justifies their behaviour. Such an action cannot be dismissed theoretically therefore, as 'guided by an interest with no normative base and . . . justified *ex post* by recourse to a norm which matches the behaviour option chosen'.[108]

106 Ibid.
107 Ibid.: 9–10.
108 Ibid.: 10.

## CONSTRUCTIVISM AND EMPIRICAL RESEARCH

As mentioned previously, it is important for constructivists to focus at this stage less on epistemological and ontological debates and more on building constructivist IR theory through empirical research.[109] The most effective starting place is testing their approaches in case studies to see what the constructivist approach yields as both an explanation and predictor, rather than just an abstract interpretation. For constructivists, the inability of neorealism and neoliberalism to explain normative transformation is seen as their key weakness and renders these approaches both historically inaccurate and predictively weak. In contrast, constructivism offers potentially 'an account of how and where change may occur'.[110] Constructivist methodology in the past has primarily set out to show how particular moral norms have influenced global politics by tracing the evolution of one clearly identified moral norm.[111] However, this book seeks to examine not one, but three norms that compete against each other for dominance. A different methodology must be employed therefore.

This book proposes to utilize a holistic approach, which examines all the transnational actors and integrates the domestic and international realms, to effect an understanding of normative transformation within global environmental regimes. The constructivism account of an empirical project provided here needs to 'revolve around the historical reconstruction of social facts . . . on the basis of interpretive narratives, practices and discourses'.[112] Arguably the best way to examine this narrative is by using a 'process tracing' methodology. This involves more than telling a mere story.[113] Rather it means 'breaking down an overarching causal relationship into a set of smaller causal links in a larger causal chain'.[114] Such an approach, while not allowing of predictive analysis, does aim to explain past and present events, social practices and interests.[115]

---

109 Adler, 'Constructivism and International Relations', 109.

110 T. Hopf, 'The Promise of Constructivism in International Relations Theory', *International Security* 23, no. 1 (1998): 180.

111 For examples of this approach, see Klotz, *Norms in International Relations: The Struggle against Apartheid*, and Price, 'Reversing the Gun Sights: Transnational Civil Society Targets Land Mines'.

112 Adler, 'Constructivism and International Relations', 109.

113 Checkel, 'Why Comply? Constructivism, Social Norms and the Study of International Institutions', 13.

114 R.B. Mitchell and T. Bernauer, 'Empirical Research on International Environmental Policy: Designing Qualitative Case Studies', *Journal of Environment and Development* 7, no. 1 (1998): 22.

115 Adler, 'Constructivism and International Relations', 109.

To underpin this approach Jeffrey Legro's test (1997) for the robustness of a norm will be employed. This book will compare and contrast three competing norms within the one environmental regime to see which has emerged as the more robust norm over time and why. Constructivist critics have maintained that constructivist theoretical designs have tended to ignore case studies where 'the dog does not bark' and where the 'outcome of interest (identity change say) does not occur'.[116] To address this critique, this book tests constructivism in relation to the 'hard case' of tropical timber, where material interests appear to prevail, and where there is no obvious normative transformation leading to identity change. The challenge facing constructivism in this type of case is to develop an interpretation or explanation of 'why the dog did not bark' that can enrich or otherwise go beyond a standard neoliberalist explanation.

To examine norm transformation over time, Finnemore and Sikkink's normative life-cycle approach has been selected. Their analysis sees norms originating in two ways:

1. Norm entrepreneurs call attention to issues or 'create' issues by utilizing language that names, interprets and publicizes the issue. There are many famous examples of norm entrepreneurs, such as Henry Dunant, who created the Red Cross.
2. Organizational platforms are created through which norm promoters at the global level are able to publicize their norms, for example Greenpeace.[117]

Tracing one individual amongst a plethora of actors is problematic, particularly if there are many potential candidates, or if there is none known, or the primary norm agent is an organization. It may be a difficult empirical task to ascertain these individuals and there may be significant overlap with organizational platforms if, for instance, decisions to push a preservationist agenda are made by an ENGO board. Despite these potential problems, the overall approach advocated by Finnemore and Sikkink remains viable, though it may need to be modified or further refined, depending on empirical findings.

Norm entrepreneurs attempt to alter other actors' perception of what is permissible behaviour.[118] It is critical to a successful argument that the norm

---

116 Checkel, 'The Constructivist Turn in International Relations Theory', 10.

117 Finnemore and Sikkink, 'International Norm Dynamics and Political Change', 900. ENGOs like Greenpeace '. . . have been "active teachers" which guide states to initiate policies that are congruent with certain international norms of behaviour . . .'. Hobson, *The State and International Relations*, 151.

118 Hoffmann, 'Entrepreneurs and Norm Dynamics: An Agent-based Model on the Norm Life Cycle'.

being promoted is seen as legitimate or appropriate in the given context, particularly if norm entrepreneurs can refer to pre-existing standards, or make analogies based on similar cases.[119] M.J. Hoffmann argues that his empirical study shows that the constructivist analysis of norm entrepreneurs is correct in principle and they do influence the birth and development of norms.[120] For Bailey, norm entrepreneurs operate only at the individual or national level, not at the global level examined here.[121] An empirical question for the research undertaken here is: can we identify supranational normative entrepreneurs operating effectively within the chosen case studies?

What must be borne in mind is that norm entrepreneurs always propose norms within a social milieu that is already characterized by other norms. Established norms are displaced when norm entrepreneurs convince other actors to change their standard of appropriateness from the old one to the new.[122] Empirically, the number and relative international power of the states that agree to abide by the replacement norm are also critical in determining whether a successor norm will arise.[123]

Hoffmann and other constructivists ignore the paradox inherent in using the terminology of norm entrepreneurs. Norms are by definition settled, in that there is a consensus as to what an appropriate standard of behaviour should be. In actuality, norm entrepreneurs are advocating a *proto-norm* or emerging norm that they are hoping will be widely accepted as a new standard of behaviour. To avoid confusion, this book will speak of emerging norms and established or settled norms. Norm entrepreneurs, which as a model of stakeholder initiative have much to offer, proffer emerging norms which may become accepted in time. It should also be borne in mind that no norm is ever truly 'settled', in that they are all subject to ongoing competition from rival formulations. Rather it is a question of degree as to how stable and robust a particular regime norm may be.

To date, one of the criticisms of constructivist research is its failure (with the exception of Finnemore and Sikkink) to focus on the individual as a unit of study. It is arguable, particularly by neoliberals, that constructivists must

---

119 Risse and Ulbert, 'Deliberately Changing the Discourse: What Does Make Arguing Effective?', 5.

120 Hoffmann, 'Entrepreneurs and Norm Dynamics: An Agent-based Model on the Norm Life Cycle'.

121 Jennifer L. Bailey, 'Arrested Development: The Fight to End Commercial Whaling as a Case of Failed Norm Change', *European Journal of International Relations* 14, no. 2 (2008): 291.

122 Hoffmann, 'Entrepreneurs and Norm Dynamics: An Agent-based Model on the Norm Life Cycle'.

123 Bailey, 'Arrested Development: The Fight to End Commercial Whaling as a Case of Failed Norm Change', 291.

examine more carefully the role of the individual in order to understand how they 'purposefully use social capital and carefully chosen words to legitimate or delegitimize opponents and sometimes entire populations' to achieve their goals, in this case normative change.[124] Utilizing the norm entrepreneur model overcomes this criticism, particularly if key norm entrepreneurs can be identified. There is also a need to understand how other key individuals can be influenced or persuaded by norm entrepreneurs into changing their beliefs as they come to realize that 'the group's dominant norms reflect reality or are more appropriate . . .'.[125]

Once norm entrepreneurs, either acting alone or through organizational platforms, have persuaded a critical mass of states to adopt new norms, the norm has reached a 'tipping point', whereby a growing number of states subscribe to the norm. How many states are required, or which ones are important as norm leaders, varies from issue to issue and is an empirical question. After tipping, Finnemore and Sikkink speak of a 'cascading effect', where more and more countries adhere to the new norms. To move from the tipping point to a normative cascade, Finnemore and Sikkink argue that states seek to determine what constitutes a violation of the agreed-to norm, and transnational influences become more important than domestic pressure for effecting change.[126] These global norms then:

> tend to exert constitutive effects on the states in the sense that it becomes the 'normal' and appropriate thing to do to sign up and to ratify the respective treaties. If you want to be a member of international society 'in good standing', a civilized member of the international community, you better sign up to the treaty at this point.[127]

Finally, norms become so widely accepted that we speak of them as internalized in that they are taken as a given. Norms can influence behaviour to the point where they become self-reinforcing, institutionalized, and as described by Finnemore and Sikkink, exhibiting a 'taken for granted' element, particularly where they have been inculcated to the point where acting consistent with the norms involved is virtually automatic.[128] The three

---

124 Adler, 'Constructivism and International Relations', 110.

125 Meyer, 'Convergence Towards a European Strategic Culture? A Constructivist Framework for Explaining Changing Norms', 536.

126 Finnemore and Sikkink, 'International Norm Dynamics and Political Change', 904; Sarah V. Percy, 'Mercenaries: Strong Norm, Weak Law', *International Organization* 61 (2007): 389.

127 Risse and Ulbert, 'Deliberately Changing the Discourse: What Does Make Arguing Effective?', 10.

128 Finnemore and Sikkink, 'International Norm Dynamics and Political Change', 904.

case studies are examined to determine whether any of the environmental norms have reached this stage.

The willingness to abide by a given norm is, in this model, dependent on how well the norm has been internalized, rather than whether compliance follows an interest calculation.[129] This stage can be hard to analyse because many norms are taken for granted and are rarely articulated or questioned. They are still powerful, however, precisely because conforming to the norm is not questioned.[130] Failure to conform to this internalized norm leads to 'rogue states' or non-state actors being identified and heavily censured (amongst other penalties) by the global community.

Agents translate ideas into normative structures and constructivists are keenly interested in the process whereby 'political actors produce the intersubjective understandings that undergird norms' (for example, see Risse et al., 1999).[131] Constructivists argue that new ideas 'resonate' because of an ideational affinity to other already embedded normative frameworks.[132] Finnemore and Sikkink hypothesize that agents deliberately try to connect new ideas to established ones when constructing persuasive messages. Such 'arguments have to "resonate" with prior knowledge, agreed-upon principles and norms, or commonly held worldviews in order to become persuasive'.[133]

Resonance can be achieved by constructing arguments that chime with previous beliefs in one of three ways: drawing analogies, referring to already established principles, and framing. In the early parts of a negotiation, delegates tend to use analogies to make their arguments appear plausible. A second approach is to refer to principles established previously in negotiations or from another regime. The arguments are perceived to be justified in terms of norms that are considered to be morally right and/or legitimate to other agents. A third approach is to frame a problem so that calling for a

---

129 Moshe Hirsch, 'Compliance with International Norms in the Age of Globalization: Two Theoretical Perspectives', in *The Impact of International Law on International Cooperation*, ed. Eyal Benvenisti and Moshe Hirsch (Cambridge: Cambridge University Press, 2004), 179.

130 Finnemore and Sikkink, 'International Norm Dynamics and Political Change', 899–905.

131 Payne, 'Persuasion, Frames and Norm Construction', 62. Persuasion is defined here as 'the process by which agent action becomes social structure, ideas become norms, and the subjective becomes the intersubjective'. Finnemore and Sikkink, 'International Norm Dynamics and Political Change', 914.

132 Margaret E. Keck and Kathryn Sikkink, *Activists Beyond Borders: Advocacy Networks in International Politics* (Ithaca, NY: Cornell University Press, 1998), 46, 65–6.

133 Risse and Ulbert, 'Deliberately Changing the Discourse: What Does Make Arguing Effective?', 11.

particular approach is in tune with the normative ideals of the listener. In this sense, a frame provides the agent a perspective that allows a difficult scenario to be clarified and acted upon.[134]

Framing a norm is critical because it reveals: 'the linkages between existing norms and emergent norms are not often obvious and must be actively constructed by proponents of new norms'.[135] Framing enables norm advocates to highlight or manufacture issues by 'using language that names, interprets, and dramatizes them'.[136] Successful norm entrepreneurs are thus able to 'frame' normative ideas in such a way that they resonate with relevant audiences. Such framing is critical to the art of successful persuasion.[137] These frames can be characterized as the basic building blocks for the creation of broadly accepted norms. Such constructs '. . . help name, interpret, and dramatize issues, allowing advocates to create or explain broader social meanings'.[138]

The more speakers are perceived as being credible and truthful, the more likely they are to be persuasive. However, if actors do not speak and act consistently, their credibility is lessened, for example the US delegation in negotiations on the Madrid Protocol.[139] Agents' arguments are likely to be persuasive if 'they are enabled and legitimated by the broader social discourse in which they are embedded', such as the argument that whales are intelligent, beautiful creatures and should not be killed.[140] Similarly, the more the message to be expounded is a simple one that norm entrepreneurs can explain easily to policy makers, and that journalists can readily regurgitate to the global public, the greater the likelihood of its being promulgated,

---

134 Ibid.: 12.

135 M. Finnemore and Kathryn Sikkink, 'International Norm Dynamics and Political Change', in *Exploration and Contestation in the Study of World Politics*, ed. P. Katzenstein, R. Keohane and Stephen D. Krasner (Cambridge, MA: MIT Press, 1999), 268.

136 Ibid. See Price's work on the banning of landmines for an example of how to construct and utilize frames successfully. R. Price, 'Reversing the Gun Sights: Transnational Civil Society Targets Land Mines', *International Organization* 62 (2008): 191–220.

137 Payne, 'Persuasion, Frames and Norm Construction', 39. A frame is defined as a persuasive device utilized to 'fix meanings, organize experience, alert others that their interests and possibly their identities are at stake, and propose solutions to ongoing problems'. M.N. Barnett, 'Culture, Strategy and Foreign Policy Change: Israel's Road to Oslo', *European Journal of International Relations*, no. 5 (1999): 25.

138 Payne, 'Persuasion, Frames and Norm Construction', 43.

139 Risse and Ulbert, 'Deliberately Changing the Discourse: What Does Make Arguing Effective?', 10–11.

140 J.T. Checkel, 'Social Constructivisms in Global and European Politics: A Review Essay', *Review of International Studies* 30 (2004): 238.

for example, Antarctica as the last fragile wilderness or whaling as murder.[141] Consequently, there is a need to establish empirically what are the conditions for effective argument that leads to changes in an actor or actors' position and that concomitantly affects negotiated outcomes.[142]

It is possible for normative entrepreneurs to reframe problems by introducing new information that causes actors to reconsider their interests.[143] By entering a discursive process, perceptions of a situation can alter, leading to changes in actors' interests and occasionally actors' identities.[144] When examining case studies, such as the ones in this book, the key to understanding normative change lies in tracing the communicative processes created by transnational actors that, in turn, generate interests.[145]

As pointed out in the introduction, Legro (and more recently Okereke) are rightly critical of the constructivist approach to normative analysis, arguing that to date such research has not focused on cases where norms compete (preferring to study one norm in isolation), nor has it investigated cases of normative failure.[146] Legro's work enables us to examine more sharply the evolution of norms and to determine their *relative robustness*. Legro proposes a three-pronged test to determine the strength of a particular norm: specificity, durability and concordance.[147]

According to Legro, a norm's strength can be judged on its specificity or 'how precisely a norm distinguishes appropriate from inappropriate behavior'.[148] Or, to put it another way, 'how well guidelines for restraint and use are defined and understood'.[149] Are they overly complex and ill defined or simple and precise? This is 'assessed by examining actors' understandings of the simplicity and clarity of the prohibition'.[150] This precision depends to a great extent on the explication of the norm in such documents as written conven-

141 Oran R. Young and Gail Osherenko, *Polar Politics: Creating International Environmental Regimes*, Cornell Studies in Political Economy (Ithaca, NY: Cornell University Press, 1993), 236.

142 Risse and Ulbert, 'Deliberately Changing the Discourse: What Does Make Arguing Effective?', 2.

143 Ibid.: 13.

144 Ibid.: 16.

145 Price, 'Reversing the Gun Sights: Transnational Civil Society Targets Land Mines', 615.

146 Okereke, 'Equity Norms in Global Environmental Governance', 27.

147 J.W. Legro, 'Which Norms Matter? Revisiting the "Failure" of Internationalism', *International Organization* 51, no. 1 (1997): 34.

148 Boekle, Rittberger and Wagner, 'Norms and Foreign Policy: Constructivist Foreign Policy Theory', 6.

149 Legro, 'Which Norms Matter? Revisiting the "Failure" of Internationalism', 34.

150 Ibid.

tions. A non-specific standard of behaviour means that there could be a wide range of behavioural possibilities that could be determined as appropriate and do not allow any straightforward assessment of whether a norm has been violated. Such unspecified norms are not suitable as a standard for appropriate behaviour and cannot be treated as an independent variable that can explain a norm's efficacy.[151]

Legro goes on to look at how *durable* a norm can be by asking us to demonstrate 'how long the rules have been in effect and how they weather challenges to their prohibitions'.[152] Are violators and violations of the norm penalized and in what way? The violation of a norm does not necessarily mean that the norm has no validity. The norm against incest is a strong one despite there being repeated infractions of the taboo. For Legro, the point is that the actors are punished or censured, either at a societal level or they sanction themselves for their transgressions.[153] Lastly, Legro examines the concept of *concordance* or commonality,[154] that is, 'how widely accepted are the rules in diplomatic discussions and treaties (that is, the degree of intersubjective agreement)'.[155] Do states agree on the acceptance of the validity of a norm? Has it been internalized? Do they put conditions on acceptance and therefore diminish it? Are these rules so taken for granted that no actor even considers violating them?[156]

The strength of the obligation inherent in a norm is determined in these cases by the units within a system who share that norm's values. Thus we can speak of a high degree of commonality if *all* actors share a certain value-based expectation of behaviour, a medium degree if a *majority* of actors share the same expectation of behaviour, and low commonality if a *minority* ascribe to the expectation of behaviour.[157] According to Legro, a norm must have at least a medium level of commonality before it can be said to be exerting any influence on a state's behaviour.[158] This can be examined by evaluating records of

151 Boekle, Rittberger and Wagner, 'Norms and Foreign Policy: Constructivist Foreign Policy Theory', 7.

152 Legro, 'Which Norms Matter? Revisiting the "Failure" of Internationalism', 34.

153 Ibid.: 35.

154 By commonality, constructivists mean 'how many actors of a social system share a value-based expectation of behavior'. Boekle, Rittberger and Wagner, 'Norms and Foreign Policy: Constructivist Foreign Policy Theory', 6.

155 Legro, 'Which Norms Matter? Revisiting the "Failure" of Internationalism', 35.

156 Ibid.

157 Boekle, Rittberger and Wagner, 'Norms and Foreign Policy: Constructivist Foreign Policy Theory', 6.

158 Legro, 'Which Norms Matter? Revisiting the "Failure" of Internationalism', 35.

national and international discussions on particular norms. The expectation of this approach 'is that the clearer, more durable, and more widely endorsed a prescription is, the greater will be its impact' and consequently its robustness.[159] The greater the level of commonality, the more robust the explanation that constructivism provides. The lower the commonality, the greater the likelihood that the expectation is not an independent variable but rather some other variable. Constructivists must demonstrate 'that certain groups assert themselves over their rivals *because* of the norms they share' and only then will that norm be the explanatory variable.[160]

Utilizing Finnemore and Sikkink's schema, bolstered by Legro's test of a norm's power, this book will seek to answer the following questions in each case area:

1. Can we identify norm entrepreneurs?
2. What organizational platforms, if any, do they utilize?
3. Can we identify a tipping point, when the norm is accepted by at least a majority of state actors?
4. Can we ever detect a cascade effect, once state acceptance has occurred?
5. Can we identify when norm entrepreneurs have used a normative framework to facilitate acceptance?
6. How does the presence of norms influence actors' behaviour in global environmental regimes?
7. How and why have norms withstood challenges from other norms for pre-eminence within a global environmental regime?
8. How are norms internalized by global actors? (Legro limits this internalization to states, but this book will investigate whether it has been internalized by other transnational non-state actors as well.)
9. What social learning mechanisms have been most or least successful, when employed by norm entrepreneurs and other actors?
10. What techniques of moral persuasion techniques have been most or least successful?
11. Does persuasion or material leverage work best to internalize norms or effect norm change?

If constructivism cannot answer these questions, its usefulness as an analytical tool may prove limited. Further, we need to examine situations

---

159 Ibid.

160 Boekle, Rittberger and Wagner, 'Norms and Foreign Policy: Constructivist Foreign Policy Theory', 6.

where if interest-based explanations are discounted, can we expect environmental norms to prevail over other normative possibilities? Such an examination will test the power of normative explanations and provide a more nuanced understanding of how norms compete.

# 3. Frozen in time: minerals and the campaign to preserve Antarctica

> We are all concerned with protection of that continent for present and future generations. (Sveneld Evteev[1])

## INTRODUCTION

Humanity has looked to Antarctica for centuries with dreams of undiscovered mineral wealth. However, it was not until the 1970s that this potential became a feasible economic reality and outside corporate forces began to pressure states to modify the existing Antarctic regime, which disallowed mining.

At the same time, various ENGOs were determined that the Antarctic environment be preserved unspoilt in perpetuity. With the support of key defecting states, in 1991 they achieved this goal with the adoption of the Madrid Protocol, allowing Antarctica to be 'locked away' for the foreseeable future.

The case of Antarctica and the fate of its mineral wealth make a fascinating test of the strengths and weaknesses of both neoliberal institutionalism and constructivism. On the one hand, it is a textbook example of cooperation, with the creation of a regime to govern the continent. This started with scientists cooperating, despite nationalist antagonisms, at the height of the Cold War. Given the privileging of consensus decisions within the resultant regime by the Contracting Parties, it might be expected that neoliberals would seek to explain normative change in regard to Antarctica as a case where states chose to cooperate to reduce uncertainty and achieve their own economic interests. However, a neoliberal analysis would also have to explain the defection of key states like Australia and France, for ostensibly altruistic reasons, in the face of a fierce veto coalition led by the United States of America. The challenge for neoliberals is to find a cogent materialistic explanation for Australia's and France's shift from a conservationist position to a preservationist one.

---

1 Sveneld Evteev, 'Antarctica and its Place in the Contemporary Environmental Movement', in *The Antarctic Treaty System in World Politics*, ed. Arnfinn Jorgensen-Dahl and Willy Ostreng (New York: St Martin's Press, 1991), 152.

Constructivism, as an analytical framework, offers a more nuanced account of the role of the negotiations to create a minerals agreement. With its focus on non-state actors, it is able to provide unique insights into the lobbying by ENGOs to designate Antarctica a world park free from mineral exploitation. ENGOs, drawing on already existing wilderness preservationist norms circulating in global discourse, were able to act as global educators for the moral position of preserving Antarctica. Constructivism is also able to provide a more complete explanation of the actions of Australia and France. Both these states opposed the introduction of a conservationist minerals regime on at least partly altruistic grounds, thus reframing and in the end reconstituting their own states' interests and identities, along with those of other regime members.

However, the constructivist approach is not without its problems. Constructivist analysis needs to show just how effective its persuasive arguments were in reframing the debate and preserving the Antarctic as a wilderness area. Can a norm-centred analysis such as the one espoused by Finnemore and Sikkink yield greater insights than an interest-centred one or does the evidence show that ENGOs resorted to coercive and/or strategic means to achieve their goal? This chapter adopts a historical narrative approach and focuses on the key events and meetings to try and historically reconstruct the social facts and positions that led to the creation of the Madrid Protocol.

## A BRIEF HISTORY OF ANTARCTICA

Antarctica has been referred to as the 'land which God gave to Cain' because of its bleak nature.[2] Its name can be traced to the Greeks, who, convinced that the world was round, reasoned there was a southern landmass to counter Eurasia. Since they had named the North Pole *arktos* (the bear), the theorized southern landmass was named 'anti-Arctic'.[3] The continent of Antarctica is a study in contrasts. It comprises an area of 14 million square kilometres (one-tenth of the globe's landmass) and it is the coldest, windiest, driest, highest and least accessible continent on earth.[4] At any given time, approximately 98 per cent of its landmass is covered with a mantle of ice approximately one mile thick. It

[2] Keith D. Suter, *World Law and the Last Wilderness* (Sydney: Friends of the Earth, 1980), 32.

[3] Ibid.: 33.

[4] Geoffrey Larminie, 'The Mineral Potential of Antarctica: The State of the Art', in *The Antarctic Treaty System in World Politics*, ed. Arnfinn Jorgensen-Dahl and Willy Ostreng (New York: St Martin's Press, 1991), 80. The lowest temperature on Earth ever recorded (–128.6 degrees Fahrenheit) was measured in 1983 at Vostok Research Station in the Eastern Antarctic interior. Christopher C. Joyner, *Antarctica and the Law of the Sea* (London: Martinus Nijhoff Publishers, 1992), 180.

receives less rainfall than the Sahara Desert (annual precipitation rarely exceeds 5 centimetres) and it is officially classed as a desert as a consequence. And yet its icecap contains 75 per cent of the world's fresh-water supplies.[5]

Antarctica is considered unique from a scientific viewpoint (for a number of reasons), a fact that ENGOs were quick to use in their arguments: it holds data as to previous atmospheric and climactic conditions trapped in its ice which are available nowhere else on the planet; it is a major determinant of the ocean's currents and it is considered a 'heat sink' by meteorologists, one that has a significant impact on the globe's weather patterns.[6] It is also one of the few wilderness areas that has not been exploited by humanity.

The nature of Antarctica, particularly its intense cold, renders the area extremely ecologically fragile and one with no mechanisms to guard against environmental damage. Antarctica's terrestrial and fresh-water ecosystems are considered particularly fragile because in such a harsh environment growth is slow and recovery times are long. Many ENGOs and scientists have argued that given this fragility, creating a strong environmental protection regime is critical, and that the emphasis must be put on 'preserving' the region as an effective way to protect what is a uniquely fragile bio-system.[7]

Up until very recently, Antarctica was the least explored continent, with only 80 per cent of the 332 000 square kilometres not covered by ice mapped at reconnaissance level and 10 per cent in detail.[8] The first official claim to Antarctic land was most likely by France, which annexed the Isles de Kerguelen in January 1893 and gave the right to exploit their resources to a private company.[9] From the 1900s onward, countries such as the UK (1908), New Zealand (1923), Australia (1933), France again (1938), Norway (1939),

---

5 Christopher C. Joyner, *Governing the Frozen Commons: The Antarctic Regime and Environmental Protection* (Columbia, SC: University of South Carolina Press, 1998), 2–7; Suter, *World Law and the Last Wilderness*, 20.

6 Evteev, 'Antarctica and its Place in the Contemporary Environmental Movement', 147; Duncan French, 'Sustainable Development and the 1991 Madrid Protocol to the 1959 Antarctic Treaty: The Primacy of Protection in a Particularly Sensitive Environment', *Journal of International Wildlife Law and Policy* 2, no. 3 (1999): 291–2; Suter, *World Law and the Last Wilderness*, 20.

7 Kelly Rigg, 'Environmentalists' Perspectives on the Protection of Antarctica', in *The Future of Antarctica: Exploitation Versus Preservation*, ed. Grahame Cook (Manchester: Manchester University Press, 1990), 69.

8 Robert Willan, David Macdonald, and David Drewry, 'The Mineral Resource Potential of Antarctica: Geological Realities', in *The Future of Antarctica: Exploitation Versus Preservation*, ed. Grahame Cook (Manchester: Manchester University Press, 1990), 25.

9 V.E. Fuchs, 'Antarctica: Its History and Development', in *Antarctic Resources Policy: Scientific, Legal and Political Issues*, ed. Francisco Orrego Vicuna (Cambridge; Cambridge University Press, 1983), 15–16.

Chile (1940) and Argentina (1942) all made territorial claims. They based these claims on (a) discovery and occupation; (b) administrative acts; and/or (c) the principles of contiguity and continuity. This group of states has come to be classified as the 'claimant states'.[10]

These claims to Antarctica were originally nationalistic ones, and were pursued in a relatively haphazard manner, due to the assumption that there was little profit to be had from such a bleak landscape. The first claim by Great Britain was so poorly drawn up that it contained parts of South America and had to be redrafted in 1917.[11] Five other countries, Belgium, Japan, South Africa, the Soviet Union and the United States, also began exploring and researching Antarctica and after World War II declared that while they did not assert any territorial claim over the area, they did not recognize any claims by other states (referred to as the 'non-claimant states'). This group argued that they could pursue their claim at any time in the future and that because the claimant states had not occupied the disputed Antarctic territory, and because Antarctica was unique, no state could legitimately claim the area as theirs.[12]

## ANTARCTICA AND THE SEARCH FOR MINERALS

In modern times, the interest in Antarctica by states was initially dominated by the desire for resource extraction, with a greater or lesser degree of concern for conservation. Two types of exploitation were immediately observable, one of living resources, and the other of mineral resources. This chapter is concerned with both.[13] Mineral resources are not easily defined, as there is much debate about how widely or narrowly to construe the term. Robert Willan et al. argue that they are best understood in expansive terms as the 'summation of hypothetical deposits and mineral reserves which have been identified'.[14] However, this definition is too wide, including as it does all possible reserves.

---

[10] John Warren Kindt, 'A Regime for Ice-covered Areas: The Antarctic and Issues Involving Resource Exploitation and the Environment', in *The Antarctic Legal Regime*, ed. Christopher C. Joyner and Sudhir K. Chopra (Dordrecht: Martinus Nijhoff Publishers), 194.

[11] Suter, *World Law and the Last Wilderness*, 33.

[12] Kindt, 'A Regime for Ice-covered Areas: The Antarctic and Issues Involving Resource Exploitation and the Environment', 195.

[13] States in the nineteenth century were initially keen to exploit the abundant living resources of the Antarctic region, for example krill, seals and whales. Exploitation of Antarctic resources centred initially around commercial sealing in the Southern Ocean. Susan J. Buck, *The Global Commons: An Introduction* (Washington, DC: Island Press, 1998), 46.

[14] Willan, Macdonald, and Drewry, 'The Mineral Resource Potential of Antarctica: Geological Realities', 27.

For the purposes of this book, mineral resources will be defined as in the 1980s Convention on the Regulation of Antarctic Mineral Resource Activities (CRAMRA), Article 1(6): 'all non-living natural non-renewable resources including fossil fuels, metallic and non-metallic minerals'.[15] Mineral resources are generally considered to be exhaustible over a given time period and are not considered to include ice.[16] Such resources, like minerals anywhere, are not considered conservable. Conservation in this case refers to ensuring that the lands (as distinct from the exhaustible minerals mined) are available to future generations in an unimpaired condition fit for other activities.

In the late nineteenth and early twentieth centuries, the presence – supposed or otherwise – of Antarctic mineral deposits served as a spur to Antarctic exploration, with several concessions and licences granted.[17] For example, in 1905 the British government granted a mining exploration licence for South Georgia Island.[18] Certainly it is now known that the earliest explorers of Antarctica did discover pockets of minerals, and coal obtained from Antarctica was utilized in various settlements.[19] However, the main problem for explorers and states wanting to exploit commercially Antarctic resources has been and remains potential rather than actual. Geological information on Antarctic mineral deposits remains scant and contradictory. While it is widely believed that minerals exist in Antarctica, this is a supposition, based on the fact that Antarctica is a continent and all other continents have yielded mineral deposits.[20]

While there have been many mineral traces discovered such as copper, gold, silver, cobalt, chromium, nickel and platinum, very few actual mineral deposits have been located.[21] Surveys indicate that there are deposits of coal

---

15 'U.S. State Department Handbook of the Antarctic Treaty System 2002' (Washington, DC: US State Department, 2002), 387.

16 Emilio J. Sahurie, *The International Law of Antarctica*, The New Haven Studies in International Law and World Public Order (New Haven, CN: New Haven Press, 1992), 425. Sahurie considers icebergs to be a mineral resource, with more than 70 per cent of the globe's fresh water contained in the Antarctic icecap. However, his view is not in accordance with the majority of commentators nor do the states party to the Antarctic regime agree with this position. Sahurie, *The International Law of Antarctica*, 357.

17 Sahurie, *The International Law of Antarctica*, 433.

18 Report of a Meeting of Experts Organised by the Fridtjof Nansen Foundation on Existing Law Relevant to the Authorisation or Prohibition of Mineral Exploration for Commercial Purposes in the Antarctic Treaty Area, 30th May–10th June 1973, reprinted in W.M. Bush, *Antarctica and International Law: A Collection of Inter-state and National Documents*, vols 1–3 (London: Oceana Publications Inc., 1982), 288.

19 Suter, *Antarctica: Private Property or Public Heritage?*, 46.

20 Sahurie, *The International Law of Antarctica*, 352.

21 Larminie, 'The Mineral Potential of Antarctica: The State of the Art', 83.

and iron, but they are currently considered uneconomic to exploit, given current technology.[22] The continent also, in the eyes of some geologists, ranks last in terms of oil potential.[23] An alternative view to the prevailing one is that there are vast resources waiting to be exploited, but they are as yet unknown. Proponents of this view estimate that there is enough iron ore in the Prince Charles Mountains to meet global demands for two hundred years. Natural gas reserves under the Ross, Weddell and Bellinghausen Seas are estimated to be in the range of tens of billions of barrels.[24] Some geologists believe that Antarctica has large reserves of gold, silver and other precious metals, as well as oil, natural gas and manganese nodules.[25]

In all, the mineral potentiality of the continent is still largely unknown, but on the balance of probabilities, it is most likely poor. The economic cost of exploiting such resources is still prohibitive and likely to remain so for the foreseeable future.[26] Given the nature of the continent, the cost of even a small commercial exploration venture is an order of magnitude higher than for other more hospitable parts of the globe.[27] Vogler argues the prevailing view that resources, such as minerals or oil, are yet to be fully mapped in Antarctica. He points out that in the foreseeable future, the sheer difficulty of extracting these resources, given current technological capabilities, makes them a non-viable commercial proposition, unless major oil or mineral shortages arise.[28]

Given the present knowledge of Antarctica and the level of technology currently available, it will be a long time before exploring and exploiting mineral resources will be cost-effective, but this has not stopped states from seeing the potential of the region, and wishing to lay claim to this potential wealth.[29] A significant feature of this case study is that the negotiations associated with Antarctic mineral exploitation took place in the context of little hard evidence about the actual location or extent of such resources, but with the hope of nonetheless tapping vast riches.[30]

---

22 Ibid.: 85.

23 Ibid.: 86.

24 Buck, *The Global Commons: An Introduction*, 62.

25 Gareth Porter and Janet Welsh Brown, *Global Environmental Politics* (Boulder, CO: Westview Press, 1991), 88.

26 Larminie, 'The Mineral Potential of Antarctica: The State of the Art', 91.

27 Ibid.: 80.

28 John Vogler, *The Global Commons: Environmental and Technological Governance*, 2nd edition (Chichester: John Wiley, 2000), 76.

29 Larminie, 'The Mineral Potential of Antarctica: The State of the Art', 82.

30 Lawrence Susskind, *Environmental Diplomacy: Negotiating More Effective Global Agreements* (New York: Oxford University Press, 1994), 66.

## BUILDING THE ANTARCTIC REGIME

The issue of the mineral exploitation of Antarctica was not tackled in any significant way in the first half of the twentieth century. The first real chance to focus on this issue came with the creation of the Antarctic regime in the late 1950s. Post-World War II interest in Antarctica peaked when both the USA and the Soviet Union became interested in the region for military strategic reasons. In the summer of 1947–48 this interest led the USA to send the largest expedition to the region, consisting of 13 ships, and over 4000 personnel. In 1949, meanwhile, the Soviet Union introduced a new holiday, 'Antarctic Day', and claimed that the Russian Admiral Bellingshausen was the first to discover the region.[31] The potential for Antarctica to become another battleground in the Cold War led the USA to suggest in August 1948 that the area be designated a 'multiple condominium', but other claimant states rejected the notion.[32]

Complicating the situation was the fact that relations between some of the claimant states had reached a perilous low point. Argentina and Chile, on one side, and Great Britain, on the other, had fallen out over plans by the first two states to create a 'South American Antarctic' that would have substantially covered the territory claimed by the British.[33] To address the escalating situation and attempt to meet these competing concerns, Argentina proposed in 1947 a Conference of Interested Parties, but this came to naught, as did a similar proposal by the USA in 1948 to have the area declared a Trust Territory under the auspices of the UN.[34]

In 1948, Chile suggested the Escudaro Declaration that outlined a plan to suspend sovereignty claims by competing Antarctic states for five years and to encourage scientific cooperation, but the suggestion was not acted upon.[35]

---

31 Fuchs, 'Antarctica: Its History and Development', 17.

32 United Nations Draft Agreement Providing for a Condominium over Antarctica (July 1948), reprinted in Bush, *Antarctica and International Law: A Collection of Inter-state and National Documents*, 464–5.

33 Lorraine Elliott, *International Environmental Politics: Protecting the Antarctic* (New York: St Martin's Press 1994), 28.

34 Ibid.: 28–9. Alfred van der Essen, 'The Origin of the Antarctic System', in *International Law for Antarctica*, ed. Francesco Francioni and Tullio Scovazzi (London: Kluwer Law International, 1996), 18. United Nations Draft Agreement for placing Antarctica under a United Nations Trusteeship (June 1948), reprinted in Bush, *Antarctica and International Law: A Collection of Inter-state and National Documents*, 461–3.

35 Joyner, *Governing the Frozen Commons: The Antarctic Regime and Environmental Protection*, 55. Chilean Statement Concerning the United States' Proposals to Internationalise Antarctica (28th October 1948), reprinted in Bush, *Antarctica and International Law: A Collection of Inter-state and National Documents*, 385–6.

That same year, the truce between the two sides (the UK versus Argentina and Chile) ended in gunfire. In May 1955, the UK brought the matter before the International Court of Justice (ICJ), but the ICJ was unable to act because neither Chile nor Argentina at that time recognized the jurisdiction of this world court. In March 1956, the Court held it could not proceed with the matter.[36]

Against this backdrop of mutual antagonism and conflict over territorial claims, scientists from several claimant nations established in 1955 20 scientific stations in Antarctica. This initiative was allowed by the claimant states for a period of 18 months.[37] Post-1956, scientists who wished to continue their research and research planning became more coordinated under the banner of the upcoming third International Geophysical Year (IGY), whose organizers were determined to marginalize political quarrels and focus on scientific cooperation.[38] The IGY ushered in a new level of cooperation regarding Antarctica, leading to the setting up of meteorological stations and a rush of scientific papers.[39] At the official conclusion of the IGY on 31 December 1958, all the Antarctic states of that period had pledged to continue scientific research into Antarctica.[40]

The success of the IGY offered the best chance yet to resolve outstanding territorial issues. Towards that end, in May 1958, the USA invited all 11 claimant and non-claimant states to Washington, DC, with the goal of avoiding potential disputes in the region, and to negotiate a treaty to oversee Antarctica. Alfred van der Essen argues that the scientific bases, which had been established by states that did not seem eager to vacate the region, provided the reason why President Eisenhower extended the invitation at this time.[41] The written request by the USA to create an Antarctic Treaty specifically mentioned that the makeup of such a treaty should include the principles of:

---

36 Suter, *World Law and the Last Wilderness*, 34. See Antarctic cases (*UK* v. *Argentina*, *UK* v. *Chile*) [1956].

37 van der Essen, 'The Origin of the Antarctic System', 18–19.

38 Elliott, *International Environmental Politics: Protecting the Antarctic*, 30; Marie Jacobsson, 'The Antarctic Treaty System: Legal and Environmental Issues – Future Challenges for the Antarctic Treaty System', in *Antarctica: Legal and Environmental Challenges for the Future*, ed. G. Triggs and A. Riddell (London: The British Institute of International Comparative Law, 2007), 15.

39 Evteev, 'Antarctica and its Place in the Contemporary Environmental Movement', 148.

40 Casarini, 'Activities in Antarctica before the Conclusion of the Antarctic Treaty', 676.

41 van der Essen, 'The Origin of the Antarctic System', 19.

(a) free scientific research in Antarctica by citizens, organizations and governments of all countries and the maintenance of the scientific international cooperation . . . carried out during the IGY;
(b) an international agreement to warrant that Antarctica . . . be used only for peaceful purposes;
(c) other peaceful purposes . . . not incompatible with those of the United Nations Charter.[42]

The USA invitation also soothed the territorial concerns of some of the invitees, as it stated that no state would have to surrender their historical or sovereign claims to Antarctica.[43]

Despite there being some resistance to the concept at the 60 preparatory meetings, negotiations opened on 15 October 1959, and the Antarctic Treaty was signed six weeks later on 1 December 1959.[44] Under Article VI, Antarctica was defined for the purposes of the Treaty as 'the area south of 60 degrees South Latitude, including all ice shelves'.[45] The signatories to the Antarctic Treaty included the 12 countries that were active in Antarctica during the International Geophysical Year of 1957–58. These parties were given the right to participate in consultative meetings under Article IX of the Treaty and were referred to as Consultative Parties. The parties now meet every year to discuss Antarctic-related issues, though prior to 1991 it was only every two years. The Consultative Parties meet:

> for the purpose of exchanging information, consulting together on matters of common interest pertaining to Antarctica, and formulating and considering and recommending to their Governments measures in furtherance of the principles and objectives of the Treaty.[46]

States that are not Consultative Parties, even if they are signatories to the Treaty, may only attend meetings as observers. The meetings themselves take

---

42 Carlos Rinaldi, 'Scar in the ATS: Conflict or Harmony?', in *The Antarctic Treaty System in World Politics*, ed. Arnfinn Jorgensen-Dahl and Willy Ostreng (New York: St Martin's Press, 1991), 154–5.

43 van der Essen, 'The Origin of the Antarctic System', 20.

44 Boleslaw A. Boczek, 'The Soviet Union and the Antarctic Regime', *American Journal of International Law* 78, no. 4 (1984): 839.

45 Duncan French, 'Sustainable Development and the 1991 Madrid Protocol to the 1959 Antarctic Treaty: The Primacy of Protection in a Particularly Sensitive Environment', *Journal of International Wildlife Law and Policy* 2, no. 3 (1999): 299.

46 'U.S. State Department Handbook of the Antarctic Treaty System 2002', 1. Since 1983, countries party to the Treaty that are not Consultative Parties have been invited to take part in these meetings. However, they cannot block any consensus decisions made by the Consultative Parties. 'U.S. State Department Handbook of the Antarctic Treaty System 2002', 1.

place in relative secrecy. It is only in the last few years that open annual reports have begun to be published.[47]

Critically, Article IV of the 1959 Antarctic Treaty annulled the various territorial claims of nations that had established a presence on the continent – Argentina, Australia, Chile, France, New Zealand, Norway and the United Kingdom.[48] The Antarctic Treaty did not settle any outstanding territorial claims. Rather, it effectively froze the status quo between the competing states by providing in Article IV that:

(1) there shall be no renunciation by any contracting party of previously asserted rights of or claims to – or even any basis of claim to – territorial sovereignty in Antarctica;
(2) no acts or activities while the Treaty is in force can constitute a basis for asserting, supporting or denying a claim; and
(3) no new claim or enlargement of an existing claim may be asserted while the Treaty is in force.[49]

Among the original parties to the Antarctic Treaty, seven (Argentina, Australia, Chile, France, New Zealand, Norway and the United Kingdom) claimed exclusive sovereign rights to Antarctic 'sectors', with the claims advanced by Argentina, Chile and the United Kingdom being conflicting and overlapping ones. Some 15 per cent of the continent was considered to be unclaimed territory. Among the non-claimant states, Japan, the United States and the Soviet Union refused to recognize any claims made by other states.[50] In recognition of the difficult history of territorial conflict, and in a bid to overcome this history, the primary purpose of the Treaty was to ensure that:

> in the interests of all mankind that Antarctica shall continue forever to be used exclusively for peaceful purposes and shall not become the scene or object of international discord. In trying to achieve this goal it prohibits 'any measures of a military nature' and the continent must be considered a 'nuclear free zone' (Article V) . . . [but does] . . . not prevent the use of military personnel or equipment for scientific research or for any other peaceful purpose.[51]

The ideal of scientific cooperation in relation to Antarctic research, which had begun with the IGY in 1957, was officially enshrined as a principle, and

---

47 Porter and Brown, *Global Environmental Politics*, 89.

48 Vogler, *The Global Commons: Environmental and Technological Governance*, 73.

49 Boczek, 'The Soviet Union and the Antarctic Regime', 840.

50 Ibid.: 840–41.

51 'U.S. State Department Handbook of the Antarctic Treaty System 2002', 2.

incorporated into Articles II and III of the Treaty.[52] The Treaty aimed to promote 'international cooperation in scientific investigation in Antarctica' and encourage 'the establishment of cooperative working relations with those Specialized Agencies of the United Nations and other international organizations having a scientific or technical interest in Antarctica'. This aim became a critical factor in allowing certain ENGOs to participate in discussions relating to treaty activities. The Antarctic Treaty contains no reference to the word 'environment', but it does allow Antarctic Treaty Contracting (or Consultative) Parties (ATCPs) to make recommendations at the meetings concerning the 'preservation and conservation of living resources'.[53]

From the date of its entry into force in 1961, the Antarctic Treaty has been evolving into a multilateral regional regime called the Antarctic Treaty System (ATS).[54] The term was originally coined by Mr Roberto Guyer and is now considered to include the Antarctic Treaty (1959), recommendations adopted at meetings of the Antarctic Treaty Parties, the Madrid Protocol on Environmental Protection to the Antarctic Treaty (also referred to as PEPAT, or the Madrid Protocol 1991), two separate conventions for the Conservation of Antarctic Seals (London 1972), and the Convention on the Conservation of Antarctic Marine Living Resources (Canberra 1980). The Convention on the Regulation of Antarctic Mineral Resource Activities (CRAMRA, Wellington 1988) has not been ratified by any state, but is considered to be part of the body of documents making up the Antarctic Treaty System. The ATS also includes the results of Meetings of Experts, the decisions of Special Consultative Meetings and, at a non-governmental level, it reflects the work of the Scientific Committee on Antarctic Research (SCAR).[55] It can also be

---

52 The Antarctic Treaty (1961) reproduced in Elliott, *International Environmental Politics: Protecting the Antarctic*, 215.

53 Article IX(1)(f). John Burgess, 'Comprehensive Environmental Protection of the Antarctic: New Approaches for New Times', in *The Future of Antarctica: Exploitation Versus Preservation*, ed. Grahame Cook (Manchester: Manchester University Press, 1990), 59; French, 'Sustainable Development and the 1991 Madrid Protocol to the 1959 Antarctic Treaty: The Primacy of Protection in a Particularly Sensitive Environment', 300.

54 Christopher C. Joyner, 'The Antarctic Legal Regime: An Introduction', in *The Antarctic Legal Regime*, ed. Christopher C. Joyner and Sudhir K. Chopra (Dordrecht: Martinus Nijhoff Publishers, 1988), 1.

55 SCAR (initially the Special Committee on Antarctic Research, now the Scientific Committee for Antarctic Research) grew out of the global scientific community concern for Antarctica, building on the cooperation evident from the IGY and predates the Antarctic Treaty. Buck, *The Global Commons: An Introduction*, 58. A Special Committee recommended that the International Council of Scientific Unions (ICSU) create a committee to examine the advantages of further scientific research on Antarctica. Rinaldi, 'Scar in the ATS: Conflict or Harmony?', 154. The primary

understood as a regime with geographical boundaries varying between 60 degrees south and the Antarctic convergence.[56]

The ATS comprises a two-tiered system in which ATCPs have full voting rights and Acceding (or Non-consultatives) have no vote.[57] The ATCPs meet regularly, as per Article IX(1):

> for the purpose of exchanging information, consulting together on matters of common interest pertaining to Antarctica, and formulating and considering, and recommending to their Governments, measures in furtherance of the principles and objectives of the Treaty.[58]

Decisions made at an ATCM require consensus by all member states present. This has become an enshrined procedural norm underpinning the regime.[59] Joyner sees the central norms underpinning the regime as peaceful use of the continent, scientific cooperation, and the promotion of international harmony.[60] However, no norm as regards the environment per se was articulated at this time.

Among commentators, there is no consensus on what the ATS model actually is and how successful it has been. Falk considers it as a model for global cooperation in that:

---

purpose of SCAR is to design and coordinate Antarctic scientific research programmes. Generally, when SCAR receives a request for scientific advice, it refers the matter to one of its National Committees. 'U.S. State Department Handbook of the Antarctic Treaty System 2002', 4. The status of the SCAR is unusual. Many academics hold it to be an ENGO despite the quasi-governmental aspects of its makeup. More accurately SCAR is a scientific organization and an IO, rather than a government organization or an NGO. Richard A. Herr and Bruce W. Davis, 'Antarctica and Non-state Actors: The Question of Legitimacy', *International Antarctic Regime Project, Fridtjof Nansens Institute*, no. 4 (1992): 8.

56 van der Essen, 'The Origin of the Antarctic System', 25; Olav Schram Stokke, 'The Relevance of the Antarctic Treaty System as a Model for International Cooperation', in *The Antarctic Treaty System in World Politics*, ed. Arnfinn Jorgensen-Dahl and Willy Ostreng (New York: St Martin's Press, 1991), 358. The Antarctic convergence is 'a belt around the continent at about 56 degrees–58 degrees south where the cold Antarctic surface water, flowing northwards, sinks beneath the warmer subantarctic water'. Maria Pia Casarini, 'Activities in Antarctica before the Conclusion of the Antarctic Treaty', in *International Law for Antarctica*, ed. Francesco Francioni and Tullio Scovazzi (London: Kluwer Law International, 1996), 628.

57 Margaret Clark, 'The Antarctic Environmental Protocol: NGOs in the Protection of Antarctica', in *Environmental NGOs in World Politics: Linking the Local and the Global*, ed. Thomas Princen and Matthias Finger (London: Routledge, 1994), 160.

58 The Antarctic Treaty (1961) reproduced in Elliott, *International Environmental Politics: Protecting the Antarctic*, 218.

59 Joyner, *Governing the Frozen Commons: The Antarctic Regime and Environmental Protection*, 63.

60 Ibid.: 64.

> The governance of Antarctica, ingeniously combining the virtues of international cooperation with the reality of state sovereignty, is the closest thing to a 'world order miracle' that the world has known.[61]

Some perceive it as a triumph of science over politics, and as avoiding hot and cold wars, so that scientific resources can benefit all humanity. Others, taking a more cynical view, argue that it is merely an example of *Realpolitik*, where clever politicians have overcome tremendous odds to achieve cooperative gains. Some have argued that the ATS is inclusive of states, while others portray the parties as a group of wealthy states that have formed an exclusionary club.[62] Krasner doubts whether the ATS constitutes a regime at all since the arrangements constitute a 'logical shambles'. For him, the arrangement is flawed because:

> Fundamental differences of principles have not been resolved while a set of 'rules and decision-making procedures, reflecting weak norms associated with scientific exploration, disarmament and environmental protection' have been put in place in order to avoid 'mutually undesirable outcomes'.[63]

While Krasner's point is well taken in that, to a certain extent, the arrangement freezes state differences, it still meets the criteria for a regime. The more important question is whether it is a strong or weak regime. For all its acknowledged faults, it has proved to be both flexible and durable in meeting the changing needs of the ATCPs. It has had no challengers to its reign as the primary Antarctic regime. This suggests that it is a strong regime.

From a neoliberal point of view, creating such a regime is a textbook case where states with the appropriate incentives come together to resolve four pressing issues. The regime resolved, or at least put in abeyance, outstanding sovereignty issues that had plagued relations between claimant and non-claimant states. It helped assuage national security fears, since no state could use the continent for military purposes nor could nuclear activities be carried out there. Further, it allowed scientists to continue to cooperate together for the betterment of all humanity and lastly, and most important to the interests of the ATCPs, it gave stability to their territorial claims.[64]

---

61 R.A. Falk, 'The Antarctic Treaty System: Are there Viable Alternatives?', in *The Antarctic Treaty System in World Politics*, ed. Arnfinn Jorgensen-Dahl and Willy Ostreng (Basingstoke: Macmillan, 1991), 399.

62 Stokke, 'The Relevance of the Antarctic Treaty System as a Model for International Cooperation', 358.

63 Stephen D. Krasner, *Structural Conflict: The Third World against Global Liberalism* (Berkeley: University of California Press, 1985), 251.

64 Donald R. Rothwell, *The Polar Regions and the Development of International Law*, Cambridge Studies in International and Comparative Law 3 (Cambridge: Cambridge University Press, 1996), 409–10.

From a constructivist perspective, while not discounting the above states' interests, the regime put in place certain critical procedural norms (for example, decision-making by consensus). It also established a framework for environmental norms to be introduced by non-state actors with scientific or technical expertise, an avenue ENGOs were quick to capitalize on by creating the Antarctic and Southern Ocean Coalition (ASOC). It also laid out the 'rules of the game' under which states could operate. As will be seen, these rules (decisions are to be by consensus with limits to certain activities that might damage the environment, such as nuclear testing) are critical for changing both the social dynamic state under which the regime operates, as well as the identities of the states involved.

## THE ANTARCTIC TREATY AND MINERAL EXPLOITATION

While the issue of mineral exploration and exploitation was discussed in the negotiations to create the Treaty, the negotiating states believed that it was premature to deal with the issue at that time.[65] First, it was considered impractical to exploit those resources and thus, in 1959 at any rate, it was not considered a pressing issue.[66] Secondly, differences between the claimant and non-claimant states were considered intractable, and with so many other more pressing issues to hand, particularly ones of sovereignty, it was agreed that this be left unresolved.

Thus, subsequent discussions on mineral exploitation were underpinned by the unresolved tension between claimant and non-claimant states. This needs to be borne in mind when examining this issue.[67] Had an agreement on mineral resources been demanded, however, the Treaty itself might not have been agreed to because it would have prejudiced the negotiations over demilitarization and scientific cooperation.[68] The Treaty is significant more for what it does not say, namely that it does not forbid mineral exploitation.[69]

---

65 'US State Department Handbook of the Antarctic Treaty System 2002', 384.

66 Rolf Trolle Andersen, 'Negotiating a New Regime: How CRAMRA Came into Existence', in *The Antarctic Treaty System in World Politics*, ed. Arnfinn Jorgensen-Dahl and Willy Ostreng (New York: St Martin's Press, 1991), 94; Sahurie, *The International Law of Antarctica*, xxiv.

67 Sahurie, *The International Law of Antarctica*, xxiv.

68 Ibid.: 433.

69 Francesco Francioni, 'The Madrid Protocol on the Protection of the Antarctic Environment', in *International Environmental Law for Antarctica*, ed. Francesco Francioni (Milan: Giuffre Editore, 1992), 22.

This does not mean that the issue was not of concern to the delegates in 1959. The issue of mineral exploitation was certainly considered by the parties, but it was not considered a pressing issue. An examination of domestic preference settings reveals that the national governments were well aware of the issues and potential problems a mineral strike might yield. For example, in evidence before the US Senate on 14 June 1960 concerning the scope of the Antarctic Treaty, Senator Aiken expressed concern as to what would be the situation under the Treaty if a vast strike of a particularly valuable resource were discovered. Mr Phleger, the leader of the US Delegation to the Antarctic Treaty, replied that the Treaty did not cover such a situation and that in any:

> discovery of value in a sector which was claimed by one of the claimant nations it would naturally claim sovereignty and the right to dictate the manner of exploitation. The United States on the other hand never having recognized the validity of that claim is in a position to assert that it has rights with respect thereto and that would be settled by whatever means the parties finally adopt and accept any control by this treaty.[70]

The fear of many states at the time was that the question of exploitation of mineral resources had the potential to derail proceedings. States like Australia worked hard to ensure that the minerals question did not become an issue that might jeopardize the creation of the regime:

> It was this Government's policy to avoid discussion on this subject at Washington, because it could easily have prejudiced the whole negotiations . . . In order to reach agreement between nations with very diverse views which are signatories to the treaty, it was necessary to confine the negotiations strictly to the purposes in hand, and that was done.[71]

The 1959 Treaty does in a limited sense address indirectly the issue of mineral exploitation, however, since it bans military activities and the dumping of radioactive wastes, and sets Antarctica aside as a 'preserve' for the carrying out of scientific research.[72] Moreover, the Antarctic Treaty did establish an approach to resource exploitation, in that it made it clear that ATCPs would regulate any future mineral activity.[73] The Antarctic Treaty did not

---

70 Bush, *Antarctica and International Law: A Collection of Inter-state and National Documents*, 114.

71 Statement by the Minister for Air (Osborne) in Australia, Parliamentary Debates, House of Representatives, vol. 29, 2, 116 (18 October 1960). Report of a Meeting of Experts Organised by the Fridtjof Nansen Foundation on Existing Law Relevant to the Authorisation or Prohibition of Mineral Exploration for Commercial Purposes in the Antarctic Treaty Area, 30 May–10 June 1973, reprinted in ibid.: 288.

72 Porter and Brown, *Global Environmental Politics*, 88.

73 Sahurie, *The International Law of Antarctica*, 433–4.

explicitly endorse environmental protection, but it did permit the ATCPs to negotiate, where thought advisable, for the preservation and conservation of Antarctic resources.[74] This design flaw, or flexibility, depending on one's perspective, has enabled normative transformation to occur to meet changing conceptions of the appropriate standard of behaviour in the region.[75]

## WHY THE PUSH TO EXPLOIT ANTARCTICA'S MINERALS?

Until about 1970, the most accurate way to describe how the ATCPs and the broader global community treated Antarctica was 'benign neglect' at best. However, the increasing global need for resources soon changed that, forcing ATCPs to confront questions of resource exploitation and/or management.[76] In the late 1960s, several ATCPs (Australia, UK and USA) were approached by domestic oil companies about the possibility of prospecting for oil within Antarctica and its surrounding oceans. At approximately the same time, New Zealand's government was asked to consider an application to prospect in the Ross Sea.[77] These entreaties first exposed the legislative and policy gap in the Treaty, in that there was no mention of mineral exploitation in the Treaty and no system for the issuing of permits or licences.[78] The issue of mineral exploitation was first discussed informally by the ATCPs at the 1970 meeting in Tokyo, but no action was deemed necessary.[79]

Several years later, the issue came to a head when the American ship, the *Glomar Challenger*, drilled into the Ross Continental shelf in 1972–73 and found gas traces in three sites indicating the potential of exploitable oil fields.[80] Several global economic developments emerged at this time that

---

74 'U.S. State Department Handbook of the Antarctic Treaty System 2002', 473.

75 Indeed, further treaty instruments decided upon by the parties have had an environmental focus. These include the Convention for the Conservation of Antarctic Seals 1972, the Convention on the Conservation of Antarctic Marine Living Resources 1980, the Convention on the Regulation of Antarctic Mineral Resource Activities 1988, and the Protocol on Environmental Protection to the Antarctic Treaty 1991. Ibid.

76 Francesco Francioni, 'Legal Aspects of Mineral Exploitation in Antarctica', *Cornell International Law Journal* 19 (1986): 163.

77 Sahurie, *The International Law of Antarctica*, 434.

78 'The Future of the Antarctic: Background for a Second UN Debate' (Greenpeace International, 1984), 13.

79 Christopher C. Joyner, 'The Evolving Minerals Regime for Antarctica', in *The Antarctic Legal Regime*, ed. Christopher C. Joyner and Sudhir K. Chopra (Dordrecht: Martinus Nijhoff Publishers, 1988), 132.

80 Suter, *World Law and the Last Wilderness*, 25.

made the issue of natural resource exploitation vital, particularly for Western states' interests. First, the Arab oil embargo of 1973–74 created a global oil shortage, and led to natural resource exploitation of Antarctica being of interest to those ATCPs which wanted to meet the shortfall with inexpensive oil.

Secondly, the ongoing United Nations Convention on the Law of the Sea (UNCLOS) negotiations were taking place between the developed and the lesser developed states. Christopher Joyner argues that the fractious nature of these discussions might well have placed added pressure on ATCPs to create a mineral regime to forestall a possible challenge from the Group of 77 that Antarctica should be subject to the common heritage principles underpinning the UNCLOS negotiations.[81] Thirdly, Antarctica was seen as a potential strategic zone if world powers went to war, because Antarctica provided a crucial base of operations for maritime communications between the Pacific and Atlantic Oceans.[82]

Both the major global powers of that period, the USA and the Union of Soviet Socialist Republics (USSR), saw Antarctica and its potential exploitable resources as a tempting prize. The United States of America had always maintained that national interest in the region included access to Antarctica's potential resources and saw Antarctica as a vital resource area of the future.[83] The other Cold War superpower, the USSR, was also cognizant of the potential mineral riches of Antarctica and it openly stated as its objective the exploitation of the resources of Antarctica for the benefit of its economy. It purposefully followed an approach, contrary to the spirit of the regime, of placing its research stations in Antarctica in strategic locations. This approach was designed to ensure that it would have the best possible bargaining basis if there were to be a future allocation of property rights over mineral deposits.[84] Combined, these issues made it imperative for the ATCPs that they develop a mineral regime to gain access to vital resources and avoid the issue becoming one that could damage the ATS as a whole. If exploitable mineral deposits were found, the parties knew that it would be hard to both assert their

---

81 Elliott, *International Environmental Politics: Protecting the Antarctic*, 106; Joyner, 'The Evolving Minerals Regime for Antarctica', 132–3.

82 Francioni, 'Legal Aspects of Mineral Exploitation in Antarctica', 164.

83 Buck, *The Global Commons: An Introduction*, 53; Gareth Porter, Janet Welsh Brown and Pamela S. Chasek, *Global Environmental Politics*, 3rd edition, Dilemmas in World Politics (Boulder, CO: Westview Press, 2000), 90. The USA historically had seen Antarctica as a region to exploit for its wealth. J.R. Rowland, 'The Treaty Regime and the Politics of the Consultative Parties', in *The Antarctic Legal Regime*, ed. Christopher C. Joyner and Sudhir K. Chopra (Dordrecht: Martinus Nijhoff Publishers, 1988), 17.

84 Boczek, 'The Soviet Union and the Antarctic Regime', 852.

authority against other nations and create a regulatory scheme against entrenched economic interests.[85]

## ENGOs AND ANTARCTIC MINERAL EXPLOITATION

NGO, as opposed to ENGO, concern about the protection of Antarctica predates the Antarctic Treaty. For example, in 1945 the Women's International League for Peace and Freedom (WILPF) argued that:

> These inclement [polar] regions are already subject to various conflicting claims which are more likely to grow extensively and intensively . . . It would seem worth while for the nations concerned to accept whatever sacrifice may be necessary in the surrender of such claims as they may have and to give this area the fullest and most equitable development, with the full status of a recognized and organized international area. It could then be run not by any one country or group of countries but by a commission acting as trustees for them all.[86]

The League recommended that the UN be tasked to create and administer such a commission. WILPF also claimed credit for influencing Indian Prime Minister Nehru's initiatives to promote peaceful management of the region in 1956 and 1958. Their aim, like many early NGO campaigns at the UN, was designed to foster international cooperation and ensure that scientific benefits from Antarctica flowed to all states.[87]

However, NGOs and ENGOs appear to have had no impact on the actual creation and framework of the Antarctic regime. Richard Herr and Bruce Davis maintain that for many years after the creation of the ATS the relative policy vacuum of the organization did not attract the attention of ENGOs, except for SCAR, and there is merit to their observation.[88] However, from the mid-1970s, ENGOs became interested in the case of Antarctica, and in particular any potential mineral exploitation that could damage the region, as part of their renewed interest in global environmental issues.[89] After the 1972 Stockholm Conference, and as the exploitation of Antarctic resources was being discussed in earnest by states, ENGOs began to investigate the Antarctic

---

85 Elliott, *International Environmental Politics: Protecting the Antarctic*, 108–9.

86 Lee Kimball, 'The Role of Non-governmental Organizations in Antarctic Affairs', in *The Antarctic Legal Regime*, ed. Christopher C. Joyner and Sudhir K. Chopra (Dordrecht, Martinus Nijhoff Publishers, 1988), 34.

87 Ibid.: 35.

88 Herr and Davis, 'Antarctica and Non-state Actors: The Question of Legitimacy', 7–9.

89 Kimball, 'The Role of Non-governmental Organizations in Antarctic Affairs', 36.

management system and states' activities, since they were concerned that the last pristine wilderness area was under threat.[90] ENGOs argued that any exploitation of mineral resources was antithetical with the ATCPs' obligations to protect the environment and should be ruled out.[91]

However, they had not decided what their environmental normative position should be. Were they looking to impose a conservationist approach or a preservationist vision? The issue came to a head at the Second World Conference on National Parks in 1972, held at the Yellowstone National Park, USA. The Conference, co-sponsored by the IUCN,[92] saw attendees argue for the creation of an Antarctic 'world park'[93] under the auspices of the UN as the best solution given the 'great scientific and aesthetic value of the unaltered natural ecosystems of the Antarctic'.[94] After much debate, the body agreed on Recommendation 5, which stated:

> That nations party to the Antarctic Treaty should negotiate to establish the Antarctic Continent and the surrounding seas as the first world park, under the auspices of the United Nations.[95]

Proponents of such a park argued that, given its fragility, any exploitation of the mineral reserves of the region could lead to an environmental catastrophe and they wanted the region to remain preserved and unmined.[96] While not binding on ENGO delegates, the recommendation appears to be the first time the debate as to the preferred ENGO normative position regarding Antarctica

---

90 Ibid.

91 Lorraine M. Elliott, *The Global Politics of the Environment* (Basingstoke: Macmillan, 1998), 109.

92 The International Union for the Conservation of Nature is a global organization whose primary members are associations with a science-based creed. This scientific basis has stood it in good stead in its dealings with other groups associated with Antarctica. It has worked with SCAR on a number of joint projects and was also the first ENGO to be granted observer status (1987 Fourteenth Meeting). It has attended every ATCM since. Herr and Davis, 'Antarctica and Non-state Actors: The Question of Legitimacy', 10.

93 A similar idea was raised at the first ATCM in 1961 by the UK delegation which promoted the idea of Antarctica as a 'natural reserve'. This appears to have been officially ignored, however, until it was revived by ENGOs. Joyner, *Governing the Frozen Commons: The Antarctic Regime and Environmental Protection*, 175.

94 James N. Barnes, 'Legal Aspects of Environmental Protection in Antarctica', in *The Antarctic Legal Regime*, ed. Christopher C. Joyner and Sudhir K. Chopra, (Dordrecht: Martinus Nijhoff Publishers, 1988), 256–7; Porter and Brown, *Global Environmental Politics*, 89.

95 'The Future of the Antarctic: Background for a Second UN Debate', Appendix 7.

96 Porter and Brown, *Global Environmental Politics*, 89.

was discussed. At that time, the IUCN sent the resolution to the ATCPs but it was never formally considered and the Non-consultative Parties were never given the chance to express an opinion on the matter.[97]

## ANTARCTIC TREATY CONSULTATIVE PARTIES AND MINERAL EXPLOITATION

In the same year as the IUCN conference, the issue of mineral exploitation was first officially discussed. This was at the Seventh Consultative Meeting held at Wellington, and occasioned the adoption of Recommendation VII-6: Antarctic Resources: Effects of Mineral Exploration. The ATCPs noted that given the 'technological developments in polar mineral exploration and the increasing interest in the possibility of there being exploitable minerals in the Antarctic Treaty area', the issue be carefully studied and included on the agenda of the next meeting.[98] Some members argued against rushing to exploit, while others such as Great Britain argued that the issue could not be avoided ad infinitum and should be addressed urgently.[99]

However, upon an examination of the literature and the official minutes, there appears to have been no state that did not define its interests in terms of being able to exploit these potential riches. The only impediment at this time to unrestrained exploitation was the fear that the issue could destroy the ATS, which had kept the lid on conflict over the region. Neoliberal analysis casts this fear of regime collapse as central to the eventual outcome. States were afraid of losing the benefits of cooperation and, in this case, the fear was well founded. One member of a European delegation was anonymously reported to have stated: 'This treaty will last till a big mineral discovery is made – then it will be every man for himself'.[100] This fear of reverting to a pre-regime 'lawless' scenario, where sovereignty disputes and unhindered exploitation are the norm, was to prove an enduring thread running through the various mineral negotiations.

The following year, from 30 May to 10 June 1973, the Nansen Foundation sponsored an informal conference of experts at Polhogda, Norway to examine whether mineral mining was compatible with the objectives of the Antarctic Treaty.[101] This Experts Meeting was the start of the ATCP's attempts to

---

97 Barnes, 'Legal Aspects of Environmental Protection in Antarctica', 256.

98 Antarctic Treaty Consultative Meeting, 'Report of the Ninth Consultative Meeting' (London, 1977), 22.

99 Elliott, *International Environmental Politics: Protecting the Antarctic*, 113.

100 Suter, *Antarctica: Private Property or Public Heritage?*, 46.

101 Deborah Shapley, *The Seventh Continent: Antarctica in a Resource Age* (Washington, DC: Johns Hopkins University Press, 1985), 158.

resolve the vexed minerals question and avoid a potential 'gold rush'. Experts came from all the ATCP states.[102] The Group's report made a number of points. It argued that considering the requests to exploit mineral resources made by oil companies:

> It is realistic to expect this interest to increase within five or ten years . . . [by which time] governments should have decided how they propose to deal with the problem; not at a much later stage when commercial exploitation may become practical.[103]

The report of that meeting shows that several states thought such commercial exploitation was antithetical to the Treaty because of the potential risks of contamination and the negative impacts on scientific research.[104] Thus the Working Group of Experts in 1973 argued:

> Commercial mineral exploration and [mining] would disturb scientific activity, would constitute a serious danger for the Antarctic ecosystem, and could cause the contamination of its seas, ice and land despite the fact that the requirements of scientific investigation are that the Antarctic should be a non-contaminated area. The attention of the Group was drawn to the preoccupation of successive Consultative Meetings with the preservation of fauna and flora, which, according to one view, was incompatible with commercial mineral exploration.[105]

Lastly, the Experts considered the issue of minerals not being mentioned in the Antarctic Treaty in the light of the theoretical suggestion that any state/group should be able to explore and exploit any mineral resources. The Experts decided that any mineral accord outside the environs of the Treaty was to be discouraged since it would lead to international discord.[106]

---

102 Elliott, *International Environmental Politics: Protecting the Antarctic*, 113; Shapley, *The Seventh Continent: Antarctica in a Resource Age*, 159–60.

103 Report of the Working Group on Legal and Political Questions of the Report of the Meeting of Experts Organised by the Fridtjof Nansen Foundation on Existing Law Relevant to the Authorisation or Prohibition of Mineral Exploration for Commercial Purposes in the Antarctic Treaty Area, reprinted in 'U.S. Policy with Respect to Mineral Exploration and Exploitation in the Antarctic', ed. US Senate Subcommittee on Oceans and International Environment of the Senate Committee on Foreign Relations (Congressional record of hearing, 94th Congress, 1st Session, 15 May 1975), 74.

104 Francioni, 'Legal Aspects of Mineral Exploitation in Antarctica', 165.

105 Report of the Working Group on Legal and Political Questions of the Report of the Meeting of Experts Organised by the Fridtjof Nansen Foundation on Existing Law Relevant to the Authorisation or Prohibition of Mineral Exploration for Commercial Purposes in the Antarctic Treaty Area, reprinted in 'U.S. Policy with Respect to Mineral Exploration and Exploitation in the Antarctic', 76–80 at para. 22.

106 Report of a Meeting of Experts Organised by the Fridtjof Nansen Foundation

In 1975, New Zealand formally proposed that Antarctica should be designated a world park and offered to cede its territorial claims if other states followed suit. Chile was generally supportive of the proposal, but was not willing to give up its territorial claims. No other party was willing to adopt the New Zealand approach, seeing it as against their interests to give up their claim, and the matter was never formally discussed at an ATCM.[107] At that point in time, the idea was seen as absurd by the ATCPs, since any such policy was considered 'conceptually fuzzy, legally undefined and internationally unenforceable'.[108]

The idea of a permanent moratorium on mining activities was much discussed by ATCPs from 1973–75.[109] By the time of the next meeting of the parties in 1975, the issue was brought into sharper focus. All the ATCPs accepted that the creation of a formal instrument was necessary and that they were the body to decide on questions pertaining to mineral exploitation within Antarctica. The majority of members favoured the imposition of a New Zealand proposal, with weak support from Argentina and Chile, which called for a moratorium on mineral exploitation in the interim.[110]

Deborah Shapley has another version of the events leading to the ban, according to which the push for such a policy was led by the Soviet Union who, it was alleged, was hoping to catch up with the Western powers in offshore oil technology. At that point, according to R. Tucker Scully of the US State Department, the USA was virtually alone in opposing such a policy, maintaining its aforementioned position that exploitation was in its interest and that it should act as the chief norm proponent. The USA refused to accede to a moratorium at the Oslo Meeting, putting considerable pressure on the other ATCPs not to impose any ban, and the issue was consequently not resolved.[111] Rather the ATCPs were urged to encourage:

---

on Existing Law Relevant to the Authorisation or Prohibition of Mineral Exploration for Commercial Purposes in the Antarctic Treaty Area, 30 May–10 June 1973, reprinted in Bush, *Antarctica and International Law: A Collection of Inter-State and National Documents* 289.

[107] Barnes, 'Legal Aspects of Environmental Protection in Antarctica', 256.

[108] Joyner, *Governing the Frozen Commons: The Antarctic Regime and Environmental Protection*, 176.

[109] Shapley, *The Seventh Continent: Antarctica in a Resource Age*, 160.

[110] Elliott, *International Environmental Politics: Protecting the Antarctic*, 114–15.

[111] Ibid.: 115. Despite their negotiating position desiring mining, the US was conscious of being perceived as a good global citizen and had refused a prospecting application in 1975, citing that there were no procedures to grant rights to Antarctica. It had also dissuaded domestic oil companies from conducting surveys of Antarctica. Rigg, 'Environmentalists' Perspectives on the Protection of Antarctica', 77; Sahurie,

> States and persons to refrain from actions of commercial exploration and exploitation while, acting as Consultative Parties, they seek timely agreed solutions to the problems raised by the possible presence of valuable mineral resources in the Antarctic Treaty Area.[112]

The parties decided to task SCAR with working out the potential environmental consequences of mineral exploitation in the region. The main documents on the issue of mineral exploitation and its consequences are the Report of the SCAR Group of Specialists on the Environmental Impact Assessment of Mineral Exploration/Exploitation (EAMREA), prepared at the request of the Eighth Consultative Meeting and the Special Preparatory Meeting (for the Ninth Consultative Meeting) held in Paris in June 1976. In 1976, SCAR reported back and offered four principles applicable to any putative mineral exploitation:

1. the Consultative Parties should continue to play an active and responsible role in dealing with the question of Antarctic mineral resources;
2. the Antarctic Treaty must be maintained in its entirety;
3. protection of the unique Antarctic environment and of its dependent ecosystems should be a basic consideration;
4. the Consultative Parties in dealing with the question of mineral resources in Antarctica, should not prejudice the interests of all mankind in Antarctica.[113]

SCAR's guidelines were subsequently approved at the Ninth Consultative Meeting in 1977 (Recommendation IX-1).[114] Cognizant of environmental concerns and possibly to forestall states trying to gain an advantage and start mineral activities now, a voluntary restraint policy was adopted in 1977 at the London Meeting by the ATCPs, that would:

> Urge their nationals and other States to refrain from all exploration and exploitation of Antarctic mineral resources while making progress towards the timely adoption

---

*The International Law of Antarctica*, 435. But the USA, for much of the decade suffering from oil scarcity, was determined under the Nixon administration to obtain exploratory permits for American oil companies in the region. This was an offset against potential oil supply problems in the future. Shapley, *The Seventh Continent: Antarctica in a Resource Age*, 160.

112 Report of the Eighth Consultative Meeting, 1976, reprinted in Bush, *Antarctica and International Law: A Collection of Inter-State and National Documents*, 296.

113 'Editorial', *SCAR Bulletin*, September, no. 69 (1981): 98–100.

114 Antarctic Treaty Consultative Meeting, 'Report of the Ninth Consultative Meeting', 12 at para. 4.

> of an agreed regime concerning Antarctic mineral resource activities. They will thus endeavour to ensure that, pending the timely adoption of agreed solutions pertaining to exploration and exploitation of mineral resources, no activity shall be conducted to explore or exploit such resources.[115]

There were several problems with the voluntary ban. The moratorium was merely a 'gentleman's agreement' that was not legally binding on ATCPs nor was it binding on other states and it was never clearly explicated as to precisely what geophysical activities were considered banned.[116] Nonetheless, there is no evidence to suggest that the ban was ever not honoured by both ATCPs and other states. States were primarily concerned that if the voluntary moratorium collapsed without any convention replacing it, there would develop a 'frontier mentality' which would allow the unrestrained exploitation of mineral resources in Antarctica by the strongest state, with no need to share with the world community.[117] The voluntary ban placed no stress on the regime as a whole, however, because there was no real pressure to mine at that time, due to technological limitations.

At this point, we can clearly observe that many states had accepted exploitation as inevitable and necessary, but the norm had not been institutionalized in any practical sense. Ted Rowlands, the UK Minister of State for Foreign and Commonwealth Affairs, argued in his speech to the 1977 ATCM in terms that seemed to speak for many states, when he framed the debate in terms of global need: 'I do not mean to imply that Antarctic resources should not be exploited – the world's need for them is probably too great for such an argument to be tenable.'[118] However, there was an understanding by Mr Rowlands and representatives of other states that such a course of action would have deleterious effects on the Antarctic environment unless 'foreseen and guarded against'.[119]

While mineral exploitation was seen as necessary to satisfy the globe's demands for raw resources, some states were concerned about the impact on the region and were calling for a conservationist approach. One of the

---

115 Ibid.: 13.

116 Lorraine M. Elliott and Australian National University, Australian Foreign Policy Publications Program, *Protecting the Antarctic Environment: Australia and the Minerals Convention*, Australian Foreign Policy Papers (Canberra, ACT: Australian Foreign Policy Publications Programme Dept. of International Relations Research School of Pacific Studies Australian National University, 1993), 21. 'The Future of the Antarctic: Background for a Second UN Debate', 14.

117 Suter, *Antarctica: Private Property or Public Heritage?*, 46.

118 Antarctic Treaty Consultative Meeting, 'Report of the Ninth Consultative Meeting', 24.

119 Ibid.

Argentinian delegates, J.C. Beltramino, argued: 'That effective conservation measures, i.e. measures conducive to rational utilisation of such resources, should be adopted seems to us to be glaringly obvious.'[120] Some delegates were in favour of the need to preserve the Antarctic environment and were willing to state such a position openly. The Chilean delegate, F. Zegers, and the US member, R.C. Brewster, highlighted the need for any mineral activities to be cognizant of preserving the unique Antarctic environment.[121] However, while there was a groundswell of concern there was not yet an acceptance of the idea that conserving the Antarctic environment was critical to any mineral regime.

SCAR, through its particular National Antarctic Committees, was asked to assess the impact of such mineral gathering.[122] The Group of Experts met between 20 and 29 September 1977 with a view to determining the current state of technology for exploring and exploiting Antarctic minerals.[123] In its report, the Group of Experts considered that were it thought possible to commence mineral exploration or exploitation in the Antarctic, guidelines would need to be drawn up with regard to any environmental impact assessment.[124] At the time, the Group felt that current technology was not capable of year-round oil production in the Antarctic, but that such technology was being developed.[125] Further, the report concluded that, to date, exploration had yielded only 1 per cent of geologically comparable areas that could contain hydrocarbon resources. Such a small area of likely candidates was unlikely at that time to lead to commercial exploitation and even exploratory drilling was unlikely in the next five to ten years.[126]

The Group of Experts' report on the technical aspects of mineral exploration and exploitation in the Antarctic revealed 'that the question of the impact of these activities on the environment has been studied very inade-

---

120 Ibid.: 26.

121 Ibid.: 31, 43.

122 'US State Department Handbook of the Antarctic Treaty System 2002', 469.

123 Ibid.: 443.

124 Ibid.: 444.

125 Ibid.: 446.

126 Ibid.: 448–9. The Group had examined the Report of the SCAR Group of Specialists on the Environmental Impact Assessment of Mineral Exploration/Exploitation in Antarctica (EAMREA), prepared at the request of the Eighth Consultative Meeting and the Special Preparatory Meeting in Paris in June 1976. 'U.S. State Department Handbook of the Antarctic Treaty System 2002', 454. The Group thought that the estimate published in the *Oil and Gas Journal* for November 1976 and quoted in the Report of the SCAR EAMREA Group that 45 billion barrels of oil and 115 trillion cubic feet of gas 'may' be extractable from the Antarctic continental margin should be considered speculation. 'U.S. State Department Handbook of the Antarctic Treaty System 2002', 456.

quately and that there is an urgent need for a further examination of this problem'.[127] The Group recommended that Antarctic environmental protection had to be determined before any mineral exploitation could be undertaken.[128] The report's recommendations presage the CRAMRA negotiations in arguing that:

> If mineral exploration or exploitation were to occur in the Antarctic it would be essential to monitor both the operations themselves and consequential changes in the environment. There would need to be a system providing immediate warning of an accident leading to significant pollution and monitoring of the dispersion and effects of the pollutants released, and of the effectiveness of any measures for containment or recovery.[129]

The Group of Experts met again in Washington, DC, between 25 and 29 June 1979.[130] The Group agreed in the Report of the Group of Ecological, Technical and Other Related Experts on Mineral Exploration and Exploitation in Antarctica, Washington 1979 that current scientific, technological and economic factors indicated little possibility of the commercial exploitation of Antarctic mineral resources except for offshore hydrocarbons for the foreseeable future. Accordingly, they recommended that future scientific programmes to deal with the impact of mining activity should be concerned primarily with oil.[131] The overall thrust of the Group's report was that while there were environmental risks associated with such activities, they were not so severe as to rule out such exploitation *ab initio*.[132]

The 1979 ATCM in Washington, DC saw the ATCPs stipulate that any agreed regime should assess the impact of any mineral resource activity and create rules to protect the environment. It was clear that some delegates to the meeting were convinced that exploitation of petroleum deposits was likely within ten years and that steps must be taken now to avoid over-exploitation.[133] The ATCPs agreed with the conservationist proposition that 'the interests of all mankind' should not be adversely affected by any minerals regime.[134] Recommendation X-1 effectively added a fifth principle to the four previously

---

127 'U.S. State Department Handbook of the Antarctic Treaty System 2002', 454.

128 Ibid.

129 Ibid.: 456.

130 Ibid.: 436.

131 Ibid.

132 Ibid.: 384.

133 Mr Merwyn Norrish of New Zealand's Statement to the ATCPs' Antarctic Treaty Consultative Meeting, 'Report of the Tenth Consultative Meeting' (Washington, 1979), 77; Mr Rene Lustig of France's Statement to the ATCPs, 'Report of the Tenth Consultative Meeting', 75.

134 Recommendation X-1, Antarctic Treaty Consultative Meeting, 'Report of the Tenth Consultative Meeting', 11–13.

accepted regime principles when it stated that any future minerals regime would designate '. . . whether mineral resource activities would be acceptable'.[135] Why states had shifted from exploitation to conservation at this time is not explored in the literature, but there are several possibilities. One is that states wanted to exploit Antarctic resources, but were afraid that such activities would be resisted unless there were environmental safeguards. Another is that there was genuine concern by states to protect the Antarctic environment, providing such regulation did not interfere with mineral activities.

Recommendation X-1 was to prove crucial in the normative battle to come, since it mandated that all parties must deem the proposed mineral regime acceptable. By 1980, the last ATCP members who had objected to the creation of such a regime, Japan and the USSR, agreed to negotiate.[136] The debate at this stage was only between those wanting a conservationist regime and those desiring exploitation. However, the negotiations to create a minerals regime would for the first time provide a forum for altruistic arguments to be tested and agreed to by the parties. This opened the door for ENGOs and their preservationist arguments.

## ENGOs DURING THE 1970s

The ENGOs spent the 1970s effectively marshalling their forces for the fight to protect the Antarctic environment. The charge was led primarily by domestic ENGOs from the developed states. In the USA, the Centre for Law and Social Policy (CLASP) became involved in Antarctic protection after the announcement that hydrocarbon gases (methane, ethylene and ethane) had been found in the Ross Sea by the American-run Deep Sea Drilling Project of 1972–73. The International Office of the America-based Sierra Club asked CLASP to represent it on Antarctic issues and the CLASP Director attended the Eighth ATCM in Oslo in 1975 and the Special Meeting on Minerals preceding the Ninth Meeting in 1976. Having no official role, the Director was limited to passing out position papers to delegates outside the meeting room. Both the Sierra Club and CLASP functioned as informational clearing-houses on Antarctic issues for the rest of the decade.[137]

In Great Britain, the International Institute for Environment and Development (IIED) implemented an Antarctic project in 1975–76 to support conservation of Antarctica. Opening up the ATS to more states and individu-

135 Shapley, *The Seventh Continent: Antarctica in a Resource Age*, 162.

136 Porter and Brown, *Global Environmental Politics*, 89–90.

137 Kimball, 'The Role of Non-governmental Organizations in Antarctic Affairs', 36.

als influenced the management of the regime. The IIED's press arm, Earthscan, also played an early vital role in raising global public awareness on Antarctica, framing the issue as one of protecting a fragile wilderness. This heightened awareness was critical, since it allowed ENGOs to convince states that any decision would be scrutinized by the world. Earthscan also provided valuable expertise to countries not part of the ATS and to concerned individuals and scholars.[138]

It was during this period that ENGOs began to be directly involved in the inner workings of the Antarctic Treaty System, access that was to prove crucial to ENGO normative policy successes in the 1980s. Following an upsurge in domestic interest in Antarctic issues, in 1977 the Director of the International Office of the Sierra Club was allowed for the first time to be a member of the US delegation to the Ninth and Tenth ATCMs.[139]

The ENGO's policy direction was influenced primarily by two documents. As noted earlier, the 1972 recommendation of the Second World Conference on National Parks, which called for Antarctica to be designated a 'world park' administered by the United Nations, was a critical starting point in the campaign to have the Antarctic declared a preserve. Initially, some ENGOs were more influenced by the second document, however, the *1980 World Conservation Strategy*, prepared by IUCN, UNEP and the WWF, part of which dealt with making the conservation of Antarctic living resources a global priority. The document was silent on the issue of mineral exploitation though.[140]

By the time of the 1981 World Parks Congress, many ENGOs had backed away from the preservationist 'world park' concept, in favour of demanding a conservationist convention. Many representatives believed that preservationism was not a viable negotiating position. This was more of a strategic decision, relatively separate from their particular beliefs, because they were convinced that advocating a preservationist position would impede their ability to influence the Antarctic policies of the states concerned. Given the virtually unanimous support amongst states for exploiting Antarctic mineral resources they calculated that the best negotiating strategy would be to push for the strongest conservationist regime.[141] Having decided their negotiating goals and strategies, the ENGOs were confident that they would be able to influence the upcoming CRAMRA negotiations.

While this was the majority decision, not all ENGOs favoured such an approach. Those more radical sought a social actor that could articulate the

138 Ibid.: 37.
139 Ibid.: 36.
140 Ibid.: 38.
141 Ibid.

preservationist position. Eventually, the Antarctic and Southern Ocean Coalition (ASOC) became the vehicle through which such views were promoted. ASOC was created in 1978 by CLASP in an effort to build a coalition of like-minded ENGOs from over 40 countries. In that year, it had met with Australian ENGOs to create the Antarctic and Southern Ocean Coalition (ASOC) and in 1981 the Antarctic Project was established in Washington, DC to take over from CLASP.[142] The framework of ASOC enabled many ENGOs to take part in Antarctic issues without having to meet large monetary or personnel expenses.[143]

If a normative entrepreneur for the preservation of Antarctica from mineral activity can be identified, it would be ASOC. However, this observation would be contentious because we cannot speak of an individual or even one organization because ASOC was an umbrella organization. It is difficult to establish any key members or individuals who were particularly active in promoting a preservationist agenda, so for the purposes of this book, we will need to treat the entire organization as the norm entrepreneur, and the platform as well.

ASOC's primary objective was '. . . to preserve the wilderness values of Antarctica by having the area declared off limits to mineral exploitation'.[144] The ASOC member groups were dedicated to creating a world park preserve and a permanent moratorium on mineral activities.[145] Towards that aim, on 12 August 1980, eight US ENGOs wrote to President Carter in an attempt to seek his support for the world park concept. They were unsuccessful.[146] Initially, ATCMs were wary of ASOC, fearing it would function only as a potential non-

---

142 Ibid.: 59. The Antarctic Project's brief is to hold states morally and politically accountable for their stewardship of Antarctica. It monitors and lobbies domestic and global forums which deal with Antarctica. Suter, *Antarctica: Private Property or Public Heritage?*, 134.

143 Clark, 'The Antarctic Environmental Protocol: NGOs in the Protection of Antarctica', 165. ASOC has remained a formal observer at all ATCMs and its members are sometimes members of state delegations. ASOC publishes *ECO*, a daily newspaper detailing updates on negotiations at major global environmental conferences, which allows delegates to stay aware of significant developments in negotiations. *ECO* was originally produced by FoE and the *Ecologist* in 1972 at the Stockholm Conference. Rather than advocating the views of any one state, it provides the position of the ENGO community. Paul Kevin Wapner, *Environmental Activism and World Civic Politics* (Albany, NY: State University of New York Press, 1996), 135. It also monitors state compliance with their agreed obligations and publicizes infractions such as the one where France built an airstrip in Terra Adelie in contravention of the Treaty. Buck, *The Global Commons: An Introduction*, 66.

144 Kimball, 'The Role of Non-governmental Organizations in Antarctic Affairs', 39.

145 Ibid.

146 Ibid.: 59, n. 19.

state 'veto group', but its work on Antarctic issues demonstrated that it could work in tandem with the other stakeholders to produce mutually beneficial outcomes. ASOC proved to be a critical player in the mineral regime negotiations of the 1980s.[147] All three normative positions were now clear and the actors espousing these views were ready to argue their various positions at the mineral negotiations and were hopeful of achieving their goals.

## THE CREATION OF THE WELLINGTON CONVENTION (CRAMRA)

The purpose of the negotiations was to establish a regulatory regime (if ever Antarctic minerals development should go forward) that balanced orderly resource extraction with environmental protection. To do this the ATCPs created what became known as the Convention on the Regulation of Antarctic Mineral Resource Activities, or the Wellington Convention. Margaret Clark evinces three reasons why state interest dictated that negotiations commence in the early 1980s: the most technologically able countries were confident they would be best able to exploit any resources and turn a profit (first in, best dressed). Further, any discovery of resources would probably lead to the dissolution of the legal freeze on territorial claims and would lead to an 'open season'. Most states were anxious to avoid this scenario and wanted an agreement in place to regulate mineral activity and avoid destroying the Antarctic regime. Lastly, some states were concerned about environmental impacts on the fragile region, and wanted a regime that allowed mineral activities that would not destroy the overall Antarctic ecosystem.[148]

Over the life of the Antarctic regime the ATCPs had developed a number of legal instruments to regulate human activity in the Antarctic. These were all negotiated in a spirit of consensus and this had changed the social dynamic under which the relevant states operated. Coupled with this consensus style has been a philosophy of attempting to regulate contentious issues before they developed into problems. When the ATCPs began to negotiate CRAMRA, these two principles of consensus and solving problems before they became intractable underpinned the proceedings and helped establish proper conduct and principles for how the states were supposed to act when negotiating.[149]

---

[147] Herr and Davis, 'Antarctica and Non-state Actors: The Question of Legitimacy', 10–11.

[148] Clark, 'The Antarctic Environmental Protocol: NGOs in the Protection of Antarctica', 168.

[149] Andersen, 'Negotiating a New Regime: How CRAMRA Came into Existence', 94–5.

This social learning was to have a major impact on both negotiations and proceedings by ensuring that they were not particularly acrimonious and the outcome was acceptable, if not internalized, by all.

At the 1981 ATCM in Buenos Aires, the parties adopted a Recommendation on Antarctic Mineral Resources that set out a schedule of Special Meetings to create a mineral regime as a matter of urgency to cover commercial exploration and exploitation.[150] The delegates to the Special Meetings were tasked with creating a mineral regime that took into account the following principles:

1. that the ATCPs continue to be the main stakeholders when dealing with issues of mineral exploitation;
2. that the Antarctic Treaty had to be maintained;
3. that the ATCPs, when deciding on this issue, be in no way prejudicing the interests of humanity in Antarctica;
4. that Article IV and its provisions on sovereignty remain unaffected; and
5. that the principles inherent in Article IV be upheld.[151]

That meeting also considered the issue of whether to continue the voluntary restraint of Antarctic mineral resource activities agreed to in Recommendation IX-1 for the interim period before the entry into force of the Convention. All the parties agreed not to engage in Antarctic mineral resource activities as defined in the Convention until CRAMRA entered into force.[152]

It should be borne in mind when examining these negotiations that the Antarctic mineral negotiations took place against a backdrop of global concern over resource exploitation generally and against a backdrop of antagonism from elements of the UN, and between states comprising the ATS and non-party states, in particular.[153] During the 1980s, the issue of global resource exploitation and its apportionment reached a zenith with the UNCLOS and CRAMRA negotiations.[154] This global atmosphere impacted significantly on the Antarctic regime in forcing the negotiators to create a regime at speed and one that did not alienate states that were not ATCPs.

Consequently the successful negotiation of CRAMRA was in the ATCPs' interests to allow for an orderly taking of resources before the intervention of, or complaints from, outside agencies or states that believed they were being

---

150 Antarctic Treaty Consultative Meeting, 'Report of the Eleventh Consultative Meeting' (Buenos Aires, 1981), 590–92.

151 Ibid.

152 'U.S. State Department Handbook of the Antarctic Treaty System 2002', 434.

153 Francesco Francioni, 'The Madrid Protocol on the Protection of the Antarctic Environment', *Texas International Law Journal* 28 (1993): 48.

154 Sahurie, *The International Law of Antarctica*, 438–42.

unfairly denied their share of Antarctic resources.[155] According to Chris Beeby, the Deputy Secretary of the New Zealand Ministry of Foreign Affairs and Chairman of the CRAMRA negotiations, without an established minerals regime ATCPs would '. . . continue to be poorly placed to resist criticism from countries . . . not become party . . . to the Treaty' and without a resolution states opposed to the ATS were likely to create a rival regime.[156]

Another background factor to the regime negotiations was the low prices minerals were fetching at that time, with non-oil commodity prices falling 28 per cent between 1980–82, the lowest price since World War II. While this may at first glance seem counter-intuitive, sustained low prices and market instability had curtailed investment and had a negative impact on future supplies of minerals from traditional sources. Subsequent low prices further discouraged investment, leading to a shutdown in non-competitive facilities. The resultant scarcity could, in the long term, have justified investment in areas of high risk such as Antarctica.[157]

ENGOS, unhappy with the idea of CRAMRA being implemented, moved strategically to create an 'alliance of interests' with states that opposed the ATS control of Antarctica, such as Malaysia. The Malaysian-led campaign for the UN to control the Antarctica idea held initial attraction for ASOC and Greenpeace since at the time the ATCPs were resistant to accepting ENGO influence in the ATS. The ENGOs were conscious that to have an impact with their own particular moral arguments, and to persuade member states, they had to ensure that the forum in which such debates occurred was receptive to their reasoning. Some ENGOs calculated that given their long association with the UN system, they would have more sway in a UN-controlled organization, and the issue split ASOC. Greenpeace, a key member, decided in 1984 that it could have direct influence in the ATS and chose to become actively involved in the negotiations, as, eventually, did ASOC for primarily the same reason.[158]

---

155 In 1983, Malaysia moved to put the issue of Antarctica and its resources on the UN General Assembly's agenda. On 15 December 1983, at the 38th Session of the UN, the General Assembly requested that the Secretary-General study all aspects of Antarctica and put on the 39th Session agenda the topic of the question of Antarctica, which affirmed that humanity as a whole, not just the ATCPs, needed to decide the future of Antarctica. 'The Future of the Antarctic: Background for a Second UN Debate', Appendix 5.

156 C.D. Beeby, 'An Overview of the Problems Which Should Be Addressed in the Preparation of a Regime Governing the Mineral Resources of Antarctica', in *Antarctic Resources Policy: Scientific, Legal and Political Issues*, ed. Francisco Orrego Vicuna (Cambridge: Cambridge University Press, 1983), 192.

157 Sahurie, *The International Law of Antarctica*, 430.

158 Herr and Davis, 'Antarctica and Non-state Actors: The Question of Legitimacy', 11–12.

In 1981 when the negotiations to create CRAMRA began, no party believed that commercial exploitation was imminent. It was deemed better to address the issue urgently, however, rather than wait for active commercial ventures to begin when technology had overcome the climactic issue with its attendant prohibitive operating costs.[159] Despite the ATCP's professed concern about environmental protection, Porter and Brown established that there was no evidence of parties carrying out an environmental impact statement of such mineral exploitation before the regime negotiations commenced. No states appear to have actively argued for exploitation without regard for its environmental consequences on the region. Of the ATCPs, those most in favour of mining were the United States, West Germany, Japan, Britain and France.[160]

The USA, along with its allies, was cognizant of the need not to undermine the existing ATS, however, and it considered that the ongoing:

> negotiations towards a minerals regime are not a concerted effort to open Antarctica to mineral exploration and exploitation, but a process necessary to create an environment in which any such mineral resource activities will not undermine the basic understandings and political compromises at the heart of the Antarctic Treaty System.[161]

The southern hemisphere nations of Australia, Argentina and Chile were all concerned that any mineral activity not be deleterious to the environment. They were all active initially in calling for strong conservationist measures to be part of the CRAMRA.[162]

In all, there were 12 formal CRAMRA negotiations and three informal intersessional meetings over six years in total. In many ways, Chris Beeby became the norm entrepreneur of the conservationist norm embodied in CRAMRA. He also became the driving force behind the negotiations, arguing for the need for a strong conservationist ethic. The participants were the current ATCPs at the time.[163] Initially, there were two draft conventions that

---

159 Lynton K. Caldwell, *International Environmental Policy: Emergence and Dimensions*, 2nd edition, Duke Press Policy Studies (Durham, NC: Duke University Press, 1990), 299. Chris Beeby, the Chair of the CRAMRA negotiations, supports this contention. While Recommendation XI-1 asks the parties to act with urgency to create a minerals regime, it does not necessarily follow that the parties believe that large-scale exploitation and enormous economic benefits are likely to occur. Beeby, 'An Overview of the Problems Which Should Be Addressed in the Preparation of a Regime Governing the Mineral Resources of Antarctica', 191.

160 Porter and Brown, *Global Environmental Politics*, 89–90.

161 David A. Colson, 'The United States Position on Antarctica', *Cornell International Law Journal* 19 (1986): 297.

162 Porter and Brown, *Global Environmental Politics*, 90.

163 Elliott, *International Environmental Politics: Protecting the Antarctic*, 121;

were known as the 'German' and the 'Beeby' drafts. Both argued that mineral activities were only permissible if a framework of environmental safeguards was in place.[164] The Beeby draft became the working draft for subsequent negotiations. Amazingly, no formal notes or records were kept of the proceedings, so it is difficult to establish individual state negotiating positions. Rather, progress was recorded by the delegates keeping mental notes of the rewriting of an informal proposal, from an agreed text, by the Chairman of the meetings.[165]

The first session of the Fourth Special Consultative Meeting was held in Wellington, New Zealand, in June 1982. Eleven other meetings took place over the course of the decade, hosted by different parties.[166] The final session of the Fourth Special Antarctic Treaty Consultative Meeting was held in Wellington from 2 May to 2 June 1988. Christopher Beeby of New Zealand was again elected as Chairman and representatives of all the Consultative Parties attended, as did the Contracting Parties and invited states (but not the ENGOs).[167] It was agreed by the negotiating parties that until negotiations

---

Suter, *Antarctica: Private Property or Public Heritage?*, 52. At the time of the First Meeting in 1982, they were Argentina, Australia, Belgium, Chile, France, West Germany, Japan, New Zealand, Norway, Poland, South Africa, the USSR, the UK and the USA. Over the course of proceedings, they were joined by states which had been granted consultative status, namely, Brazil, China, East Germany, India, Italy and Uruguay. States that were not party to the proceedings were also invited to attend and Austria, Bulgaria, Cuba, Czechoslovakia, Denmark, Ecuador, Finland, Greece, Hungary, the Republic of Korea, the Netherlands, Papua New Guinea, Peru, Romania, Spain and Sweden all accepted the invitation and attended sessions of the negotiations. Suter, *Antarctica: Private Property or Public Heritage?*, 52.

[164] Francioni, 'Legal Aspects of Mineral Exploitation in Antarctica', 178–9.

[165] Andersen, 'Negotiating a New Regime: How CRAMRA Came into Existence', 96–7.

[166] Further sessions were held in:

- Wellington, 17 to 28 January 1983;
- Bonn, 11 to 22 July 1983;
- Washington, DC, 18 to 27 January 1984;
- Tokyo, 23 to 31 May 1984;
- Rio de Janeiro, 26 February to 12 March 1985;
- Paris, 23 September to 6 October 1985;
- Hobart, 14 to 25 April 1986;
- Tokyo, 27 October to 12 November 1986;
- Montevideo, 11 to 20 May 1987;
- Wellington, 18 to 29 January 1988.

'U.S. State Department Handbook of the Antarctic Treaty System 2002', 432.

[167] Ibid. Argentina, Australia, Belgium, Brazil, Chile, China, France, German Democratic Republic, Federal Republic of Germany, India, Italy, Japan, New Zealand,

were concluded and a new mineral regime installed, a voluntary moratorium would remain in place.[168]

## ENGO RESPONSES TO THE CRAMRA NEGOTIATIONS

The response to the CRAMRA negotiations by the ENGOs was fractured. As noted previously, there was dissension between the various ENGOs making up ASOC as to what their objective in the CRAMRA negotiations should be. Should they seek to preserve the region via the creation of a world park or bow to what many believed would be the inevitable minerals convention and seek stronger environmental provisions in the CRAMRA?[169] Many individual ENGOs had as policy the complete denial of mineral development in Antarctica, declaring it an internationally protected site. For example, Greenpeace International circulated an 'Antarctic Declaration' which emphasized the principles of the Antarctic Treaty as justifying 'full protection' status.[170] Another faction of ASOC members favoured promoting environmental safeguards to the CRAMRA negotiations as the appropriate negotiating strategy.[171]

However, over time the preservationist faction within ASOC appears to have achieved ascendency. The IUCN resolution in 1981 to designate Antarctica a world park was endorsed by the World National Parks Congress in Bali in 1982. It was resolved that 'the concept of a world park and other appropriate designations should be developed more urgently'.[172] Greenpeace,

---

Norway, Poland, South Africa, USSR, UK, USA and Uruguay participated in the session. On the invitation of the Consultative Parties, representatives of 13 Contracting Parties to the Antarctic Treaty that are not Consultative Parties, Bulgaria, Canada, Czechoslovakia, Denmark, Ecuador, Finland, Greece, Republic of Korea, the Netherlands, Papua New Guinea, Peru, Romania and Sweden, also participated in the session.

168 Francisco Orrego Vicuna, 'The Definition of a Regime on Antarctic Mineral Resources: Basic Options', in *Antarctic Resources Policy: Scientific, Legal and Political Issues*, ed. Francisco Orrego Vicuna (Cambridge: Cambridge University Press, 1983), 201.

169 Rowland, 'The Treaty Regime and the Politics of the Consultative Parties', 29.

170 Barnes, 'Legal Aspects of Environmental Protection in Antarctica', 257. Greenpeace became involved in the protection of the Antarctic in 1983 just after the CRAMRA negotiations began. It put an enormous amount of resources into the campaign, even going so far as to create its own scientific station – World Park Base – which acted as if it was any other scientific mission created by an ATCP. Herr and Davis, 'Antarctica and Non-state Actors: The Question of Legitimacy', 11.

171 Kimball, 'The Role of Non-governmental Organizations in Antarctic Affairs', 39.

172 'The Future of the Antarctic: Background for a Second UN Debate',

one of the more preservationist ENGOs, joined up with ASOC in 1983 after concerns about the direction of the ATCP's mineral negotiations in 1982. As a result, ASOC took on a more preservationist edge as a whole.[173]

Using a constructivist multi-level approach to examine actions of the ENGO, we can observe their campaign to promote altruistic environmentalist norms. Their determination to sway states to a adopt a preservationist perspective echoes Putnam's analysis of states as implementing 'positive reverberation' campaigns, designed in this case to convince the domestic populations of the ATCPs to force their negotiators to adopt a preservationist approach.[174] Over this decade, ASOC circulated world park petitions globally, while Greenpeace created a publicity campaign that included expeditions to the region in 1985–86 and 1986–87 that focused on the idea of a world park. They also established 'World Park Week' every year in February and the creation of 'World Park Embassies' in some capital cities. They published a pamphlet on the idea in October 1986 that was circulated during the UN debate on the Question of Antarctica in November. The umbrella group ASOC published numerous articles on world parks in its magazine *ECO* and handed out a briefing paper to the Antarctic Treaty states in 1986.[175]

ASOC was not above employing strategic actions designed to embarrass the ATCPs about their preference for mineral exploitation. After the Special Meeting in January 1983 in Wellington, a working draft of a minerals regime was created. This working paper was obtained by ASOC, which published it in the ENGO publication *ECO*, bearing the headline caption 'Beeby's Slick Solution' to underscore the ENGO's opposition to the CRAMRA text. The *ECO* editors were scathing in their criticism of the CRAMRA draft in the article:

> The document gives the lie to the negotiators ... who assert that concern for the pristine Antarctic environment is their first consideration. It reveals that providing a political solution to the Treaty partners' internal conflicts is an objective that has overridden protection of the environment. Political expediency has triumphed over sound management.[176]

---

Appendix 7, 3. The IUCN General Assembly in 1985 passed a slightly amended document with substantially the same point. Barnes, 'Legal Aspects of Environmental Protection in Antarctica', 258.

173 Kimball, 'The Role of Non-governmental Organizations in Antarctic Affairs', 39.

174 Robert D. Putnam, 'Diplomacy and Domestic Politics: The Logic of Two-level Games', *International Organization* 42, no. 3, Summer (1988): 454. Such reverberation occurs when international pressure tips the domestic balance in favour of a particular outcome. Ibid.: 454. Such pressure can be positive or negative in that such actions cause a domestic backlash. Ibid.: 456.

175 Barnes, 'Legal Aspects of Environmental Protection in Antarctica', 257.

176 'Antarctic Mineral Regimes, Beeby's Slick Solution', *ECO* 23, no. 1 (1983): 1.

The ENGOs were in one sense forced to employ such tactics since the CRAMRA negotiations provided few avenues for ENGO participation. Only the Scientific Advisory Committee could receive 'views' from 'international organizations', and only in circumscribed circumstances.[177] However, the ENGOs set upon a strategy of infiltrating the negotiations by joining sympathetic state delegations. Since 1983, a representative from either ASOC or Greenpeace has been on the delegations of Australia, New Zealand and Denmark at ATCMs. They were thus a presence, albeit minimal, during the CRAMRA negotiations.[178] For example, ASOC was able to call for the creation of an Antarctic Environmental Protection Agency during the CRAMRA negotiations, albeit without success.[179]

At the same time, ENGOs set about becoming an official part of the ATS system through a series of strategic partnerships with established non-state stakeholders. The start of the negotiation for a minerals regime in 1982 also brought increased scientific community concern that any such development would harm the pristine nature of Antarctica. In 1982–83, IUCN's Ecology Commission contacted SCAR about a possible collaborative effort to conserve Antarctica. In April 1985, the two groups met in Bonn, Germany and in late 1985, a joint IUCN/SCAR Working Group was created to focus on long-term conservation strategies for Antarctica. The IUCN saw SCAR's special position in the ATS as a conduit to better promote conservationist policies, but there is no evidence of their explicit agreement to act in this manner.[180]

The ENGOs led the charge to declare Antarctica a world park and they lobbied national delegates vociferously to achieve that aim. When this position was rejected by those states which saw their interests being linked to mining, they argued for the most stringent environmental protections possible.[181] When the negotiations were considered complete, the Consultative Parties adopted the Convention on the Regulation of Antarctic Mineral Resource Activities that opened for signature in Wellington on 25 November

---

177 Barnes, 'Legal Aspects of Environmental Protection in Antarctica', 265.

178 Kimball, 'The Role of Non-governmental Organizations in Antarctic Affairs', 39. Rowland, 'The Treaty Regime and the Politics of the Consultative Parties', 29. Wapner, *Environmental Activism and World Civic Politics*, 135. By 1990, the strategy was so successful that ASOC was asked as a group to be present at the 1990 Special Meeting as an expert party and has attended all subsequent ATCMs in that guise. Herr and Davis, 'Antarctica and Non-state Actors: The Question of Legitimacy', 10–11.

179 Sahurie, *The International Law of Antarctica*, 458.

180 Kimball, 'The Role of Non-governmental Organizations in Antarctic Affairs', 39–40.

181 Christopher C. Joyner, 'CRAMRA: The Ugly Duckling of the Antarctic Treaty System?', in *The Antarctic Treaty System in World Politics*, ed. Arnfinn Jorgensen-Dahl and Willy Ostreng (New York: St Martin's Press, 1991), 167–8.

1988.[182] The CRAMRA text attempted to put in place a conservationist regime to allow for the taking of minerals without damaging the Antarctic environment in the long term.

While CRAMRA was not designed to promote sustainable mining, an oxymoron at best, it was intended to balance the rational taking of resources without significant damage to the Antarctic environment in order to conserve the region for other uses and future generations. As noted in the introduction, CRAMRA Article 1(6) defined mineral resources as 'all non-living natural non-renewable resources including fossil fuels, metallic and non-metallic minerals'.[183] CRAMRA Article 1(7) defined Antarctic mineral resource activities as 'prospecting, exploration or development, but does not include scientific research activities within the meaning of Article III of the Antarctic Treaty'.[184] CRAMRA's area of application was considered to be similar to the Antarctic Treaty definition, the Antarctic continent, the islands, the ice shelves south of 60 degrees latitude, and the seabed and subsoil of adjacent offshore areas, but not the deep seabed.[185]

The Preamble of the Convention acknowledged the ENGO campaign to link Antarctica with environmental principles that while exploitable mineral resources may exist in Antarctica, the region has unique ecological, scientific and wilderness value which the parties had to recognize and take into account.[186] Article 2(1) of CRAMRA supported this proposition by stating:

> No Antarctic mineral resource activity shall take place until it is judged, based upon assessment of its possible impacts on the Antarctic environment and on dependent and associated ecosystems, that the activity in question would not cause . . . damage to Antarctica's environment and global weather patterns.[187]

Article 4, paragraph 2 mandated that environmental impact statements must be made before exploration and development could occur, while paragraph 3 stated that 'significant adverse impacts' on global climate and weather must be taken into account in any development decision. Article 8 made an operator liable for damage to Antarctica caused by their mineral activities, and Article

---

182 'U.S. State Department Handbook of the Antarctic Treaty System 2002', 434.

183 Ibid.: 387. On a curious note, the Special Meeting delegates argued that the definition of mineral resources, as defined in Article 1(6) of the Convention, excludes ice and opened the door for the harvesting of that resource if it became feasible in the future. 'U.S. State Department Handbook of the Antarctic Treaty System 2002', 434.

184 'U.S. State Department Handbook of the Antarctic Treaty System 2002', 387.

185 Joyner, *Antarctica and the Law of the Sea*, 163.

186 'U.S. State Department Handbook of the Antarctic Treaty System 2002', 385.

187 Joyner, 'CRAMRA: The Ugly Duckling of the Antarctic Treaty System?', 166.

12 allowed for inspections of all mineral resource activities.[188] Further under CRAMRA, Antarctic mining was banned in any Specially Protected Area or at a Site of Special Scientific Interest under Article IX(1) of the treaty.[189]

CRAMRA proposed, under Article 3, to prohibit any mineral mining outside its rules and procedures, while imposing strict environmental impact criteria on any proposal to mine Antarctica. It also created a skeleton framework of rules governing exploration and exploitation of minerals that was intended to be fully fleshed out over time.[190] The Convention required consensus by all members of the commission for any mineral exploitation to occur that might have *substantial* environmental impact. No exploration for minerals was to occur without a consensus of members agreeing that such activity would not break environmental standards, thus reversing the previous standard laid down under CCAMLR that exploitation was possible unless there was consensus on measures to limit it.[191]

The Beeby text required decisions on Antarctic mineral exploitation to be made on an ad hoc and individual basis and set up a Commission to serve as a broker between the various competing interests. An attempt to exploit the Antarctic mineral resources would start with a sponsoring state informing the Commission that a private company under its jurisdiction desired to prospect a particular region. The sponsoring state would then submit a request, with an environmental impact statement attached, to open such an area for exploration to the Commission that would forward such a request to an advisory committee comprising one expert from every member state. This body was to consider the request and recommend a decision.[192]

Once allowed, a Regulatory Committee, comprising eight states specifically chosen to reflect the pattern of Antarctic political interests and always to include the USSR and the USA, would oversee the exploration and exploitation until the exploitation was concluded. The Committee was charged with putting in place a management scheme specific to that operation which contractually bound the developers, that is, the state(s) whose area was being exploited and the superpowers. Such a management scheme was meant to specify: whether civil or criminal law applies to the project, any licensing, taxes and royalty arrangements, technical and safety specifications, monitoring proposals, emergency plans, reporting criteria and the circumstances under

---

188 Ibid.: 166–7.

189 Joyner, *Governing the Frozen Commons: The Antarctic Regime and Environmental Protection*, 76.

190 Vogler, *The Global Commons: Environmental and Technological Governance*, 87.

191 Porter and Brown, *Global Environmental Politics*, 90–91.

192 Shapley, *The Seventh Continent: Antarctica in a Resource Age*, 164–5.

which a permit could be withdrawn. Under the scheme, developers were granted secure tenure and the sole right to apply for a development permit in the future. The proposal was submitted to the Commission, to approve or veto.[193]

The Final Act of the Fourth Special ATCM on Antarctic Mineral Resources urged 'their nationals and other States to refrain from Antarctic mineral resource activities as defined in the Convention pending its timely entry into force'.[194] Against this background of negotiations, it remained a moot point as to whether the moratorium was in force throughout the 1980s. One view states that with the adoption of CRAMRA, the moratorium was no longer in effect and any state could have exploited the mineral resources. The opposing view argues that because a large segment of the ATCPs were not yet willing to sign and ratify CRAMRA, the moratorium was in continuance until a treaty was concluded. The negotiations themselves do not shed light on which version is correct.

Later, at the Vina del Mar Special Meeting, France, Italy and Germany put forth an informal proposal that the parties should confirm in explicit terms that the moratorium still held but Chile, the UK and the US rejected the proposal strenuously and vociferously. Francesco Francioni believes that the ban was not in force by the end of the decade, but there is no evidence that any ATCP or other states began exploitation of the region.[195] At this point in time, there was still a normative and regulatory void regarding mining, since the rule and standards of behaviour had not yet been decided, let alone entrenched.

Joyner considers that CRAMRA did evince a strong environmental protection ethic as demonstrated by Article 4. Here are outlined the principles to be used in evaluating mineral activities, with decisions to be based on 'sufficient information'[196] as to any potential unacceptable damage that might be caused by such activity.[197] However, Joyner concedes that this formulation was broad enough to be open to multiple interpretations, since the term 'sufficient information' was imprecise at best.[198] Other critical terms utilized under the

---

193 Ibid.: 165–6.

194 W.M. Bush, *Antarctica and International Law: A Collection of Inter-state and National Documents* (London: Oceana Publications Inc., 1994), 1.

195 Francioni, 'The Madrid Protocol on the Protection of the Antarctic Environment', 66–7.

196 This test required that before mineral exploitation could occur, sufficient information had to be gathered by decision-makers to determine whether unacceptable damage would be done to the Antarctic environment. Joyner, 'CRAMRA: The Ugly Duckling of the Antarctic Treaty System?', 166.

197 Joyner, *Antarctica and the Law of the Sea*, 164.

198 Joyner, 'CRAMRA: The Ugly Duckling of the Antarctic Treaty System?', 166.

Convention were also hard to quantify in a meaningful way, for example, Article 4 and the definition of 'significant adverse effects' or 'substantial risk' when applied to mining activities.[199] Further, the Beeby proposal made no provision for the right of humanity as a whole to share in the mineral wealth of Antarctica.[200] Such shortcomings made the Convention an easy target for those stakeholders unhappy with the normative direction of the proposal or the impact on their interests.

Three views of differing states' interests were immediately apparent and were to have an impact on the chances of the Convention being ratified. One was that for some states and groups, the very existence of CRAMRA was seen as approval for the mining of Antarctica that they opposed. Secondly, the approval of CRAMRA would be seen as granting security of title to any potential claim that could impact on what some states regarded as their territory.[201] A corollary to this view was the old fear that many of the sovereignty issues, frozen by the Antarctic Treaty, would erupt again, potentially ruining the ATS. Thirdly, to achieve the requisite consensus, all parties had to compromise their interests to some extent, leading to many states feeling aggrieved at the Convention itself.

Most of the delegates were happy that the long negotiations were finally over. The French Delegate Head and Chief Negotiator Jean-Pierre Puissochet, in his statement on the adoption of CRAMRA, gave no hint of the furore that would develop later internally over France's position on the Convention, when he wished on behalf of the French government that CRAMRA enter into force in a short period of time.[202] He stated that in his opinion:

> The texts we have just adopted represent a happy balance between concern for the protection of the environment and the wish to allow, if it ever becomes necessary and possible, a reasonable exploration and exploitation of Antarctic mineral resources.[203]

CRAMRA was opened for signature on the 25 November 1988 in New Zealand. However, out of the 33 eligible states, only nine states signed on immediately: the Soviet Union, New Zealand, Norway, Finland, Brazil, South Korea, South Africa, Sweden and Uruguay. The USA, the UK, Chile and

---

[199] Vogler, *The Global Commons: Environmental and Technological Governance*, 87.

[200] Shapley, *The Seventh Continent: Antarctica in a Resource Age*, 166.

[201] Vogler, *The Global Commons: Environmental and Technological Governance*, 87.

[202] Bush, *Antarctica and International Law: A Collection of Inter-state and National Documents*, 4.

[203] Ibid., Booklet AL88E, D. AL02061988D, p. 4.

Argentina promised to sign as rapidly as possible. To reach the tipping point of ratification, the treaty needed at least 16 ATCPs to enter into force. Many states at this stage were ambivalent about the Convention.[204]

The reason why so many ATCP states remained disenchanted with CRAMRA is not clearly expressed in the writings on the negotiations, but several explanations are possible. One, the short-term rewards offered by mining in Antarctica were not seen as sufficient by certain states, which might well have feared more technologically advanced states, such as the USA, and the advantage they had. Secondly, the campaign by ENGOs in the 1980s, coupled with growing global public awareness of environmental issues, may have caused governments to reconsider their positions either on altruistic grounds or simply to obtain a boost in domestic polls.

## ENGO OPPOSITION TO CRAMRA

The ENGOs observed this reticence and determined to drive a wedge between the ATCPs and prevent CRAMRA from being ratified. Environmentalists saw the purpose of the treaty as setting up procedures to exploit Antarctic resources more effectively and believed that the proposed twin objectives of orderly mineral exploitation and environmental protection were mutually exclusive. Further, they were doubtful that the ATCPs could be relied on to put environmental protection ahead of economic gains from any race to exploit such resources, leading to a 'slippery slope' of increased exploitation.[205] They worried that such a treaty created a legal framework that would enhance investor confidence, leading to more exploration and development in the short term. Lastly, the ENGOs were concerned that CRAMRA opened the door for potential armed disputes over resource exploitation between the parties to protect their interests, contrary to the nature of the ATS, whose *raison d'être* was to promote peace.[206]

Following the opening up for signature in June 1988, the ENGOs adopted a strategy of convincing certain states to refuse to sign or ratify CRAMRA and/or delay its implementation. They initially targeted the seven claimant states, Italy, West Germany, the USA and the Soviet Union, since if any claimant state or superpower failed to ratify the Convention, it would lapse. Their tactics to achieve their aims were traditional and similar to their campaign to stop CRAMRA being negotiated. They again launched publicity

---

204 Suter, *Antarctica: Private Property or Public Heritage?*, 57.

205 Porter and Brown, *Global Environmental Politics*, 91.

206 Joyner, 'CRAMRA: The Ugly Duckling of the Antarctic Treaty System?', 170–72.

campaigns through the media, designed to influence domestic constituencies. They obtained signatures on petitions, lobbied domestic politicians and gave evidence to legislative committees – all designed to increase the pressure on negotiators not to sign on.[207]

The two main ENGO groupings, the Antarctic and Southern Ocean Coalition and Greenpeace, maintained a preservationist approach, arguing that a complete ban on mining in Antarctica was the only way to protect this fragile environment and that the region had to be designated a world park or preserve.[208] ENGOs such as Greenpeace attempted to frame the debate by appealing to the higher values of wilderness. Greenpeace argued that, as far as it was concerned: 'In all decision-making on Antarctica, preservation of the continent's wilderness values should be paramount.'[209] Greenpeace's approach resonated with people who had an ideational affinity with the wilderness concept and feared that a unique wilderness was in danger of being lost. Greenpeace argued that:

> The proposed mineral regime, if brought into operation, could allow the destruction of wilderness by a gradual, cumulative process, without any decision being made regarding protection of the overall character of the region.[210]

However, Greenpeace was quite willing to utilize interest-based arguments if it aided its cause, by pointing out, for example, that a moratorium on mineral activities would defuse state territorial disagreements and increase the chance of peace in the region, allowing scientific research to be better carried out unhindered.[211]

ENGOs were particularly active domestically in encouraging public debate about, and opposition to, CRAMRA in Australia and France, and in Belgium and Italy, where they sought to narrow what Robert Putnam refers to as the government's 'win sets' and prevent ratification.[212] Both the Australian

---

207 Elliott, *International Environmental Politics: Protecting the Antarctic*, 163–4.

208 'The Future of the Antarctic: Background for a Second UN Debate', 1; Clark, 'The Antarctic Environmental Protocol: NGOs in the Protection of Antarctica', 169.

209 Suter, *Antarctica: Private Property or Public Heritage?*, 134.

210 'The Future of the Antarctic: Background for a Second UN Debate', 23.

211 Ibid.: 21–2.

212 Laurence Cordonnery, 'The Implementation of the Protocol on Environmental Protection to the Antarctic Treaty: The Interplay between Law and Environmental Management' (University of Tasmania, 1997), 10–11; Putnam, 'Diplomacy and Domestic Politics: The Logic of Two-level Games', 454. Putnam refers to 'win sets' as the set of all negotiated agreements that could gain acceptance and be ratified. The larger the win sets, the more the likelihood of its being ratified. The converse also applies. Traditionally done by governments, to achieve their own goal of ratification of

Conservation Foundation (ACF) and Greenpeace Australia lobbied politicians, created a national petition and letter-writing campaign, and talked to community groups, all the time highlighting the weaknesses of the Convention.[213] Initially, the Australian Environmental Minister, Graeme Richardson, favoured signing the Convention, because he personally believed that mining was inevitable. He publicly stated that modern drilling and shipping practices were so sophisticated that there would be no problems, but a few days later the *Exxon Valdez* incident undercut his argument, weakening his position with the Australian populace.[214]

This was just one of a spate of environmental problems that year that influenced global attitudes to CRAMRA. In Antarctica, the Argentine supply ship *Bahia Paraiso* hit rocks on 28 January 1989, spilling 250 000 gallons of diesel fuel into the ocean and killing thousands of seabirds, penguins and krill. On 7 February, the British resupply ship *Endurance* hit an iceberg near Deception Island apparently (not confirmed) causing an oil spill in Esperanza Bay.[215] Then on 28 February a research ship from Peru, the *BIC Humboldt*, ran aground, leaking oil into Fildes Bay. On 24 March, the *Exxon Valdez* hit a reef in the Prince William Sound, off the coast of Alaska, and 11 million barrels of crude oil spilled into the sea, creating a 45-mile pollution zone which killed thousands of marine creatures.[216] The ENGOs were able to harness global outrage at the wreck of the Argentine ship, the *Bahia Paraiso*, in Antarctic waters and the *Exxon Valdez* disaster to convince many people that damage to the fragile Antarctic environment would inevitably follow mineral activities there and needed to be prevented.[217]

Domestic state interest was also a factor. In September 1988, the Australian Treasurer Paul Keating wrote to the Foreign Affairs Minister Gareth Evans, arguing that Australia should not sign on to CRAMRA in its current incarnation because of the lack of provisions dealing with royalties and taxes in the

---

an agreement, they seek to expand each other's win sets through activities such as financial aid and persuading leaders of the necessity of contacting opposition parties. Putnam, 'Diplomacy and Domestic Politics: The Logic of Two-level Games', 454.

[213] Elliott and Australian National University. Australian Foreign Policy Publications Program, *Protecting the Antarctic Environment: Australia and the Minerals Convention*, 31.

[214] Clark, 'The Antarctic Environmental Protocol: NGOs in the Protection of Antarctica', 171.

[215] Joyner, *Governing the Frozen Commons: The Antarctic Regime and Environmental Protection*, 150.

[216] Ibid.; Rigg, 'Environmentalists' Perspectives on the Protection of Antarctica', 71.

[217] Francioni, 'The Madrid Protocol on the Protection of the Antarctic Environment', 49.

text and how this undermined Australian sovereignty.[218] The Treasury Department was against signing CRAMRA, since it feared that acquiescing to the agreement would be tantamount to admitting that Australia was not the legal owner of its claimed territory and that the proposed revenue-sharing scheme costs under CRAMRA were prohibitive.[219]

The Resources Ministry opposed the Convention because it feared that a possible loophole in the document could allow any state to bankroll mining for strategic purposes. Australia, as a net exporter of minerals, was particularly concerned to have in the CRAMRA text a section banning subsidized mineral production. Senator Richardson, the Environmental Minister, put forth the Australian position when he stated in the Australian Parliament that:

> In general terms we sought a provision proscribing substantial types of incentives for the development and disposal of mineral resources which might give some sort of unfair advantage to mining in Antarctica compared with elsewhere in the world. We received support, through negotiations, from Chile and Argentina on that question. Unfortunately at the end of the day we finished up practically alone on that point.[220]

At the same time as concerns were being raised over CRAMRA's economic worth to Australia, the domestic political landscape within Australia was altering. In May 1989, for the first time in Australia, the state of Tasmania voted into its Parliament five 'green' candidates who ended up with the balance of power. This coincided with the Australian public's growing awareness, as part of a growing global consciousness, of green issues such as the 'ozone hole'.[221] Politicians across the country scrambled to appear more 'environmental', prompting even the conservative federal opposition, which had showed little interest in environmental issues before, stating that Australia should not sign onto CRAMRA.[222] Polls indicated that environmental issues were important at both the state and national levels and concern peaked at the time CRAMRA was tabled in the Federal Parliament. With public and parliamentary support

---

218 Elliott and Australian National University. Australian Foreign Policy Publications Program, *Protecting the Antarctic Environment: Australia and the Minerals Convention*, 29.

219 Clark, 'The Antarctic Environmental Protocol: NGOs in the Protection of Antarctica', 171–2.

220 *Parliamentary Debates; Daily Hansard*, Senate, 1439, 12 April 1989, reprinted in Bush, *Antarctica and International Law: A Collection of Inter-state and National Documents*, 6.

221 Paul Kevin Wapner, 'Politics Beyond the State: Environmental Activism and World Civic Politics', *World Politics* 47, no. 3 (April) (1995): 323–4.

222 Suter, *Antarctica: Private Property or Public Heritage?*, 62–3.

for signing ebbing, the Cabinet responded to the public mood and indicated it would not sign.[223]

Meanwhile, in France, Jacques Cousteau, the oceanographer and national icon, campaigned strenuously against France signing onto CRAMRA. His foundation had collected approximately 1.2 million signatures to petition the French government to 'Save the Antarctic'. Cousteau believed that the mining treaty increased the risk of oil spills and other environmental damage and that there was no need to pursue hypothetical mineral resources when humanity was currently experiencing a glut of such resources.[224] In April 1989, the French Prime Minister said – ostensibly because of the sinking of the *Exxon Valdez* – that France would not sign the Convention and that negotiations should be reopened. Thus France became the first ATCP to openly question CRAMRA.[225] Given the need for consensus within the ATS, this represented a real blow to the states hoping to ratify the Wellington Convention. However, it was still possible for CRAMRA to pass if the negotiations were reopened and France's concerns were satisfied.

The academic analysis of this decision is almost uniform in ascribing to France interest-based reasons for its *volte face*. For many decades, France had been perceived by the global community as one of the parties that were among the least interested states when it came to global environmental protection.[226] Clark argues that France's decision to refuse to sign onto CRAMRA can be traced to its desire to be seen as a good international environmental citizen, following the criticism it received for building an airbase in Antarctica by levelling a chain of islands, as well as for its Pacific nuclear testing programme.[227] The decision to forgo CRAMRA by France also had the added benefit of placating ENGOs and the French green vote at relatively little cost to itself.[228] Furthermore, as Willy Ostreng argues (supported by Peter Beck), the French support for a wilderness reserve was driven by a desire to protect their sovereign claims to Antarctica.[229]

---

223 Elliott and Australian National University. Australian Foreign Policy Publications Program, Protecting the Antarctic Environment: Australia and the Minerals Convention, 40.

224 Suter, *Antarctica: Private Property or Public Heritage?*, 63.

225 Elliott and Australian National University. Australian Foreign Policy Publications Program, *Protecting the Antarctic Environment: Australia and the Minerals Convention*, 31.

226 Elliott, *International Environmental Politics: Protecting the Antarctic*, 170.

227 Clark, 'The Antarctic Environmental Protocol: NGOs in the Protection of Antarctica', 170.

228 Ibid.; Suter, *Antarctica: Private Property or Public Heritage?*, 63.

229 Willy Ostreng, 'The Conflict and Alignment Pattern of Antarctic Politics: Is a New Order Needed?', in *The Antarctic Treaty System in World Politics*, ed. Arnfinn Jorgensen-Dahl and Willy Ostreng (New York: St Martin's Press, 1991), 443.

A neoliberal would, using Putnam's defection analysis, characterize France's decision as an instance of involuntary defection, where a state is unable to ratify an agreed negotiated position because of a lack of domestic support.[230] Initially, as seen by the French negotiator's comments at the end of the CRAMRA, the French political elite were happy with the outcome of the negotiations. The French public were heavily influenced by the passionate pleas of Jacques Cousteau, however, a national icon for decades. At the domestic level, the French government was unable to build coalitions among disaffected groups strong enough to overcome Cousteau's opposition, thus shrinking the win-set options open to the government, and by extension, to the negotiators. This domestic discord placed pressure on the French government to alter its international negotiating stance from conservation to preservation to satisfy domestic concerns. Doing so necessitated abandoning CRAMRA, since it was never designed to promote, indeed was antithetical to, preservationist ideals.

Elliott is the only commentator to concede that there may have been an altruistic element at work as well in the French government's decision.[231] A further point which has been overlooked in the neoliberal analysis to date is that the environmental beliefs of the newly elected socialist government of France helped constitute their government's identity. The new Environmental Minister Brice Lalonde was a founding member of the French Friends of the Earth. The French National Assembly was also upset that it had not been involved significantly in the CRAMRA negotiations, and the President of the Assembly, M. Fabius, argued in early April that France should not sign the Convention.[232] A more contextual understanding of France's decision not to sign must encompass this notion that the identity of the new French government included a strong environmental component that opposed damaging the environment, particularly the fragile and unique Antarctic biosphere.

At the same time, the Australian Cabinet was divided over whether to sign and the anti-CRAMRA faction in Cabinet was boosted by the French announcement.[233] Prime Minister Hawke of Australia found himself assailed from all sides by members of the Senate lobbying for and against the

---

[230] Putnam, 'Diplomacy and Domestic Politics: The Logic of Two-level Games', 438.

[231] Elliott, *International Environmental Politics: Protecting the Antarctic*, 170.

[232] Ibid. The Parliamentary Committee examining CRAMRA went even further and recommended other avenues of approach rather than the Convention and proposed legislation to make it illegal for French nationals to participate in Antarctic mineral activity. Elliott, *International Environmental Politics: Protecting the Antarctic*, 170.

[233] Elliott and Australian National University. Australian Foreign Policy Publications Program, *Protecting the Antarctic Environment: Australia and the Minerals Convention*, 31.

Convention, while Jacques Cousteau wrote to him personally seeking to dissuade him from signing the document. The French Prime Minister Rocard flew to Australia in person to outline the reasons behind France's decision not to sign. Even the Liberal opposition declared it was against CRAMRA. On 22 May 1989, the Australian Cabinet stated it would not sign on.[234]

The Australian Prime Minister, Bob Hawke, in November 1989, put the case for his country's opposition to signing CRAMRA in the following terms:

> The most urgent and relevant action we can take is to ensure that this irreplaceable environment is never put at risk by mining. That is why Australia has decided not to sign the Minerals Convention. This position is based on two simple propositions. First, the Antarctic environment is extremely fragile and critically important to the whole global ecosystem. Second, mining in Antarctica will always be dangerous, and could be catastrophically so. In the light of those propositions, we are convinced that the Minerals Convention is basically flawed. It is based on the clearly incorrect assumption – current in the 1970s – that mining in the Antarctic could be consistent with the preservation of the continent's fragile environment. But any mining operation, with its accompanying infrastructure and bulk transport needs, would have a lasting and major impact on the area in which it takes place.[235]

Bob Hawke also referred to the recent *Exxon Valdez* sinking as one reason why Australia no longer supported CRAMRA in July 1989:

> The grounding of the *Exxon Valdez* in Alaska is testimony to the damage that an oil spill can do to such an environment. In Australia's view, mineral exploitation in Antarctica poses unacceptable risks to the Antarctic environment.[236]

Again, the scholarly explanations for why Australia refused to sign CRAMRA are mostly interest based and are characterized as a case of involuntary defection. The negotiated treaty texts were not ratified due to domestic considerations. Leaders prize these considerations, in most circumstances, above international objectives. Joyner argues that Australia's about face was due both to a domestic political desire to please the green vote and, at the global level, a desire to retain Australia's sovereign influence within the ATS.[237]

---

234 Clark, 'The Antarctic Environmental Protocol: NGOs in the Protection of Antarctica', 171.

235 R.J.L. Hawke, 'Antarctica's Future – Speech by the Prime Minister to the 16th National Conference of the Australian Institute of International Affairs, 18 November 1989', *Department of Foreign Affairs and Trade: The Monthly Record* 60, no. 11 (1989): 627.

236 R.J.L. Hawke, 'Our Country, Our Future: Statement on the Environment by the Prime Minister of Australia' (Canberra: Australian Government Publishing Service, Canberra, 1989), 26.

237 Joyner, *Governing the Frozen Commons: The Antarctic Regime and Environmental Protection*, 150.

Elliott echoes these charges when she maintains that from Australia's perspective CRAMRA was flawed in that it left Australia with little authority over any mineral activity in the region. From Australia's perspective, CRAMRA also critically failed to clearly outline the rules governing decisions on claims nor did it demand that prospectors seek prior authorization before commencing (although any prospecting had to be carried out within the rules established by the Convention).[238] Elliott points out that both the Treasurer Paul Keating and the Minister for Resources Peter Cook opposed CRAMRA because it did not guarantee a royalty payment scheme that they believed would not undermine Australian sovereignty, and because CRAMRA had no anti-subsidy provisions which would not put Australian mining firms at a competitive disadvantage.[239]

Elliott maintains that the factors of sovereignty and potential economic loss were part of the reason why Australia did not sign CRAMRA, but she concedes that there was also a genuine commitment by the government to environmental protection of the continent, for example, its prevention of the building of the Franklin dam in Tasmania. Australia had long seen itself as an advocate of global environmental protection and in a number of forums, for example, whaling. It had consistently argued that Antarctic environmental protection would be best met with a comprehensive agreement rather than the piecemeal approach of CRAMRA.[240] Australia had been a leading advocate for just such an agreement, having first tabled one in 1983. It had been arguing before the Fifteenth ATCM that there was a need for an all-encompassing agreement.[241]

The Australian states' identity as a global citizen in the 1980s was bound up with its belief in the need for strong global environmental protection. This is not to say that Australia was not interested in pursuing its global interests, but rather that its belief in the need for environmental protection for the region both framed and disciplined its approach. Joyner supports this contention when he notes that environmental concerns may well have been crucial to Australia's decision not to sign onto CRAMRA, because there were four environmental disasters in polar waters in early 1989 that highlighted the fragility

238 Elliott and Australian National University. Australian Foreign Policy Publications Program, *Protecting the Antarctic Environment: Australia and the Minerals Convention*, 25–7.

239 Elliott, *International Environmental Politics: Protecting the Antarctic*, 168.

240 Elliott and Australian National University. Australian Foreign Policy Publications Program, *Protecting the Antarctic Environment: Australia and the Minerals Convention*, 39.

241 Elliott, *International Environmental Politics: Protecting the Antarctic*, 169.

of the polar environment.[242] These ships' accidents, combined with the campaigns of the ENGOs, seem to have heightened the Australian public's concern for protecting Antarctica, an issue that until then had not registered on the Australian political landscape.[243] Combining Australia's traditional conception of itself as an environmental advocate on the global stage, the ENGO campaign aimed at both the government and the populace and the newly recognized public concern for environmental issues. This made for a powerful troika of influences opposed to CRAMRA.

The Australian defection from CRAMRA was not well received by the other ATCPs who were quick to criticize the decision. They argued that it threatened the ATS as a whole.[244] On 18 August 1989, the French and Australian Prime Ministers issued a joint statement on Antarctica that cited environmental grounds for their decision:

> [i]n the light of their shared concerns about the Antarctic Minerals Convention and other factors affecting the environment in the Antarctic . . . [M]ining in Antarctica is not compatible with protection of the fragile Antarctic environment . . . the two countries will be proposing that the Treaty Parties negotiate a Comprehensive Environmental Protection Convention which will turn the Antarctic into a wilderness reserve.[245]

The main opponents to changes to CRAMRA took the view that Australia and France would eventually cave in to the united opposition of the other ATCPs, but this was not to be the case. In fact, other states were beginning to show their support for a world reserve, such as Belgium, India and Italy.[246] Of particular significance was the Soviet Union's decision to accept the French and Australian position. On 19 January 1990, at the World Forum on Environment and Development in Moscow, President Gorbachev told the assembled delegates that his country was 'ready to participate in the survival of the Antarctic, of this world reserve, which is our common natural laboratory'.[247]

In Britain, the Labour Party opposition, in defiance of long-standing bipartisan support on Antarctica, voted against the domestic legislation, approving

---

242 Joyner, *Governing the Frozen Commons: The Antarctic Regime and Environmental Protection*, 150.

243 Elliott, *International Environmental Politics: Protecting the Antarctic*, 167.

244 Ibid.: 166.

245 R.J.L. Hawke and M. Rocard, *Joint Statement on International Environmental Issues Agreed by Prime Ministers Hawke and Rocard*, Canberra, 18 August 1989, 1, reprinted in Elliott and Australian National University. Australian Foreign Policy Publications Program, *Protecting the Antarctic Environment: Australia and the Minerals Convention*, 50.

246 Ibid.: 49.

247 Elliott, *International Environmental Politics: Protecting the Antarctic*, 184.

the signing onto CRAMRA in the House of Commons in July 1989. The European Parliament also passed two resolutions pertaining to Antarctic protection and the economic significance of the region. The Belgian Parliament forbade any Belgian national or corporation from exploiting Antarctic mineral resources. The Italian Parliament passed a unanimous motion on 28 September 1989 that bound the government 'not to subscribe to and not to ratify the Minerals Convention and to support and promote the proposal to transform Antarctica into the first world natural park among the Consultative Parties of the Antarctic Treaty'.[248]

By the time of the Fifteenth Consultative Meeting in Paris, France, in October 1989, only 15 states had signed onto CRAMRA and none had ratified it.[249] Thus the Wellington Convention never reached a tipping point where enough states agreed that a conservationist approach to Antarctic mining should be put in place. Concerns over CRAMRA's ability to safeguard the environment for future generations led to the Consultative Parties discussing the matter at the Fifteenth Meeting.[250] The refusal of France and Australia to follow the usual protocols of consensus on any ATS business opened the door for a radical re-evaluation of both mining, and the proper role of the Antarctic regime in environmental conservation.[251]

The Australian and French governments submitted a joint proposal, in the form of two working papers, to the Fifteenth ATCM in October 1989, with a view to convening a Special Consultative Meeting to create this new Convention.[252] The proposal declared that there should be a ban on mineral activity and drew heavily on the ENGO approach.[253] The proposal argued that Antarctica should be designated a wilderness reserve and that the new Convention should take an all-embracing approach to environmental protec-

248 Burgess, 'Comprehensive Environmental Protection of the Antarctic: New Approaches for New Times', 55.

249 Elliott, *International Environmental Politics: Protecting the Antarctic*, 179.

250 Cordonnery, 'The Implementation of the Protocol on Environmental Protection to the Antarctic Treaty: The Interplay between Law and Environmental Management', 11.

251 Vogler, *The Global Commons: Environmental and Technological Governance*, 77–8.

252 A Joint Australian–French Proposal in the form of a Paper including a Draft Recommendation for ATCM XV: Working Paper Submitted by Australia and France (XV ATCM/WP/2), Franco-Australian Draft Working Paper of Possible Components for a Comprehensive Convention for the Preservation and Protection of Antarctica: Working Paper submitted by Australia and France (XV, ATCM/WP/3). Antarctic Treaty Consultative Meeting, 'Report of the Fifteenth Consultative Meeting' (Paris, 1989), 220–29.

253 Wapner, *Environmental Activism and World Civic Politics*, 137.

tion.[254] The proposal specifically referred to preserving Antarctica for its uniqueness. Both France and Australia, now acting as norm entrepreneurs for a preservationist approach, agreed in their working paper that: 'The value of Antarctica's wilderness qualities is recognized by Consultative Parties. There is value in the preservation of these qualities for their own sake.'[255]

Joyner argues that other ATCPs were 'stimulated' by this approach and seeing that CRAMRA was not going to succeed, Chile, New Zealand, the USA and Sweden submitted their own environmental proposals.[256] Opponents of the initiative, led by the USA and the UK, however, argued that if Australia and France continued with their intransigent position, then it could lead to a scenario where a moratorium crumbled in the face of determined opposition and there would be no rules to protect the region.[257] The US State Department was convinced that Australia would retreat from its decision if sufficiently pressured, but failed to consider that Australia's, and France's, moral position now constituted their identity, and there was no 'going back'.[258] They had assumed the role of moral crusaders for the environment in the sense that it was now part of their global identities to promote environmental norms both narrowly in the case of Antarctica, but also broadly in other cases such as whaling and tropical timber.

Critics dismissed the wilderness idea as little different to the ENGOs' conception of a world park, which was probably correct. What the French and Australian governments meant by the term was not explained. Certainly it was a convenient rhetorical device to reinforce the notion that Antarctica should not be exploited, but the positive dimensions of the idea were never developed. Rather, the concept metamorphosed into the term 'natural reserve – land of science' to show that scientific activity was still permissible and to put political distance between the proposal and the ENGOs' construction.[259] Both the UK and the USA were adamant that a ban should not be implemented, while arguing that they had no intention of commencing mining operations in the short or medium term and were prepared to act as a blocking coalition against the French and Australian proposal. Rather, they wanted to reserve the right to mine in the future. The USA went so far as to say that a minerals ban was not

---

[254] Antarctic Treaty Consultative Meeting, 'Report of the Fifteenth Consultative Meeting', 220–29.

[255] Ibid.: 220.

[256] Joyner, *Governing the Frozen Commons: The Antarctic Regime and Environmental Protection*, 150.

[257] Elliott and Australian National University. Australian Foreign Policy Publications Program, *Protecting the Antarctic Environment: Australia and the Minerals Convention*, 52.

[258] Elliott, *International Environmental Politics: Protecting the Antarctic*, 179.

[259] Ibid.: 176–7.

negotiable.[260] Both the USA and the UK[261] argued that any reserve should arise organically from negotiations but not be an element delimiting them. Japan and the Republic of Korea also opposed the concept to ensure mineral exploitation would be allowed under the framework of CRAMRA.[262]

Australia and France built their own veto coalition of states (Italy, India, Spain, Austria, Bulgaria and Greece plus Poland and Belgium, nearly all of whom were recent signatories) to support their proposal and oppose CRAMRA in the face of the considerable veto coalition led by the United States of America.[263] The preservationist coalition of states agreed at the Fifteenth Consultative Meeting in Paris in 1989 to create a comprehensive system for the protection of the Antarctic environment and its ecosystems.[264] To achieve this goal, a Special Antarctic Treaty Consultative Meeting was held in November 1990 in Vina del Mar, Chile, to explore all proposals for the comprehensive protection of the Antarctic environment and its dependent and associated ecosystems.[265] This Special Meeting was the organizational platform that ENGOs, France and Australia were looking for to push their preservationist agenda. Now the task was to convince like-minded states to support the proposal and reach a tipping point.

Following the Fifteenth Meeting, Australia and France continued lobbying other states for the nature park and a ban on exploitation, with particular emphasis on the Latin American countries and the United States. In Great Britain, Greenpeace and the WWF instituted a public campaign designed to educate the British public about the issue and influence the UK's negotiating stance to support a world park. In Germany, a petition distributed by the WWF calling for a permanent ban on mineral exploitation garnered over 300 000 signatures. Jacques Cousteau met with the Prime Minister of New Zealand and the President of the United States in an effort to dissuade them from their support for CRAMRA.[266] The ENGOs knew that they now had an opportunity

---

260 Ibid.: 175.

261 The UK was heavily committed to mining Antarctica and was the only state to have passed an Act of Parliament to allow British corporations to begin commercial activities. Suter, *Antarctica: Private Property or Public Heritage?*, 66.

262 Francioni, 'The Madrid Protocol on the Protection of the Antarctic Environment', 61.

263 Cordonnery, 'The Implementation of the Protocol on Environmental Protection to the Antarctic Treaty: The Interplay between Law and Environmental Management', 11.

264 Recommendation XV-1, Antarctic Treaty Consultative Meeting, 'Report of the Fifteenth Consultative Meeting', 6.

265 'U.S. State Department Handbook of the Antarctic Treaty System 2002', 481.

266 Elliott and Australian National University. Australian Foreign Policy Publications Program, *Protecting the Antarctic Environment: Australia and the Minerals Convention*, 57–8.

to resubmit the idea of a world park to what was a more receptive audience. ENGOs argued for the criticality of designating Antarctica a world park by posing the stark choice: leave a minerals gap in the heart of the ATS or negotiate a permanent mining ban.[267]

ENGOs argued that constituting Antarctica as a world park would set a precedent, since no other part of the globe had been declared an international reserve. They maintained that a [relatively] untouched wilderness would enable scientists to monitor worldwide environmental change. Further, it would create a pristine environmental laboratory for research, as well as reducing the risk of oil spills (bearing in mind recent spills from ships) or well blowouts that harmed commercial krill fishing offshore. It would also prevent the region from state exploitation, which fostered state animosity over resource allocation, leading to conflict.[268] The growing strength and determination of those ENGOs with backgrounds in both science and politics, which pushed the world park concept, were critical in reframing the issues of mineral exploitation, which until then had been set by states, bureaucrats and scientific groups.[269] In effect, they reframed the debate from exploitation versus conservation to exploitation versus preservation.

One of the leading ENGOs, Greenpeace, was quite clear that at the core of the world park proposal it supported was 'the primacy of "wilderness values", and that the Antarctic species and their environment had an intrinsic aesthetic and scientific importance that must override all other considerations'.[270] However, Greenpeace was not above pandering to the interests of the ATCPs. Early in the proceedings, Greenpeace realized that issues of sovereignty were critical and so stated:

> One can imagine a Protocol to the World Heritage Convention dealing specifically with Antarctica, which incorporates the creative approach of Article IV of the Antarctic Treaty regarding claims to sovereignty, and which includes all other principles of the Treaty. All nations could nominate the totality of their perceived 'rights, titles and interests' for 'protection status'.[271]

---

267 Joyner, 'CRAMRA: The Ugly Duckling of the Antarctic Treaty System?', 176.

268 Barnes, 'Legal Aspects of Environmental Protection in Antarctica', 266; Joyner, 'CRAMRA: The Ugly Duckling of the Antarctic Treaty System?', 175.

269 Clark, 'The Antarctic Environmental Protocol: NGOs in the Protection of Antarctica', 180.

270 Vogler, *The Global Commons: Environmental and Technological Governance*, 82.

271 'The Future of the Antarctic: Background for a Second UN Debate', 25.

ENGOs arguing for the need to preserve Antarctica found kindred spirits in scientists who wished to make their views publicly known and built a strategic coalition with them. Scientists, particularly those involved in Antarctic research, from Great Britain, Germany and New Zealand, all signed petitions to the effect that Antarctica should be preserved.[272] Joyner argues this position was adopted because scientists were keen to keep inviolate the area as a 'laboratory' to enable research to continue, rather than have Antarctica usurped by mining.[273] While they were not to play a significant role in this debate, they neutralized the conservationist arguments put forth by SCAR scientists who had argued that a world park would limit scientific research, thereby strengthening the persuasiveness of ENGO arguments.[274]

In February 1990, after a prolonged campaign by both domestic and global ENGOs, New Zealand agreed that it would not sign CRAMRA and stated that it was open to the prospect of a long-term mineral exploitation ban. In July, Prime Minister Palmer went further and stated the New Zealand position was now one of supporting a permanent ban. The acquiescence by New Zealand was important since it had, under Chairman Beeby, been the main driving force behind the CRAMRA negotiations. The UN General Assembly passed a Malaysia-sponsored resolution[275] which supported a world park that banned mineral activities and declared that the global community should be included in the negotiations. However, this resolution was not accepted or even formally acknowledged by the ATCPs.[276] This global pressure, combined with the defections of key states, left the potential blocking states of the USA and the UK increasingly isolated and unable to convince defecting states of the need to sign onto CRAMRA.[277]

---

[272] Elliott and Australian National University. Australian Foreign Policy Publications Program, *Protecting the Antarctic Environment: Australia and the Minerals Convention*, 58–9.

[273] Joyner, 'CRAMRA: The Ugly Duckling of the Antarctic Treaty System?', 167.

[274] Elliott, *International Environmental Politics: Protecting the Antarctic*, 195.

[275] Question of Antarctica (Agenda Item 70), Forty-fourth Session, A/C.1/44/L.69.

[276] Cordonnery, 'The Implementation of the Protocol on Environmental Protection to the Antarctic Treaty: The Interplay between Law and Environmental Management', 4–5.

[277] Elliott, *International Environmental Politics: Protecting the Antarctic*, 184–6. At the same time, the chief advocate for CRAMRA, the USA, was having its official negotiating position undermined by domestic Congressional dissent. On the 26 September 1989, ten US senators led by Senator Al Gore put forth a Joint Resolution that called on the US to start negotiations on a new Convention with the aim of protecting Antarctica by declaring the region a global ecological commons. Congressional Record, Senate, Washington, DC, 26 September 1989, S11, 906–8. In February 1990, Representative Conte introduced to the US House of Representatives a bill that would

With the imminent collapse of CRAMRA, the parties feared that a stampede of states attempting to gain mineral resources without caring about the impact on other states or the environment would badly impact on their interests in the region.[278] Member states had feared all along that if minerals were discovered and appropriate technologies developed, then the rush to claim these resources could doom the entire Antarctic Treaty System. With the collapse of CRAMRA, that fear was close to realization. Thus member states, concerned about the viability of the entire Antarctica regime, were willing to consider the joint Australian–French proposal.

The idea of a world park, privileging preservation of the Antarctic environment, as promulgated by the ENGOs and given a fillip by the French and Australian initiative, had no traction until it became clear that CRAMRA was doomed. Thus delegates either had to renegotiate the treaty after six long years of negotiation or replace it with something new. Given the need to maintain the overall regime, member states were willing to entertain the concept of a world park because it met their current needs and carried forward many of the prohibitions specified in the Antarctic Treaty, such as no military or nuclear activities.[279]

## WHY DID CRAMRA FAIL TO BE RATIFIED?

So, why did CRAMRA fail to gain acceptance by the ATCPs? Davor Vidas lists four reasons: the fear that any adoption of CRAMRA would alter the sensitive balance of sovereignty imposed by the Antarctic Treaty; the use of the UN General Assembly by Lesser Developed Countries to critique the current system, political pressure applied by ENGOs, and domestic policy considerations.[280] Certainly, in the case of Australia, it can be observed that

---

prevent US exploitation of Antarctica and would have bound US negotiators to work towards banning mineral exploitation and preserving the area in perpetuity. The US Antarctic Protection Act 1990 HR 3977, December 1990; Burgess, 'Comprehensive Environmental Protection of the Antarctic: New Approaches for New Times', 56; Francioni, 'The Madrid Protocol on the Protection of the Antarctic Environment', 2. As per Putnam's analysis, these actions undercut the US negotiating position, making it difficult for the government to satisfy these domestic pressures while arguing that the official US position had broad support at home.

278 Sahurie, *The International Law of Antarctica*, 425.

279 Clark, 'The Antarctic Environmental Protocol: NGOs in the Protection of Antarctica', 173.

280 Davor Vidas, 'Entry into Force of the Environmental Protocol and Implementation Issues: An Overview', in *Implementing the Environmental Protection Regime for the Antarctic*, ed. Davor Vidas (Boston, MA: Kluwer Academic Publishers, 2000), 3.

sovereignty issues were of concern to the government, but there is no evidence that the concern was critical to the decision to preserve the region. The pressure applied by Lesser Developed Countries, fearful of missing out on any spoils from mining or just wanting to use the issue to embarrass developed states, certainly played a part in keeping the issue in the public eye, but again was not critical to the decisions of both Australia and France.

Porter and Brown agree with Vidas about the importance of environmental issues in domestic parliamentary elections and certainly this was an important factor in both Australia and France's decision not to sign the Convention. Environmental considerations did affect domestic election results.[281] An analysis, without a consideration of the moral context and the social actors, does not explain how or why such considerations became central, however. This is what a constructivist approach can provide. There had been a change in the domestic French government, which came to openly espouse both a socialist and environmental doctrine. Jacques Cousteau's campaign to preserve Antarctica, and the ability of his arguments to resonate with the French domestic populace, were also critical factors. In Australia's case, similarly, the domestic landscape had changed, with both a new left-leaning Labor government and an electorate that had become more receptive to the environmental message transmitted by ENGOs.

For neoliberals, the defection of France and Australia can be analysed in involuntary terms, that is, one where negotiators were undermined by domestic political considerations, to which domestic leaders were forced to accede. Neoliberals may argue that France was only looking after its own interests and cynically only took this decision to embellish its global green credentials after they had been tarnished by Pacific nuclear tests and the Rainbow Warrior incident. However, this analysis tends to marginalize the significance of the changed domestic political situation in France. Nor can the fact that France's decision put it at odds with the rest of the global community be explained in neoliberal terms. Young argues that the defection of both France and Australia created the most serious crisis in the history of the ATS and left many other states with concerns about the reliability of France and Australia as negotiating partners.[282] The decision by France and Australia to defect, given this suspicion of their reliability by other states, goes against their material, strategic interests, and therefore challenges the standard neoliberal analysis.

Such an analysis does not capture the 'moral dimension' either. Both individual leaders and populaces were persuaded that preserving Antarctica was

281 Porter and Brown, *Global Environmental Politics*, 92.

282 Oran R. Young, 'Fairness Matters: The Role of Equity in International Regimes' (paper presented at Environmental Justice: Global Ethics for the 21st Century, University of Melbourne, 1–3 October 1997), 23.

the 'right' thing to do. Adopting such a preservationist position meant reconstituting both Australia's and France's global identity. Their international personas became increasingly bound up with being good global environmental citizens and they became active norm proponents in trying to convince other states of their stance. Even if the initial impetus to defect was governed primarily or partly by sovereignty issues and material incentives, over time both states became increasingly convinced of the 'rightness' of their normative positions to the point where the sovereignty/material incentives disappeared into the background.

An explanation of this 'persuasion' cannot be offered without an examination of the role played by ENGOs. They used moral persuasion techniques to convince domestic constituents and states (as domestic and international actors) of the necessity of preventing the ratification of CRAMRA. Their moral arguments stressed the fragility and wilderness aspects of the region and were successful because they were simple, easy to communicate, and able to appeal to 'higher ideals' that resonated with state leaders and domestic constituents. Their campaign tactic was to bombard member states with information, combined with a strategy to link meetings to larger global concerns about Antarctic fragility and damage. This approach was crucial in both raising global public awareness of the issues and directly influencing government policy in critical states.[283]

However, ENGOs were able to sharpen this message by appealing to the strategic as well as moral interests of states. They argued that a moratorium on mineral activities would defuse state territorial disagreements and increase the chance of peace in the region, which would in turn allow scientific research, a core concern in the founding of the regime, to be better carried out. They exploited the fear of certain states that open access exploitation would be detrimental to their state interests in the short term and highlighted to domestic populaces that accidents (such as the *Exxon Valdez*) were inevitable and would damage the area. Even if people never intended to visit Antarctica, many people nonetheless liked the prospect of its being unsullied and the ENGOs tailored their message to appeal to this sentiment. The ENGOs made common cause with other like-minded states and scientists to nullify criticism of their solution and to ensure that their goal – the prevention of CRAMRA – would win acceptance.

---

[283] Elliott and Australian National University. Australian Foreign Policy Publications Program, *Protecting the Antarctic Environment: Australia and the Minerals Convention*, 143; Vogler, *The Global Commons: Environmental and Technological Governance*, 82.

## THE NEGOTIATION OF THE MADRID PROTOCOL

The defeat of CRAMRA was not the end of the normative struggle. The debate now turned to what would replace it. The differing sides continued to offer their interpretations of what would be best for the Antarctic environment. On 16 March 1990, Australia and France prepared a 'Revised Australian–French Paper on the Components of a Comprehensive Regime for the Protection of the Antarctic Environment and its Dependent and Associated Ecosystems', which argued that Antarctica should be designated a 'nature reserve – land of science'.[284]

The Eleventh Antarctic Treaty Special Consultative Meeting was held, in accordance with the provisions of Recommendation XV-1 adopted by all the Antarctic Treaty Consultative Parties in Paris in October 1989, in order to explore proposals to achieve a comprehensive environmental protection of Antarctica. On 16 October 1990, Australia, Belgium, France and Italy produced an 'Indicative Draft of a Convention for the Comprehensive Protection of the Antarctic Environment', which again argued that Antarctica should be designated a 'nature reserve – land of science', but that its protection should be outlined in a convention rather than a protocol.[285]

New Zealand responded on 25 October 1990 with its own Draft Protocol to the Antarctic Treaty on Environmental Protection that allowed 'mineral resource activities' balanced against the protection of the region in an attempt to keep open the option of mining.[286] On 18 November 1990, New Zealand presented its 'Introduction to the New Zealand Draft Protocol to the Antarctic Treaty on Environmental Protection' and Draft Protocol to the Antarctic Treaty on Environmental Protection for discussion prior to the Special Consultative Meeting in Chile.[287] On the same day, the British put forth their draft Environmental Protocol Supplementing the Antarctic Treaty that stressed in Section 2 that 'Human activities in Antarctica shall avoid significant adverse impacts on the Antarctic environment and dependent and associated ecosystems'.[288] The Draft Protocol left the door ajar for mining activities that did not *significantly* affect the region, however.[289] The USA presented its own Draft Environmental Protocol Supplementing the Antarctic Treaty, also on the same

[284] W.M. Bush, *Antarctica and International Law: A Collection of Inter-state and National Documents* (London: Oceana Publications Inc., 1992), 5.

[285] Ibid.: 24.

[286] Ibid.: 42.

[287] Ibid.: 1–4.

[288] Ibid.: 4.

[289] Ibid.: 4–13.

day. This also stressed the need to avoid significant impacts to the area, but still effectively allowed mining under controlled conditions.[290]

The Special Meeting took place in Vina del Mar from 19 November to 6 December 1990.[291] At the negotiations, the ATCPs were divided into three warring camps. The first coalition comprised what came to be called the 'group of four' (Australia, France, Belgium and Italy) and other like-minded states (such as New Zealand). It acted as preservationist norm proponent in arguing for a permanent moratorium to be put in place. A second grouping of the USA, Argentina and Chile argued a conservationist position that there should be a limited ban, with the eventual allowance of CRAMRA to enter into force. The third coalition again put forth a similar conservationist position, where states such as the UK and Japan were against any such ban, but favoured the entry into force of CRAMRA immediately.[292]

On 20 November 1990, there was an Outline submitted by Argentina, Norway, United Kingdom, United States and Uruguay of a Protocol on Environmental Protection Supplementing the Antarctic Treaty, the 'Comprehensive Measures for the Protection of the Antarctic Environment and its Dependent and Associated Ecosystems: Outline of a Protocol Supplementing the Antarctic Treaty'. This again stressed, under section 8(b), that any 'activities must avoid significant adverse impacts on the environment'.[293] No actual mention was made of mining, but again the Protocol would allow such actions if the collateral environmental damage was considered less than significant.

The Opening Statements by the various Heads of Delegations at the Eleventh Special Consultative Meeting revealed the pressure the various states felt about the importance of the issue. The German address given by Dietrich

---

[290] Ibid.: 13.

[291] 'U.S. State Department Handbook of the Antarctic Treaty System 2002', 471. Representatives of the Antarctic Treaty Consultative Parties, Argentina, Australia, Belgium, Brazil, Chile, China, Ecuador, Finland, France, Germany, India, Italy, Japan, the Netherlands, New Zealand, Norway, Peru, Poland, the Republic of Korea, South Africa, Spain, Sweden, the Union of Soviet Socialist Republics, the United Kingdom, the United States of America and Uruguay all attended. Mr Oscar Pinochet de la Barra, Head of the Delegation of Chile, acted as Chairman for this First Session Report. 'U.S. State Department Handbook of the Antarctic Treaty System 2002', 471.

[292] Francioni, 'The Madrid Protocol on the Protection of the Antarctic Environment', 67. For example, the Opening Statement by the Head of the US Delegation, E.U. Curtis Bohlen, revealed that the US was still committed to putting in place a new mineral agreement and, as a concession, was willing to ban mineral activities until one was agreed. Reprinted in Bush, *Antarctica and International Law: A Collection of Inter-state and National Documents* 63.

[293] Bush, *Antarctica and International Law: A Collection of Inter-state and National Documents*, 56.

Granow refers to the delegation having received thousands of letters from concerned German citizens (a tactic of the ENGOs) to pressure states demanding comprehensive protection for the Antarctic region. He remarked that globally people had become more conscious of the value of pristine environments and the need to preserve such areas.[294] Such remarks indicate that the campaign to pressure state negotiators, with ENGOs putting pressure on domestic constituents, appeared to have worked.

Australia submitted its own paper to the Eleventh Special ATCM at Vina del Mar, Chile, 1990, entitled 'Protection of the Antarctic Environment and its Dependent and Associated Ecosystems: A Review of Existing Measures'. The paper noted the piecemeal attempts at environmental protection over the years by the parties and argued for a more comprehensive approach to the subject matter.[295] ASOC introduced a draft set of principles and objectives at the Vina del Mar (Chile) Meeting, designed as a model protection convention, but it was not accepted.[296]

At the first session in Chile, Rolf Trolle Andersen of Norway put forward an informal draft document that was accepted by the parties as a 'valuable basis' on which to proceed.[297] Delegates were prepared to use this draft, but it was not considered a 'negotiating text' as such. The USA and the UK, acting as a blocking coalition, were not prepared to move much from their stated negotiating position. However, in the face of continued international opposition, the USA proposed, in a diplomatic note, a fixed-term moratorium that would require consensus amongst the ATCPs to extend it. In a similar vein, the UK, in March of 1991, indicated it would support a temporary moratorium to achieve a consensus decision.[298]

After the 1990 Special Consultative Meeting, the Group of Four continued to attempt to garner support for its position. They had identified eight other states who they hoped they could convince: India, New Zealand, Finland, Denmark, Greece, Austria, Romania and Ecuador. In January 1991, the four met in Paris to discuss their response to the Andersen draft and on the second day the eight states met with the four. These 12 states met again in March in Rome to consolidate the changes they proposed to make at the Second Special Meeting, with the aim of strengthening the environmental provisions, such as

---

[294] Ibid.: 60.

[295] Ibid.: 20–33.

[296] Clark, 'The Antarctic Environmental Protocol: NGOs in the Protection of Antarctica', 174.

[297] Francioni, 'The Madrid Protocol on the Protection of the Antarctic Environment', 50.

[298] Elliott, *International Environmental Politics: Protecting the Antarctic*, 191.

the environmental impact statements.[299] At this point, it was clear that a tipping point had been reached and that the majority of states were firmly in the preservationist camp.

The second session took place in three parts in Madrid from 22 to 30 April, from 17 to 22 June, and from 3 to 4 October, 1991.[300] For the first time, many non-state groups were invited to participate at the meeting (with certain restrictions), including:

- the Antarctic and Southern Ocean Coalition;
- the Commission of the European Communities (CEC);
- the Commission for the Conservation of Antarctic Marine Living Resources (CCAMLR);
- the International Union for the Conservation of Nature and Natural Resources;
- the Intergovernmental Oceanographic Commission (IOC);
- the Scientific Committee on Antarctic Research;
- the World Meteorological Organization (WMO).[301]

In Madrid, many ENGOs had representatives on state delegations as advisors. For example, ASOC and Greenpeace members were part of the Australian delegation and Greenpeace was also on the official Danish party, while the Wilderness Society had personnel on the USA delegation. Many ENGOs were present as observers at meetings though they were excluded from Heads of Delegation Meetings. Further, many ENGOs monitored the proceedings from outside the official meeting and circulated various documents and information

---

299 Elliott and Australian National University. Australian Foreign Policy Publications Program, *Protecting the Antarctic Environment: Australia and the Minerals Convention*, 65; Elliott, *International Environmental Politics: Protecting the Antarctic*, 191–2.

300 The Madrid Session was chaired by Mr Carlos Blasco Villa, Head of the Delegation of Spain. Representatives from all the Consultative Parties took part in the Madrid Session, Argentina, Australia, Belgium, Brazil, Chile, China, Ecuador, Finland, France, Germany, India, Italy, Japan, the Republic of Korea, the Netherlands, New Zealand, Norway, Peru, Poland, South Africa, Spain, Sweden, the Union of Soviet Socialist Republics, the United Kingdom, the United States of America and Uruguay. At the invitation of the Consultative Parties to the Antarctic Treaty, representatives from all of the Contracting Parties which were not Consultative Parties, also attended: Austria, Bulgaria, Canada, Colombia, Czechoslovakia, Cuba, Denmark, Greece, Guatemala, Hungary, the Democratic People's Republic of Korea, Papua New Guinea, Romania and Switzerland. 'U.S. State Department Handbook of the Antarctic Treaty System 2002', 472.

301 Ibid.

broadsheets, such as *ECO*.[302] For the first time, the ENGOs' activities had enabled them to be accepted as part of the ATS, which positioned them to exert influence, both internally as well as externally, through the more traditional approach.

Andersen again was able to produce a second draft with input from the group of four.[303] The amendments to the draft document by the group of four included a reference to an Antarctic world park, adopted the language of the ENGOs, and called for the creation of an Antarctic 'natural reserve, land of science'.[304] However, the issue of a ban on mineral activity remained a sticking point. The USA initially proposed a temporary prohibition of 20 or 30 years. The intransigent group saw that inevitably CRAMRA would fail and began to accept that some form of ban would be implemented. At the same time, the group who supported the ban began to see that they had to compromise and that a time limit, albeit of considerable length, would be the compromise position (Article 25, paras. 2, 3).[305]

Andersen proposed a two-stage process to lift any future ban. After 50 years, a majority of all parties, including a majority of ATCPs, could amend the protocol but it could only enter into force if ratified by three-quarters of the ATCPs, including all of the current ATCPs.[306] The compromise, which required a consensus to remove the ban and to adopt a further mineral regime, represented a clear victory for the environmental coalition.[307]

In April of that year, we can see a norm cascade effect occurring, with the Japanese and German governments bowing to the growing clamour to institute a ban.[308] On 10 May, the UK Prime Minister, John Major, decided to support PEPAT over the objections of his own bureaucrats in the Foreign Office and the Departments of Energy, and Trade and Industry. The USA refused to concede defeat and continued to be an effective blocking state, albeit now

---

[302] Clark, 'The Antarctic Environmental Protocol: NGOs in the Protection of Antarctica', 176.

[303] Elliott, *International Environmental Politics: Protecting the Antarctic*, 192.

[304] Draft Convention for the Comprehensive Protection of the Antarctic Environment, 16 October 1990, article 3, paragraph 2, reprinted in Bush, *Antarctica and International Law: A Collection of Inter-state and National Documents*, 17.

[305] Francioni, 'The Madrid Protocol on the Protection of the Antarctic Environment', 67–8.

[306] Elliott, *International Environmental Politics: Protecting the Antarctic*, 192.

[307] Francioni, 'The Madrid Protocol on the Protection of the Antarctic Environment', 68–9.

[308] Elliott and Australian National University. Australian Foreign Policy Publications Program, *Protecting the Antarctic Environment: Australia and the Minerals Convention*, 66–7; Elliott, *International Environmental Politics: Protecting the Antarctic*, 193.

virtually alone.[309] Early in June, before the next session, the USA stated that it had a problem with the consensus requirement to lift a ban on a moratorium on mineral exploitation and wanted it changed to a three-quarters majority which any state could walk away from if the required majority was not met within three years.[310]

When the Madrid Session reconvened on 17 June, the session was initially mired in controversy. ENGOs who had attended the Second Meeting were not given official invitations. The reason for this oversight remains unclear, with perhaps Spain thinking that it did not need to send an invitation since the first invitation sent was meant to cover all subsequent meetings. Another view was that it was an attempt to limit ENGO interference in proceedings, but many ENGOs were able to attend as observers, including ASOC and the IUCN, while other environmental groups monitored events and broadcast it to the world to increase the pressure on delegates, who knew that their every word was being heavily scrutinized.[311]

The USA was still determined to play a spoiler role. In an effort to negate the USA, Australia led a group of 15 states at a closed session on 19 June, where the group's displeasure with the USA and its intransigence was conveyed to the USA. The Session Chair proposed an amendment where a three-quarters majority would be needed to adopt an amendment to end the moratorium and where withdrawal provisions would apply to the protocol in its entirety.[312] Thus US intransigence was able to win a 'walk away' clause within the proposed Protocol on Environmental Protection (Article 25(5)(a)). The proposed article allowed any member state to opt out (walk away) and exploit Antarctica's mineral wealth if the agreement was not ratified in five years. Further, it stated that for the first 50 years after PEPAT entered into force, the ban could only be lifted if all ATCPs agreed. After 50 years, the moratorium could be ended with the agreement of three-quarters of the ATCPs and then ratified by the same fraction of the ATCPs, including all 26 of the current members.[313]

On the last day of the meeting, the USA informed the other delegates that its government wanted more time to consider the changes. The chance to sign

---

309 Elliott and Australian National University. Australian Foreign Policy Publications Program, *Protecting the Antarctic Environment: Australia and the Minerals Convention*, 65.

310 Ibid.: 67.

311 Clark, 'The Antarctic Environmental Protocol: NGOs in the Protection of Antarctica', 176.

312 Elliott, *International Environmental Politics: Protecting the Antarctic*, 193.

313 Clark, 'The Antarctic Environmental Protocol: NGOs in the Protection of Antarctica', 177.

the Proposal on the 30th Anniversary of the Antarctic Treaty was missed.[314] Global public reaction to this decision was highly critical, with the USA being seen virtually as a rogue state. The leaders of Australia, the European Community, the former Soviet Union and Japan went so far as to individually write to US President Bush expressing their displeasure at this tactic and the general negotiating position of the United States.[315] In the face of this level of criticism, even a superpower must listen and on 3 July, the USA publicly announced it would sign PEPAT.[316] It is unclear why they acceded to the wishes of the other delegates in this matter. Perhaps the US delegates realized that their negotiating position was doing more harm than good to their international reputation as a good environmental actor and was unsustainable.

Alternatively, the US negotiators may have realized it was better to cut their losses and negotiate for the exploitation of Antarctica at a future date. However, constructivism allows for another explanation. This is not interest-based, but rather related to the intersubjective nature of the regime itself. In this case, the norm of consensus decision-making had become such an ingrained part of the process that, once the USA was effectively isolated, it felt compelled to 'follow the rules' and acquiesce to the overwhelming majority, rather than endanger the regime itself.

At the conclusion of the Madrid Sessions, the Representatives of the Consultative Parties, including the USA, adopted by consensus the Protocol on Environmental Protection to the Antarctic Treaty, known as the 'Madrid Protocol', of which four annexes form the key documents, namely, environmental impact assessment, conservation of Antarctic fauna and flora, waste disposal, and management and prevention of marine pollution.[317] Under the

---

314 Elliott and Australian National University. Australian Foreign Policy Publications Program, *Protecting the Antarctic Environment: Australia and the Minerals Convention*, 67; Elliott, *International Environmental Politics: Protecting the Antarctic*, 193.

315 Clark, 'The Antarctic Environmental Protocol: NGOs in the Protection of Antarctica', 177.

316 Elliott and Australian National University. Australian Foreign Policy Publications Program, *Protecting the Antarctic Environment: Australia and the Minerals Convention*, 67–8.

317 'U.S. State Department Handbook of the Antarctic Treaty System 2002', 473. The final Act of the Special Consultative Meeting was adopted, whereby the Protocol would be opened for signature in Madrid on 4 October 1991, and thereafter in Washington, DC until 3 October 1992. Elliott, *International Environmental Politics: Protecting the Antarctic*, 194. The Fifth Annex was adopted under Recommendation XVI-10 at the Sixteenth Antarctic Treaty Consultative Meeting on 17 October 1991 in Bonn. Annex V entered into force on 24 May 2002. The US signed the Protocol on 4 October 1991 and the Senate consented to ratification on 7 October 1992. 'U.S. State Department Handbook of the Antarctic Treaty System 2002', 473.

Protocol, the parties committed themselves to the comprehensive protection of the Antarctic environment (and the current constraints on mineral resource activity) and designated Antarctica as a natural reserve devoted to peace and science. It was agreed by the parties that the harvesting of ice was still allowable if technologically feasible, but the voluntary moratorium, in place since 1977, was to continue until ratification of the Protocol took place by all 26 ATCPs.[318]

The Madrid Protocol was intended to supplement the Antarctic Treaty and under Article 4(1), neither modified nor amended the original treaty.[319] Rather, it consolidated all previous environmental protection legislation and recommendations into a single legal instrument.[320] The Protocol aimed, as per the Preamble, to provide 'protection of the Antarctic environment and dependent and associated ecosystems'.[321] The Preamble of the Madrid Protocol made no mention of preservation but rather reaffirmed the 'conservationist principles of the Convention on the Conservation of Antarctic Marine Living Resources'.[322]

Despite the conservationist language, Article 2 of the Protocol saw the parties agree to 'the comprehensive protection of the Antarctic environment and dependent and associated ecosystems' and designated the region as a 'natural reserve, devoted to peace and science'.[323] The eventual designation of the park as a nature reserve/land of science departed somewhat from the world park concept espoused by the ENGOs, but still embodied many of the qualities of that ideal. The designation of Antarctica as a natural reserve under Article 2 had both symbolic value and legal force in that:

> it is functional to the norms of the Protocol and of the Annexes which concern the limitation of various freedoms of use, in relation, for example, to the protection of flora and fauna and to the operation of new norms on the subject of environmental impact assessment of any human activity in the Antarctic even that of a scientific matter.[324]

---

318 'U.S. State Department Handbook of the Antarctic Treaty System 2002', 474; Elliott, *International Environmental Politics: Protecting the Antarctic*, 194.

319 Vidas, 'Entry into Force of the Environmental Protocol and Implementation Issues: An Overview', 5.

320 Joyner, *Governing the Frozen Commons: The Antarctic Regime and Environmental Protection*, 80.

321 Protocol on Environmental Protection to the Antarctic Treaty, Doc XI ATSCM/2, 21 June 1991, adopted 4 October 1991; 'Final Report of the Eleventh Antarctic Treaty Special Consultative Meeting' (Spain, 1991).

322 Joyner, *Governing the Frozen Commons: The Antarctic Regime and Environmental Protection*, 81.

323 'The Protocol on Environmental Protection to the Antarctic Treaty', the Antarctic Treaty Committee for Environmental Protection website, http://www.cep.aq/default.asp?casid=5074.

324 Francioni, 'The Madrid Protocol on the Protection of the Antarctic Environment', 17.

Article 3 of the Madrid Protocol included language that explicitly referred to preserving the Antarctic environment. For example, Article 3(1) of PEPAT read:

> The protection of the Antarctic environment and dependent and associated ecosystems and the *intrinsic* [my italics] value of Antarctica, including its wilderness and aesthetic values and its value as an area for the conduct of scientific research, in particular research essential to understanding the global environment, shall be fundamental considerations in the planning and conduct of all activities in the Antarctic Treaty area.[325]

The Protocol introduced new concepts for the southern polar region, among them aesthetics, wilderness values and geomorphological values (which until this time had been absent). While the term preservation was not explicitly mentioned, the language of the section, with its reference to intrinsic values (including wilderness ideals), would seem to indicate clearly that preservationism was at the heart of the Article, and that the standard of behaviour of all who visit Antarctica should conform to preservationist ideals. Article 3 was in many respects identical to Article 4 of CRAMRA, except that the latter related only to mineral activity, while Article 3 was truly comprehensive. It applied to all human activity, mining or scientific.[326] The Madrid Protocol further created the Committee for Environmental Protection (CEP), of which every party could be a member. It was tasked with overseeing compliance with the Protocol, but had no independent capabilities, enforcement capabilities or decision-making authority. Rather, it provided advice and recommendations to ATCMs. States had to ensure compliance.[327]

Article 7 of the Madrid Protocol simply stated, with regard to minerals, that: 'Any activity relating to mineral resources, other than scientific research, shall be prohibited.'[328] When examined in isolation, it appeared to place a permanent ban on mining. But when read with subsequent provisions (Article 25), it was widely interpreted to have created a 50-year ban, though due to the US amendments, it was subject to review and potential revisions at the end of that period.

Two views of the Article 7 ban can be discerned here. One view was expressed by Tristan Garel-Jones, a UK minister who argued that the parties had no right to stop future generations accessing Antarctic resources, and that

---

325 'The Protocol on Environmental Protection to the Antarctic Treaty'.

326 Laura Pineschi, 'The Madrid Protocol on the Protection of the Antarctic Environment and its Effectiveness', in *International Law for Antarctica*, ed. Francesco Francioni and Tullio Scovazzi (London: Kluwer Law International, 1996), 262.

327 Joyner, *Governing the Frozen Commons: The Antarctic Regime and Environmental Protection*, 79.

328 'The Protocol on Environmental Protection to the Antarctic Treaty'.

there might well be a need to exploit these resources when the ban's time limit expired. This conservationist view seems to see the ban as locking away resources for 'a rainy day'. The other view is that Antarctica should be considered off-limits in perpetuity to preserve the pristine nature of the continent, and that any mining is incompatible with the proper environmental protection of the region.[329] In the short to medium term, the latter view has prevailed, with the possibility that the former may hold currency at the end of 50 years.

Article 7 renders the issue of sovereignty, and the state appetite for resources, moot in the short to medium term. The Article also has the effect of neutralizing the developing states' critique by acceding to their long-standing demand for such a ban.[330] Vidas argues that Article 7 was little different to CRAMRA's requirement that a consensus of ATCPs was required before mining could commence. However, given the conflict between the parties on this issue, it seems likely that, under CRAMRA, a state would sooner rather than later have been tempted to exploit Antarctic mineral resources.[331]

Chile argued that its understanding of Article 7 was that the term 'mineral activities in all their phases' also outlawed prospecting for resources in the region and that this would seem to be the correct and accepted interpretation.[332] Thus no mineral exploring, prospecting or related activity can be carried out save for scientific purposes, which must by nature be small scale and subject to environmental impact assessment as per Article 8.[333]

As noted previously, Article 7 must be read in conjunction with Article 25 to determine the strength of the prohibition on mineral resource activity. Section 1 of Article 25 allows amendments to be made at any time pursuant to Article XII of the Antarctic Treaty. Section 2 allows that after 50 years from the date of entry into force, any party may convene a conference to review the operation of the Protocol to date. Section 3 states that any modification or amendment moved at that conference must be adopted by a majority of parties, and at least three-fourths (20) must be ATCPs as of 1991. Section 4 outlines that any change must be ratified by three-fourths of the ATCP and again must include all those parties as of the adoption of the Protocol.[334]

---

329 French, 'Sustainable Development and the 1991 Madrid Protocol to the 1959 Antarctic Treaty: The Primacy of Protection in a Particularly Sensitive Environment', 326–7.

330 Vidas, 'Entry into Force of the Environmental Protocol and Implementation Issues: An Overview', 4.

331 Ibid.: 1.

332 Bush, *Antarctica and International Law: A Collection of Inter-state and National Documents*, 24.

333 'The Protocol on Environmental Protection to the Antarctic Treaty'.

334 'The Protocol on Environmental Protection to the Antarctic Treaty', Committee for Environmental Protection, www.cep.aq/apa/legal_docs/protocol.htm.

This proposed 'veto' of activities by any party was of the greatest concern to the USA. The USA insisted that Article 25, Section 5, be altered to counter this.[335] Section 5(a) imposes an indefinite ban on mineral activity. If there is a change to the ban, a legal regime must be established that: (1) clarifies whether mineral activity can occur; (2) imposes conditions under which such activity can occur; and (3) puts forward safeguards designed to protect the interests of all states as per Article IV of the Antarctic Treaty. Section 5(b), the so-called 'walkout clause', was proposed by the USA with the aim of nullifying Section 4. It reads:

> if any such modification or amendment has not entered into force within 3 years of the date of its adoption, any Party may at any time thereafter notify the Depository of its withdrawal from this Protocol, and such withdrawal shall take effect two years after receipt of the notification by the Depository.[336]

The new wording to Article 25 maintained a nexus between the possible ending of the ban and the beginning of mineral exploitation by providing 'an agreed means for determining whether, and, if so, under which conditions, any such activities would be acceptable' (Article 25(a)). The intent of such a provision was to assuage the claimant states' concerns that after the 50-year period there could be unilateral moves to exploit the mineral resources of Antarctica. To further reinforce this point, the final wording of Article 25(a) contained a clause stating that any potential mineral regime 'shall fully safeguard the interests of all states referred to in article IV of the Antarctic Treaty and apply the principles thereof'.[337] There has been a suspicion, particularly by ENGOs, that scientific research may well be a 'Trojan horse' to allow mineral exploitation to continue post-moratorium.[338]

The question of whether 'scientific activity' should take place within a 'world park' is still an open one among academics. Kelly Rigg seems to argue that Greenpeace's official position is that any scientific activity should be

---

335 Article 25(5)(a): 'With respect to Article 7 the prohibition on Antarctic mineral resource activities . . . shall continue unless there is in force a binding legal regime on Antarctic mineral resource activities that includes an agreed means for determining whether and, if so, under which conditions, any such activities would be acceptable. This regime shall fully safeguard the interests of all States referred to in Article IV of the Antarctic Treaty and apply the principles thereof.' Ibid.

336 Joyner, *Governing the Frozen Commons: The Antarctic Regime and Environmental Protection*, 167–8.

337 Francioni, 'The Madrid Protocol on the Protection of the Antarctic Environment', 69–70.

338 David J. Drewry, 'Conflicts of Interest in the Use of Antarctica', in *Antarctic Science: Global Concerns*, ed. Gotthilf Hempel (Berlin, Germany: Springer-Verlag, 1994), 15.

limited since it might be damaging. David Drewry maintains that, on balance, it would seem that the position held by Greenpeace and other ENGOs who have an interest in Antarctica is that science still has a place under the moratorium on commercial activity within the region.[339] However, the notion of preservationism allows for the treatment of an area as a silo, and providing that scientific research is not a cover for mineral activities, seeing it as no threat to the underlying norm of preservation.

## CONCLUSION

As befitting the two states that worked hardest to see the Protocol accepted by the global community, France ratified PEPAT on 5 February 1993, and Australia on 6 April 1994, before any other states.[340] The main opponent of the Protocol, the USA, deposited the instrument of ratification on 17 April 1997.[341] With Japan agreeing to ratify the Protocol in late 1997, the Protocol entered into force on 14 January 1998.[342] The global community, including Malaysia, appears to have accepted the Protocol and given it their seal of approval, as expressed by the UN General Assembly, which passed a consensus resolution in 1994 that expressly stated that the ATS had conducted itself meritoriously over its stewardship of the Antarctic continent in this regard.[343]

The combination of a ban on mineral activities and the designation of Antarctica as a natural reserve confirms that a strong preservationist norm now underpins the Antarctic regime. But how robust is the norm of preservation within the minerals regime? In terms of Legro's test for measuring the robust-

---

339 Ibid.: 21.

340 'U.S. State Department Handbook of the Antarctic Treaty System 2002', 471.

341 Christopher C. Joyner, 'The United States: Legislation and Practice in Implementing the Protocol', in *Implementing the Environmental Protection Regime for the Antarctic*, ed. Davor Vidas (Boston, MA: Kluwer Academic Publishers, 2000), 422. In 1996, the thrust of the Protocol was turned into US domestic legislation without much fanfare with an amendment to the 1990 Antarctic Protection Act. This made permanent the interim ban on drilling and mining. Section 202(a) of the Act made it '. . . unlawful for any person to engage in, finance, or otherwise knowingly provide assistance to any Antarctic Mineral activity' (Antarctic Science, Tourism, and Conservation Act (US) (ASTCA), Title II; USC, Vol. 16, section 2643). Since the ban came into force in 1990, no US corporation has publicly evinced a desire to mine Antarctica. Joyner, 'The United States: Legislation and Practice in Implementing the Protocol', 422.

342 'U.S. State Department Handbook of the Antarctic Treaty System 2002', 471.

343 United Nations General Assembly (UNGA) Resolution 49/80, reprinted in Vidas, 'Entry into Force of the Environmental Protocol and Implementation Issues: An Overview', 15.

ness of a norm according to its specificity, concordance and durability, preservationism is deeply entrenched, with a high degree of commonality. Certainly it is specific in its categorical stipulation that no mineral activity is allowed except on clear scientific grounds. To date there has been minimal argument as to its implementation. There is strong and widespread concordance insofar as it is virtually taken for granted by ATCPs, to the point where we can speak of the norm being internalized, as per Finnemore and Sikkink, at least in the short to medium term.

The question of the durability of the norm is not quite so straightforward. While there are no recorded instances of violations, many academics remain unconvinced of the durability of the norm. Joyner argues that the Madrid Protocol cannot be considered to have created a world park because it does not provide permanent protection for the area.[344] Given that the technological ability to economically exploit mineral deposits in Antarctica has not yet been developed, there has been little economic pressure to exploit Antarctic minerals that are available far more cheaply in other parts of the globe.[345] The test will come either during a global period of resource scarcity or if technology improves sufficiently to allow commercial mining at a relatively low economic cost. Any attempt to exploit minerals or hydrocarbons in the Antarctic appears at least several decades away. Most authorities believe that given the uncertainty regarding mineral deposits and the concomitant difficulties of transport, terrain and climate, there will be no mining industry on Antarctica for the foreseeable future.[346]

The Protocol does allow a loophole for mineral activities in the future. Article 25.5(a) states that any moratorium will stay in place 'unless a compulsory regime governing such activities is agreed between Antarctic Treaty Parties'. Laurence Cordonnery believes that the need to refer to such a regime 'strongly foreshadows a future revival of CRAMRA' and that 50 years is about the time it will take to develop cost-effective techniques to facilitate commercial exploitation.[347] Further, the Wellington Convention, while having no chance at present of entering into force, is still a binding legal instrument covering mineral exploitation. If the ban is ever reconsidered, it provides a ready-made framework to provide for future mineral exploitation.[348]

---

344 Joyner, *Governing the Frozen Commons: The Antarctic Regime and Environmental Protection*, 173.

345 Suter, *Antarctica: Private Property or Public Heritage?*, 48–9.

346 Vogler, *The Global Commons: Environmental and Technological Governance*, 87.

347 Cordonnery, 'The Implementation of the Protocol on Environmental Protection to the Antarctic Treaty: The Interplay between Law and Environmental Management', 25.

348 Elena Sciso, 'Are Mineral Resource Activities Still Compatible with the

In the short term, the argument that preservationism is the governing norm appears to be unassailable, however. As John McCarthy, Head of the Australian Delegation, points out in his Statement to the Eleventh Special Consultative Meeting, the objective of comprehensive protection of the Antarctic environment will only be achieved by actual application of the Protocol.[349] Article 7 has been incorporated into states' policies when dealing with Antarctica and is virtually unquestioned.[350] A search of the Antarctic Treaty Meeting minutes of the 1990s and 2000s reveals that there have been no recorded violations of the moratorium and that the issue is presumed to be settled and therefore off the agenda for the foreseeable future. States appear so faithful to the ban that it can be concluded that they have internalized the ban. Whether this holds true when the moratorium is due to end in 2048 is unknowable, but given the speed with which the moratorium has been internalized by states, there is an excellent chance that the ban will hold.

The neoliberal approach utilized here allows for an examination of the coalitions both for and against a world park, and a ban on mineral activities, as well as an exploration of the interest calculations of key regime members. Putnam's two-game analysis allows us to understand the involuntary defection of both Australia (buying off the domestic electorate) and France (placating domestic interest groups), but doesn't convey the whole picture because it does not account for the positive reverberations of the domestic campaigns undertaken by ENGOs to shape the behaviour and identities of the ATCPs.[351]

An examination of the veto coalitions that sprang up against both CRAMRA and the Madrid Protocol can help with an examination of the negotiating position of certain states, but does not adequately explain the situation. Rather, there is a need to explore how domestic preferences were formed in key states – something that a conventional neoliberal approach is unable to do. Porter and Brown argue that the norm of consensus was a powerful weapon

---

Protection of the Antarctic Environment', in *International Environmental Law for Antarctica*, ed. Francesco Francioni (Milan: Giuffre Editore, 1992), 262–3.

349 'Final Report of the Eleventh Antarctic Treaty Special Consultative Meeting', 165.

350 For example, the document 'Quarrying in Antarctica: An Environmental Policy Statement', prepared by the Australian Antarctic Division in May 1996, directs that any quarrying undertaken must be cognizant of PEPAT. British, Italian and Korean observers, in an inspection in early 1993 of 16 stations on the South Shetland Islands and the Antarctica Peninsula, found that most national expeditions (for example, the UK base Rothera) were aware of PEPAT's conditions and many had already been implemented. Pineschi, 'The Madrid Protocol on the Protection of the Antarctic Environment and its Effectiveness', 267.

351 Robyn Eckersley, *The Green State: Rethinking Democracy and Sovereignty* (Cambridge, MA: MIT Press, 2004), 93.

that could be wielded by veto coalitions.[352] Their approach cannot then explain the failure of the US-led veto coalition to prevent the Madrid Protocol, however, despite the norm of consensus being operational.

Neoliberalism can easily explain why states would want to exploit Antarctica, with its potential mineral wealth serving as a magnet for states seeking resources. It can also show that conservationist practices are in states' interests to secure resources for future generations. Neoliberalism is incapable, however, of explaining those moral dimensions of a preservationist position that cannot be captured by interest calculations. Rational choice theory seems unable to explain the range of human motivations involved, particularly in the environmental political field, and why wilderness values can have such a significant impact, even though they are not in states' material interests.[353] The neoliberal approach is meant to show institutionalized long-term interest calculations, and perhaps one can explain France and Australia's refusal to sign onto CRAMRA as having long-term benefits with regard to being perceived as a good global citizen. This characterization does unduly stretch the meaning of the term 'interest', however, and neglects any altruistic motivations by the states.[354]

Neoliberals could argue that, since the mineral wealth was only ever speculative, states' short-term interests were not really affected by the Madrid Protocol and that the real test is still to come. Alternatively, they could argue that France and Australia's stance conferred on them a form of 'reputational advantage'. If both these states are perceived as altruistic, trustworthy states, looking out for the globe's interests, it may confer some relative advantage on their negotiating positions in the future. Perceived superior moral positioning can influence both debate and negotiation. However, such an explanation of France and Australia's behaviour fails to understand that their principled stance might have had repercussions for states *not* trusting them. Neither state could know at the time whether their refusal to sign CRAMRA might have led to a diminution of their material interests. However, the idea of reputational advantage is an interesting point, and a possible point of intersection with the constructivist approach that will be explored more fully in the Conclusion to this book.

---

352 Porter, Brown and Chasek, *Global Environmental Politics*, 91–2.

353 John Vogler, 'Taking Institutions Seriously: How Regime Analysis Can Be Relevant to Multilateral Environmental Governance', *Global Environmental Politics* 3, no. 2 (2003): 27.

354 Audie Klotz, *Norms in International Relations: The Struggle against Apartheid*, Cornell Studies in Political Economy (Ithaca, NY: Cornell University Press, 1995), 26.

A constructivist approach allows us to account for the motivations and actions of ENGOs and the states of France and Australia in a more coherent and complete way, while still allowing for interest calculations by individual states. It allows us to chart how the new environmental norm of preservation emerged and stabilized from within previously existing social institutions, in this case ENGOs.[355] Further, it allows us to examine the moral positions put forth by key states, and can account more fully for the changed negotiating positions of France and Australia. Such an analysis reveals that France and Australia's identity changed along with their interests. We can observe that the idea of their being good environmental citizens came to constitute their identity and their actions. Both France and Australia became powerful proselytizers for the preservationist position. The strength of their change can be demonstrated by their willingness to fight for a world park despite the powerful states opposed to their stance. This change in France and Australia's identity shows that the neoliberal conception of states with fixed interests is incorrect and that state identity is a more fluid concept than neoliberals admit.

Holistic constructivism, with its multi-level, multi-actor analysis, points to the significance of the domestic situation, particularly in France and Australia, but also in other key veto states like the USA. It allows an understanding of how French elites, who had initially supported CRAMRA, could split from a French populace that had been influenced by Cousteau's one-man crusade.[356] A newly installed socialist government, itself sensitive to ecological concerns, heeded the popular demand and refused to ratify CRAMRA. Likewise, understanding the Australian domestic situation, with its recently ecologically aware electorate, receptive to the message being advocated by the ENGOs, is crucial to a greater understanding of why Australia's negotiating position and identity altered. Constructivism also allows an analysis of the domestic criticism that undermined the US negotiating position at crucial points in the negotiation. It enables a more nuanced understanding of state identity, one that includes the influence of moral factors on domestic leaders and shows how and why Australia and France became altruistic proponents for a preservationist position.

Holistic constructivism shows the impact of ENGOs upon negotiations. ENGOs were successful in increasing the global public's awareness of the Antarctic issues and were able to mobilize public and political support to

---

355 Ibid.: 22.

356 Cordonnery, 'The Implementation of the Protocol on Environmental Protection to the Antarctic Treaty: The Interplay between Law and Environmental Management', 6–7.

change states' support for CRAMRA.[357] The nature of the regime allowed ENGOs to gain increasing respect and legitimacy, based on their credible participation in the regime itself. This allowed them to act as effective norm entrepreneurs.[358] In many ways, ENGOs acted as normative teachers to states, with their emphasis on educating domestic constituencies on the need for Antarctic preservation. The ENGOs' framing of the issue as preserving a unique fragile wilderness circumscribed the terms of the debate. They successfully appealed to 'higher values', such as wilderness, that resonated with the populace and had an ideational affinity to the already embedded domestic norm of maintaining wilderness.

The ENGOs used the fears of the ATCPs to sharpen their message. They exploited the fear of states that the regime could collapse, pitching them back into a situation where the strongest, most technologically advanced states would have a significant relative advantage. They also utilized the concern ATCPs felt that if Antarctica could no longer be managed by their club alone, it would be opened up for all states to get a share. The ATCPs were aware that the UN was watching their negotiations and if any agreement was not perceived to be equitable or did not contain strong environmental provisions, then the matter might have been taken out of their hands and decided by the UN.

Despite the persuasive success enjoyed by the ENGOs, they also resorted to strategic methods to bolster their message. For example, they backed away from a preservationist position at the CRAMRA negotiations, until the climate was receptive to their more radical message. This appears to indicate that while ENGOs wanted to preserve the Antarctic, they were conscious of their relative strength as an agent of change and were most concerned with gaining the strongest protective regime possible. Once their publicity campaign, aided by strategic alliances with groups such as Antarctic scientists, allowed for other possibilities, they quickly reverted to their preferred position.

Lastly, constructivism allows for a greater understanding of why the USA stopped acting as a veto state and allowed the Madrid Protocol to pass. The Antarctic regime itself, with its structure and norms promoting consensus decision-making, set the boundaries of what was permissible behaviour for a state. This helped to frame and discipline the naked interest of states like the USA. In this case, the USA did not want to endanger the entire regime over one issue and arguably chose to preserve the integrity and spirit of the regime

---

[357] Elliott and Australian National University. Australian Foreign Policy Publications Program, *Protecting the Antarctic Environment: Australia and the Minerals Convention*, 72.

[358] Clark, 'The Antarctic Environmental Protocol: NGOs in the Protection of Antarctica', 180.

by ultimately accepting the Madrid Protocol. The socializing effect of the regime, with its emphasis on 'fitting in', may have had a powerful effect on the USA, which did not want to be perceived as a rogue state.

By incorporating a constructivist approach, this book is able to better explain the decision by ATCPs to incorporate a preservationist norm, as well as provide a greater understanding of the role played by non-state actors. Further, it enables a more nuanced understanding of the failure of a conservationist approach to become entrenched, as states such as France and Australia chose to adopt environmental positions that became part of their state identity. Without a more comprehensive understanding of a normative stance more altruistic than that provided by neoliberals, our working knowledge of Antarctic regime change is deficient, as is our ability to extrapolate lessons learned to other environmental regimes.

# 4. The International Whaling Commission and the elusive great white whale of preservationism*

> The moot point is, whether Leviathan can long endure so wide a chase, and so remorseless a havoc; whether he must not at last be exterminated from the waters, and the last whale, like the last man, smoke his last pipe, and then himself evaporate in the final puff. (Herman Melville, *Moby Dick*, 1851)

## INTRODUCTION

The fight by ENGOs to preserve whales is considered to be the first modern, global environmental campaign and in many ways the whale is still regarded as the symbol of the ENGO transnational movement.[1] Environmentalists often cite this campaign as a model of how to achieve environmental goals. Yet these claims belie a more complex history, characterized by a morass of competing interests and positions regarding the killing of whales that continues to this day.[2] This chapter will examine the modern exploitation of whales and the attempt to introduce conservationist programmes to manage whaling stocks on a sustainable basis, along with the drive to preserve whales by ENGOs and states like Australia and the United States of America. The primary arena of normative contestation to be examined is the meetings to regulate the whaling industry held primarily under the auspices of the International Whaling

* A version of this chapter appears as 'The International Whaling Commission and the Elusive Great White Whale of Preservationism', *William and Mary Environmental Law and Policy Review*, 3, no. 2 (2009): 375–447.

1 Niels Einarsson, 'All Animals are Equal but some are Cetaceans: Conservation and Culture Conflict', in *Environmentalism: The View from Anthropology*, ed. Kay Milton (London: Routledge, 1993), 73; Paul Kevin Wapner, 'Horizontal Politics: Transnational Environmental Activism and Global Cultural Change', *Global Environmental Politics* 2, no. 2 (2002): 48.

2 Wapner, 'Horizontal Politics: Transnational Environmental Activism and Global Cultural Change', 48.

Commission (IWC), as well as other forums held to regulate the practice of whaling.

A constructivist analysis allows an exploration of how non-state actors, such as whaling industry representatives, NGOs and scientists, acted as catalysts in effecting normative change in an effort to control the whaling regime.[3] Constructivists need to answer certain hard questions, however. One key question is whether ENGOs bring about normative change through persuasion and discussion – as constructivists believe they do – or whether they use strategic means. Secondly, can constructivists satisfactorily account for the behaviour of rogue states such as Japan and Norway (who have consistently refused to honour the prevailing norm of preservationism) without resorting to strategic interest explanations?

On the face of it, the neoliberal perspective has an easier time explaining the evolving whaling regime, at least up to a certain point. As the need to exploit whale products economically declined, due to substitution of other goods, it was no longer in the interests of many states to continue whaling. The remaining whaling states then dedicated themselves to conserving a dwindling resource. They created a regime to encourage normative change from exploitation to conservation to ensure an adequate resource base for future generations. However, the pursuit of short-term economic interests, and the failure to put in place a stronger conservationist approach, ensured that exploitation remained dominant until it was challenged by a new set of players, that of the ENGOs, with a new normative claim of preservationism.

Neoliberal analysis needs to defend the superiority of its explanation against altruistic explanations of normative change, however. It needs to demonstrate that an interest-based approach can account for the successful drive to install a preservationist norm by certain states like the US and by non-state agents such as ENGOs. Further, neoliberals must adequately explain how states' self-interests in the case of whaling are satisfied without resorting to domestic preference formation analyses, which are not part of the majority of neoliberal analyses.

---

[3] M.J. Peterson, 'Whalers, Cetologists, Environmentalists, and the International Management of Whaling', in *Knowledge, Power, and International Policy Co-ordination*, ed. Peter M. Haas (Columbia, SC: University of South Carolina Press, 1992), 148; Tora Skodvin and Steinar Andresen, 'Nonstate Influence in the International Whaling Commission, 1970–1990', *Global Environmental Politics* 3, no. 4 (2003): 62.

## GLOBAL INDUSTRIAL EXPLOITATION OF WHALES[4]

Whalemeat has been eaten by humans for over a thousand years, and it remains a prized food in parts of Japan.[5] For centuries, humans treated whales as a 'free resource', a gift from nature to be exploited by anyone who could catch them.[6] However, until the development of more efficient harvesting technologies, over-exploitation of whales was not a problem.[7] In the fifteenth century, whales were so plentiful off the coast of (what became) Newfoundland, that mariners regarded them as a greater hazard than '. . . fog, ice or unchartered rocks'.[8]

Modern whaling is considered to have commenced in 1864 when Svend Foyn of Norway first used explosive grenade harpoons fired by cannon to hunt whales from the north-east coast of Norway.[9] This enabled whalers to hunt larger, swifter rorqual whales such as blue, fin, sei and minke.[10] The advent of these new technologies enabled whalers for the first time to begin harvesting whales in large numbers, to the point that they threatened the viability of several species of pelagic whales. These new whaling technologies enshrined exploitationist practices as the global standard.

Although it soon became readily apparent that human hunting of whales was having a negative impact on whale stocks, whaling continued at ever increasing rates.[11] Robert Ellickson points out that at this early industrial

---

4 Elizabeth R. DeSombre, *The Global Environment and World Politics*, International Relations for the 21st Century (London: Continuum, 2002), 122; Farley Mowat, *Sea of Slaughter: A Chronicle of the Destruction of Animal Life in the North Atlantic* (Shelburne, VT.: Chapters Publishing Ltd, 1996), 208; F.D. Ommanney, *Lost Leviathan* (London: Hutchinson, 1971), 70.

5 Ommanney, *Lost Leviathan*, 55–65.

6 Anthony D'Amato and Sudhir K. Chopra, 'Whales: Their Emerging Right to Life', *The American Journal of International Law* 85 (1991): 28.

7 DeSombre, *The Global Environment and World Politics*, 123.

8 Mowat, *Sea of Slaughter: A Chronicle of the Destruction of Animal Life in the North Atlantic*, 210.

9 'International Whaling Statistics 1931' (Oslo: The Committee for Whaling Statistics, 1931), 15; Peter J. Bryant, 'Biodiversity and Conservation: A Hypertext Book', http://www.dbc.uci.edu/~sustain/bio65/Titlpage.htm; Ray Gambell, 'The International Whaling Commission and the Contemporary Whaling Debate', in *Conservation and Management of Marine Mammals*, ed. John R. Twiss Jr and Randall R. Reeves (Melbourne, Victoria: Melbourne University Press, 1999), 179–80. Svend Foyn's first use of the harpoon gun was not auspicious. He managed to become entangled in the line and was hurled into the water, but was rescued. Ommanney, *Lost Leviathan*, 95.

10 'International Whaling Statistics 1931', 5.

11 DeSombre, *The Global Environment and World Politics*, 123; Ommanney, *Lost Leviathan*, 92. European whalers such as the British, French and the Germans

period there would have been short-term economic incentives for states to promote excessive hunting to prevent other whaling nations from exploiting a global resource.[12] This type of state interest would have prevented a conservationist regime from being put in place, as states jostled to secure relative gains over other states, leading to a classic instance of the 'tragedy of the commons'. Each new state that undertook whaling '. . . passed through a phase of fierce competition and ruthless exploitation with improving techniques and ended at length in diminishing resources, exhaustion and failure'.[13] By the twentieth century, whaling had developed into a global industry supplying the world economies with whale oil and other by-products in vast quantities.[14] By the season of 1904–05, the newly developed factory whaling ships had reached the hitherto pristine Antarctic waters.[15] The use of steam was followed by diesel-powered floating factories to process the catch at sea.[16]

The increased scale of exploitation caused concern in the traditional whaling states of Scandinavia, which attempted to regulate domestic whalers. In 1902, Norway passed a law strictly limiting its whaling companies' activities, with the aim of conserving whale stocks as a valuable state asset. The new law stipulated that each whaling station was to have only one catcher and the stations must be 50 miles apart.[17] Iceland was the first state to put in place a domestic whaling moratorium on whaling – for 20 years, starting from 1915.[18] However, the taking of whales by other states continued virtually unabated.[19] The seriousness of the plight of whales was captured by Lewis Radcliffe, the Deputy Commissioner of the US Bureau of Fisheries, who argued in 1928 that:

---

continued large-scale hunting of Greenland bowhead whales and Biscayan right whales throughout the nineteenth century, leading to the decimation of these whale populations. D'Amato and Chopra, 'Whales: Their Emerging Right to Life', 28–29.

12 Robert C. Ellickson, 'A Hypothesis of Wealth-maximizing Norms: Evidence from the Whaling Industry', *Journal of Law, Economics, and Organization* 1 (1989): 96.

13 Ommanney, *Lost Leviathan*, 69.

14 'International Whaling Statistics 1931', 4.

15 Ibid.: 14.

16 Ibid.: 5. 'International Whaling Statistics 1931', 14. In 1923, factory ships were made even more efficient when they were built with a ramp at the stern to enable an entire whale to be brought aboard in a matter of minutes. 'International Whaling Statistics 1931', 15.

17 'International Whaling Statistics 1931', 10.

18 Chris Stroud, 'The Ethics and Politics of Whaling', in *The Conservation of Whales and Dolphins*, ed. Mark P. Simmonds and Judith D. Hutchinson (Chichester: John Wiley & Sons, 1996), 59–61.

19 'International Whaling Statistics 1931', 7. For example, in 1920 it is estimated that 11 369 whales were caught globally. However, by 1929, 27 566 whales were being harvested annually. 'International Whaling Statistics 1931', 7.

> At no stage in the history of whale fisheries, have whales been harassed in so many parts of the globe . . . That any one who has made even a casual study of the history of the whale fisheries of the globe can honestly advance the thought that there has been little or no diminution in the number of whales in the waters of the globe, seems little short of absurdity. That the whale supply will long stand up under the losses in numbers of 18,000 or more killed a year, seems extremely doubtful.[20]

The taking of so many whales in the early part of the twentieth century led to proposals for limited international regulation, starting in 1918, of the harvesting of whales by the whaling industry. Some elements were cognizant that the industry relied on viable numbers of whales to be profitable, but the effort came to naught and regulation was not agreed to. The imminent collapse of the whaling industry became an issue of global concern. The League of Nations representatives going to the International Council for the Exploration of the Seas (ICES) argued in 1929 that:

> The enormous expansion of the whaling industry in recent years constitutes a real menace to the maintenance of the stocks of whales and that, if the expansion continues at the present rate, there is a real risk of those stocks being so reduced as to cause serious detriment to the industry.[21]

At approximately the same time, the issue of managing global marine resources as a whole began to emerge as a state issue. Many leaders and diplomats, while acknowledging the need to protect these resources from exploitation, felt they lacked the technical knowledge to guide their actions. As a result, they tended to leave the regulation of different marine species to those states with the greatest interest in harvesting them.[22]

Organizations such as the Whaling Committee, established under the International Council for the Exploration of the Sea, comprised those states that regularly whaled. This started a long trend of whalers being allowed to govern themselves, with disastrous results for whale stocks. The Whaling Committee did attempt to regulate the industry at the 1927 Meeting, where the Norwegian delegate recommended curbing an open access approach to whaling. He argued that a system of licences should be implemented. This plea was unsuccessful, however, and exploitation continued unabated.[23]

---

20 Kristen M. Fletcher, 'The International Whaling Regime and U.S. Foreign Policy', in *The Environment, International Relations, and U.S. Foreign Policy*, ed. Paul G. Harris (Washington, DC: Georgetown University Press, 2001), 219.

21 Ibid.

22 Ibid.

23 D'Amato and Chopra, 'Whales: Their Emerging Right to Life', 30. The Whaling Sub-committee did, however, introduce changes that enabled states to begin to assess the size of the problem confronting it. It met in London in 1929 and recom-

## BUILDING A GLOBAL WHALING REGIME

Prior to the establishment of the IWC in the post-World War II period, there were earlier attempts to create a whaling regime. They were hampered by a lack of commitment from the relevant parties (Germany, Japan, Norway and the UK), despite ample long-term economic imperatives to do so.[24] In the early 1930s, the killing of blue whales hit such heights that it depressed whale oil prices.[25] Anthony D'Amato and Sudhir Chopra argue that at this point whaling nations began to recognize the need to regulate the taking of whales to prevent the extinction of the major whale species, acting out of their own self-interest to maintain profits.[26] The whalers themselves had also realized that the national controls proposed by states such as Norway and Iceland were not sufficient and that a global regulatory system aimed at stabilizing prices was needed.[27]

After four years of negotiation between the states attached to the League of Nations, the first Convention for the Regulation of Whaling was created in 1931 in Geneva, Switzerland (the Geneva Convention). The Convention covered all waters (Article 9), including states' territorial waters (Article 1), and it enforced the licensing of whaling vessels (Article 8).[28] It also exempted coastal aboriginal peoples, providing they utilized 'canoes, pirogues or other exclusively native craft propelled by oars or sails' and did not use firearms or employ non-aboriginals in their whaling activities.[29]

---

mended that the Norwegian government be asked to establish a central repository to collect whaling statistics yearly from all countries, including whales caught, the number of whaling companies operating and the number of catchers employed. The aim was to determine the biological conditions of whales at the time. This central repository was given the name the Committee for Whaling Statistics. The primary way of collecting the information was hardly ideal, though, since it consisted of logging information on forms filled out by each whaling expedition. 'International Whaling Statistics 1931', 1–2. All statistics collected under the auspices of the Committee for Whaling Statistics must be viewed with caution, therefore, as such a methodology enabled great scope for whalers to underreport their catches. They do, nonetheless, indicate the size of the problem, to a limited extent.

24 Shirley V. Scott, 'Intergovernmental Organizations as Disseminators, Legitimators, and Disguisers of Hegemonic Policy Preferences: The United States, the International Whaling Commission, and the Introduction of a Moratorium on Commercial Whaling', *Leiden Journal of International Law*, no. 21 (2008): 589.

25 'International Whaling Statistics 1935' (Oslo: The Committee for Whaling Statistics, 1935), 4. In 1930–31, 42 874 whales were taken. 'International Whaling Statistics 1935', 4.

26 D'Amato and Chopra, 'Whales: Their Emerging Right to Life', 29.

27 Peter John Stoett, *The International Politics of Whaling* (Vancouver, BC: UBC Press, 1997), 57.

28 D'Amato and Chopra, 'Whales: Their Emerging Right to Life', 31.

29 Alexander Gillespie, *Whaling Diplomacy: Defining Issues in International*

For the first time, conservation as a concept was applied globally to whaling, though D'Amato and Chopra persuasively argue that the norm was limited to merely protecting the long-term viability of the whaling *industry* rather than the welfare of whales.[30] The Convention, while outlawing the '. . . killing of calves, immature whales and female whales accompanied by calves', still allowed the hunting of adult whales virtually unhindered.[31] Furthermore, Japan, Germany and the USSR, all of which were prolific whaling states, did not sign on to the Convention, since the economic incentives, in their eyes, were not sufficient to do so. Without several of these key players, which accounted for approximately 30 per cent of whales harvested, the Convention was a collective failure and ineffective in its aims.[32]

The failure of the Geneva Convention opened the door for whaling companies to attempt to stabilize the situation. They created 'a regime of mutual production restraint', known as the International Association of Whaling Companies, to stabilize world oil prices by limiting production of whale oil.[33] For the 1933–34 whaling season, the major Antarctic whaling companies agreed to restrict their actions via this production agreement. However, two British companies and one Norwegian company refused to join the cartel and harvested 34 521 barrels of whale oil.[34] Due to the defections of the British and Norwegian companies, and the collapse of the accord, in the 1934–35 period, whaling in Antarctica increased to 26 087 from 24 327 whales taken, as compared to the previous year. The global total was reported to the Committee for Whaling Statistics as being 32 167.[35]

John Vogler argues that the behaviour of the whaling companies was motivated more 'by the need to maintain and support oil prices in a depressed

---

*Environmental Law* (Cheltenham, UK and Northampton, MA, USA: Edward Elgar, 2005), 194; Jeremy Firestone and Jonathan Lilley, 'Aboriginal Subsistence Whaling and the Right to Practice and Revitalize Cultural Traditions and Customs', *Journal of International Wildlife Law and Policy* 8, no. 2 (2005): 194; Randall R. Reeves, 'The Origins and Character of "Aboriginal Subsistence" Whaling: A Global Review', *Mammal Review* 32 (2002): 72.

30 D'Amato and Chopra, 'Whales: Their Emerging Right to Life', 31.

31 Ibid. Both Germany and Japan did not sign on to the Agreement because they considered it contrary to their interests at that time. Germany was using whale oil to lessen its need for importing edible oil and Japan was using the sale of whale oil to pay for its imperial ambitions in China and Manchuria. D'Amato and Chopra, 'Whales: Their Emerging Right to Life', 31.

32 DeSombre, *The Global Environment and World Politics*, 124.

33 'International Whaling Statistics 1935', 1, John Vogler, *The Global Commons: Environmental and Technological Governance*, 2nd edition (Chichester: John Wiley, 2000), 49.

34 'International Whaling Statistics 1935', 1.

35 Ibid.: 4.

market rather than any concern with long-term sustainable management'.[36] The refusal of some companies to amend their behaviour led to the Association collapsing, like many voluntary arrangements. This manifests the predictable problem of collective action, as it gets ignored when it goes against particular agents' interests, is subject to freeriding and is not recognized by more aggressive members, like whaling nations such as Japan.[37]

In 1937, another global agreement was attempted between the whaling nations of Argentina, Australia, Germany, the Irish Free State, New Zealand, South Africa, the United Kingdom and the United States of America. All agreed to implement the International Agreement for the Regulation of Whaling (1937). This is noteworthy because the Convention concerned covered for the first time shore-based operations and was the first comprehensive global whaling agreement.[38] The Convention outlawed the taking of both grey whales and right whales, limited hunting areas (by time and geographic area), and regulated the length of the whaling season in order to protect young and immature whales.[39] The problem was again the way the main whaling states of this period (Japan, Germany, Chile, Argentina and the USSR) refused to be bound by its provisions.[40] In 1938, a Protocol to the Convention 'banned

---

36 Vogler, *The Global Commons: Environmental and Technological Governance*, 49.

37 DeSombre, *The Global Environment and World Politics*, 124. With the failure of international accords, some whaling states attempted to put in place domestic controls again. Norway, at this point in time a leading proponent of a conservationist ethic to be applied to global whaling, enacted a law on 26 June 1934 which limited the hunting season in Antarctic waters from 1 December to 31 March from the 1934–35 season. Foreign whaling companies, except the Southern Whaling and Sealing Co. Ltd and the Kerguelen Sealing and Whaling Co. Ltd, agreed to adhere to the time limit affixed by the Norwegian Act of 1934. 'International Whaling Statistics 1936' (Oslo: The Committee for Whaling Statistics, 1936), 1–2. In 1935, the Act's purview was extended when new regulations were adopted under the Norwegian Whaling Act which limited the catching of baleen whales southward of 40 degrees south latitude. This could only take place between 1 December to 15 March of any year. 'International Whaling Statistics 1936', 2. On 6 July 1935, a second production agreement was decided for the 1935–36 season and agreed to by 21 whaling companies. The Norwegian companies who refused to adhere to the production agreement had quotas set for them by the Norwegian government. The Japanese Whaling Co. Ltd refused to be bound by any restrictions. 'International Whaling Statistics 1936', 2. The number of defectors from the production agreements soon doomed the agreement to collapse, as those adhering to the accord were unwilling to allow the freerider companies to derive economic advantage from it.

38 'Eighth Report of the Commission' (London: International Whaling Commission, 1957), 3.

39 D'Amato and Chopra, 'Whales: Their Emerging Right to Life', 31.

40 Karen Oslund, 'Protecting Fat Mammals or Carnivorous Humans? Towards

the taking of humpback whales for two years except in the area south of 40 degrees south latitude, where a one-year ban was imposed'. In 1939, the Protocol was amended to slightly increase protection for the humpback whale.[41] The problem remained that despite these added paper protections, the exploitation of whales in the 1930s continued virtually unchecked.[42]

By the 1937–38 season, the number of whales taken by whalers had risen to 54 873.[43] Patricia Birnie argues this was for many reasons, including the 'inadequacy of the scope of regulations; inadequate scientific data; non-cooperation by some major whaling nations; poor enforcement of agreements and no international supervision or control; and lack of global interest'.[44] To this impressive list of regulatory failures can be added that it was in the economic interest of whalers to continue harvesting, what was perceived by many, to be a 'free' resource, to be taken as quickly as technology allowed.

The only thing that prevented complete extinction of major whale species at this time was the advent of World War II. Naval interdictions confined most floating factories to port, while others were destroyed or utilized in the war effort.[45] For example, only 6197 whales were caught in the 1943–44 season (about 10 per cent of pre-war figures), allowing whale stocks to recover slightly. However, there were still attempts by whaling states to better regulate the industry.[46] At the height of World War II, in 1944, it was agreed by whaling states that they would attempt to regulate the whaling industry on the basis of how much oil particular whales contained, and to restrict the size of a catch to a standard measure, known as the Blue Whale Unit (BWU), regardless of the whale species being hunted.[47]

---

an Environmental History of Whales', *Historical Social Research* 29, no. 3 (2004): 70; Stoett, *The International Politics of Whaling*, 57.

41 D'Amato and Chopra, 'Whales: Their Emerging Right to Life', 31.

42 Ibid.

43 'International Whaling Statistics 1953' (Oslo: The Committee for Whaling Statistics, 1953), 13.

44 Patricia W. Birnie, *International Regulation of Whaling: From Conservation of Whaling to Conservation of Whales and Regulation of Whale-watching* (New York: Oceana Publications, 1985), 129–30.

45 'Eighth Report of the Commission', 3.

46 'International Whaling Statistics 1953', 13.

47 DeSombre, *The Global Environment and World Politics*, 124. The BWU, however, was a scientifically dubious measurement devised in the 1930s as a way to quantify the oil produced from various species of whale. Gregory Rose and George Paleokrassis, 'Compliance with International Environmental Obligations: A Casestudy of the International Whaling Commission', in *Improving Compliance with International Environmental Law*, ed. James Cameron, Jacob Werksman and Peter Roderick (London: Earthscan Publications Ltd, 1996), 161. One BWU was considered equal to one blue whale, which was equal to two fin whales, which equalled two and a half humpbacks and six sei whales. 'International Whaling Statistics 1950' (Oslo: The

In the post-World War II period, edible fat was in short supply, causing an upsurge in interest by even traditionally non-whaling states for this resource.[48] At the close of World War II the victorious Allies resumed negotiations, under the auspices of the 1937 Agreement, to facilitate the orderly exploitation of whales. A new set of regulations was quickly drafted to apply for the 1945–46 season, which incorporated the new BWU measure. It was agreed that the Antarctic season should be ended when whalers had taken the equivalent of 16 000 BWUs.[49] In the 1946–47 season, the number of whales taken jumped to 34 720, and by the following season it had increased to 43 378 BWUs.[50]

The concomitant decrease in whale stocks alarmed environmentalists and those who saw this example of overfishing as leading to not only the extinction of whales, but the extinction of the whaling industry. This formed a powerful convergence of interests.[51] Combined with this was a burgeoning understanding that whales should no longer be seen as the property of individual states but as a global resource. In 1946, Dean Acheson, the US Secretary of State, encapsulated the new mood when he declared: 'The world's whale stocks are a truly international resource in that they belong to no one single nation, nor to a group of nations, but rather they are wards of the entire world.'[52]

## THE INTERNATIONAL CONVENTION FOR THE REGULATION OF WHALING (1946)

In this atmosphere of a reinvigorated whaling industry and a greater appreciation of the nature of whales as a global resource, it is clear that most whaling nations recognized that there was a need for a new and more effective convention to prevent over-exploitation. Heeding this call, the United States, architect of much of the post-World War II political landscape, spearheaded a call for

---

Committee for Whaling Statistics, 1950), 2. The imprecision of such calculations only exacerbated the situation, since the methodology employed treated whales merely as an exploitable resource, taking the focus away from the number of whales killed and putting it on what each species economically provided.

48 Sebastian Oberthur, 'The International Convention for the Regulation of Whaling: From Over-exploitation to Total Preservation', in *Yearbook of International Co-operation on Environment and Development 1998/9*, ed. Olav Schram Stokke (London: Earthscan, 1998/99), 31.

49 'Eighth Report of the Commission', 3.

50 'International Whaling Statistics 1953', 13.

51 G.J. Aplin, *Global Environmental Crises: An Australian Perspective* (Melbourne: Oxford University Press, 1995), 239–41; Vogler, *The Global Commons: Environmental and Technological Governance*, 49.

52 Stoett, *The International Politics of Whaling*, 30.

an international conference to re-examine the issues.[53] Out of this conference came a new International Convention for the Regulation of Whaling (ICRW). This superseded all previous agreements, coming into effect on 10 November 1948. It established the IWC as the pre-eminent body regulating the global whaling industry.[54] It introduced maximum catch quotas (16 000 BWUs) for the total season for Antarctic pelagic whaling and initially encompassed only the great whales.[55]

The Preamble to the Convention highlighted that whales needed to be protected against overfishing and that the delegates' aim was to manage exploitation of the great whales.[56] The Preamble's language incorporated the more conservationist goals of intergenerational equity, however, and the safeguarding of endangered species, particularly when it spoke of:

> (1) recognizing the interest of the nations of the world to safeguard for future generations the great natural resource represented by the whale stocks;
> (2) that in view of the 'history of whaling' [which] has seen over-fishing of one area after another and of one species of whale after another to near extinction, it is essential to protect all species of whales from further over-fishing;
> (3) confining whaling operations to those species best able to sustain exploitation in order to give an interval for recovery to certain species of whales now depleted in numbers;
> (4) establishment of a system of international regulation for the whale fisheries to ensure proper and effective conservation and development of whale stocks . . .[57]

The Preamble to the ICRW thus outlined the Convention as being about the orderly development of a commercial whaling industry and the conservation of existing whaling stocks. The inherent tension between these dichotomous aims would lead to much acrimony between member states, as they could not be easily reconciled.[58] Vogler argues that whilst the Preamble paid lip service

---

53 D'Amato and Chopra, 'Whales: Their Emerging Right to Life', 32.

54 'First Report of the Commission' (London: International Whaling Commission, 1950), 3; Reeves, 'The Origins and Character of "Aboriginal Subsistence" Whaling: A Global Review', 72. The Convention was signed by the delegates of Argentina, Australia, Brazil, Canada, Chile, Denmark, France, the Netherlands, New Zealand, Norway, Peru, the United Kingdom including Northern Ireland, the United States of America and the Union of Soviet Socialist Republics on 2 December 1946. 'First Report of the Commission', 3.

55 D'Amato and Chopra, 'Whales: Their Emerging Right to Life', 32; Vogler, *The Global Commons: Environmental and Technological Governance*, 53.

56 Vogler, *The Global Commons: Environmental and Technological Governance*, 49.

57 Appendix 1: The 1946 International Convention for the Regulation of Whaling, 'First Report of the Commission', 9.

58 Rose and Paleokrassis, 'Compliance with International Environmental Obligations: A Casestudy of the International Whaling Commission', 29.

to the norm of conservation, it was essentially an arrangement between states with an interest in commercially exploiting whales.[59] Certainly conservation was understood to be merely the facilitation of an orderly resource allocation regime, rather than the maintenance of sufficient stock for future generations. The ICRW did enable the opening up of a discourse between whaling states, however, whereby it was permissible to consider protecting whales as an objective.[60]

The Preamble's language reveals further a fundamental misunderstanding of the nature of whaling by the delegates when it mistakenly refers to 'whale fisheries'. The delegates assumed that, like fish, whales were quick to mature and were available to harvest in vast numbers. In fact, the opposite holds true.[61] In treating whaling like any other fishery agreements, the drafters of the agreement placed too great an emphasis on short-term economic considerations in overcoming the shortage of whale fats and oils at the expense of legitimate scientific concerns about the effects of over-exploitation on existing stocks.[62]

The Convention created the IWC as a supra-authority with the power to issue binding regulations to protect whales.[63] Its establishment as the global regulatory body for whaling meant that the norms underpinning the organization would reflect those operating in the broader world. The IWC was initially composed of delegates of the signatory whaling nations, but was open to all states who paid fees and was to meet annually to review the schedule on non-allowed whaling activities.[64] The allowing of other states to join the IWC,

---

59 Vogler, *The Global Commons: Environmental and Technological Governance*, 50. The UK delegation to the Meeting in 1945 argued that it would be in his view a '... tragedy if any international machinery was to get in the way of increased production' and this was indicative of the position of all the whaling nations. Vogler, *The Global Commons: Environmental and Technological Governance*, 50.

60 D'Amato and Chopra, 'Whales: Their Emerging Right to Life', 32; Skodvin and Andresen, 'Nonstate Influence in the International Whaling Commission, 1970–1990', 71.

61 Rose and Paleokrassis, 'Compliance with International Environmental Obligations: A Casestudy of the International Whaling Commission', 151.

62 J.L. McHugh, 'The Role and History of the International Whaling Commission', in *The Whale Problem: A Status Report*, ed. W. Schevill (Cambridge, MA: Harvard University Press, 1974), 318.

63 Rose and Paleokrassis, 'Compliance with International Environmental Obligations: A Casestudy of the International Whaling Commission', 29.

64 Charlotte Epstein, *The Power of Words in International Relations: Birth of an Anti-whaling Discourse* (Cambridge, MA: MIT Press, 2008), 80; Skodvin and Andresen, 'Nonstate Influence in the International Whaling Commission, 1970–1990', 70–71. Initially, only 15 nations participated in meetings, and overwhelmingly they were whaling nations. Skodvin and Andresen, 'Nonstate Influence in the International

whether whaling nations or not, was to prove a critical factor in norm transformation. This step would not have occurred in the absence of this new view that whales should be considered a global resource and not just the property of whaling states. The provision allowed states to circumvent potential veto coalitions by recruiting like-minded allies, a tactic used by both pro and anti-whaling forces.[65] The powers of the ICW to protect whales from exploitation are enumerated in a Schedule which allowed the body to:

> fix protected and unprotected species; open and close seasons; open and close areas, including sanctuaries; limitations on the size of species taken; methods and intensity of whaling, including maximum catch; types of gear and equipment used; methods of measuring whales taken; the requirement that returns be made of catch; and statistical and other biological information.[66]

The IWC operates under a majority-voting rule that requires a three-quarters majority of present members to vote to approve changes to the Schedule that contains the operative rules governing the global whaling regime.[67] The ICRW also allows dissenting states to opt out of any decision arrived at within the IWC by filing an objection within 90 days, applying for an exemption under Article V(3), a loophole that would allow rogue whaling states significant wiggle room in evading IWC directives.[68] Objections were so common in the first few decades of the IWC that it was rendered virtually impotent. Enforcement was left to individual member states as well, whose interests dictated continuing whaling unhindered, so were unlikely to police themselves rigorously. Further the Commission was powerless to regulate the activities of non-member countries since the Convention was not applicable to non-members.[69]

---

Whaling Commission, 1970–1990', 71. However, the key whaling states of Germany and Japan were initially excluded. Epstein argues that such practices started an initial dynamic of inclusion/exclusion for IWC states that reverberates to this day. Epstein, *The Power of Words in International Relations: Birth of an Anti-whaling Discourse*, 82.

65 Gareth Porter, Janet Welsh Brown and Pamela S. Chasek, *Global Environmental Politics*, 3rd edition, Dilemmas in World Politics (Boulder, CO: Westview Press, 2000), 78.

66 D'Amato and Chopra, 'Whales: Their Emerging Right to Life', 34.

67 Vogler, *The Global Commons: Environmental and Technological Governance*, 51.

68 Oberthur, 'The International Convention for the Regulation of Whaling: From Over-exploitation to Total Preservation', 30.

69 Adrienne M. Ruffle, 'Resurrecting the International Whaling Commission: Suggestions to Strengthen the Conservation Effort', *Brooklyn Journal of International Law* 27 (2002): 2.

The ICRW allowed under its 'primary rules' (the regulations attached to the Schedule to the ICRW) for the creation of conservationist programmes to enhance the protection of existing and future whale stocks.[70] It also allowed for potential preservationist outcomes, in that the IWC had the power to create whaling sanctuaries and ban the taking of particular whale species. At this point in time, however, IWC members could not even frame the question as to what whale preservation meant, let alone answer it, since no member states thought of whales as intrinsically worth saving.[71]

The ICRW Schedule also banned the taking of grey, humpback and right whales in certain areas (although it allowed aboriginal subsistence whaling in the Soviet Union – a loophole to be exploited later by many whaling states).[72] However, this restriction, combined with seasonal time limits and quotas, was unsuccessful in stopping the ongoing exploitation of whales, despite the emphasis on limited conservationist aims in the ICRW.[73] This highlights one of the weaknesses of the constructivist normative approach, particularly as articulated by Finnemore and Sikkink. Their approach presumes that once a norm has gone through the normative life cycle and been accepted by states, it becomes operational. In fact, the whaling regime created by the ICRW reveals that while a norm can be 'accepted' as appropriate behaviour by states, in that they agree to abide by it at negotiations, the practice may not reflect such promises.

---

70 Rose and Paleokrassis, 'Compliance with International Environmental Obligations: A Casestudy of the International Whaling Commission', 154. To amend the constitution requires the agreement of all IWC member states, but amendments to the Schedule Regulations, under Article III, can be passed with merely a three-quarters majority. These regulations are also binding on all members, whether they vote for them or not. Rose and Paleokrassis, 'Compliance with International Environmental Obligations: A Casestudy of the International Whaling Commission', 154. These two factors were to have a profound effect on the normative direction of the organization, since most normative advocacy focused on changing the regulations due to the relative ease of doing so.

71 Milton M.R. Freeman, 'Political Issues with Regard to Contemporary Whaling', in *Who's Afraid of Compromise?*, ed. Simon Ward (Tokyo: Institute of Cetacean Research, 1990), 2–3, http://luna./pos.to/whale/icr_wac_freeman.html, accessed 24/01/05.

72 'First Report of the Commission', 5. Yet the IWC, as one of its first acts, passed Resolution 11, which permitted the hunting of 1250 humpback whales south of 40 degrees south latitude in both the 1949–50 and 1950–51 seasons. 'First Report of the Commission', 5; Gillespie, *Whaling Diplomacy: Defining Issues in International Environmental Law*, 195.

73 The initial IWC Regulations were similar to those in force in the 1937–38 season. The maximum pelagic catch of baleen whales was set at 16 000 BWU. The harvest period was fixed from 15 December 1948 to 1 April 1949 and whaling from shore stations was fixed at six months. 'International Whaling Statistics 1950', 1. If the level of 16 000 BWUs was reached before the end of the hunting season, then operations were to stop immediately. 'International Whaling Statistics 1950', 2.

For neoliberals, this is a clear case of involuntary defection. The whaling states were unable to back up the promises made by their negotiators because of domestic considerations, in this case economic interests. Despite many states discontinuing whaling due to economic imperatives, for many others, particularly traditional whaling nations, their economies were tightly bound up with the continuation of whaling. As states competed for a shrinking resource pool, the exploitation only increased. Neoliberals would argue that in the case of whaling, fixed economic interests compelled continuing exploitative behaviour.

In fact, the restrictions on taking certain whale species have had the opposite effect to the one intended. It set in train a technological race to create better ships and more advanced killing technologies to achieve designated quotas as rapidly as possible, leading to whalers referring to the period as the 'Whaling Olympics'.[74] During this period, in the late 1940s, whalers raced the clock to catch whales before the season ended, in an effort to beat the competition. From 1946 to 1951, the whaling season shrank from 112 days to only 64, but the catching technologies became more efficient. An unintended consequence of the new, deadlier ships, however, was a significant increase in the cost of outfitting a whaling fleet. By 1960, some nations had ceased whaling on economic grounds, due to the prohibitive capital costs against returns.[75]

Problematically, the IWC set initial whaling quotas too high to ensure whaling states would not pull out of the IWC, yet even so the quotas were usually exceeded.[76] By the 1948–49 season, whaling had rebounded from the World War WII interregnum and 31 262 whales were taken.[77] Throughout the 1950s, the whale catch continued to increase, despite the presence of the IWC and its conservationist edicts.[78] IWC prohibitions to ban the taking of certain

---

74 Rose and Paleokrassis, 'Compliance with International Environmental Obligations: A Casestudy of the International Whaling Commission', 161.

75 DeSombre, *The Global Environment and World Politics*, 127. While the number of floating factory ships and catchers was down from pre-World War II numbers, the average size of the catchers' ships had increased, as had their engine power. The average horsepower of the catcher ships had increased from 1100 before the war to 1562 in 1948–49, enabling a greater taking capacity. 'International Whaling Statistics 1950', 11.

76 DeSombre, *The Global Environment and World Politics*, 118. For example, see the 'Third Report of the Commission' (London: International Whaling Commission, 1952), 15. The report stated that the 16 000 BWU limit had been exceeded by 413 for that year.

77 'International Whaling Statistics 1950', 10.

78 The IWC responded to the ongoing situation by resolving at the Fourth Meeting to stop taking: blue whales smaller than 70 feet; sei whales smaller than 40 feet; and humpback whales smaller than 35 feet. The same meeting banned factory ships and catchers from catching baleen whales in certain areas. 'Fourth Report of the Commission' (London: International Whaling Commission, 1953), 12–13. At the 1955

species for a limited time were met by numerous states lodging objections, including Canada, Japan, the USA and the Soviet Union. This enabled these states to continue to be able to exploit whales unchecked.[79] In the 1950–51 whaling period, the greatest yet whale kills were recorded, with 55 795 whales taken globally.[80] By the 1957–58 season, the number of floating factories operating in Antarctic waters had increased to 20, with two shore stations and 257 catchers and by the following season, 64 586 whales, a new high, were being killed annually.[81]

At the Tenth Meeting of the IWC, the British Commissioner argued that it was apparent to all that there had been a marked decrease in the number of fin whales caught in Antarctica. At the same time, the number of factory ships operating in the region was rising. He proposed that the main Antarctic whaling states work together to resolve this situation.[82] Consequently, in November 1958, the whaling nations of Japan, the Netherlands, Norway, the United Kingdom and the USSR met in London to create a separate allocating system.[83] However, the attendees could not agree how to equitably distribute the remaining catch, leading to the near collapse of the IWC.[84]

Norway and the Netherlands gave notice of their withdrawal from the Convention from 29 and 31 December respectively and Japan indicated it would follow suit on 6 February 1959, if the matter was not settled to their satisfaction.[85] The Netherlands and Norway withdrew from the forum and other states refused to consider the issue with them being absent.[86] After

---

IWC Meeting, conservationist measures were approved, with prohibitions placed on the taking of any blue whales in parts of the North Pacific Ocean and humpback whales in the North Atlantic Ocean for five years. Similar prohibitions banned the taking of sperm or minke whales, except as permitted by contracting governments. IWC, 'Sixth Report of the Commission' (London: International Whaling Commission, 1955), 5. In 1955, the Scientific Sub-committee recommended that the Pacific Sanctuary be reopened, which was accepted, but the delegates refused to reduce the BWU limit by 500, negating the decision. 'Sixth Report of the Commission', 17, 19.

79 'Seventh Report of the Commission' (London: International Whaling Commission, 1956), 6; Ruffle, 'Resurrecting the International Whaling Commission: Suggestions to Strengthen the Conservation Effort', 5.

80 'International Whaling Statistics 1953', 2.

81 'International Whaling Statistics 1959' (Oslo: The Committee for Whaling Statistics, 1959), 1; 'International Whaling Statistics 1960' (Oslo: The Committee for Whaling Statistics, 1960), 1.

82 'Tenth Report of the Commission' (London: International Whaling Commission, 1959), 5–6.

83 Ibid.: 24.

84 Ibid.: 6.

85 Ibid.

86 Rose and Paleokrassis, 'Compliance with International Environmental Obligations: A Casestudy of the International Whaling Commission', 154.

intense behind-the-scenes negotiations, the issue of quotas was worked out in 1962 and the states rejoined the Commission. The threat of states breaking away led to the setting of exploitative quotas, however, which did nothing to ameliorate the situation.[87]

D'Amato and Chopra characterize the period 1948 to 1960 as 'wasted years', in that states continued to argue mainly over quota allocations, backed by grandstanding threats of withdrawal from the IWC.[88] Before 1960, the whaling industry dominated the IWC, mostly through their national governments' delegates. The IWC was still 'a whalers' club' and the majority of members were themselves whaling nations, whose interests were synonymous with whaling industry interests.[89]

Indeed, not only were many state delegations filled with members with a pro-whaling bent, the IWC was also attended, from the Second Meeting onwards, by representatives of the Association of Whaling Companies.[90] The IWC in this period had little sense of urgency when it came to protecting whales, perceiving them only as a resource to be utilized. For many states, the establishment of a regime was considered to have 'solved' the problem, despite the voluminous evidence that the problem was worsening. Frustrated delegates to the IWC, who wanted to promote a conservationist platform, could not alter the situation in a context where there was little public knowledge of whaling issues and practices.[91]

## SCIENTISTS AND THE INTERNATIONAL WHALING COMMISSION

A holistic constructivist approach enables an examination of other critical regime actors that are often overlooked, including cetologists who attempted to alter the normative direction of the IWC by strengthening the conservationist norm. By the 1960 IWC Meeting in London, it was clear to most IWC

---

87 DeSombre, *The Global Environment and World Politics*, 127. For example, in 1964 the Scientific Committee recommended a level of 2833 BWUs but the IWC set the quota at 8000 BWUs to placate member states. Gregory Rose, 'International Law and the Status of Cetaceans', in *The Conservation of Whales and Dolphins*, ed. Mark P. Simmonds and Judith D. Hutchinson (Chichester: John Wiley & Sons, 1996), 31.

88 D'Amato and Chopra, 'Whales: Their Emerging Right to Life', 34.

89 Skodvin and Andresen, 'Nonstate Influence in the International Whaling Commission, 1970–1990', 63.

90 'Second Report of the Commission' (London: International Whaling Commission, 1951), 3.

91 Peterson, 'Whalers, Cetologists, Environmentalists, and the International Management of Whaling', 158–9.

members, based on their own compiled figures, that stocks of blue whales, fin whales and humpback whales had declined to crisis levels.[92] With the situation at crisis point, the delegates turned to a hitherto ignored group, cetologists (initially whale biologists), to provide a new policy direction.[93]

Up until this point, scientists had been perceived, and had acted, as virtual mouthpieces for their states, with their policy prescriptions tending to reflect nationalistic demands for whale products.[94] To ensure that scientific advice given to the member states was not tainted by states' interests, the United Kingdom proposed that a committee of three independent scientists (later four) be established and the motion was passed. The committee's role would be to quantify potential catch reductions to allow policy to be determined on more objective grounds.[95]

Once freed of the constraints of serving as states' spokesmen, the scientists quickly exhibited a high degree of independence in their scientific advice. Given that most cetologists' backgrounds were in biology, it was not surprising that their advice regarding whaling reflected that background and focused on the conservation of whale stocks. Acting as normative entrepreneurs, they

---

92 'Twelfth Report of the Commission' (London: International Whaling Commission, 1961), 14–15. In 1962, the IWC introduced national quotas, but due to the ongoing crashing whale stock, the quotas could not be met. Epstein, *The Power of Words in International Relations: Birth of an Anti-whaling Discourse*, 40.

93 Joji Morishita and Dan Goodman, 'Role and Problems of the Scientific Committee of the International Whaling Commission in Terms of Conservation and Sustainable Utilization of Stocks', *Global Environmental Research* 9, no. 2 (2005): 158. Scientific advice had always been integral to the structure of the IWC and scientists had always had a formal, institutionalized place within the IWC structure. Such scientific interest predates the organization. In 1929, American scientists, representing six zoological organizations, founded the Council for the Preservation of Whales. Epstein, *The Power of Words in International Relations: Birth of an Anti-whaling Discourse*, 75. In 1949, at the First Meeting of the IWC, a Joint Standing Scientific and Technical Committee was created to provide advice and experience to IWC member states. Skodvin and Andresen, 'Nonstate Influence in the International Whaling Commission, 1970–1990', 63. During the first few years of the IWC, the scientific representation to the Committee was sporadic, with few states sending representatives and the state of knowledge of whaling stocks minimal and disputed. While scientific advice was cursorily considered, it was generally ignored by states. Jose Truda Palazzo Jr, 'Whose Whales? Developing Countries and the Right to Use Whales by Non-lethal Means', *Journal of Wildlife Law & Policy* 2, no. 1 (1999): 69; Skodvin and Andresen, 'Nonstate Influence in the International Whaling Commission, 1970–1990', 71.

94 Gareth Porter and Janet Welsh Brown, *Global Environmental Politics* (Boulder, CO: Westview Press, 1991), 80–81; Skodvin and Andresen, 'Nonstate Influence in the International Whaling Commission, 1970–1990', 76.

95 Skodvin and Andresen, 'Nonstate Influence in the International Whaling Commission, 1970–1990', 75–6.

advocated quotas to protect scientifically determined, fragile whale stocks, to impose temporary moratoriums, and to reduce the overall catch.[96]

Despite their efforts, their efficacy as advocates was severely limited by a number of factors. They were only ever small in number, 30 at most, and their advice was merely advisory in nature, advice which member states were free to disregard or object to if it was not in accordance with their interests.[97] Problematically, cetologists also lacked the theoretical models and a consensus amongst themselves as to the correct policy prescriptions, without which they could not plausibly convince whaling states to abandon exploitationist practices.[98]

Further, they were unable to link their arguments with higher values that would persuade whaling states to adopt conservationist practices. Lastly, they were constrained by the platform from which they had to communicate. Unlike the Finnemore and Sikkink conception of a normative organizational platform where the norm entrepreneur creates a vehicle for their views to be heard, here the scientists were forced to conform to the agenda and operating norms of the IWC. This limited their effectiveness.[99] It limited their ability to communicate the need for conservationist mores and, despite their best efforts, the overall harvest rate was not limited for a further 18 years.[100]

In the 1960s, however, the ongoing exploitationist practices (which ensured set quotas were not being met) were beginning to affect the whaling industry and it was clear that as a global business whaling had peaked.[101] The IWC

---

96 Peterson, 'Whalers, Cetologists, Environmentalists, and the International Management of Whaling', 153; Rose and Paleokrassis, 'Compliance with International Environmental Obligations: A Casestudy of the International Whaling Commission', 154.

97 Porter and Brown, *Global Environmental Politics*, 79; Peterson, 'Whalers, Cetologists, Environmentalists, and the International Management of Whaling', 154.

98 Oberthur, 'The International Convention for the Regulation of Whaling: From Over-exploitation to Total Preservation', 31; Peterson, 'Whalers, Cetologists, Environmentalists, and the International Management of Whaling', 160–61, 69–70.

99 Skodvin and Andresen, 'Nonstate Influence in the International Whaling Commission, 1970–1990', 71.

100 Rose and Paleokrassis, 'Compliance with International Environmental Obligations: A Casestudy of the International Whaling Commission', 154. The scientists knew that if they actually did inform the IWC of the scale of the problem, their advice would not be heeded due to the ongoing desire to keep exploiting whale stocks. Jennifer L. Bailey, 'Arrested Development: The Fight to End Commercial Whaling as a Case of Failed Norm Change', *European Journal of International Relations* 14, no. 2 (2008): 295.

101 'International Whaling Statistics 1965' (Oslo: The Committee for Whaling Statistics, 1965), 12. For the 1964–65 season, whaling in BWUs was set at 8000 units, but only 6986.1 BWUs were harvested, down from a peak of 16 433.5 in 1960–61. 'International Whaling Statistics 1965', 12.

responded by reducing quotas and signalling that there would need to be further reductions to ensure a steady supply.[102] The major whaling states of Norway, Japan, the Netherlands and the USSR would only agree to a 'voluntary' catch of 8000 BWUs, however – 3500 higher than first proposed.[103]

By the 1967 Meeting in London, the Joint Parliamentary Under-Secretary of State for Scotland, Mr Buchan, in his opening speech to the IWC, revealed some sobering statistics regarding the parlous state of global whale stocks. In 1937, there were approximately 100 000 blue whales in the oceans. By 1967 there were around 1000.[104] The official BWU catch limit set at that meeting was only 3500, but there were reports that whalers were going after younger whales.[105] By the 1971 Meeting, it was clear that whale stocks were not recovering but were going backwards. In a breakthrough, however, the USA decided, due to domestic pressure, to put eight types of whales on the domestic Endangered Species List and that, as a country, it would no longer issue licences for its whalers to hunt.[106] This defection by the USA from the whalers' faction would prove a critical factor in the normative battles ahead, since its relative economic power in the global system ensured states were wary of crossing it for fear of sanctions or other retributive action.

It was clear that the IWC as an entity was unable to change the exploitationist ways of its members in view of the vested economic interests at play, which were dedicated to preserving the status quo.[107] However, the sea change in the US foreign policy on whaling led them to seek another forum to raise the matter, which they duly did at the 1972 UN Conference on the Human Environment in Stockholm, Sweden.[108] The USA at Committee Two of the

---

102 'Fifteenth Report of the Commission' (London: International Whaling Commission, 1965), 6.

103 Ibid.: 18.

104 'Ninteenth Report of the Commission' (London: International Whaling Commission, 1969), 15.

105 Ibid.; Porter and Brown, *Global Environmental Politics*, 79.

106 D'Amato and Chopra, 'Whales: Their Emerging Right to Life', 38.

107 Epstein maintains that states at this point were already leaning towards a conservationist approach to whaling, but the whaling figures of the period, evidence from scientists and the approach of the IWC do not support this position. Charlotte Epstein, 'The Making of Global Environmental Norms: Endangered Species Protection', *Global Environmental Politics* 6, no. 2 (2006): 51. They were still very much exploiting whale stocks, despite conservationist rhetoric.

108 David D. Caron, 'The International Whaling Commission and the North Atlantic Marine Mammal Commission: The Institutional Risks of Coercion in Consensual Structures', *The American Journal of International Law* 89, no. 1 (1995): 156. The US was the main advocate at the UN Conference on the Human Environment for a ten-year ban on whaling. Scott, 'Intergovernmental Organizations as Disseminators, Legitimators, and Disguisers of Hegemonic Policy Preferences: The

Conference, which examined questions of natural resource management, called for a ten-year moratorium (Resolution 33) on whaling to enable stocks to replenish.[109] States at this point were still advocating the conservation of species for future use. Predictably, whaling nations like Japan automatically opposed such a measure since it was not in their interests. Over their objections the motion was passed 53–0 and included in the conference recommendations despite the IWC's Scientific Committee arguing that any such action was not scientifically valid.[110]

The passing of the motion by such an overwhelming margin indicates that saving the whales was now perceived by much of the world as an issue of critical importance. Further, the IWC as an organization was put on notice that its ineffective approach to date was being challenged from without. D'Amato and Chopra argue it is difficult to pinpoint when measures undertaken to protect the whaling industry started '... to become transformed into protective measures undertaken for the survival and longevity of whales as a species' because it is difficult to measure when global psychological change becomes reflected in legal texts.[111]

---

United States, the International Whaling Commission, and the Introduction of a Moratorium on Commercial Whaling', 594. The move came as a particular shock to the Japanese delegation, since the issue had not been raised at the Preparatory Committee stage. Atsushi Ishii and Ayako Okubo, 'An Alternative Explanation of Japan's Whaling Diplomacy in the Post-moratorium Era', *Journal of International Wildlife Law and Policy* 10, no. 1 (2007): 57. Japan's response was to label the moratorium proposal as 'dramatic and emotional'. Ruffle, 'Resurrecting the International Whaling Commission: Suggestions to Strengthen the Conservation Effort', 4. Charlotte Epstein maintains that the US, which at the forum was under attack, both from domestic and international critics, for other environmental stances, was able to stifle criticism for these policies by introducing the whaling ban. Epstein, 'The Making of Global Environmental Norms: Endangered Species Protection', 43. Tora Skodvin and Steinar Andresen argue that the US acted from state self-interest since it no longer had any whaling operations of its own and given the strength of domestic ENGOs, spearheading the anti-whaling drive was a cheap way to appear environmentally friendly. Tora Skodvin and Steinar Andresen, 'Leadership Revisited', *Global Environmental Politics* 6, no. 3 (2006): 21. Such arguments do a disservice to the strength of moral commitment amongst many in the US, not just ENGOs, to ending whaling. The US did not need to lead the global push for a moratorium; it could merely have supported the end of whaling, yet it choose to become actively involved. Skodvin and Andresen's argument does, however, point to the need to be able to open the black box of domestic considerations, something neoliberal analysis is not able to do, but which constructivism allows, to better understand normative evolution in global negotiations.

[109] Stoett, *The International Politics of Whaling*, 65; Rex Weyler, *Greenpeace: An Insider's Account: How a Group of Journalists, Ecologists and Visionaries Changed the World* (London: Rodale, 2004), 211.

[110] D'Amato and Chopra, 'Whales: Their Emerging Right to Life', 38.

[111] Ibid.: 32.

For the purposes of this book, it is not strictly necessary to know the exact point in time when global change occurred, although, due to the confluence of a number of factors, it can be narrowed down to between the late 1960s and early 1970s.[112] As previously stated, the lack of great whales to catch played a part, as did the USA raising the issue at the United Nations Conference on Environment and Development (UNCED) and the failure of scientists to put in place conservationist programmes. The economic collapse of the whaling industry, due to its products being substituted for others, was critical too. The economic imperative to hunt whales was declining for many IWC member states. A further factor was the ability of the ICRW to alter its composition to allow new members to join, a loophole the newly interested and energized ENGOs were to employ strategically to achieve their aims.[113]

To focus on the economic or institutional arguments is to overlook the moral sea change in general attitudes to the depletion of whale stocks, however. Critically, the issue of over-exploiting whales was becoming of global concern at a time when the global public was becoming more worried and better educated on global environmental issues. This global concern provided both a backdrop and a fillip to ENGO articulations of a preservationist position and in the attempt to persuade the IWC members of the need to alter their behaviour.[114]

## ENGOs AND THE INTERNATIONAL WHALING COMMISSION

Any understanding of the shift in the IWC's operating norm must account for the role played by ENGOs, which in the 1970s pushed a preservationist agenda both within the IWC and to the global society in general. Using the Finnemore and Sikkink norm life-cycle analysis is once again complicated, however, by the fact that it is difficult to identify any central norm entrepreneur.[115] As was

---

112 Ibid.: 37–40.

113 Oberthur, 'The International Convention for the Regulation of Whaling: From Over-exploitation to Total Preservation', 31; Vogler, *The Global Commons: Environmental and Technological Governance*, 50. The flexible nature of the IWC founding charter allowed for new nations to become members even if they were not whaling, or indeed, had never whaled. Porter and Brown, *Global Environmental Politics*, 79.

114 Oberthur, 'The International Convention for the Regulation of Whaling: From Over-exploitation to Total Preservation', 31; Vogler, *The Global Commons: Environmental and Technological Governance*, 50.

115 There are many individuals who helped publicize and drive the anti-whaling campaign, such as Joan McIntrye of Project Jonah and Christine Stevens of the Animal

the case in the Antarctic case study, the ENGOs here seem to have functioned collectively as norm entrepreneurs. Consequently, the structure they operated under provided an organizational platform from which to advocate their preferred norm position.

Initially, ENGOs had little interest in the IWC and they did not even attend until the Fifteenth Meeting when Major K.R.C. Priestley represented the International Society for the Protection of Animals.[116] In the 1960s, the environmental movement's arguments on whaling were in accord with the position of scientists, namely, that conservationist programmes were needed.[117] However, the decision by the IWC in 1970 to allow ENGOs to make statements opened the door for the more forceful articulation of environmental positions to the IWC members.[118] Despite this availability, it was not until Greenpeace, an organization founded on a 'biocentric philosophy that challenged the idea that humans were the supreme beings on the face of the planet', became involved (in the mid-1970s) that a preservationist normative position was put forth.[119] For environmentalists, whales became a potent symbol of the entire environmental movement's commitment to save the planet and bring about a more ecologically aware society.[120]

---

Welfare Institute. Epstein, *The Power of Words in International Relations: Birth of an Anti-whaling Discourse*, 140. However, no one person seems to fit the template of a normative entrepreneur as outlined by Finnemore and Sikkink.

116 'Fifteenth Report of the Commission', 11.

117 Skodvin and Andresen, 'Nonstate Influence in the International Whaling Commission, 1970–1990', 73.

118 Arne Kalland, 'The Anti-whaling Campaigns and Japanese Responses', in *Japanese Position on Whaling and Anti-whaling Campaign* (Tokyo: The Institute of Cetacean Research, 1998), 4; Peterson, 'Whalers, Cetologists, Environmentalists, and the International Management of Whaling', 149. Representatives of Friends of the Earth, the Fauna Preservation Society, the International Society for the Protection of Animals, the International Union for the Conservation of Nature and Natural Resources and the World Wildlife Fund all made statements. 'Twenty-second Report of the Commission' (London: International Whaling Commission, 1972), 20.

119 Peterson, 'Whalers, Cetologists, Environmentalists, and the International Management of Whaling', 184. A Greenpeace calendar from 1990 encapsulates their preservationist position: 'Save the whales. Whales and humans share a common enemy – humankind itself. Our blind greed has pushed the whale to the brink of extinction. We are arguably not far behind. Whales are beautiful and intelligent creatures, each of which has the innate right to survive . . . Greenpeace is committed to ending all commercial whaling once and for all.' Einarsson, 'All Animals Are Equal but Some Are Cetaceans: Conservation and Culture Conflict', 77.

120 Arne Kalland, 'Whale Politics and Green Legitimacy: A Critique of the Anti-whaling Campaign', *Anthropology Today* 9, no. 6 (1993): 5; Scott, 'Intergovernmental Organizations as Disseminators, Legitimators, and Disguisers of Hegemonic Policy Preferences: The United States, the International Whaling Commission, and the Introduction of a Moratorium on Commercial Whaling', 593; Peter J. Stoett, 'Of

ENGOs like Greenpeace, the WWF, the International Fund for Animal Welfare and the Environmental Investigation Agency were able to tap into, articulate and publicize the Western public's horror of whaling.[121] Stoett argues that they were able to 'corner the emotional marketing of the issue', thus gaining the moral highground over their whaling opponents.[122] Their tactics were to use mostly peaceful protests and public information campaigns to highlight the brutality of whaling and its impact on whaling species and persuade the global populace to end whale hunting and reframe the debate from one of exploitation or conservation to preserving all whales in perpetuity.[123]

Their aim was to put pressure on the regime states to change their expectations, behaviours and identities. Kalland maintains that the strictures of the IWC required ENGOs to primarily put their arguments against whaling in scientific terms.[124] While some arguments in certain forums were made in scientific terms, DeSombre argues that utilizing a non-scientific approach was more effective. Rather than use science to advance their position, the ENGOs conducted both an internal and external campaign that focused on brutality, capturing images that promoted their view that whaling was barbarous and should be ended.[125] They linked their arguments to higher values that highlighted the intelligence and uniqueness of whales and argued that they therefore

---

Whales and People: Normative Theory, Symbolism, and the IWC', *Journal of International Wildlife Law and Policy* 8, no. 2 (2005): 153. Arne Kalland argues that ENGOs were successful in creating an ideal of a 'superwhale' which embodied the traits of a number of cetaceous species. ENGOs were also able to cast whalers as easily identifiable villains and argue that, due to whales being allegedly endangered, whaling must stop as a matter of urgency. Kalland, 'Whale Politics and Green Legitimacy: A Critique of the Anti-whaling Campaign', 4–5. Stoett argues, without adducing any evidence, that the reifying of the whale has been highly influential in certain areas (presumably the West), but has had little traction elsewhere. Stoett, 'Of Whales and People: Normative Theory, Symbolism, and the IWC', 154. The growing global level of interest in whale-watching, the growing numbers of members of the IWC, and the reduced number of whalers, however, reveal an ongoing intrigue with whales by many differing cultures that recognize that whales are unique creatures which should not be hunted.

121 Vogler, *The Global Commons: Environmental and Technological Governance*, 50.

122 Stoett, 'Of Whales and People: Normative Theory, Symbolism, and the IWC', 161.

123 Stoett, *The International Politics of Whaling*, 95.

124 Kalland, 'Whale Politics and Green Legitimacy: A Critique of the Anti-whaling Campaign', 4.

125 DeSombre, *The Global Environment and World Politics*, 136. Greenpeace was particularly adept at using visual images to portray the barbarity of whaling practices. Epstein, *The Power of Words in International Relations: Birth of an Anti-whaling Discourse*, 97.

deserved to live unhindered.[126] Framing their approach in this way helped their arguments resonate with the global public in a way scientists had been unable to do thus far. This put increased pressure on states to alter their behaviour. By the early 1980s, over 50 ENGOs were represented at the IWC in an effort to influence debates, either through persuasion, direct action or putting states on notice that the constituents they represented were watching.[127]

The IWC's own downplayed, but still worrying, figures backed up the ENGOs' case that the methods of conserving whales utilized to date were not working. Initially anti-whaling groups concentrated on arguing their case in terms of extinction. However, when nations like Japan were able to argue plausibly that there was no threat of extinction of certain species, for example, minke whales, anti-whaling states and ENGOs shifted ground to argue that it was simply unethical to kill whales.[128]

Initially, the ENGOs made little headway despite the global paradigm shift in thinking on the issue that had begun to manifest itself. At the Twenty-third Meeting in 1971, the IWC members decided that in view of Antarctic minke stocks being relatively unexploited, they could be sustainably harvested annually at the rate of 5000 and that the level of harvesting pelagic whales in the Antarctic should be 1100 BWUs. This was over the objections of Japan, which wanted 2125 whales killed.[129] However, there were signs that the member states knew that their approach to date had not been effective in promoting conservationist practices. For example, upon the advice of the Scientific Committee, the IWC voted to discard the BWU measurement in favour of

---

126 Bailey, 'Arrested Development: The Fight to End Commercial Whaling as a Case of Failed Norm Change', 297; Wapner, 'Horizontal Politics: Transnational Environmental Activism and Global Cultural Change', 48. ENGOs mounted a campaign to educate the global public about the anthropomorphic qualities of whales using photographs, film and audio recordings purporting to show 'evidence' of the intelligence and uniqueness of whales. Some ENGOs pursued direct action methods against whalers and promoted these mini-dramas to global media outlets to emphasize their points. Wapner, 'Horizontal Politics: Transnational Environmental Activism and Global Cultural Change', 48.

127 Oberthur, 'The International Convention for the Regulation of Whaling: From Over-exploitation to Total Preservation', 31. These included such well-known ENGOs as Friends of the Earth, Greenpeace International, the WWF, the Whale Coalition and Whale Project and some lesser-known ENGOs such as the Assembly of Rabbis and the International Transport Workers' Federation statements. 'Annual Report of the International Whaling Commission 31' (London: International Whaling Commission, 1981), 35.

128 Isao Miyaoka, *Legitimacy in International Society: Japan's Reaction to Global Wildlife Preservation* (New York: Palgrave Macmillan, 2004), 90–91.

129 'Twenty-third Report of the Commission' (London: International Whaling Commission, 1973), 9, 19.

fixing catch limits by species for the future. The larger issues of catch size remained off-limits, though.[130]

## THE PUSH TO IMPOSE A MORATORIUM

At the 1972 IWC Meeting in London, Maurice Strong, the UN Secretary-General attended, and put the case to the members that as the UN Conference had resolved that there should be a ten-year moratorium on all commercial whaling, the IWC should address the issue. The United States and the United Kingdom delegations moved a global moratorium motion, arguing that the current assessment of whale stocks was so poor that it would be prudent to stop whaling. Epstein argues that at this point in time, it was clear that the whale had become symbolic of an ecological sensibility in the majority of states.[131] However, subsequent voting patterns in the IWC reveal that such an outlook was not yet fully internalized by the majority of members.

Such a moratorium on whaling was initially perceived as a conservationist measure that would allow stocks to recover over time. However, the Scientific Committee argued successfully that a blanket ban should not be imposed since whaling was better regulated at the individual species level and a moratorium would lead to a reduced research programme on whales and possibly the unregulated taking of whales.[132] Despite a 'green turn' in some key states, the IWC voted the motion down with four countries voting for the proposal and seven against, with three abstentions.[133] To make matters worse, the IWC yet again set quotas that were higher than the previous year's catches.[134]

At both the 1973 and 1974 IWC Meetings, the US delegation, backed by Argentina and France, again called for the moratorium to be implemented, citing new research that whaling populations had been reduced from four to five million down to a few hundred thousand.[135] A similar appeal for a ban, backed by Mexico, was also made to the IWC in 1974.[136] The petitions were

---

130 Ibid.: 9.

131 Epstein, *The Power of Words in International Relations: Birth of an Anti-whaling Discourse*, 106.

132 Laurence Davies, 'The International Whaling Commission: Scientific Fact?', *Environmental Ethics* 1 (2007): 3.

133 'Twenty-fourth Report of the Commission' (London: International Whaling Commission, 1974), 24–5.

134 Weyler, *Greenpeace: An Insider's Account: How a Group of Journalists, Ecologists and Visionaries Changed the World*, 215.

135 'Twenty-fifth Report of the Commission' (London: International Whaling Commission, 1975), 26.

136 'Twenty-sixth Report of the Commission' (London: International Whaling Commission, 1976), 25.

unsuccessful in the face of opposition from Japan and the USSR, who, acting in concert, argued that stocks of fin, sei and sperm whales were still plentiful enough to hunt.[137] However, it did open the door in 1974 for delegates from the Food and Agriculture Organization (FAO), the United Nations Environmental Programme (UNEP) and the IUCN to formally play a part at IWC Meetings as a compromise measure. The participation of these IOs was to prove crucial as it paved the way for alternative non-state arguments to be presented.[138]

At this point in history, the IWC member states were unclear in their language as to what the normative position of the IWC should be. At the 1974 meeting, an amending resolution to the global moratorium on commercial whaling, proposed by Australia and Denmark, argued there was a need 'to *preserve* [my italics] and enhance whale stocks as a resource for future use and taking into consideration the interests of consumers of whale products and the whaling industry as required by the International Convention on Whaling'.[139] The resolution was adopted by the members with the amendment of 'present' being added before the term 'future', demonstrating that the member states were still primarily focused on the short term at the expense of future generations of whalers and whales.[140]

The same IWC Meeting attempted to introduce a new conservationist measure to replace the BWU designation with new terminology. The Australian delegate put forth a selective moratorium schema called the New Management Procedure (NMP). The Procedure placed each whale species into three distinct groupings as designated by the Scientific Committee. It was intended to manage whale stocks by utilizing the idea of 'Maximum Sustainable Yield' (MSY).[141] This programme was implemented in 1975 and reduced quotas for whales to be taken until the beginning of the 1980s.

---

137 Weyler, *Greenpeace: An Insider's Account: How a Group of Journalists, Ecologists and Visionaries Changed the World*, 215.

138 D'Amato and Chopra, 'Whales: Their Emerging Right to Life', 40.

139 'Twenty-sixth Report of the Commission', 25.

140 Ibid.: 26.

141 Ibid.: 11; Rose and Paleokrassis, 'Compliance with International Environmental Obligations: A Casestudy of the International Whaling Commission', 161; Stroud, 'The Ethics and Politics of Whaling', 77. The MSY was calculated by analysing whale stocks according to three criteria. Level one was 'Protected Stocks', where hunting was banned until whale stocks had recovered to acceptable levels. If a whale type was designated 'at or near' MSY levels, they were meant to be maintained at those numbers (Sustained Management Stocks). The third grouping was a situation where whale stocks of a certain species were above the MSY level (Initial Management Stocks); they could be lowered, presumably by hunting, to the designated MSY. 'Twenty-sixth Report of the Commission', 11.

However, the programme was ineffective in preventing the exploitation of whales due to poor biological data on whale species and their decline. This was critical to determining the correct levels to be set.[142]

The creation of the NMP did not achieve its primary conservationist goal. It did improve the tenor of scientific practices that influence decision-making, however. Before, scientific members gave a unanimous 'best estimate' of whale stocks without any concomitant scientific basis. Now, in response to outside pressure from both scientists and ENGOs, committee members created a more open model by which scientific papers were published and criticism sought. This enhanced the credibility of the cetologists as advocates.[143]

Despite being allowed to attend as observers by the IWC in 1977, cetologists were unable to speak with a unified voice, fracturing over questions of 'uncertainty' when applied to whale stocks and whether a moratorium was scientifically justified.[144] By 1982, the Committee was so at war internally between conservationists and preservationists that it was unable to even discuss the content of any paper submitted to it for approval.[145] M.J. Peterson argues that the rift was so wide that cetologists were unable to function as a coherent lobby group between 1974 and 1982, opening the door for ENGOs to become the primary normative advocates on whaling issues.[146]

The ENGOs, building on their successes in altering domestically the whaling policies of states like Australia, Argentina, Uruguay and the Netherlands, were determined to translate their policies into action in the global sphere.[147] As of 1979, ENGOs were able to attend IWC Meetings officially in the dual

---

142 'Twenty-sixth Report of the Commission', 11; Rose and Paleokrassis, 'Compliance with International Environmental Obligations: A Casestudy of the International Whaling Commission', 161; Stroud, 'The Ethics and Politics of Whaling', 77.

143 Skodvin and Andresen, 'Nonstate Influence in the International Whaling Commission, 1970–1990', 72.

144 Davies, 'The International Whaling Commission: Scientific Fact?', 3; Peterson, 'Whalers, Cetologists, Environmentalists, and the International Management of Whaling', 169–70.

145 High North Web, http://highnorth.no/iwc2000/briefings/Moratorium.htm, accessed 25/05/04.

146 Peterson, 'Whalers, Cetologists, Environmentalists, and the International Management of Whaling', 169–70.

147 DeSombre, *The Global Environment and World Politics*, 137–8. For example, in Australia this occurred through domestic electoral pressure winning the support of the Liberal/National government post-1977. In the case of the Netherlands, it had stopped whaling but remained in the IWC, committed to preventing commercial whaling. Peterson, 'Whalers, Cetologists, Environmentalists, and the International Management of Whaling', 175; DeSombre, *The Global Environment and World Politics*, 138.

role of observers, and in some cases, delegation members.[148] Vogler argues that their activities were particularly effective with regard to nations that had stopped whaling (because it was no longer a viable business) as well as with traditional non-whaling states.[149]

The 1977 Meeting in Canberra set a new benchmark for ENGO protests and political actions. The ENGOs were determined to make their point forcibly that whales were not to be hunted. ENGO tactics to pressure the IWC included a coalition of ENGOs, with the Whale and Dolphin Coalition and Project Jonah at the forefront. They placed a 12-metre inflatable white whale in the lake next to the meeting place.[150] At the same meeting, Jean-Paul Forton-Gouin, a wealthy Frenchman who supported the ENGO position, managed to gain entrance to the IWC by funding a Panamian delegation and having himself declared a Commissioner, a tactic which the ENGOs would later use to great effect.[151]

That meeting also saw, for the first time, a ban on aboriginal whaling of the Arctic bowhead whale, the most threatened whale species, though the ban was subsequently lifted (in 1978) at the request of the USA, where domestically indigenous groups had sued, arguing that this infringed their constitutional rights. The United States had been at the vanguard of the moratorium approach, so this perceived climbdown weakened its moral legitimacy. Peru advanced two more moratorium proposals but these were quickly taken off the table when it was obvious they would not be successful.[152]

Despite its lack of moral legitimacy, the US was willing to use its economic power to achieve its goal of imposing a global moratorium on whaling.[153] Under the US Pelly Act provisions, the US certified Chile, Peru and South Korea in 1978 for continued whaling.[154] Under this pressure from a significant

---

148 'Annual Report of the International Whaling Commission 29' (London: International Whaling Commission, 1979), 31.

149 Vogler, *The Global Commons: Environmental and Technological Governance*, 51.

150 'Whale Vote Leaves Japan out in the Cold' (Greenpeace Australia, 1994), on file with the author. The whale was eventually discovered blocking the entrance to the Japanese assembly room, leading to a situation where hotel staff and police destroyed the inflatable whale with knives in front of the media's television cameras in a wonderful publicity coup for the ENGOs.

151 Weyler, *Greenpeace: An Insider's Account: How a Group of Journalists, Ecologists and Visionaries Changed the World*, 472.

152 'Twenty-ninth Report of the International Whaling Commission' (London: International Whaling Commission, 1979), 18.

153 Skodvin and Andresen, 'Nonstate Influence in the International Whaling Commission, 1970–1990', 74.

154 In 1972, the US Congress enacted the Marine Mammal Protection Act (MMPA) that put in place a moratorium on harvesting and importing marine mammal

trading partner, all agreed to be bound by IWC decisions in future. The US also certified Taiwan, which was not a signatory to the ICRW, in 1980. Fearful of alienating a powerful trading partner, Taiwan decided to ban all foreign whaling from its waters and then imposed a ban on whaling in 1981.[155] Despite the US actions, commercial whaling continued and it was evident that whalers were being forced to catch more immature whales. In 1932, the average whale caught weighed 67 tonnes, but by 1978 the average was 20 tonnes.[156]

The reason why the USA chose to become such an ardent protector of whales is not entirely clear from the literature or Annual Reports. While whaling was no longer an economic imperative for the USA, it was not in its economic interest to threaten sanctions against long-standing trading partners. It is arguable that the USA might have gained a 'reputational advantage' in being perceived as a good environmental citizen. As Vogler argues, for states

---

products unless a waiver had been granted. The Pelly amendment of that year also supported the broad strokes of the MMPA, in that it allowed the Secretary of Commerce to certify to the President actions such as sanctions, providing they were not prohibited under the then General Agreement on Tariffs and Trade (GATT), against foreign states that abrogated global nature conservation initiatives. Stephen S. Boynton, '"Whaling Policy" of the United States Yesterday, Today and Tomorrow' (paper presented at the ISANA No. 11, 1994), 2, http://luna.pos.to/whale/jwa–v11–boy.html, accessed 12/08/04. The threat to invoke the Pelly amendment by the US government saw the routine defiance of the IWC by whaling states over the previous decades become a thing of the past by the mid-1970s. In 1979, the Packwood–Magnuson Amendment allowed the US government to limit the amount of fish from the American Exclusive Economic Zone (EEZ) a state could fish if the USA believed the state was not implementing the IWC's decisions. The use of this power has been inconsistently applied to various states depending on US interests. In 1986 and 1987, the USA threatened to use the Amendment to impose sanctions on the Republic of Korea for wanting to initiate its own 'scientific research' mission. The provision was also held over the heads of Peru and Chile to get them to join the IWC. However, the USA did not impose sanctions on Iceland for three years from 1986–88, despite threatening to do so, over the sale of whale meat by Iceland to Japan, probably because the Icelandic government stopped the construction of a North Atlantic Treaty Organization (NATO) base being built in Iceland. In the case where sanctions were actually imposed, on Japan, in 1987 for failing to stop its whale research programme, the US stopped short of banning certain imports because Japan threatened to reduce its imports of American fish, worth US $1.5 billion annually. It is clear that the USA was willing to threaten sanctions and impose limited sanctions to back up its position at the IWC. Rose and Paleokrassis, 'Compliance with International Environmental Obligations: A Casestudy of the International Whaling Commission', 170. However, the fear of losing fishing quotas in the US EEZ led to Japan reluctantly dropping its objection to the whaling ban and signing the Murazawa–Baldridge Pact. Keiko Hirata, 'Why Japan Supports Whaling', *Journal of International Wildlife Law and Policy* 8, no. 2 (2005): 132.

155 DeSombre, *The Global Environment and World Politics*, 134.

156 Aplin, *Global Environmental Crises: An Australian Perspective*, 239.

like the USA, Great Britain and France, opposing the taking of whales was '. . . a relatively cost-free way of establishing "green" credentials . . .' both domestically and internationally, since none of these states had hunted whales for decades.[157] However, the economic costs in pursuing such a path were most likely greater than the potential reputational benefit since it risked trade relations. Thus some other factors beyond economic considerations must have been in play.

Here constructivism holds an analytical edge since it is plausible to surmise that the large and vocal contingent of domestic ENGOs, and their ongoing publicity campaign, had an effect on official USA government policy. It appears that the USA heeded the arguments of ENGOs about the intrinsic worth of whales and incorporated them into its global identity when dealing with other actors, acting as a normative advocate for the preservation of whales. Certainly, we can point to the passing of the Pelly Amendment as evidence that the US was concerned about the protection of whales and was willing to enforce on other states a moral position above strategic economic interests.

By the 1979 Meeting, the number of members attending the IWC had grown to 23, due in part to US economic pressure on non-member states that were whaling to agree to attend.[158] The other factor in the growth of new IWC members was the ENGOs' strategic plan to end commercial whaling by adding new non-whaling members to the IWC in order to tip the balance in favour of a moratorium and usher in a new era of preservationism.[159] Realizing that moral persuasion was not working quickly enough and that whale species were threatened with extinction, ENGOs elected to act strategically. Although never officially confirmed by Greenpeace, a former Greenpeace consultant recounted that there was a plan to add:

> at least six new anti-whaling members from 1978 to 1982 through the paying of annual dues, drafting of membership documents, naming of a commissioner to represent these countries, at an annual cost of more than USD 150,000.[160]

---

[157] Vogler, *The Global Commons: Environmental and Technological Governance*, 51. Epstein agrees with Vogler that for the US signing on to preserve whales was an easy way to burnish environmental credentials. Epstein, 'The Making of Global Environmental Norms: Endangered Species Protection', 47.

[158] 'Annual Report of the International Whaling Commission 30' (London: International Whaling Commission, 1980), 25. Sweden and the Seychelles joined the IWC in 1979. 'Annual Report of the International Whaling Commission 30', 25.

[159] This was possible because, unlike the Antarctic regime, there is no requirement to actually whale for a state to become a member of the IWC, leading to such anomalies as landlocked Switzerland being able to become a member. Vogler, *The Global Commons: Environmental and Technological Governance*, 51–2.

[160] Skodvin and Andresen, 'Nonstate Influence in the International Whaling

However, the neoliberal analysis of Porter and Brown argues that the recruiting of anti-whaling states was actually conducted by the US, Sweden and other conservationist states. They maintain that the Seychelles was recruited, followed by seven other states (not named), all dedicated to the ideal that the oceans and their resources should be viewed as 'the common inheritance of mankind'.[161] While it is impossible to be certain as to which actors put in place a plan to 'stack' the IWC, an examination of the membership list of that period reveals that this is in fact what happened, with countries like Switzerland and the Seychelles joining the IWC.[162] Further, some states joined the IWC to 'fit in' with the global society of states. Materially, there was no reason for Kenya or Finland to join the IWC except to be perceived by other states as a good 'environmental citizen'.[163]

On the balance of probabilities, there appears to be more evidence supporting the contention that this was the ENGO strategy. Alongside the Greenpeace statements already mentioned, it is clear from the record that the Seychelles delegation appointed naturalist Lyall Watson as their plenary delegate and marine biologist Sidney Holt as the scientific committee member, both of whom were linked to ENGOs.[164] Environmentalists maintain they recruited the Seychelles to their cause as a counterbalance to Panama, which had been offered a sugar deal by Japan that ENGOs feared would influence their IWC vote.

In addition to their state infiltration strategy, the ENGOs planned to assemble a three-quarters majority of anti-whaling nations to vote along preservationist lines and ban whaling outright.[165] Since they could not match the incentives on offer by states like Japan, they approached traditionally non-whaling states that they felt would be more easily persuaded that banning whaling was the correct moral decision. One view is that it was in the interests of these non-whaling states to join, because it was an easy way to acquire the kudos of being a good 'green' international citizen without suffering any economic costs.[166] However, doing so ignores the work done by ENGOs to

---

Commission, 1970–1990', 81. DeSombre tells a tale of an IWC secretary who alleges that an '. . . unnamed member state . . . simply signed over the check from an environmental organization to pay its dues'. Skodvin and Andresen, 'Nonstate Influence in the International Whaling Commission, 1970–1990', 81.

161 Porter, Brown and Chasek, *Global Environmental Politics*, 78.

162 'High North Web: Whaling Today', High North Alliance, http://www.highnorth.no/iwc2000/briefings/Whaling.htm.

163 Epstein, *The Power of Words in International Relations: Birth of an Anti-whaling Discourse*, 159.

164 Weyler, *Greenpeace: An Insider's Account: How a Group of Journalists, Ecologists and Visionaries Changed the World*, 540–41.

165 'High North Web: Whaling Today'.

166 Rose, 'International Law and the Status of Cetaceans', 30.

convince both state leaders and domestic populations that whaling was morally repugnant.

The ENGO strategy had the support of both conservationist and preservationist groups initially. The drive to install a moratorium appealed, in the short term, to the 'wise use' philosophy of conservationists to allow stocks to recover, while preservationists were interested in making it permanent. This marriage of convenience could only ever be a short-term strategy, however, because the end goal was different. Eventually there would be a split in direction.[167]

At the 1979 IWC Meeting, Australia announced that its position, both domestically and globally, would be to prohibit whaling in its own waters and oppose the taking of whales in international waters. The reasons cited by the Australian delegation for this new direction were: the probable high intelligence of whales; an understanding that such actions were immoral and methods of taking were inhumane; whaling products were economically substitutable and the survival of some whale species was in doubt, thus requiring a 'change in emphasis from one of the conservative utilization of whale stocks to promoting a policy of banning whaling and protecting whale populations'.[168] The emphasis on the intelligence of whales and the immorality of whaling is an indication that the ENGOs' publicity campaign was affecting state direction and identity.

This meant that two traditional whaling states, the US and Australia, were now staunch advocates of a global commercial whaling moratorium. President Carter of the USA went so far as to send a letter asking the Commission to carry out 'effective action to ensure the survival of the great whales'.[169] Both states put forward proposals for a global moratorium on the taking of whales. The USA argued that a moratorium should be imposed on the commercial taking of whales until the current conservation programme was completely overhauled. It is clear that given the resources put into the global moratorium, this was no mere strategic decision by the USA and Australia, but rather symptomatic of a change in their very identity, from passive bystanders to active norm proponents.

Panama and Sweden proposed that there should be a vote on a commercial ban on the taking of whales (excluding minke whales) by factory ships and land stations. The first moratorium was agreed to, much to the dissatisfaction of Japan and the USSR, but land stations were allowed to continue whaling.[170]

---

167 Peterson, 'Whalers, Cetologists, Environmentalists, and the International Management of Whaling', 155.

168 D'Amato and Chopra, 'Whales: Their Emerging Right to Life', 42.

169 Ibid.: 42

170 'Annual Report of the International Whaling Commission 31', 26.

However, moratorium proponents were able to put in place a recommendation to ask the Technical Committee to examine the possible procedures necessary to put in place a worldwide ban on whaling and the potential hardships inherent in such a move, with a view to reporting back at the next meeting.[171]

The early 1980s saw the idea of a global moratorium become the central issue within the IWC, testing both its identity and future direction. On the one side, there were the states and ENGOs that espoused a preservationist creed and wanted '. . . to ban all whaling, irrespective of whether a particular species is stable or endangered'.[172] Opposing them was the whale industry that, at best, favoured a conservationist perspective, but in reality had been exploiting whales for decades.[173] Such diametrically opposed positions meant whalers and preservationists were unable to reach any accord, leading to an escalation in what became known colourfully as 'the whale wars'.[174]

The Thirty-second Meeting of the IWC had 24 nations (Oman and Switzerland having recently joined) attend, with three moratorium proposals put up: 'a worldwide moratorium, a moratorium on commercial whaling, and a moratorium on sperm whaling'.[175] The US put forward a moratorium amendment to a proposal by France, arguing it was necessary because the IWC had been unable to stop the over-exploitation of whale stocks. The amendment failed to get through, but the vote was close, with 13 votes in favour, nine against and two abstentions.[176] Iceland, Canada and South Africa all spoke of the need for a policy 'which recognises whales as a harvestable resource subject to the needs of conservation'.[177] The global ban that had been promoted by Australia in 1979 and had been considered by a Working Group of the IWC was rejected when the Group's report argued such a course of action would probably have adverse economic effects and '. . . result in the direct loss of over 7,000 jobs and an indirect loss of over 35,000 jobs'.[178]

By the 1981 Meeting, global interest in the issue of whaling saw the number of member nations within the IWC increase by 33 per cent. New members like Costa Rica and India came out in favour of whale preservation.[179] Despite the change in the composition of the members, a United Kingdom proposal for a global ban on the taking of whales at the 1981

---

171 'Annual Report of the International Whaling Commission 30', 33.

172 D'Amato and Chopra, 'Whales: Their Emerging Right to Life', 37.

173 Ibid.: 45.

174 Ibid.: 45.

175 Ibid.: 43.

176 'Annual Report of the International Whaling Commission 31', 18–19.

177 Ibid.: 18.

178 Ibid.: 18–19.

179 'Annual Report of the International Whaling Commission 32' (Cambridge: International Whaling Commission, 1982), 17.

Meeting, which was supported by the United States, Sweden, France and New Zealand, was again not passed, with 16 in favour, eight against and three abstentions.[180] Also unsuccessful were plans for a ban in the North Atlantic, a ban on minke whaling, and a global phase-out of commercial whaling over the next five years. The only proposal to gain any traction was one put up by the United Kingdom, France, the Netherlands and the Seychelles that called for a ban on the culling of sperm whales, which had been hunted in such large numbers that they were virtually extinct.[181]

At the 1982 Meeting in Brighton, UK, more than 37 members of the IWC were present, including eight who had never had whaling industries, and 51 ENGOs.[182] At that meeting, the IWC received five moratorium proposals from the Seychelles,[183] UK, USA, France and Australia.[184] The Seychelles argued for a phase-out of commercial whaling, leading to a negotiated ban, because such an approach would:

> facilitate the adjustment that whaling nations will have to make if the whale is to be saved from extinction, and at the same time [would] safeguard the future work of the Commission as a growing alliance of nations committed to *preserving* [my italics] all cetaceans for posterity.[185]

Japan argued that as per the Scientific Committee Reports, there was no scientific basis for a blanket moratorium since some whale stocks had replenished. Further, in Japan's eyes, such a move would be hypocritical and contrary to the Convention, since it would also ban traditional aboriginal subsistence whaling. Norway, Iceland and the Republic of Korea all opposed the ban on scientific grounds. Uruguay, Mexico, Argentina, Peru, Brazil, Chile and Costa Rica supported a moratorium, but expressed worries over the issue

---

180 Ibid.: 18.

181 Ibid.: 19–20.

182 Vogler, *The Global Commons: Environmental and Technological Governance*, 52.

183 The tiny island nation of the Seychelles ended up playing a critical role in the decision to impose a moratorium on whaling, since the document was introduced by that nation. Behind that flag of convenience were NGOs determined to push their own preservationist agenda at the IWC Meeting. The Seychelles delegation included Sidney Holt, a key player in the Save-the-Whale movement who had been chairman of Greenpeace UK and had been employed for ten years by the International Fund for Animal Welfare (IFAW). In partnership with the director of Greenpeace International, David McTaggart, he had worked tirelessly to recruit new, non-whaling nations to the IWC. 'High North Web: Whaling Today'.

184 'Annual Report of the International Whaling Commission 33' (Cambridge: International Whaling Commission, 1983), 20–21.

185 D'Amato and Chopra, 'Whales: Their Emerging Right to Life', 45.

of the sovereign rights of coastal states to access their resources within their 200-mile exclusive economic zones. Australia argued that a moratorium would best balance the competing interests of the whaling industry and the conservation of whales.[186]

The amendment was eventually passed 25 to seven, with five abstentions. The deciding vote was cast by Spain, till then a whaling state. Given the overwhelming numbers voting for the ban, it is arguable that a 'critical mass' of states had agreed to be bound by the preservationist norm.[187] The imposed blanket ban was not species specific and applied regardless of the status of individual whale populations.[188] Holt characterizes the ban as being more of a 'pause', where catch limits were set at zero until overturned by the members.[189] Whaling states were granted a three-year grace period to phase out their hunts to lessen the economic impact of the moratorium (to comply with the IWC Preamble). However, the ban exempted aboriginal subsistence whaling (particularly of the endangered bowhead species, hunted by the Inuit in the Arctic regions).[190] Paragraph 10 was amended to read:

> Notwithstanding the other provisions of paragraph 10, catch limits for the killing for commercial purposes of whales from all stocks for the 1986 coastal and the 1985/86 pelagic seasons and thereafter shall be zero. This provision will be kept under review, based upon the best scientific advice, and by 1990 at the latest the Commission will undertake a comprehensive assessment of the effects of this decision on whale stocks and consider modification of this provision and the establishment of other catch limits. (Paragraph 10(e), IWC Schedule, February 1983)[191]

The ENGO twin strategies of bringing in new non-whaling member-states and publicizing the issue to the world, combined with the economic pressure applied by the USA, tipped the balance within the IWC. With the passing of the commercial whaling moratorium in 1982, to become operational in 1986, preservationism became ascendant, if not totally dominant, over both conservationism and exploitation. However, it was not a clean victory, as the moratorium was confined to commercial whaling and it allowed exemptions if registered with the IWC, which countries like Japan and Norway were quick

---

186 'Annual Report of the International Whaling Commission 33', 21.

187 Bailey, 'Arrested Development: The Fight to End Commercial Whaling as a Case of Failed Norm Change', 298.

188 Davies, 'The International Whaling Commission: Scientific Fact?', 3.

189 Sidney J. Holt, 'Whaling: Will the Phoenix Rise Again?', *Marine Pollution Bulletin* 54 (2007): 1081.

190 D'Amato and Chopra, 'Whales: Their Emerging Right to Life', 46.

191 'Annual Report of the International Whaling Commission 33', 40.

to exploit.[192] Japan immediately lodged an objection under Article V(3) which allowed them to legally continue whaling, while Canada, an ardent whaler, left the IWC entirely.[193]

Using the Finnemore and Sikkink analysis to gauge where in the norm cycle preservation took hold, it appears the tipping point (more than one-third of members had signed on) and the cascade occurred at the same meeting when the moratorium passed. It is arguable that certain states (such as the USA and Australia) had internalized the norm of preservation as part of their state identity. However, many other states were neutral or, to use neoliberal terminology, merely bystanders. Other states with a traditional culture of whaling tied into their state identity, such as Japan, Norway and Iceland, adamantly opposed the ban and were resolved to work against it actively.

Peterson maintains that the passing of the moratorium, while a victory for environmentalists in general, may not have been one for those pushing a preservationist agenda, since it '. . . can be read as either conservationist or preservationist in inspiration'.[194] The arguments made by the preservationist proponents within the IWC also reflect this ambivalence. Preservationist proponents' arguments were never advanced in terms of preserving whales.[195] Rather, these arguments were defended within the IWC as providing a chance for whaling stocks to rebound, which left the door open for whaling to continue at a later date, which is consistent with a conservationist position.[196] This, however, looks more like a strategic decision by proponents to argue in terms they knew would be acceptable to the other delegates. Proposing an indefinite ban would most likely not have been accepted or would have split the IWC to the point where many states would leave, destroying the regime.

There were many reasons why states were willing to stop commercial whaling at this particular point. From a self-interested perspective, the fact that for many states whaling had become a marginalized economic activity, with a declining demand globally for whale products, certainly played its part. The

192 Ibid. Interestingly, when the moratorium was finally introduced, some ENGOs from the USA opposed it, fearing it was too weak to prevent commercial whaling under other pretexts. Miyaoka, *Legitimacy in International Society: Japan's Reaction to Global Wildlife Preservation*, 75. Time will tell if they were correct.

193 Reeves, 'The Origins and Character of "Aboriginal Subsistence" Whaling: A Global Review', 90; Ruffle, 'Resurrecting the International Whaling Commission: Suggestions to Strengthen the Conservation Effort', 4.

194 Peterson, 'Whalers, Cetologists, Environmentalists, and the International Management of Whaling', 148.

195 Miyaoka, *Legitimacy in International Society: Japan's Reaction to Global Wildlife Preservation*, 92.

196 Peterson, 'Whalers, Cetologists, Environmentalists, and the International Management of Whaling', 148.

inexorable laws of supply and demand allowed states to change their stance from pro- to anti-whaling at minimal cost to their interests.[197] Further, many non-whaling states supported a moratorium because of domestic political pressure to appease voters, who thanks to the ENGO publicity campaign, perceived whaling as a morally repugnant activity. Voting for the moratorium cost domestic governments little strategically and appeased domestic voters.[198]

One must also consider the interest many states had of being seen as a good international citizen, with the concomitant reputational advantage to states of being perceived as good global environmental citizens. Further, US threats to impose sanctions under the Pelly Act had an important effect in convincing reluctant states to adhere to the moratorium or risk losing lucrative export markets.[199]

All these interest-based arguments ignore the fact that for many states and their citizens there was great concern about declining whale numbers and that many states acknowledged that whaling had been badly regulated. Also a proper conservationist ethic had not taken hold either within the IWC or in the broader world.[200] Further, it can be seen that some states (for example, Australia, the USA and the Netherlands) had come to accept that whales had an intrinsic right to live. This altered their identity within global society. For these states and most of the ENGOs, whaling was a barbaric practice and the taking of even one whale was anathema. These states have been at the forefront of strengthening the commercial moratorium in the hopes of stopping the taking of any whales. By voting for the moratorium, the preservationist states internalized a new moral reality, played out on the global stage of the IWC, that killing whales was wrong and was to be opposed.[201]

The moratorium at least put an end to the large-scale exploitation of whale stocks even if it did not end whaling altogether. Rather, the normative debate appeared to have become one of proponents advocating conservation, or proselytizing a preservationist position. The moratorium subsequently saw a recovery in some whale species in certain areas. For example, in the cases of Southern California grey, blue and humpback whales, stocks rebounded. One

---

197 DeSombre, *The Global Environment and World Politics*, 140; Stoett, *The International Politics of Whaling*, 59.

198 Oberthur, 'The International Convention for the Regulation of Whaling: From Over-exploitation to Total Preservation', 35.

199 DeSombre, *The Global Environment and World Politics*, 136; Oberthur, 'The International Convention for the Regulation of Whaling: From Over-exploitation to Total Preservation', 33.

200 DeSombre, *The Global Environment and World Politics*, 139, 141.

201 Epstein, *The Power of Words in International Relations: Birth of an Anti-whaling Discourse*, 66.

of the most threatened species, the bowhead whale, has seen a fivefold increase from 1500 in 1976 to 7500 by the mid-1990s. North Atlantic humpback whales increased in numbers from 5505 in the 1980s to approximately 11 000 by the mid-1990s.[202]

## AFTER THE WHALING MORATORIUM

The granting of the moratorium did not end the normative contestation within the IWC and globally as to the standard of behaviour to be applied to whales. In many ways, the debates became more acrimonious as positions hardened. The contest also shifted to other normative battlegrounds both within the IWC and without. For the pro-whaling states, the battle to define the whaling regime was not over and they sought to '. . . refocus the whaling debate from a philosophical dilemma to the practical question of sustainable activity'.[203] While preservationism is now ascendant, it hangs by a slim thread that is challenged yearly at IWC Meetings by those seeking to roll back the ban. The tactics and strategies used by the ENGOs to bring about a moratorium have now been copied by states like Japan to end the ban.

Japan for the last two decades has led, in neoliberal terms, a new veto coalition, comprising states that allegedly have been offered inducements to vote against preservationist programmes. The whaling regime at this point can be modelled in game-theoretic terms in a number of ways. The actions of the coalition of pro-whaling states indicate that the whaling regime is in a situation of 'asymmetric deadlock', with whaling states having no intention of cooperating with other states to preserve whales. The same model could be applied to the preservationist camp as well. Neither side has approached the negotiating table with a willingness to compromise because no diminution of position is possible given the moral and cultural belief structures at stake. These (a constructivist would argue) cannot be reducible to material interests.

From the perspective of many states, the regime could also be modelled as an example of an 'assurance game'. Most states are willing to comply with the moratorium provided they see that other states are not whaling and thus not deriving any economic benefit. As can be observed when examining the history of the IWC, after the ban was put in place, this kind of 'play' was constantly reiterated across a host of different issues (examined below) without reaching a conclusion satisfactory to either side.

---

202 Raymond L. Bryant and Sinead Bailey, *Third World Political Ecology: An Introduction* (New York: Routledge, 1996), 3–4.

203 Fletcher, 'The International Whaling Regime and U.S. Foreign Policy', 224.

If examined from a constructivist perspective, however, in many ways Japan and its allies have become norm entrepreneurs for conservation, arguing for its entrenchment as the dominant norm in the regime. Given this coalition's previous behaviour, there is a need to be wary about the genuineness of its professed desire to conserve whales. However, it is arguable that these states have learned that their previous exploitative behaviour has led to this outcome, and have therefore learned to be genuine in their willingness to whale according to conservationist mores. The fact that this group had violated the norm of preservation does not detract from the veracity of the conservationist norm. It still exerts a powerful effect on many states, defining their appropriate behaviour and constituting their identities, as well as the practices of many whalers.

To further their own interests in continued whaling, states like Norway have left the IWC in an attempt to create their own alternative whaling organization, albeit with limited success. Preservationist states and ENGOs have attempted to widen the moratorium into a comprehensive ban on all whaling by creating whale sanctuaries and encouraging whale-watching enterprises, while other states like Japan campaign to put in place ostensibly conservationist programmes. Despite the global social censure directed at Japan and its allies for refusing to submit to the discursive outcome of the ban, the coalition continues to flout the accepted standard in order to carry out 'scientific whaling'.

Constructivism also allows a deeper, more contextual examination of the pro-whaling states' interests in continuing whaling. Japan's intransigent attitude to ending whaling is puzzling to many, particularly in the West. The whaling industry contributes little to the overall economy and internationally Japan pays a heavy price for its position. Thus, regime theory has a hard time explaining the Japanese position, since it is not a response to hegemonic threats nor is it in Japan's material interests to hold out.[204] The traditional constructivist position is also problematic as an explanatory device, since Japan has as yet failed to adhere to the anti-whaling norm through global socialization.[205]

K. Hirata's work offers insight into Japan's traditions and cultural practices, however, pertaining to whaling and the domestic impediments to change. At the domestic level, Japanese political and cultural structures have prevented normative entrepreneurs against whaling from gaining any purchase, as they are not part of the domestic decision-making process. Consequently, they have been unable to gain the access necessary to dissuade policy leaders and the

---

[204] K. Hirata, 'Beached Whales: Examining Japan's Rejection of an International Norm', *Social Science Japan Journal* 7, no. 2 (2004): 177–8.

[205] Ibid.: 178.

general public to abandon their position to date.[206] Further, Japanese society members have traditionally equated whales to fish, and the eating of whale-meat as no different to the Western custom of eating beef or pork.[207]

The cultural significance of eating such food, combined with a proud history of whaling, has become woven into the national identity of these states and is not easily discarded. States like Norway and Japan perceive whaling as not just a commercial imperative, but rather as a question of protecting their traditional and legal rights to access such culturally significant resources. These factors must be borne in mind when examining their behaviour at the IWC.[208] The remainder of this chapter will examine key actors and issue flash-points in the whaling saga in order to determine whether the norm of preservationism has strengthened or weakened since the implementation of the commercial ban on whaling. Further, it will seek to analyse the behaviour of the key veto actors, particularly Japan, through the lens of norms and historical traditions intrinsic to that culture, as an alternative explanation to material arguments for their desire to continue whaling.

As mentioned previously, Japan immediately registered an objection to the moratorium on the grounds that the ban was not justified given the available scientific evidence, a theme it has consistently pushed since then.[209] Of the six remaining active whaling states at that time, three filed formal objections to the ban (Norway, Peru and the USSR), while three other nations, together with one of the absentees (Brazil, Chile, Iceland and the Republic of Korea), decided at that point to take no action. Peru decided at the meeting to withdraw its objection, leaving only the three whaling nations of Norway, Japan and the USSR as formal objectors. This made the latter increasingly isolated.[210]

The United States of America then informed Norway and Japan that under the Pelly Amendment it would seek to impose an embargo, banning the importation of their fish products to force them to comply with the IWC decision. The USA was unable to use such pressures on the USSR, since the US did not import fish products from the Soviet Union.[211] The threats by the USA to

206 Ibid.: 179.

207 Ibid.: 193. The Japanese culturally see whales as fish rather than mammals and this influences their approach to IWC negotiations. Andrew R. Miller and Nives Dolsak, 'Issue Linkages in International Environmental Policy: The International Whaling Commission and Japanese Development Aid', *Global Environmental Politics* 7, no. 1 (2007): 70.

208 Stroud, 'The Ethics and Politics of Whaling', 56.

209 'Annual Report of the International Whaling Commission 34' (Cambridge: International Whaling Commission, 1984), 13.

210 D'Amato and Chopra, 'Whales: Their Emerging Right to Life', 46.

211 Ibid.: 46.

impose sanctions were not enacted, however, since they were found to be illegal under the GATT – a decision that eliminated a key weapon of coercion used to force states to abide by IWC decisions.[212]

At the Thirty-sixth Meeting in 1984, Brazil and the Republic of Korea agreed to amend their stated position and support the ban. Japan renewed its objections, however, based on technical, economic (particularly in relation to the viability of coastal communities) and legal grounds, with the USSR also objecting on technical grounds. Japan altered its position at the 1985 Meeting. While informally objecting on technical grounds, to avoid upsetting the United States of America, it withdrew its formal objection to the ban. The Philippines, however, which had previously argued for continued scientific research on whales, now announced it was intending to cull whale stocks that were not endangered.[213]

At the same time, the Soviet Union declared that whilst it would, for technical reasons, temporarily discontinue commercial whaling in the Antarctic, it would uphold its objection to the ban, arguing that the decision had been illegal.[214] In the eyes of many, the IWC was rapidly becoming an anti-whaling body. The new member state of India, through its Prime Minister Rajiv Gandhi, argued in a missive to the Commission that India wished to have a seat at the Commission, despite not whaling, to 'join other nations . . . in their endeavor to save this most fascinating and remarkable member of our planet's living fraternity'.[215]

By 1986, Brazil had agreed to abide by the moratorium and Japan had decided to stop its commercial whaling activities by 1987. The five-year moratorium on commercial whaling was re-examined at the 1990 Meeting, but the Commission refused to change the moratorium's conditions. D'Amato and Chopra believe that from this point in time, commercial whaling of the larger whale species had become obsolete. The situation is more complex and not settled, however. States like Japan, Iceland and Norway continue to hunt using the pretext of scientific research, or alternatively, refuse to recognize the authority of the IWC, thereby casting themselves as rogue states in the eyes of much of the world.[216]

---

212 Aplin, *Global Environmental Crises: An Australian Perspective*, 241.

213 D'Amato and Chopra, 'Whales: Their Emerging Right to Life', 47.

214 Ibid.: 47.

215 Ibid.: 47.

216 Ibid.: 48. For example, Norway stated in 1993 that it would restart the harvesting of minke whales despite the IWC moratorium. Aplin, *Global Environmental Crises: An Australian Perspective*, 241. Norway continues to flout the IWC moratorium and continues whaling, taking approximately 600 minke whales yearly. Norway sets itself an annual quota in a bid to be considered conservationist, which in 2001 was 549 minke whales, which yield approximately 730 tons of meat and sell for about US $2.9 million. Bryant, 'Biodiversity and Conservation: A Hypertext Book'.

Japan has emerged as the leader of a veto coalition determined to roll back the moratorium, prevent the ban widening and replace it with conservationist whaling practices.[217] It appears to have learnt from its ENGO opponents' strategies, in that it has been accused by ENGOs of attempting to 'stack' the IWC by using the leverage of potential fisheries markets and aid money to convince South Pacific and Caribbean states to join the organization, despite global criticism.[218]

Such allegations have been widely reported, such as the case of the Solomon Islands and the Caribbean states reputedly receiving 'aid money' to support Japan at the IWC.[219] The two states' voting records certainly indicate a pro-whaling bias, but this is not conclusive evidence in and of itself.[220] The Japanese have traditionally denied such aid is linked to votes, and accusations of this nature are impossible to prove, given that Japanese aid is distributed to over 150 states.[221] However, in 2003 the Japanese Ambassador to New Zealand stated baldly its diplomatic game:

> [T]o defend our own stance we have to persuade our friends . . . We are an international player so it is very natural for the Japanese government to ask for votes . . . overseas aid is very good leverage so they can support our position in general, including whaling.[222]

Japan has also learnt to tailor its message to become more persuasive, as well as being selective about its intended audience. For example, it is exploit-

---

[217] Andrew Darby, *Harpoon: Into the Heart of Whaling* (Crows Nest, NSW: Allen & Unwin, 2007), 212.

[218] Matthew Denholm, 'Push to Harpoon Ban on Whaling', *The Australian*, 21 January 2005, 3.

[219] Gillespie, *Whaling Diplomacy: Defining Issues in International Environmental Law*, 433–4.

[220] *Greenpeace Australia Magazine*, Spring 1994. On file with the author, 3. During the 2005 IWC Meeting, there were again many allegations of Japan attempting to buy votes. The Solomon Islands National Planning and Aid Coordination Minister, Fred Fono, reportedly agreed to support the Japanese position after meeting the Japanese delegation, who offered the Solomon Islands an extended aid package of US $39 million. Peter Alford, 'Whaling Ban Faces Extinction as Japan Splashes Cash', *The Australian*, 20 June 2005, 4. Japan has recently been discovered paying the IWC's annual levies on behalf of Grenada and the Solomon Islands. In the case of Grenada, support for the Japanese position was bought, according to Grenada's former IWC Commissioner, Michel Baptiste, in exchange for support of Grenada's fishing industry. Clay Lucas, 'Evidence of Whale Vote Bribery', *The Age*, 18 July 2005, 4.

[221] Peter Alford, 'Defeated Whalers Sense Tide Turning', *The Australian*, 25–6 June 2005, 16.

[222] Gillespie, *Whaling Diplomacy: Defining Issues in International Environmental Law*, 435.

ing the fear of developing states that a permanent ban on whaling will inevitably lead to bans on other marine resources. Such resources are crucial to many developing states' economies and such arguments can be extremely persuasive, since they strike at the heart of states' economic interests.[223]

Japanese attempts to convince states to support their position at the IWC had an initial success (the St Kitts and Nevis Declaration in 2006), but by the 2007 Meeting preservationist forces had also recruited heavily and an impasse was again reached.[224] Despite the attempts by Japan to overturn the moratorium, it has continued to be applied since Japan has not yet rallied the two-thirds majority to overturn it.[225] Japan is playing a long diplomatic game to achieve its objectives, knowing that it will take at least three years to overturn the ban even if it gets the votes at the next meeting in Portugal in 2009.[226]

## CONTESTING THE DEFINITION OF 'CONSERVATION' IN THE ICRW

The Japan-led veto coalition has also tried to change the terms of the debate linguistically in arguing for a clearly understood definition of the term 'conservation'. They seek not only to define and limit the debate over the direction of the IWC to terms favourable to themselves, but in constructivist terms, to reshape the material world by influencing the social world. If Japan and its allies can limit and define the normative contest within the IWC as one of only debating conservationist mores and practices, it knows that it has an excellent chance of eventually being allowed to whale legally again. At the Thirty-sixth Meeting of the IWC in 1984 in Argentina, Japan and the USSR both argued that the 1946 Convention clearly spoke of the consumptive uses of whales to ensure a greater emphasis on conservation of whale stocks and greater IWC policy responsiveness.[227]

---

223 Alford, 'Defeated Whalers Sense Tide Turning', 16.

224 Mike Iliff, 'The International Whaling Regime Post 2007', *Marine Policy* 32 (2008): 526.

225 The issue of the moratorium was apparently not offically raised at the 2008 Meeting. Rather, Japan is pinning its hopes on a breakthrough in discussions on the future of the IWC (see following sections). Currently, there are 84 members of the IWC, with both preservationists and pro-whalers actively seeking allies. IWC member countries and Commissioners, http://iwcoffice.org/commission/members.htm, accessed 12/01/09.

226 Alford, 'Defeated Whalers Sense Tide Turning', 16.

227 'Annual Report of the International Whaling Commission 35' (Cambridge: International Whaling Commission, 1985), 20.

At the 1986 IWC Meeting, the USSR proposed – supported by representatives from Norway, Iceland and Japan – that the 1946 Convention be revised to better reflect both scientific research and conservation mores. New Zealand, representing the anti-whaling forces, opposed the need for such a review, noting that the Convention had proved capable of evolution to meet 'changing conditions', a view supported by the USA, Sweden and West Germany. Since there was no consensus achieved, the Chairman decided to retain the item on the agenda for the next meeting to allow governments to evaluate the matter further.[228] In 1987, the USSR proposed that a Special Working Group be established to consider the issue, one that would meet in November/December 1987 and was agreed to by the members.[229]

The tensions between the conservationist-arguing states and the preservationist-leaning nations flared again at the Thirty-ninth Annual Meeting, when the Working Group to Examine Questions Related to the Operation of the International Convention for the Regulation of Whaling, created at the previous meeting, met.[230] Issues raised included the operation of the Convention and whether it needed to be revised, in particular whether the Convention should focus more on conservation. However, other members (not identified in the Chairman's Report), argued that the current Convention was sufficient and there was no pressing need to alter the Convention at this time, if ever.[231] The Working Group met annually, but never seemed to make progress in its stated aims, due to intransigence by preservationist states. By the Forty-second Meeting, the USSR was complaining that the issue was not being debated seriously and that the progress to date was unacceptable.[232]

At the Forty-third Meeting, the issue of the operation of the Convention was revisited. Again the same fault lines were present, with some states arguing that the IWC had departed significantly from the original Convention. The anti-whaling coalition of states argued that change was unwarranted, since

---

228 'Annual Report of the International Whaling Commission 37' (Cambridge: International Whaling Commission, 1987), 10.

229 'Annual Report of the International Whaling Commission 38' (Cambridge: International Whaling Commission, 1988), 10.

230 'Annual Report of the International Whaling Commission 39' (Cambridge: International Whaling Commission, 1989), 10. The membership of the Committee comprised both preservationist and conservationist states, including representatives from Australia, Brazil, People's Republic of China, Denmark, Iceland, Japan, Republic of Korea, Mexico, New Zealand, Norway, Seychelles, Spain, Sweden, Switzerland, USSR, UK and the USA. 'Annual Report of the International Whaling Commission 39', 10.

231 'Annual Report of the International Whaling Commission 39', 10.

232 'Annual Report of the International Whaling Commission 41' (Cambridge: International Whaling Commission, 1991), 11.

there were no fundamental changes in circumstances or to existing international law.[233] After much debate at the plenary discussion, it was agreed to create terms of references for the Working Group to enable it to initiate a thorough review and with the advice of experts, to ascertain those parts of the Schedule that needed altering. It was to report to the IWC by 31 October 1991.[234] Japan continued to press for adherence to conservation protocols, but at the 1993 Meeting in Kyoto it was dealt a severe blow when the Working Group decided it could not proceed until the Revised Management Scheme (RMS) was implemented. To this day, this has not occurred.[235]

Preservationist states have attempted in response to control the terms of the debate by using conservation rhetoric against whaling states to undermine their arguments. Both sides to the debate have used conservationist rhetoric for their own ends, rather than actually discussing exploitation and preservation. The IWC Meeting in Mexico in 2003 saw Mexico introduce a draft resolution, the Berlin Initiative on Strengthening the Conservation Agenda of the International Whaling Commission. It aimed to create a Conservation Committee (with appropriate funding) composed of all Contracting Parties to the Convention, to provide the institutional structure to examine conservation issues and to overcome what Mexico saw as the 'stagnation' of the IWC and install a conservationist ethos.[236]

Australia argued that such a resolution was a milestone in the evolution of the organization. New Zealand posited that it had the potential to meet the obligations imposed by the Preamble to protect whale stocks for future generations. The US, which was in support of the proposal, maintained that the proposal was not necessarily anti-whaling and supported the draft. Ireland hoped that such an entity could reinvigorate the moribund Revised Management Scheme debate.[237] However, the traditional whaling states, and their allies, all spoke out against the proposal, arguing it was an attempt to

---

[233] 'Annual Report of the International Whaling Commission 42' (Cambridge: International Whaling Commission, 1992), 11.

[234] Ibid., Appendix 1, 46.

[235] 'Annual Report of the International Whaling Commission 44' (Cambridge: International Whaling Commission, 1994), 11.

[236] 'Annual Report of the International Whaling Commission 53' (Cambridge: International Whaling Commission, 2003), 7–8; Gail Osherenko, 'Environmental Justice and the International Whaling Commission: Moby-Dick Revisited', *Journal of International Wildlife Law and Policy* 8, no. 2 (2005): 237. Mexico moved the motion on behalf of the co-sponsors Australia, Brazil, Finland, France, Germany, Ireland, Italy, Kenya, Monaco, the Netherlands, New Zealand, Portugal, San Marino, South Africa, Spain, Sweden, the UK and the US. 'Annual Report of the International Whaling Commission 54' (Cambridge: International Whaling Commission, 2004), 7.

[237] 'Annual Report of the International Whaling Commission 53', 8–9.

prevent whaling.[238] Denmark was concerned that the resolution did not consider the role played by the North Atlantic Marine Mammals Commission (NAMMCO) (a rival entity set up by Scandinavian whaling states) and gave too much power to NGOs to set IWC priorities. Iceland, Norway, the Republic of Korea, Antigua and Barbuda, China, Dominica, the Russian Federation, Japan, Grenada, St Lucia and Morocco were all opposed to the creation of such an entity, arguing that it would '. . . create a radical and lasting change in the character of the IWC'.[239]

However, the resolution was adopted with 25 votes for, and 20 against. The Chair argued in closing the debate that 'the establishment of the Conservation Committee would not solve the problems within [sic] IWC' and stressed the need to continue to work to find a balance between conservation and preservation, without directly referring to this balance in these terms.[240] The problems the Chair alluded to appear to be intractable, with neither faction willing to engage in a legitimate dialogue.

At the Fifty-sixth Meeting, the Conservation Committee met for the first time. The Annual Report states that the IWC delegates all agreed they 'were committed to conservation', but the term is not analysed in any coherent way. While the Committee did discuss the issue in conservationist terminology (for example, what constitutes 'sustainable use'), it felt it could not give a definitive answer at this point in time. Other pro-whaling states were concerned the term would not be examined in the context of achieving 'the orderly development of the whaling industry', which for them was the key aim.[241]

At the same meeting, Japan attempted to regain the policy initiative by giving a presentation to the other members under the heading 'The Centennial of Antarctic Whaling – From the History of Over-harvesting to the Creation of New Sustainable Whaling' that focused on learning from what Japan regarded as past mistakes in the region to create a new sustainable regime. The paper provided a contextual argument highlighting Japan's traditional whaling culture and how various legal instruments state the need for the full utilization of whales. It concluded with an analysis of how whaling should be conducted in the future and how any Revised Management Procedure (RMP) should

---

[238] Osherenko, 'Environmental Justice and the International Whaling Commission: Moby-Dick Revisited', 237. At this time, the veto coalition included Denmark, Iceland, Norway, the Republic of Korea, Antigua and Barbuda, China, Dominica, Russia, Japan, Grenada, St Lucia and Morocco. 'Annual Report of the International Whaling Commission 53', 9.

[239] 'Annual Report of the International Whaling Commission 53', 9–10.

[240] Ibid.: 10–11.

[241] 'Annual Report of the International Whaling Commission 55' (Cambridge: International Whaling Commission, 2005), 64–5.

reflect the ICRW's original objectives. It defended the practice of scientific whaling as necessary and argued that the whales taken should be fully 'utilized' by being used as a food source. Japan requested that this item be placed on the agenda for future meetings. Although the Chair acquiesced, to date the issue has not proceeded any further.[242]

At the 2006 Meeting, Japan, with a view to 'normalizing' relations within the IWC, responded with the 'St Kitts and Nevis Declaration', which demanded a return to a literal interpretation of the ICRW and its conservationist principles (with an emphasis on the orderly development of the whaling *industry*), as well as a rejection of the ban.[243] Japan knew if it passed this motion it could argue that a majority (but not a three-quarters majority) wanted a resumption of commercial whaling. The vote was on a knife edge until the Senegalese Commissioner turned up to vote (curiously, afterwards the Senegalese President said he was unaware of the vote). The vote was 33 for, 32 against and one abstention, and, for the first time in 14 years since the Southern Ocean Sanctuary vote, the preservationist forces had lost.[244] After the St Kitts conference, Japan set up a 'normalization meeting' to put whaling on a 'proper course' which was shunned by preservationist states and a report by the Chair was submitted to the IWC, but there has been no action on the issues discussed to date, since it did not address the fundamental disagreements between the two camps.[245]

At the 2007 Meeting in Anchorage, Alaska, the Conservation Committee met, but again could not agree on establishing the terms of reference, with the Chair deciding to try to deal with the issue before the next meeting in Chile.[246] The Committee met in Chile in 2008, but again did not consider the RMS issue.[247]

---

242 Ibid.: 67–8.

243 'Annual Report of the International Whaling Commission 58', Resolution 2006–1, 1; Mike Iliff, 'Normalization of the International Whaling Commission', *Marine Policy* 32 (2008): 333.

244 'Annual Report of the International Whaling Commission 58', 64–5; Darby, *Harpoon: Into the Heart of Whaling*, 243–4; Iliff, 'Normalization of the International Whaling Commission', 336.

245 'Conference for the Normalization of the International Whaling Commission', IWC/59/7, 13–15 February 2007, Tokyo Japan; Darby, *Harpoon: Into the Heart of Whaling*, 245; Mike Iliff, 'Modernisation of the International Convention for the Regulation of Whaling', *Marine Policy* 32 (2008): 403.

246 'Annual Report of the International Whaling Commission 59', 11.

247 'Revised Draft Agenda, Conservation Committee, 60th Annual Meeting of the International Whaling Commission', IWC/60/CC1Rev. http://www.iwcoffice.org/_documents/, accessed 01/09/08.

Instead the issues facing the Conservation Committee have been subsumed under the broader remit of the Intersessional Meeting on the Future of the International Whaling Commission, which met for the first time in London in March 2008.[248] The Intersessional Meeting, hosted by the Chair of the IWC, Bill Hoggarth of the USA, is tasked with overcoming the polarized nature of the IWC and putting forward suggestions on improving practice and procedures, with the overall aim of rebuilding trust in the organization.[249] The IWC has agreed to continue negotiations on the substantive issues raised by the Intersessional Meeting.[250]

Given the impasse at the last few meetings between conservationist and preservationist forces, it seems unlikely that this mechanism can resolve the normative tensions between the two camps. Pro-whaling states have been unable to get anti-whaling states to agree to their preferred version of conservation, either rhetorically or in practice. As neither side was willing to compromise, the increasingly bitter debate has switched to other issues.

## WHALING AND SOCIO-ECONOMIC CONSIDERATIONS

Since the middle 1980s, Japan has attempted to persuade other states that the whaling moratorium has affected its citizens' spiritual, psychological, physical and cultural well-being and that the IWC owes a 'moral debt' to those people affected by the decision. In 1985, the IWC constituted an ad hoc Working Group to investigate the domestic socio-economic impact of the zero catch limit.[251] A report was submitted by the Chair of the Working Group (T.M.M. Quintella of Brazil) at the 1986 Meeting, and was adopted by the IWC, which allowed states that had prohibited whaling to make submissions on its impact using three criteria: economic input factors, economic output factors and employment.[252]

---

248 'Annotated Provisional Agenda, 60th Annual Meeting of the International Whaling Commission', Santiago, Chile, 23–7 June 2008. C:\IWC60/60-2. http://www.iwcoffice.org/_documents/, accessed 01/09/08, 8.

249 'Chair's Report of the Intersessional Meeting on the Future of the IWC, Renaissance London Heathrow Hotel', UK, 6–8 March, 2008. C:\IWC60/60-7. http://www.iwcoffice.org/_documents/, accessed 01/09/08, 8.

250 'IWC Press Release, Day 2, Tuesday 24 June', http://www.iwcoffice.org/meetings/meeting2008.htm, accessed 10/07/08.

251 'Annual Report of the International Whaling Commission 36' (Cambridge: International Whaling Commission, 1986), 11. The members of the Working Group were Australia, Brazil, Iceland, Japan, the Republic of Korea, Mexico, the Philippines, Spain and the USA. 'Annual Report of the International Whaling Commission 36', 11.

252 'Annual Report of the International Whaling Commission 37', 11. Ironically,

Despite the success of other states in adjusting easily to a post-whaling era, Japan saw the creation of the Working Group as an opportunity to press its pro-whaling cause. At the Forty-first Annual Meeting in 1989, Japan's argument to the Socio-economic Working Group was that the moratorium had 'affected the spiritual, psychological, physical and cultural well-being of people who depended on whaling'.[253] Spain and Iceland submitted a document with a similar tale of difficulty experienced by some of its populace and, in the case of Iceland, arguing that the ban was impacting negatively on the state's overall marine research programmes. Other states, led by the UK, reacted with disbelief to Japan's submission, pointing to what they claimed were exaggerations in the Japanese text. The Working Group promised to examine the documents and call for further meetings before the next Annual Meeting if warranted.[254]

At the Forty-second IWC Meeting, Iceland, Japan and Norway changed their arguments on the socio-economic implications of the moratorium to emphasize the impact on localized whaling communities and Japan's paper asked that if aboriginal whaling was permitted, then a special class of whaling, one of small-types coastal whaling, should be recognized.[255] The Working Group was unwilling to alter its 1989 stance where it argued that:

> The Working Group agreed that it was clear that the zero catch limits have several levels of socio-economic impacts and that it is important for the commission to have these facts and opinions as they proceed with their deliberation . . . Some of the socio-economic effects are serious, but governments at times have to take painful actions that affect their citizens . . . Though governments can successfully take actions to mitigate change, some are permanent and cannot be remedied.[256]

At the same meeting, a Japanese proposal for an interim relief quota for small-type whaling from the Okhotsk Sea–West Pacific stock of 50 minke whales to ameliorate the 'socio-economic hardship suffered' by some Japanese citizens was rejected.[257] Since that time, and at every subsequent meeting,

---

the first submission received was by a pro-preservationist state, Australia, in 1987, on the 1978 closure of its Western Australian whaling operation. The report highlighted that the cessation of whaling activities had no long-term deleterious effects on the local community. Any short-term economic and employment factors had been resolved quickly and alternate employment in the form of a whaling museum and a whale-watching industry had been established. 'Annual Report of the International Whaling Commission 38', 11.

[253] 'Annual Report of the International Whaling Commission 40' (Cambridge: International Whaling Commission, 1990), 12.

[254] Ibid.: 13.

[255] 'Annual Report of the International Whaling Commission 41', 32–3.

[256] Ibid.: 33.

[257] Ibid.: 36.

Japan has asked for relief in the form of a request to be allowed to hunt minke whales, but this has been rejected by the other delegates as unnecessary, given the condition of the Japanese coastal peoples concerned and as a thinly veiled attempt to abrogate the moratorium.[258]

Britain, Australia, New Zealand, France and some smaller states have been staunch advocates of the moratorium and have consistently rallied support to ensure that Japan's requests have been unsuccessful. Following Japan's approach, Iceland and Norway requested, at the Forty-third Meeting of the IWC, if they could carry out small-type coastal whaling, citing economic hardships for their peoples. The motion was defeated (six votes for, 14 against and nine abstentions) with the US speaking for the dominant view in arguing that this was another form of commercial whaling.[259] Norway continued to try at the next two meetings, but was rebuffed and has subsequently stopped asking.[260]

Despite the tenacity of the Japanese, and their year-to-year appeals, it is unlikely that the other IWC members will accept the idea of a moral debt to Japanese coastal whalers over this issue. Most other states' citizens who have stopped whaling have adjusted to this change in life circumstances and have not been severely economically disadvantaged. While continuing to call for a vote may be a strategic decision of the Japanese government, it also reflects the Japanese viewpoint that this issue is a question of morally looking after

258 'Annual Report of the International Whaling Commission 42', 33–6; 'Annual Report of the International Whaling Commission 43' (Cambridge: International Whaling Commission, 1993), 17; 'Annual Report of the International Whaling Commission 44', 13–14; 'Annual Report of the International Whaling Commission 45' (Cambridge: International Whaling Commission, 1995), 17–18; 'Annual Report of the International Whaling Commission 46' (Cambridge: International Whaling Commission, 1996), 18; 'Annual Report of the International Whaling Commission 47' (Cambridge: International Whaling Commission, 1997), 48; 'Annual Report of the International Whaling Commission 48' (Cambridge: International Whaling Commission, 1998), 17–19; 'Annual Report of the International Whaling Commission 49' (Cambridge: International Whaling Commission, 1999), 3–4; 'Annual Report of the International Whaling Commission 50' (Cambridge: International Whaling Commission, 2000), 7; 'Annual Report of the International Whaling Commission 51' (Cambridge: International Whaling Commission, 2001), 12; 'Annual Report of the International Whaling Commission 52' (Cambridge: International Whaling Commission, 2002), 28; 'Annual Report of the International Whaling Commission 53', 35–7; 'Annual Report of the International Whaling Commission 54', Summary of Decisions; 'Annual Report of the International Whaling Commission 55', 52–3; Chair's Report of the 58th Meeting 2006, Summary of Main Outcomes, 6; Chair's Report of the 59th Meeting 2007, Summary of Main Outcomes, 2; Revised Chair's Report of the 60th Meeting, 2008, 26.

259 'Annual Report of the International Whaling Commission 42', 33–6.

260 'Annual Report of the International Whaling Commission 43', 17; 'Annual Report of the International Whaling Commission 44', 13–14.

disadvantaged traditional coastal whaling towns. At the 2008 Meeting Japan again raised the issue of the hardship suffered by its coastal communities (to satisfy its honour), but did not call for a vote due to perceived progress in the ongoing 'Future of the IWC' discussions.[261] Despite the non-vote by Japan, the issue is far from settled and will continue to be argued for at future meetings in one way or another.

## IWC SCIENTIFIC PERMITS AND WHALING

The issuing of scientific permits has been a particularly bitterly fought topic between preservationist-minded states and those states dedicated to continuing whaling. Under the IWCR, states are allowed to issue their own scientific permits to hunt whales and the IWC has few powers to prevent such permits for activities it might regard as scientifically dubious, a loophole whaling states have ruthlessly exploited.[262] For example, since 1987 Japan, under its declared scientific whaling programmes, has killed over 10 000 whales, more than four and a half times the rate taken for research by all other states since 1952.[263] Preservationist states have attempted over the years to tighten the regulations pertaining to the issuance of individual states' scientific permits, but in the face of the intransigence of states such as Japan and Norway, they have to date been unsuccessful.[264]

Japan, Iceland, Russia and Norway have continued to award themselves scientific permits in the face of global condemnation of the twisting of the term 'scientific'. They have justified this decision on the grounds that whale numbers for certain species have recovered enough for such activities, or alternatively, that killing whales is necessary to better understand them.[265] For preservationist-minded states, these explanations appear dubious and are perceived as attempts to circumvent the moratorium. However, under the rules of the ICRW, states are allowed their own scientific programmes and so the sceptics have been limited to calls to stop such activities.

---

261 'Revised Chair's Summary Report of the 60th Annual Meeting', Santiago, Chile, June 2008. http://www.iwcoffice.org/_documents/, accessed 01/01/09, 6.

262 Rose and Paleokrassis, 'Compliance with International Environmental Obligations: A Casestudy of the International Whaling Commission', 157.

263 Phillip J. Clapham et al., 'The Whaling Issue: Conservation, Confusion and Casuistry', *Marine Policy* 31 (2007): 315.

264 Rose, 'International Law and the Status of Cetaceans', 38.

265 Ibid.: 38–9. For example, in the 1987–88 season, Japan undertook a research programme with the nebulous aim of determining a better understanding of the population dynamics of minke whales in Antarctica, which apparently meant killing 300 whales a year. Stroud, 'The Ethics and Politics of Whaling', 69–70.

Following on from the IWC Meeting that imposed the moratorium in 1985, Japan argued at the Joint Working Group of the Technical and Scientific Committees (chaired by K. Yonezawa of Japan) that there was a need to create better conceptual approaches. The delegate argued the aim should be to better inform the IWC, with effective scientific advice and recommendations, as well as setting out a timetable for a detailed assessment of whale stocks. The report was accepted by the Commission and this has allowed Japan and other whaling states to argue that scientific whaling was necessary.[266]

Preservationist states clashed with whaling states in a number of meetings in the 1980s over the regulation of scientific permits. At the 1985 Meeting, there was vigorous debate as to whether such catches should be allowed to enter into international trade and whether special permit catches should be allowed from protected stocks. A new resolution was adopted by consensus.[267] The Resolution on Special Permits for Scientific Research recommended:

> That Contracting Governments when considering proposed research permits and the Scientific Committee when reviewing such permits . . . should take into account whether:
> (1) the objectives of the research are not practically and scientifically feasible through non-lethal research techniques;
> (2) the proposed research is intended, and structured accordingly to contribute information essential for rational management of stock.[268]

Following on from the 1986 decision to review special permits, Iceland, the Republic of Korea and Japan all submitted proposals to be allowed to catch whales under a scientific permit. All three requests were turned down by the IWC, citing, in the case of Korea, that it would not contribute information that answers significant management questions, while arguing in Iceland's case that the request did not meet the 1986 criteria.[269] Japan was asked not to take whales while the Scientific Committee examined its proposed research methods.[270] The following year both Norway and Iceland applied for special permits but both applications were rejected by the IWC.[271]

At the Forty-first Meeting, Iceland stated it would not seek scientific permits to hunt sei whales as it had lost faith in the IWC as an organization.

---

[266] 'Annual Report of the International Whaling Commission 35', 9–10.

[267] 'Annual Report of the International Whaling Commission 37', 11–12.

[268] Ibid.: 25.

[269] Appendix 2, 'Annual Report of the International Whaling Commission 38', 28; Appendix 3, 'Annual Report of the International Whaling Commission 38', 28.

[270] Appendix 4, 'Annual Report of the International Whaling Commission 38', 29.

[271] Appendices 1, 2, 'Annual Report of the International Whaling Commission 39', 30–31.

Japan, Norway and initially the Soviet Union sought official permission to kill whales for scientific purposes but have found themselves consistently refused by the other delegates.[272] At the Forty-fifth Meeting, Norway decided not to ask for a scientific permit, leaving Japan isolated as the only state still claiming that whaling is a scientific activity.[273]

In the 1990s, the preservationist states have sought to limit scientific research carried out by IWC members to research that primarily uses non-lethal means. In 1995, the UK (acting on behalf of Australia, Brazil, France, the Netherlands, New Zealand, Oman, South Africa and the USA) introduced a resolution that research should be conducted primarily by non-lethal methods, and that lethal methods should only be used in 'exceptional' circumstances, in order to address vitally important scientific questions.[274]

There was much debate about the meaning of 'exceptional'. St Vincent and the Grenadines argued this was a moral issue and wondered what made whales so special that they should not be killed. India responded that, in its particular case, it did not carry out lethal research on tigers, elephants, lions and rhinos. On being put to a vote, the resolution was passed (23 for, five against and two abstentions).[275]

At the Fiftieth Meeting, the IWC members passed a resolution on whaling under special permit which regretted that Japan was still carrying out lethal research and recommended that the taking of whales should be done in a manner consistent with Section III of the Schedule.[276] At the Fifty-fifth Annual Meeting, the IWC isolated Japan even further when as an entity it:

---

272 'Annual Report of the International Whaling Commission 40', 36; Appendices 1, 2, 'Annual Report of the International Whaling Commission 41', 47–8; Appendices 2, 3, 'Annual Report of the International Whaling Commission 42', 46–7; 'Annual Report of the International Whaling Commission 43', 49; 'Annual Report of the International Whaling Commission 44', 33; 'Annual Report of the International Whaling Commission 45', 29; Appendix 7, Resolution 1996–7, 'Annual Report of the International Whaling Commission 47', 51–2; Appendix 6, Resolution 1997–6, 'Annual Report of the International Whaling Commission 48', 47–8; Appendix 2, IWC Resolution 1998–1, 'Annual Report of the International Whaling Commission 49', 42; Appendix 4, Resolution 1999–3, 'Annual Report of the International Whaling Commission 50', 52–3; Resolution 2000–4, Resolution 2000–5, 'Annual Report of the International Whaling Commission 51', 56; Resolution 2001–7, 2001–8, 'Annual Report of the International Whaling Commission 52', 57; 'Annual Report of the International Whaling Commission 54', Summary of Decisions; Resolution 2007–1, 'Annual Report of the International Whaling Commission 59', 5.

273 'Annual Report of the International Whaling Commission 45', 29.

274 'Annual Report of the International Whaling Commission 46', 30.

275 Ibid.

276 Appendix 5, IWC Resolution 1998–4, 'Annual Report of the International Whaling Commission 49', 43.

> expressed deep concern that the provision permitting special permit whaling enables countries to conduct whaling for commercial purposes despite the moratorium on commercial whaling . . . (and that doing so was . . . contrary to the spirit of the moratorium on commercial whaling and the will of the Commission).[277]

Despite being virtually alone within the IWC, Japan (and again recently Iceland) continues to take whales for 'scientific purposes'.[278] Their decision to continue this programme has seen them subjected to global censure.[279] Despite their continued intransigence, the fact that they continue whaling in small numbers does not invalidate the preservationist norm. Quite the contrary, Japan and Iceland stand out as the exception that proves the norm, which is becoming more deeply entrenched among IWC members.

## THE REVISED MANAGEMENT PROCEDURE

For several decades the pro-whaling sections of the IWC have been attempting to put in place a conservationist approach to maintaining whaling stocks. This goes by the rubric of the aforementioned Revised Management Procedure (RMP). Prior to the implementation of the moratorium in 1980, a Special Working Group proposed an RMP. The group's Report established that an operating principle of the IWC should be to 'set a target level for each stock and that the level of catches, if any, should be that which would bring the stock to target level in a fixed term of years'.[280]

The Scientific Committee supported the RMP concept in principle and a Technical Committee was tasked with setting up a Working Group of the two committees to set up proposals for the 1981 Annual Meeting.[281] ENGOs have been especially critical of the RMP since it relies on catch data, both historical and current, provided by whalers. They have historically proven unreliable at best when it comes to this type of information. To them, the programme is flawed in conception and should be abandoned.[282]

---

277 'Annual Report of the International Whaling Commission 54', Summary of Decisions.

278 In the 2007–08 season, Japan issued permits for the taking of minke, fin and humpback whales (for the first time). Japan killed 551 Antarctic minke whales in the season. Iceland up to 2007 took 200 minke whales as part of its scientific programme. 'Revised Chair's Summary Report of the 60th Annual Meeting', Santiago, Chile, June 2008. http://www.iwcoffice.org/_documents/, accessed 01/01/09, 6.

279 Resolution 2007–1 (40 for, two against, one abstention, with 27 states not participating) required the Japanese government to suspend the lethal aspects of its research programme. 'Annual Report of the International Whaling Commission 59', 5.

280 'Annual Report of the International Whaling Commission 31', 19.

281 Ibid.

282 Stroud, 'The Ethics and Politics of Whaling', 78.

Throughout the 1980s, the Technical Committee worked at creating such a procedure, but the idea was overtaken by events when the moratorium was introduced. However, at the Forty-third Meeting in 1991, Norway put forward a resolution for the IWC to accept the Scientific Committee's recommendation to create an RMP, based on the 'C Procedure', that set an acceptable catch level of 66 per cent. Iceland, St Vincent and the Grenadines and Japan favoured the proposal, but Australia, the USA, the UK, the Netherlands and Germany all opposed the motion as flawed. Upon being put to a vote, the resolution was defeated (seven for, 19 against and three abstentions).[283]

However, the IWC agreed to an alternative RMP resolution, applying only to baleen whales (18 for, six against and five abstentions).[284] Australia, the UK, the USA and the Netherlands all sponsored or supported the resolution as a means of moving forward. New Zealand abstained because it favoured preserving these 'great natural resources' and opposed the resumption of commercial whaling.[285]

Japan and Norway voted against the resolution, citing a distortion of the Scientific Committee's recommendations, in Japan's eyes, by 'non-scientists', and because, as Norway argued, of the lack of knowledge regarding the instructions to the Scientific Committee.[286] Despite these objections, the IWC approved, under the scheme, a conservationist catch limit algorithm created by the Scientific Committee. It was meant to be implemented with a new observation and inspection system to replace the failed previous efforts.[287]

At the Forty-fifth Meeting, Norway and Japan proposed a resolution that the IWC should show greater initiative and put in place the RMP. However, the resolution was voted down (18 against, six in favour and six abstentions) as most states were concerned about the current state of the RMP document.[288]

---

283 'Annual Report of the International Whaling Commission 42', 25.

284 The resolution agreed that any such procedure must include the following provisions:
'1. Commercial whaling shall only be permitted for populations in areas and seasons for which catch limits are in force. These catch limits shall have been calculated by the Scientific Committee, and forwarded to and approved by the Commission in conformity with all the provisions of the Revised Management procedure. Catch limits for all other populations in all areas and seasons shall be zero.
3. To permit depleted stocks (i.e. stocks below 54% of the unexploited level) to recover to more productive levels, catch limits under the Revised Management Procedure shall only be greater than zero in cases when the stock is determined to be above 54% of its unexploited level.' Ibid. Appendix 4, 47–8.

285 Ibid.: 26.

286 Ibid.

287 Rose, 'International Law and the Status of Cetaceans', 35.

288 'Annual Report of the International Whaling Commission 44', 19–20.

The following year the mooted RMP was reviewed and in Appendix 5 the IWC reaffirmed that the RMP was not yet ready to be implemented and said that if it were to be initiated, its provisions could not obviate the ban on commercial whaling.[289] The issue of implementing an RMP was stymied for several years because states such as Australia would not accept its entering into force since they were implacably opposed to it under any circumstances.[290] At the Fifty-first Meeting Japan, which was desperate to get the conservationist scheme operating, asked for a date for this issue to be finalized, noting that the paragraph supporting the ban, 10(e), was meant to have been reviewed in 1990, but had still not been finalized.[291]

There was some movement on this issue prior to the Fifty-sixth Meeting, with the USA changing its previous position and indicating approval for the idea of an RMS. A small group, comprising delegates from Denmark, Iceland, Ireland, Japan, the Netherlands, Spain, Sweden and the USA met to try to determine how to progress the RMS. All but Ireland were able to attend and an RMS 'package' was deliberated by the delegates that called for 'a phased in approach to the resumption of whaling' and that 'for an initial period (for example, five years after the lifting of the moratorium), commercial whaling would only be allowed in waters under national jurisdiction'.[292]

In commenting on the plan to the other Commissioners, Denmark stressed the need for whale conservation and whale management as critical elements of any package. The USA stated, somewhat problematically, that while it supported the moratorium, it was committed to the RMS being completed in a timely manner. Consequently, Denmark (on behalf of the other co-sponsors, Ireland, Iceland, the Republic of Korea, Japan, the Netherlands, Spain, Sweden, Switzerland and the USA) proposed a resolution to proceed at haste to complete the text and the technical details for adoption at the next Annual Meeting. To facilitate this, the US proposed an intersessional plan of action to meet this deadline.[293]

After an amendment by Australia, which attempted to stall the start-up of the scheme, the resolution's operative paragraph was altered to read '. . . with the aim of having the results ready for consideration, including for possible adoption at IWC/57 and/or to identify any outstanding policy and technical issues'.[294] The resolution was adopted by consensus by the other IWC delegates.[295] However,

289 'Annual Report of the International Whaling Commission 45', 43–4.
290 'Annual Report of the International Whaling Commission 48', 36.
291 'Annual Report of the International Whaling Commission 49', 27.
292 'Annual Report of the International Whaling Commission 55', 33.
293 Ibid.: 41.
294 Ibid.
295 Ibid.: 33–40.

despite the defection of the US, apparently to appease Japan, to date the RMS has not been implemented. This is due to a successful stalling campaign by the preservationist states; even though it is technically ready to be deployed, discussions had broken down due to an inability to agree on the wording of the scheme.[296] Recognizing this reality at the 2008 Meeting, the RMP was not included in official discussions by pro-whaling states, but was folded into the ongoing 'Future of the IWC'discussions.[297]

## THE 'IRISH PROPOSAL' FOR THE FUTURE OF THE IWC

In an attempt to break the conservationist/preservationist deadlock, the Irish Commissioner, Michael Canny, was asked at the Forty-ninth IWC Meeting to consult with the other Commissioners regarding the Irish proposal with a view to seeking consensus. The proposal would allow coastal whaling to resume once again (but not to be traded), but would still continue to ban whaling on the high seas.[298] As a trade-off for the preservationist forces, whaling for 'scientific purposes', and the global trade in whale commodities, would also be forbidden under the proposal. The submission stipulated that whaling 'should be restricted to coastal areas only', but it is unclear as to how it would define 'coastal'.[299]

Despite holding an intersessional meeting in February 1998, attended by 17 states in Antigua and Barbuda, Ireland could not put forward a formal proposal at the next meeting, due to the US, the UK and Australia supporting the moratorium. The only exception members were willing to entertain was that of aboriginal whaling. They were willing to retain the item on the agenda though. At the Fiftieth Meeting, debate ensued and it was clear that there was a vast gulf in views between the two factions. Brazil declared it wished to see a South Atlantic Ocean Sanctuary created, while Denmark argued it was critical to preserve whale stocks. Japan was dismissive of this argument, however,

---

[296] Andrew Darby, 'Whale Sighting', *The Age*, 28 April 2005, 14; Iliff, 'Modernisation of the International Convention for the Regulation of Whaling', 403.

[297] 'Revised Chair's Summary Report of the 60th Annual Meeting', Santiago, Chile, June 2008. http://www.iwcoffice.org/_documents/, accessed 01/01/09, 5. At the 2007 Meeting, the Japanese Commissioner stated that, in his opinion, the RMS was 'postponed for ever'. Iliff, 'The International Whaling Regime Post 2007', 523.

[298] Gillespie, *Whaling Diplomacy: Defining Issues in International Environmental Law*, 180.

[299] 'Annual Report of the International Whaling Commission 49', 35. The submission does not make it apparent whether it is it the 200 nautical mile Exclusive Economic Zones, the 12 nautical mile fisheries limit, or the 4 nautical mile territorial zones.

stating that its position was that the 'IWC has turned into an organization to protect whales, whereas it should consider the sustainable use of ocean resources and the total ecosystem'.[300]

At the Fifty-first Meeting, in a debate over the Irish proposal, Norway argued that the IWC was not adhering to its Convention and had become 'a protectionist organization with no will to lift the moratorium'.[301] Denmark thought that both sides must give up something to keep the organization functioning. The UK wanted to see a permanent global ban except for aboriginal subsistence whaling, and argued that whale-watching as 'a benign and sustainable way of exploiting natural resources' was a better way forward.[302] Japan chided the UK for talking in terms of 'conservation' when new whaling sanctuaries were annually proposed and a coalition of preservationist states was implacably opposed to whaling.[303]

At the Fifty-second IWC Meeting, the Chair reported that, despite there not yet being consensus, there was at least support for a process with the aim of reaching compromise.[304] However, while the RMS proposal advocates such a conservationist stance, it will not succeed in supplanting the preservationist stance of the IWC any time soon, since renewing coastal whaling is seen by the majority of states as the thin edge of the wedge to undermine the moratorium. Many preservationist states were opposed to the RMS because of the fear that it would lead to new whaling colonies being established globally, undermining the moratorium.[305]

However, the Irish compromise has exposed the real positions of IWC states behind their negotiating stances. States like the US and the UK, which had opposed the resumption of whaling on ethical grounds, but couched their rhetoric in scientific terms, were met with a plan that would meet their stated scientific goals. If the RMS were implemented, Norway and Japan, which have hidden their intentions to continue commercial whaling, would be forced to concede their true intentions.[306] Given that neither side wants the compromise implemented fully, it appears the compromise has failed to break the normative impasse, and to date it has not been implemented.[307]

---

300 Ibid.: 35–6.

301 'Annual Report of the International Whaling Commission 50', 42.

302 Ibid., 47.

303 Ibid., 43.

304 'Annual Report of the International Whaling Commission 51', 50.

305 Palazzo Jr, 'Whose Whales? Developing Countries and the Right to Use Whales by Non-lethal Means', 77.

306 DeSombre, *The Global Environment and World Politics*, 142.

307 Ibid. There is no mention of the issue being discussed at all at the 2007 Meeting in Alaska or the 2008 Meeting in Chile and it appears to have been allowed to lapse.

## WHALE-WATCHING AS AN ALTERNATIVE

Preservationist states and ENGOs have sought to entrench the preservationist norms in a variety of ways. One strategy they have employed has been to promote whale-watching as an alternative to the slaughtering of whales, with the aim of convincing states that it is in their economic interests. In 1993, the UK introduced a paper outlining that over the previous ten years there were now whale-watching companies established on all continents with revenues estimated at US $320 million and rising at an average of 49 per cent every year. It asked the IWC, via a resolution, to play a role in this burgeoning industry, by collecting information and setting regulations for it. France, Spain, New Zealand, Brazil, Australia, Monaco, the Netherlands, St Lucia, Argentina and India all favoured the resolution. It was agreed that the resolution should be adopted and that a Working Group should be set up to examine the issues.[308]

Opponents of the moratorium, such as Japan, Norway and Russia, have consistently argued that activities such as whale-watching are outside the scope of the Convention and should not be discussed or regulated by the IWC. This position appears to be in the minority, though.[309] More and more states are coming to understand the financial benefits available to its peoples in creating whale-watching businesses. Whale-watching has become a more critical economic activity, with a turnover of US $23 million on the East Coast of the US alone. Ironically, given the stance adopted by Japanese leaders, whale-watching is becoming an increasingly popular activity amongst Japanese tourists, indicating that domestic attitudes to the issue may be changing.[310]

The IWC is currently investigating the effect of whale-watching on whale populations, with a view to developing more legally enforceable codes of conduct regarding the activities. Such actions undercut the pro-whaling states' determination that the issue should not fall under the IWC and broadens the

---

308 'Annual Report of the International Whaling Commission 44', 23–4; Appendix 9, 'Annual Report of the International Whaling Commission 44', 33–4.

309 'Annual Report of the International Whaling Commission 53', 9.

310 Rose, 'International Law and the Status of Cetaceans', 50. By 1999, the UK valued the income from whale-watching in the Caribbean at US $10 million annually. The following year Senator Robert Hill, the then Australian Minister for the Environment, pointed out in his Address of Welcome that Australia made more income from protecting whales than it ever had in hunting them. Other states had arrived at the same conclusion and were shifting their positions to take advantage of this burgeoning business. In the process, they were helping to further entrench preservationism within the IWC. 'Annual Report of the International Whaling Commission 50', 9–10; 'Annual Report of the International Whaling Commission 51', 11.

remit of the organization from one concerned merely with whaling to one covering all whale-related activities.[311]

## ABORIGINAL SUBSISTENCE WHALING

An analysis of the case of aboriginal subsistence whaling is critical when examining the normative debate underlying the IWC because it raises three issues.[312] The first issue is best phrased as a question: how strong can the preservationist norm within the IWC be if whales are still killed under the pretext of aboriginal subsistence whaling? If whaling still continues, even if only a few are taken, then the preservationist norm has not been fully entrenched, but is limited in its application.

The second issue is the attempt by pro-whaling states, in particular whaling states with indigenous populations, to continue to push for the expansion of the ambit of such activities. Countries like Japan and Norway have attempted to use this issue as a wedge to reopen the broader issue of commercial whaling, arguing that some of their traditional cultural activities should fall under this category. Meanwhile, the USA, which opposed commercial whaling, has sought to sanction such whaling since it has a large indigenous population which has hunted whales for centuries. The USA has sought to defend their interests within the IWC, despite being one of the main sponsors of the moratorium against commercial whaling.

The third issue raised is the normative confusion over this issue adopted by states like the US as well as the various ENGOs. The USA, despite its staunch opposition to commercial whaling, has also been a supporter of aboriginal whaling, chiefly for its own domestic reasons, differentiating it from industrial whaling. ENGOs have also been strangely quiet on this issue, not wishing to

---

311 'Revised Chair's Summary Report of the 60th Annual Meeting', Santiago, Chile, June, 2008. http://www.iwcoffice.org/_documents/, accessed 01/01/09, 8.

312 As per the IWC's ad hoc Technical Committee Working Group on Development of Management Principles and Guidelines for Subsistence Catches of Whales by Indigenous (Aboriginal) Peoples, aboriginal subsistence whaling is defined as 'for purposes of local aboriginal consumption carried out by or on behalf of aboriginal, indigenous or native peoples who share strong community, familial, social and cultural ties related to a continuing traditional dependence on whaling and on the use of whales'. 'Report of the International Whaling Commission (Special Issue 4): Aboriginal/Subsistence Whaling (with Special Reference to the Alaska and Greenland Fisheries)' (Cambridge: International Whaling Commission, 1982), 83. Conversely, the IWC has never defined the term 'commercial whaling', thus any practice not considered to be 'aboriginal subsistence' is deemed commercial. Reeves, 'The Origins and Character of "Aboriginal Subsistence" Whaling: A Global Review', 76.

offend aboriginal organizations whose rights they have traditionally supported in other forums. Their silence on the issue, however, undercuts their moral persuasiveness in the eyes of their opponents and to some extent, the rest of the world. The vexed issue of aboriginal subsistence whaling is one that preservationist groups must come to terms with by declaring which set of rights is more important, aboriginal group rights or the intrinsic right of whales to exist.

The rights of aboriginal groups have been enshrined for decades within the IWC.[313] Initially, the right to hunt was felt to be a narrow one and was designed to help indigenous peoples whose economy and culture was based on the traditional hunt for whales.[314] However, the capacity for such a loophole to allow full-blown commercial whaling under the guise of subsistence whaling was spotted and corrected by the IWC. In 1964, after a submission by the United States of America to the IWC, the following revision of paragraph 2 of the Schedule was carried unanimously to avoid abuse of the rights of aboriginal groups by commercial interests:

> It is forbidden to take or kill gray whales or right whales except by aborigines or a Contracting Government on behalf of aborigines and only when the meat and products of such whales are to be used exclusively for local consumption by the aborigines.[315]

In 1981, just prior to the imposition of the moratorium, but at the height of discussion about taking whales, it was agreed by the contracting members to the IWC that the three broad management objectives for the aboriginal subsistence whaling scheme would be:

> (1) to ensure that the risks of extinction to individual stocks are not seriously increased by aboriginal whaling;
> (2) to enable aboriginal people to harvest whales in perpetuity at levels appropriate to their cultural and nutritional requirements, subject to the other objectives; and
> (3) to maintain the status of whale stocks at or above the level giving the highest net recruitment and to ensure that stocks below that level are moved towards it, so far as the environment permits.[316]

---

313 Gillespie, *Whaling Diplomacy: Defining Issues in International Environmental Law*, 195.

314 Fletcher, 'The International Whaling Regime and U.S. Foreign Policy', 221.

315 'Sixteenth Report of the Commission' (London: International Whaling Commission, 1966), 20.

316 The Report of the Technical Committee Working Group on Development of Management Principles and Guidelines for Subsistence Catches of Whales by Indigenous (Aboriginal) Peoples in 'Report of the International Whaling Commission (Special Issue 4): Aboriginal/Subsistence Whaling (with Special Reference to the Alaska and Greenland Fisheries)', 84.

It is clear that the IWC always meant aboriginal whaling to be a legitimate exemption to the overall commercial ban, providing such activities did not threaten the survival of whale species. Over the years the IWC has designated the following whaling operations as qualifying for aboriginal subsistence whaling: the Greenland hunt for minke and fin whales; the hunt for humpback whales in the Lesser Antilles; for bowhead and grey whales in Alaska; and for grey whales in Russia. In the 1990s bowhead whaling in Chukotka, Russia, and grey whaling by the Makah in the US State of Washington, were also authorized.[317]

The US, in particular, has traditionally stated that it supports the concept of aboriginal subsistence whaling when applied to its own citizens, following on from the IWC formulation '. . . when it does not negatively impact whale stocks and when the hunt fulfils nutritional, spiritual, and cultural needs of a traditional whaling people'.[318] This has in theory been applied to the Inuit (comprising the indigenous peoples of Arctic Canada, Alaska, Greenland and Siberia), who have also, in previous centuries, hunted whales for food as a means of survival.[319]

However, in practice the United States of America allowed Alaskan Inuits to take bowhead whales in the 1970s despite evidence of the stocks being endangered. The IWC halted the Alaskan quota in 1977 and the US lobbied hard against its doing so, with the IWC eventually agreeing to a 'limited and strictly controlled hunt'.[320] D'Amato and Chopra contend that the US's fierce advocacy of the Inuit whaling claims over the years is because the Inuit can vote in US elections, whereas whales are barred. This argument certainly has merit.[321] However, it could equally be argued that segments of the American populace support the right of indigenous peoples to carry out traditional activities.

In 1987, the US again lobbied for the Makah Indians of the Olympic peninsula in the northwest of the United States to be allowed to hunt grey whales.[322] The Makah consider whales a gift from the sea and the hunting of whales represents the spiritual and technological proficiency of their society.[323] Traditionally, the Makah have hunted whales for two centuries, but by the

317 Reeves, 'The Origins and Character of "Aboriginal Subsistence" Whaling: A Global Review', 77.

318 Fletcher, 'The International Whaling Regime and U.S. Foreign Policy', 217.

319 D'Amato and Chopra, 'Whales: Their Emerging Right to Life', 57.

320 Fletcher, 'The International Whaling Regime and U.S. Foreign Policy', 221.

321 D'Amato and Chopra, 'Whales: Their Emerging Right to Life', 58.

322 Fletcher, 'The International Whaling Regime and U.S. Foreign Policy', 221.

323 World Council of Whalers, 'WCW Profile', http://www.worldcouncilofwhalers.com/wcwprofile/history.htm.

1920s the grey whale faced extinction and domestic policies were put in place to prevent hunting. Over the years, the species has rebounded and it was taken off the US Federal Endangered Animals list in 1994. The Makah asked the US government to present a case for them to the IWC to be allowed to whale once more.[324]

First, the US needed to determine its own position on aboriginal whaling, however. The criteria until that point had been 'cultural and subsistence needs', but this was redrafted by the IWC to state that 'there must be a demonstration of cultural *and/or* subsistence needs'.[325] Preservationist-leaning groups were appalled, arguing that such a regulation 'opened the door to cultural whaling in the United States of America, and, by example, around the world'.[326] They were afraid that the more loosely worded definition would allow other whaling nations to be able to claim that their indigenous populations should also be allowed to hunt.[327] If enough states could claim an exemption, this would effectively circumvent the moratorium and allow large-scale slaughtering of whales.

In 1996, the US went to the IWC on the Makah's behalf, but it was met with animosity. When it became clear that it would not gather the required three-quarters majority, the USA withdrew the motion. In 1997, the USA tried again without success, so they arranged a deal with Russia to effectively trade quotas that enabled the Makah to hunt. Most IWC members denounced this arrangement. Their sentiments are best summed up by the Australian delegate, who argued that '[t]he only aboriginal people who are authorized to take Gray whales are those whose traditional aboriginal subsistence and cultural needs have been recognized'.[328]

At the Forty-eighth IWC Annual Meeting, the US put forward a request from the Makah tribe to be allowed to catch five grey whales. The USA stipulated that it had an agreement with the Makah tribe that there would be no commercial whaling, and that the request conformed to the criteria for an aboriginal subsistence quota. France and the Netherlands opposed the motion, asking, in the case of France, how it could be a cultural event if modern technologies were to be used, and querying whether it met the definition of subsistence if the tribe had managed for 70 years without hunting whales. The Netherlands was concerned whether this request met the current definition of aboriginal subsistence whaling and questioned the Makah tradition, citing that

324 Fletcher, 'The International Whaling Regime and U.S. Foreign Policy', 221–2.

325 Ibid.: 221.

326 Ibid.: 222.

327 Ibid.: 223–4.

328 Ibid.: 222–3.

their whaling had been of a commercial nature. Further discussion exposed that there was clear division on this issue, with Japan, the Republic of Korea and the Russian Federation supporting the proposal, but many other members (Australia, Spain, Chile, New Zealand, China and Mexico) opposing the motion. Before it could be put to a vote, the item was adjourned in favour of informal discussions.[329]

At the Fifty-fourth Meeting, the issue was again raised. A joint US/Russian proposal to renew the existing aboriginal subsistence whaling quota for hunting bowhead whales for the next five years was introduced. After fierce debate, the motion was defeated, as it did not reach the three-quarters majority necessary for it to pass (32 for, 11 against, two abstentions). However, it was not the preservationist states that voted down the motion. The vote appears to have been an example of payback by whaling states, with Japan leading a coalition of states arguing that aboriginal whaling was the 'moral' equivalent of Japanese small-type coastal whaling, and if that was not allowed, then aboriginal whaling should also be banned.[330] Despite the setback, the US has still authorized the Makah to take whales domestically. Doing so does undercut their moral legitimacy, however, and has allowed some states to argue for increased whaling through the device of aboriginal whaling.[331]

With indigenous people's populations rebounding in certain areas, particularly in the USA and Siberia, there is a growing demand to take whales by these parties. There are concerns that such groups may potentially hunt in commercial quantities and undermine the moratorium. This has placed some anti-whaling states with indigenous populations in a terrible quandary, as well as ENGOs who have traditionally supported indigenous rights.[332] D'Amato and Chopra are rightly critical of leading ENGOs such as the Sierra Club and Friends of the Earth, which have been silent on the issue of protecting the endangered bowhead whale because they are hamstrung by their support for the rights of indigenous peoples.[333]

---

329 'Annual Report of the International Whaling Commission 47', 26–7.

330 'Annual Report of the International Whaling Commission 53', 19–22.

331 Fletcher, 'The International Whaling Regime and U.S. Foreign Policy', 225. With the allowing of the Makah hunt, the US has created a new permissible type of whale killing, that of 'cultural whaling', for those aboriginal people with a cultural desire to hunt but not a subsistence need. Despite its actions on aboriginal whaling, the US still argues it holds to the position of being anti-whaling and the US public supports this position. Fletcher, 'The International Whaling Regime and U.S. Foreign Policy', 227–8.

332 Rose, 'International Law and the Status of Cetaceans', 41.

333 D'Amato and Chopra, 'Whales: Their Emerging Right to Life', 58. Greenpeace, in particular, with its emphasis on a biocentric approach to the planet, has a problem, since its ethos as the 'warriors of the rainbow' draws on the mythology of

Their silence runs the danger of undercutting their authority as norm teachers, leaving them open to accusations of hypocrisy by pro-whaling forces. Rather than being drawn into a moral and public battle they may not be able to win, most ENGOs have avoided the issue. Rather, they have supported the right of aboriginal groups, with a long history of whaling, to continue, provided the whales being hunted are not endangered and that precautionary monitoring and management protocols are in place.[334] This tension raises the wider question: does support for aboriginal whaling necessarily undermine the preservationist norm as a whole? The IWC and its member nations have always recognized the right of indigenous groups to hunt whales in their traditional manner, so does this mean the norm of preservationism is limited, and if so, by how much?

Whilst it is arguable that the practice of aboriginal subsistence whaling could be said to undermine the preservationist norm, one tightly circumscribed exception in this regard does not negate the fact that the majority of states seem implacably opposed to the taking of whales on a commercial level. Preservationist-leaning states may eventually hope that the practice will eventually cease, but to date have not felt that it was in their interests to push the matter, especially since the United States is so keen for indigenous whaling to continue. The fear is that pushing the issue may lead to a reopening of the moratorium debate. Rather, they have focused on ensuring that the exception is not widened, and to date they have been successful in this goal.

## WHALING SANCTUARIES

The provision of whale sanctuaries has been another critical battleground between conservationists and preservationists. Preservationists have attempted to widen the scope of the preservationist norm by advocating that sections of the high seas be declared sanctuaries under Article V of the ICRW.[335] Pro-whaling states are just as determined to prevent new sanctuaries bolstering the ban. There is a long history of such sanctuaries being created by the IWC, but the issue took on new significance after the passing of the moratorium.[336]

the Inuit tribe of Alaska. Frank Zelko, '"Make It a Green Peace": The History of an International Environmental Organization', *GHI Bulletin* 34, Spring (2004): 131.

334 Reeves, 'The Origins and Character of "Aboriginal Subsistence" Whaling: A Global Review', 73.

335 Rose, 'International Law and the Status of Cetaceans', 37.

336 Cassandra Phillips, 'Conservation in Practice: Agreements, Regulations, Sanctuaries and Action Plans', in *The Conservation of Whales and Dolphins*, ed. Mark P. Simmonds and Judith D. Hutchinson (Chichester: John Wiley & Sons, 1996), 460. The IWC established one in the Southern Ocean (south of 40 degrees, between 160

Neoliberal institutionalism has some difficulty in explaining the preservationist states' push to create whaling sanctuaries. On the face of it, it does not appear to be in the interest calculations of states like Great Britain, France, Brazil and Australia to advocate for such regions, particularly in the face of the strident opposition of traditional trading partners like Japan. From the neoliberal perspective, such actions could be construed as wanting to be perceived as a good global environmental citizen, which may pay off in the future in terms of reputational advantage. However, utilizing a constructivist approach allows us to understand that the desire by certain states to create these sanctuaries is because their identities have been altered by having internalized preservationist norms and practices. Having done so, it is logical they would want to proselytize their position to others and help strengthen this norm as the appropriate behaviour globally.

## The Indian Ocean Sanctuary

With whale stocks approaching extinction for some species, preservationist-minded states proposed an old solution for an old problem, that of sanctuaries. In 1979, the ENGO-infiltrated Seychelles put forward a proposal for a sanctuary in the Indian Ocean to the Scientific Committee, but no consensus was reached, despite it being the expressed opinion of several neighbouring countries that it was a good idea and that it satisfied the criteria of being an area of ecological coherence. Such a sanctuary, the proposal argued, would enable breeding and other activities to be carried out unhindered. The Technical Committee, after debate as to the length of the review period, agreed (16 votes for, three against and three abstentions) to a new paragraph to be inserted into the Schedule establishing a new Indian Ocean Sanctuary for an initial period of ten years.[337]

The Indian Ocean Sanctuary protects baleen and sperm whales for most of the year, except when the whales migrate to Antarctic waters to feed.[338] Japan objected to the creation of a sanctuary, arguing that such a concept was

degrees west and 70 degrees west) in 1946, but it was really the same sanctuary set up in 1938 under the auspices of the 1937 International Agreement for the Regulation of Whaling. Whalers accepted the 1946 sanctuary because the region quarantined was not considered economically viable due to whales being scarce in the region. However, when blue and fin whale stocks became scarce, whaling states succeeded in convincing the IWC to rescind sanctuary status to the area and exploitation continued. Gillespie, *Whaling Diplomacy: Defining Issues in International Environmental Law*, 250; Phillips, 'Conservation in Practice: Agreements, Regulations, Sanctuaries and Action Plans', 460.

337 'Annual Report of the International Whaling Commission 30', 34.

338 Phillips, 'Conservation in Practice: Agreements, Regulations, Sanctuaries and Action Plans', 460.

contrary to the conservationist objectives of the Convention, a position it has consistently maintained in the face of strong opposition.[339] Traditionally, the region chosen has not been a commercial whaling region, which is probably why whaling states, even Japan, agreed to its implementation.[340] The sanctuary created has some flaws, in that there are no monitoring or enforcement provisions to oversee the initiative, but it does exert a moral force that most states have accepted.[341]

Again in 1989, as the ten-year period was drawing to a close, the Seychelles, supported by Australia, put forth a proposal that the Indian Ocean Sanctuary created in 1979 should be extended for three years. Both Japan and Iceland were against the creation of any sanctuaries and Iceland opposed the continuation of the sanctuary because few states bordering the area were interested in the issue. Many other states, including France, Spain, India, Antigua and Barbados, Oman, UK, Argentina, Brazil, Mexico, the Netherlands and the USA, supported the proposal. In the face of such strong support for the proposal, Japan and Iceland agreed not to oppose the provision, which was consequently accepted.[342] At the 1992 Meeting, it was agreed that the status of the sanctuary would be reviewed every ten years.[343] To date this area has retained that status.

## Southern Hemisphere Sanctuary

Emboldened by their success in achieving the Indian Ocean Sanctuary, preservationist-minded states argued for the expansion of whaling sanctuaries throughout the 1980s and early 1990s. At the Forty-fourth IWC Meeting, France put forward a proposal that a sanctuary be created in the Southern Hemisphere, but while many members supported the gist of the proposal, most thought that it was better to seek input from the Scientific Committee first. Japan believed that such a motion was antithetical to the spirit and objectives of the ICRW, but the sanctuary proposal was supported by many IWC members as falling within the ambit of the Convention. It was decided that any debate would be deferred to the following meeting to allow the Scientific Committee to more fully examine the idea.[344]

---

339 'Annual Report of the International Whaling Commission 30', 27.

340 Rose, 'International Law and the Status of Cetaceans', 37.

341 Ibid.

342 'Annual Report of the International Whaling Commission 40', 21–2.

343 'Annual Report of the International Whaling Commission 43', 26.

344 Ibid.: 26–7; Annex IWC/44/19: A Southern Whale Sanctuary Proposal by the Government of France, 'Annual Report of the International Whaling Commission 43', 41–8.

At the Forty-fifth Meeting, the IWC endorsed the concept of creating a Southern Sanctuary, with Australia offering to hold an intersessional open-ended Working Group to address outstanding issues so that a decision could be taken at the next meeting (Appendix 6).[345] At the Forty-sixth Meeting, the delegates, following on from the decision taken the previous year, voted (23 in favour, one against and six abstentions) to create a Southern Sanctuary for baleen and toothed whales, to be reviewed in ten years.[346] The creation of the Southern Ocean Sanctuary was resisted strenuously by Japan, which attempted to 'stack' the IWC with small states to influence the vote.[347] Norway argued that doing so was contrary to the ICRW and Japan attempted to utilize conservationist arguments that such resources should not be denied future generations. Their arguments went unheeded.[348]

Several factors were instrumental in the success of the sanctuary proposal. First was the support of several influential states, specifically, France, Ireland, Australia and New Zealand. Second was the outside pressure exerted by ENGOs like Greenpeace and the WWF.[349] Robert Kelman of Greenpeace Australia notes that the organization had 15 members lobbying at the Conference, including a representative on both the Australian and the US delegation. Other ENGO tactics employed included educating and building global public support and the individual lobbying of key states to bring about the sanctuary.[350]

Phillips argues that the key factor in building support for the sanctuary was the discovery in November 1993 that the Soviet whaling fleet had been consistently underreporting its catch figures.[351] These revelations, made just prior to the Norfolk Island Meeting in February 1994, showed that whalers had been ignoring IWC directives. This undercut the argument that whalers could be trusted to regulate their activities.[352] This revelation was so morally shocking

---

345 'Annual Report of the International Whaling Commission 44', 32.

346 'Annual Report of the International Whaling Commission 45', 28.

347 Phillips, 'Conservation in Practice: Agreements, Regulations, Sanctuaries and Action Plans', 460.

348 'Annual Report of the International Whaling Commission 45', 28.

349 Phillips, 'Conservation in Practice: Agreements, Regulations, Sanctuaries and Action Plans', 461.

350 *Greenpeace Australia Magazine*, Spring 1994, 3.

351 The Soviet whaling fleet, from 1948 to 1973, reported taking a mere 2710 humpback whales, but it was later revealed by Russia that the real take was over 48 000. Bryant, 'Biodiversity and Conservation: A Hypertext Book'; Caron, 'The International Whaling Commission and the North Atlantic Marine Mammal Commission: The Institutional Risks of Coercion in Consensual Structures', 171.

352 Phillips, 'Conservation in Practice: Agreements, Regulations, Sanctuaries and Action Plans', 461.

to the other states that it proved to be a critical factor in the successful vote to create a whale sanctuary in the region in May 1994.[353]

Japan was not prepared to concede defeat, however. It lodged an objection and thus can still legally hunt minke whales in the region.[354] Japan continues whaling in the Southern Ocean Sanctuary in the name of 'science', but it is the only state to do so. This is despite the fact that, at the Forty-seventh Meeting, the IWC agreed that within both sanctuaries member states should utilize only non-lethal research methods and refrain from issuing special permits that allowed the taking of whales.[355]

At the Forty-eighth IWC Meeting, Japan introduced three papers from a legal workshop held in Tokyo in January 1996. The workshop addressed the issues of the legal status of the moratorium and whether the IWC could extend it indefinitely. A majority of members did not accept Japan's contention that a 'change in the objectives of the Convention based solely on majority interpretation should not be permitted' and thus the establishment of the Southern Ocean Sanctuary was not permitted by the Convention's objectives.[356] At the Forty-ninth Meeting, France, Chile, the Netherlands, the USA, Austria, Brazil, Spain and New Zealand all reiterated their view that the creation of the Southern Sanctuary was legal 'as the will of the countries in conference for the protection of whales and the ecosystem'.[357]

At the Fiftieth Meeting, a resolution proposed by Japan, Antigua, Dominica, Grenada, St Lucia and St Vincent and the Grenadines to abolish the Southern Ocean Sanctuary was declared out of order.[358] At the Fifty-first Meeting, Japan attempted to lift the prohibition on hunting minke whales in the Southern Ocean Sanctuary. The motion was defeated (nine votes in favour, 22 against and one abstention).[359] The US argued that the robust nature of the minke whale population was not a factor in determining the validity of the sanctuary.[360]

At the Fifty-third Meeting, Japan changed its strategy and attempted to modify the Southern Ocean Sanctuary by amending the schedule to state that any prohibition would be applied if so advised by the Scientific Committee.

---

353 Caron, 'The International Whaling Commission and the North Atlantic Marine Mammal Commission: The Institutional Risks of Coercion in Consensual Structures', 172.

354 Rose, 'International Law and the Status of Cetaceans', 37–8.

355 Appendix 9, 'Annual Report of the International Whaling Commission 46', 46; Stroud, 'The Ethics and Politics of Whaling', 70.

356 'Annual Report of the International Whaling Commission 47', 36.

357 'Annual Report of the International Whaling Commission 48', 36.

358 'Annual Report of the International Whaling Commission 49', 28.

359 'Annual Report of the International Whaling Commission 50', 10.

360 Ibid.

The amendment was not passed (13 votes for, 23 against and one abstention).[361] At the Fifty-sixth Annual Meeting, Japan again tried to have the Southern Ocean Sanctuary abolished, but it was not able to get the required three-quarters majority (19 for, 30 against, and two abstentions).[362] Japan seems determined to continue raising the issue until it is successful, however.

The creation of the Southern Hemisphere sanctuary represents a highwater mark in the attempt to preserve whales through the mechanism of sanctuaries. A proposed South Pacific Sanctuary, put forth by Australia and New Zealand since the late 1990s, has not received a three-quarters majority, nor has a joint proposal by Brazil and Argentina to create a South Atlantic Whale Sanctuary been successful.[363] Advocates of the conservationist position, such as Japan, are still contending with those like France, Australia, Brazil and Argentina who have sought to expand the scope of such sanctuaries to other parts of the oceans.

The fact that the sanctuaries were meant to be temporary is significant in that preservationist states have managed to have their sanctuary status continued indefinitely, in the face of contrary scientific advice.[364] At both the 2006 and 2007 meetings, proposals for a new sanctuary in the South Atlantic were defeated without going to a vote.[365] A Japanese motion at the 2006 Meeting to abolish the Southern Ocean Sanctuary was defeated again (28 votes for, 33

---

361 'Annual Report of the International Whaling Commission 52', 17.

362 'Annual Report of the International Whaling Commission 55', 46–7.

363 'Annual Report of the International Whaling Commission 51', 15–17; 'Annual Report of the International Whaling Commission 52', 17–19; 'Annual Report of the International Whaling Commission 53', 33–5; 'Annual Report of the International Whaling Commission 54', 24–7; 'Annual Report of the International Whaling Commission 55', 48–50; 'Revised Chair's Summary Report of the 60th Annual Meeting', Santiago, Chile, June 2008. http://www.iwcoffice.org/_documents/, accessed 01/01/09, 6. At the 2008 Meeting, the issue was again raised but not taken to a vote to allow the 'Future of the IWC' talks to go on unimpeded.

364 Mark A. Zacharias, Leah R. Gerber, and K. David Hyrenbach, 'Review of the Southern Ocean Sanctuary: Marine Protected Areas in the Context of the International Whaling Commission Sanctuary Programme', *Journal of Cetacean Resource Management* 8, no. 1 (2006): 9–10. Andrew Darby, in *The Age* newspaper, cited a report being prepared by scientists for the 2004 IWC Meeting in Sorrento, Italy which argues that the creation of the Southern Ocean Sanctuary was not ecologically justified since it did not conform to the principles of marine reserve design, nor did it protect the whale's habitat. Rather the sanctuaries, the three American scientists argued, were a political and social compromise, not based on any hard scientific data. Despite these criticisms, the author expected the sanctuary to remain, given that anti-whaling states were unlikely to vote for the sanctuary to be opened up. Andrew Darby, 'Scientists Attack Whale Sanctuary', *The Age*, 13 July 2004, 5.

365 'Annual Report of the International Whaling Commission 58', 34–6; 'Annual Report of the International Whaling Commission 59', 4.

against with four abstentions) and was not raised at the 2007 Meeting.[366] At the 2008 Chile Meeting, Brazil, Argentina and South Africa were going to again call for the creation of a South Atlantic Sanctuary. However, in a spirit of amity they did not, citing that they did not wish to call for a vote on the issue while ongoing negotiations were occurring on the future of the IWC.[367]

At the moment, there appears to be a normative deadlock, with neither group able to expand their sphere of influence. This situation appears set to continue for the foreseeable future, with neither faction able to progress their agendas.[368]

## CONCLUSION

Undoubtedly the whaling moratorium has had a positive effect in terms of reversing decades of exploitation and allowing whaling stocks to recover.[369] However, the question of how entrenched the norm of preservation has become is the subject of fierce debate amongst researchers in the field.[370] It is

---

366 'Annual Report of the International Whaling Commission 58', 36–7.

367 'IWC Press Release, Day 4, Thursday 26 June', http://www.iwcoffice.org/meetings/meeting2008.htm, accessed 10/07/08.

368 Ibid.

369 At the Fiftieth Meeting, Dr Peter Bridewater, past Australian Chairman, noted that in the past decade there had been a recovery in the population of most whale species. 'Annual Report of the International Whaling Commission 49', 23. At the Fifty-fourth Meeting, the Japanese Minister of Agriculture, Forestry and Fisheries, Mr Tsutomo Takebe, noted that there had been such a rapid recovery in many whale species, since the imposition of the moratorium, that this opened the door for the consumption of whale meat again. 'Annual Report of the International Whaling Commission 53', 5.

370 Kristen Fletcher maintains that since the moratorium, the IWC is split between preservationists and conservationists and has become a forum merely to air grievances. Fletcher, 'The International Whaling Regime and U.S. Foreign Policy', 226. Brian Hodges argues that despite an acceptance of the norm of preservation in the global community towards whales, the preservationist norm has not become customary international law, or supplanted the settled law of the ICRW. Rather, because the norm of conservation has been entrenched in global environmental law in such documents as the 1972 Stockholm and the 1992 Rio Declarations, conservation rather than preservation is the operating norm. Brian Trevor Hodges, 'The Cracking Façade of the International Whaling Commission as an Institution of International Law: Norwegian Small-Type Whaling and the Aboriginal Subsistence Exemption', *Journal of Environmental Law and Litigation* 15, no. 2 (2000): 2. Jennifer Bailey maintains that what she calls the 'anti-commercial whaling norm' (preservationism) has failed to become dominant at the global level because the remaining whaling states do not adhere to it. Bailey, J.L., 'Arrested Development: The Fight to End Commercial Whaling as a Case of Failed Norm Change', *European Journal of International*

clear that for the moment preservationist norms are ascendant and that most members of the IWC favour the total extinction of the whaling industry.[371]

Utilizing Legro's test for the robustness of the norm, it is observable that, as regards specificity, the commercial moratorium is reasonably understood and adhered to. However, the exemptions allowing for scientific and aboriginal subsistence whaling complicate the operation of the ban.[372] The vexed anomaly of aboriginal whaling continues, and given the ENGOs' reluctance to tackle the issue, shows no sign of being limited or annulled. While Japan and Iceland are the only states still continuing 'scientific research' on whales, such research seems set to continue for the foreseeable future.

The issue of the durability of the norm is also complicated. While the moratorium has been in effect for over 20 years, the question of its continuation has been revisited on a yearly basis at the IWC Annual Meeting. While there have been violations of the preservationist norm by states like Japan and Norway, the majority of states do at present accept the ban as legitimate. As Stoett acknowledges, '. . . it may be argued that there is sufficient normative consensus to maintain the present non-consumptive philosophic outlook in the IWC and the broader whaling regime'.[373] Other researchers such as Vogler are not so sure, arguing that the failure of the Irish proposal, and the RMP, threatens the long-term survival of the moratorium.[374]

---

*Relations*, 14 no. 2 (2008): 289–318. However, most researchers agree that preservationism is now dominant within the IWC. For example, Victor argues that preservationist values are now pervasive and, combined with the global public losing a taste for whale products, this means there is no need to alter the IWC. Rather, Victor believes evolving norms are bringing about reform. David G. Victor, 'Whale Sausage: Why the Whaling Regime Does Not Need to Be Fixed', in *Toward a Sustainable Whaling Regime*, ed. Robert L. Friedheim (Seattle: University of Washington Press, 2000), 294. Anders Blok argues that the preservationist norm 'has gained a near global diffusion, if not acceptance'. Anders Blok, 'Contesting Global Norms: Politics of Identity in Japanese Pro-whaling Countermobilization', *Global Environmental Politics* 8, no. 2 (2008): 43. D'Amato and Chopra argue that, due to the efforts of the ENGOs, we can now speak of '. . . an emergent entitlement of whales – not just "on behalf of" whales – to a life of their own'. D'Amato and Chopra, 'Whales: Their Emerging Right to Life', 22.

371 Victor, 'Whale Sausage: Why the Whaling Regime Does Not Need to Be Fixed', 292.

372 Since the moratorium was put in place, there are estimates that over 14 000 whales have been killed under the guise of aboriginal whaling, commercial kills, pirate and scientific whaling. Chris Stroud argues that the moratorium has never been honoured by some whaling states. Stroud, 'The Ethics and Politics of Whaling', 76. Approximately 2300 whales will be killed annually under the four categories of scientific whaling, aboriginal subsistence whaling, accidents or pirate whaling. Peter Alford, 'Whales Off the Menu', *The Australian*, 22 June 2005, 13.

373 Stoett, *The International Politics of Whaling*, 133.

374 Vogler, *The Global Commons: Environmental and Technological Governance*, 55.

Delegate numbers are still finely balanced. Both sides seek to attract new members supporting their respective positions. Japan still targets poor states wanting foreign aid, Mali and Kiribati having recently joined. They are expected to support conservationist measures. However, to overturn the moratorium requires a three-quarters majority of members. This seems unlikely in the near future given that faction numbers are so evenly balanced.[375]

At the 2005 IWC Meeting in Ulsan, South Korea, Japan appeared to have the numbers to overturn crucial votes. However, three of the putative pro-whaling states – Naaru, Togo and Gambia – failed to present themselves for crucial votes. As a result, pro-whaling states lost all the contested votes, including failing to block progress on new whale sanctuaries (new non-whaling zones in the South Pacific and South Atlantic) and on conservation and animal welfare items. It is unclear if this was a strategic blunder on behalf of these states or a deliberate policy to avoid offending anti-whaling forces.[376]

At recent meetings, Japan has been unable to advance its position significantly at the IWC. Despite being confident initially of success, it has found that the proxy states which receive Japanese aid do not always vote for Japanese positions at the IWC.[377] Consequently, Japan seems to be losing faith in the process altogether. At the 2007 Meeting, Japan, when asked to vote, called out that they would 'not participate' and threatened to quit the IWC and set up an alternative organization based on sustainable utilization.[378] Despite this threat, they still attended the 2008 Meeting, perhaps hoping to use the talks on the 'Future of the IWC' to advance their cause. In the near future, these talks will be the primary normative battleground as both preservationists

---

375 Agence France-Presse (AFP), 'Hunters Push to Harpoon Whaling Ban', *The Australian*, 20 July 2004, 8. Epstein argues that the pendulum has swung back towards 'controlled exploitation', but adduces no evidence for this position. Epstein, 'The Making of Global Environmental Norms: Endangered Species Protection', 47. As of 2008, the numbers of pro- versus anti-whaling states remains evenly matched. However, Epstein's point that the IWC has not evolved from an emphasis on whale species to an ecosystemic approach is correct. C. Epstein, 'The Making of Global Environmental Norms: Endangered Species Protection', 48.

376 Peter Alford, 'Japan's Whaling Friends a No-show', *The Australian*, 21 June 2005, 5.

377 Alford, 'Japan's Whaling Friends a No-show', 5. In 2006, the meeting appeared set for a showdown, since it seemed that the whalers had enough members (a simple majority) to push the IWC in a conservationist direction. The first test was over the meeting's agenda. Japan started by proposing to eliminate debate on small cetaceans, but surprisingly lost the vote (30–32–1). Several states like Gambia and Togo couldn't vote because they had not paid back dues, but states like Senegal, despite back fees being paid, did not attend the vote. Darby, *Harpoon: Into the Heart of Whaling*, 240–43.

378 Ibid.: 245–6.

and whalers attempt to influence the ongoing direction of the IWC. However, given the intransigence of the two positions, it is more likely the stalemate will continue.

The issue of concordance is also not settled since not all states agree with preservationist ideals. As noted, not all states, such as Japan, Norway and Iceland, accept preservationist ideals. Proponents of preservationism do not dare make arguments with preservationist language because they know they will not succeed, so they strategically couch their claims in conservationist rhetoric instead. Since both sides use such rhetoric, it can appear to the outside that the points of contention are smaller. However, the philosophical gulf between the two sides is much greater than the formal rhetoric, which suggests that it is highly unlikely that there will be any increase in concordance over core treaty norms in the near future.

Some states are pessimistic about the acceptance of the moratorium. They argue that a whaling regime that does not include the major whaling states is futile and that it might be better to relax the ban.[379] However, Friedheim argues that we can observe within the whaling regime that 'the preservation norm has gone through a "tipping point" and has "cascaded" throughout the world community, and all that needs to be done is to have it "internalised" by the peoples and governments of the world'.[380]

Friedman's analysis is mostly correct, but he fails to understand that many states have already internalized the preservationist norm. States such as Australia, France, the Netherlands and the USA appear to have internalized preservationist values as part of their state identities and as a consequence they have become powerful norm proponents.[381] While preservationist proponents may not yet have brought about a universal shift sufficient to end the normative debate, they have been remarkably successful in a relatively short period of time in changing how whales, and the practice of whaling, are perceived globally.[382] Few, if any, norms ever acquire this universalist character, however. It is sufficient that a clear majority have that belief and that the minority respect the wishes of the majority of the global community. Japan

---

379 DeSombre, *The Global Environment and World Politics*, 141.

380 Robert L. Friedheim, 'Introduction: The IWC as a Contested Regime', in *Towards a Sustainable Whaling Regime*, ed. Robert L. Friedheim (Seattle: University of Washington Press, 2001), 9.

381 DeSombre provides an example of how deep the norm has been internalized, in the speech by the UK delegate to the Fiftieth IWC Meeting. He stated: 'We do not believe that any whaling is justified' and wanted '. . . the introduction of a permanent, comprehensive moratorium on all whaling other than aboriginal subsistence whaling', DeSombre, *The Global Environment and World Politics*, 141.

382 Stoett, *The International Politics of Whaling*, 134.

and its allies seem unlikely to do this in the near future, although. Taking the three factors of specificity, durability and concordance into account, we can only speak of the norm being of medium-to-high commonality.

Both the neoliberal and constructivist analyses have something to offer when examining the whaling regime. Neoliberalism allows for an economic understanding of normative change within the IWC. Initially, industrial whaling was run on a boom-to-bust cycle – a case of an unmanaged common resource. For many states, as the economic imperative to kill whales faded with the advent of substitutable goods, there was no economic reason to continue what was becoming an unprofitable enterprise.

From a neoliberal perspective, there is an institutional barrier that is preventing the regime from operating properly. The IWC is unable to enforce its collective will because its provisions allow states like Japan to construct veto coalitions. The ICRW allows states unhappy with a decision to lodge an objection, secure in the knowledge that the IWC members will have to acquiesce. This has led to the absurd situation where 'scientific whaling' continues despite all sides knowing that it is a farce.

A neoliberal analysis also allows us to demonstrate the importance of the USA as an actor in achieving normative change within the whaling regime. Even before 1982, both whaling groups and NGOs knew that the US was the most important actor, because it was willing to apply economic duress to enforce its conclusion that whales should be protected and that the authority of the IWC should be heeded.[383]

It is tempting to argue that the crucial role of the USA in the 1970s in pressuring states was the definitive factor in changing IWC norms and conduct, but this is not the whole story. As Peterson argues, '[i]n the case of whaling, no single country or group ever exerted hegemony in the Gramscian sense of winning all others over to its preferred categories for defining and dealing with the problems'.[384]

Examining only the role of the USA and its economic power does not explain why the USA waited so long to exercise its strength, nor does it explain why it used its relative strength as it did. There is a need to examine the role of individuals or groups that directly or indirectly influence or control

---

[383] Caron, 'The International Whaling Commission and the North Atlantic Marine Mammal Commission: The Institutional Risks of Coercion in Consensual Structures', 157; DeSombre, *The Global Environment and World Politics*, 121; Peterson, 'Whalers, Cetologists, Environmentalists, and the International Management of Whaling', 172.

[384] Peterson, 'Whalers, Cetologists, Environmentalists, and the International Management of Whaling', 149.

its policy.[385] Without an understanding of the role played by ENGOs in changing the public perception of whaling, and therefore domestic preference formation, there can be no comprehending why the US position on whaling changed. The only answer neoliberals can propose is that of reputational advantage, but in this case, and given the level of economic power the USA enjoys, it seems highly unlikely that this was the only or primary goal the USA sought.

It is the altruistic dimension of whaling where neoliberals seem most unable to provide a cogent explanation. While they can adequately explain why states would be willing to cooperate to end exploitation and impose a conservationist regime, they are seemingly incapable of explaining why states would choose to preserve whales. In explaining the sway of the preservationist argument, constructivism has the edge. Constructivism also enables us to go beyond the 'veil of statehood' and examine the role of other global actors such as the scientists and ENGOs who acted as norm teachers for their various normative positions.

Scientists were not able to convince states to abandon exploitationist practices and adopt conservationist mores, because they were unable to link their arguments to higher values, nor stop arguing amongst themselves about the correct conservationist approach. However, ENGOs' arguments for preserving whales were made in terms of the uniqueness, intelligence and intrinsic beauty of whales, coupled with a campaign to demonstrate the barbarity of whaling as an activity.[386] This ENGO-led campaign resonated with the global populace, leading to a domestic outcry in key states, including the USA, to end the practice. This bears out Michael Mason's point that claims by ENGOs' campaigns achieve more if they fit with other existing norms such as harm prevention and fair treatment.[387] In this case, ENGOs were able to argue successfully that whale stocks were in danger of extinction (harm prevention) and that such creatures were morally worthy of fair treatment.

Evidence indicates that the ENGOs did not only resort to persuasive techniques, however. They also utilized strategic means. They pushed to become observers to the IWC, had themselves seconded to various state delegations, and in the case of the Seychelles, appear to have used that state as a stalking horse to achieve their goals. These twin strategies enabled ENGOs to achieve their overriding aim of a global moratorium on commercial whaling.

---

385 Ibid.

386 Wapner, 'Horizontal Politics: Transnational Environmental Activism and Global Cultural Change', 48.

387 Michael Mason, 'The Governance of Transnational Environmental Harm: Addressing New Modes of Accountability/Responsibility', *Global Environmental Politics* 8, no. 3 (2008): 19.

However, the strength of the ENGO position was weakened after the moratorium was put in place. This was due to a number of factors, including a split between conservationist and preservationist ENGOs. Conservationists and preservationists can, in some circumstances, agree to implement the same policy for different reasons (for example, zero quotas on endangered species). However, because their underlying principles are so radically different, they cannot form a secure alliance for the longer term. With whale stocks rebounding, the fragility of temporary alliances is exposed.[388] Further, preservationist ENGOs have lost some of their moral legitimacy, and consequently their persuasiveness, because they seem incapable of reconciling the issues of aboriginal whaling with the intrinsic right of whales to exist. The failure to confront this philosophical point head on has opened them up to charges of hypocrisy, which the pro-whaling coalition is only too happy to exploit.[389]

Constructivism allows for an understanding of the way the normative position against whaling has become part of particular states' identities and affects how they interact within the global community. The fact that states like Australia, the US and others had been whaling states, demonstrates that a state's identity is not fixed but is fluid. States, like individuals, can alter their identities even from one extreme to another.[390] States like Australia, the Netherlands, the UK and the USA have all internalized the preservationist norm and act accordingly. Epstein maintains that the IWC has thus become a site for state identity construction.[391] For preservationist states, the IWC is a forum in which to be perceived as a 'good environmental citizen' bonded by the normative position that killing whales is unethical.[392]

However, a case can be made that even notorious exploiters of the past such as Japan, Russia and Norway have moved away from a position of unrestrained exploitation towards a conservationist approach and identity.[393]

---

388 Peterson, 'Whalers, Cetologists, Environmentalists, and the International Management of Whaling', 184.

389 Bailey contends that whalers have been able to reframe the whaling debate from that of an environmental issue to one of nationalistic cultural imperialism and the protection of aboriginal rights. Bailey, 'Arrested Development: The Fight to End Commercial Whaling as a Case of Failed Norm Change', 313. While whaling states are certainly happy to argue these issues, it is drawing a long bow to say the debate has been reframed in this way.

390 Epstein, *The Power of Words in International Relations: Birth of an Anti-whaling Discourse*, 200–201.

391 Ibid.: 218.

392 Ibid.

393 Bailey argues that ENGOs have forced whalers to adopt a conservationist approach (utilizing scientific management of whaling stocks) to justify whaling. Further, by arguing in terms of culture, whalers have distanced themselves from the old exploitationist practices that may well limit the use of whale products in the future.

Only if the pro-whaling states were successful in overturning the moratorium would their position be revealed as either mere posturing or a reflection of a deeper change, one that allows for an environmental component to their state identity.

Lastly, constructivism allows for an understanding of why rogue states such as Japan, Iceland and Norway continue to vehemently pursue policies to return to full-scale whaling, despite the global opprobrium they face. The decision to do so cannot be reduced to economic or other material considerations, but rather must allow for other factors such as culture.[394] In this case, constructivism reveals that cultural and historical conditions drive the ongoing campaign and without an understanding of the strength of the effect of these factors, it is impossible to understand the normative dynamics operating within the IWC.

Despite the whaling tradition in Japanese culture, there are signs that the domestic populations of states like Japan are no longer wedded to the hunting of whales. Porter and Brown and Stoett point out that many Japanese now oppose killing whales, are losing their desire to eat whale meat and many enjoy whale-watching vacations.[395] Miller and Dolsak note that a recent Gallup Poll held in Japan found that while the majority did not oppose whaling as such, they were opposed to eating whale meat.[396] Blok maintains that support for whaling, particularly amongst young Japanese, is fragile at best.[397] This is perhaps a sign of a breakdown between the Japanese people and their leaders, who, at least at the IWC, continue to press for whaling to recommence. In response to this shift in public attitude, a number of Japanese children are being served whale meat for school lunch in an effort to inculcate a taste for whale meat, which many Japanese not born in the post-World War II generation have lost, as well as to reconnect them with the supposed Japanese whaling tradition.[398]

---

Bailey, 'Arrested Development: The Fight to End Commercial Whaling as a Case of Failed Norm Change', 314.

[394] Miller and Dolsak, 'Issue Linkages in International Environmental Policy: The International Whaling Commission and Japanese Development Aid', 88.

[395] Porter, Brown, and Chasek, *Global Environmental Politics*, 81; Stoett, 'Of Whales and People: Normative Theory, Symbolism, and the IWC', 167.

[396] Miller and Dolsak, 'Issue Linkages in International Environmental Policy: The International Whaling Commission and Japanese Development Aid', 71.

[397] Blok, 'Contesting Global Norms: Politics of Identity in Japanese Pro-whaling Countermobilization', 61.

[398] Peter Alford, 'Japan's Whalers Bite Off Too Much', *The Australian*, 8 November 2005, 9; Holt, 'Whaling: Will the Phoenix Rise Again?', 1084. Blok describes an effort by the Group to Preserve Whale Dietary Culture to drum up interest by holding a public symposium in Ishinomaki to introduce to people whale food culture. Only 450 people turned up, most in their fifties and sixties who remembered

Young argues that convincing individual states like Japan and Norway to stop their current whaling practices is too costly.[399] He may be correct in the case of Japanese leaders, but perhaps not in the case of Japanese society. ENGOs have shown themselves to be adept at conducting public education campaigns. If preservationist mores are to become more deeply entrenched in the IWC, then these leading norm teachers need to focus on domestic populaces in the recalcitrant states, and to suggest to their citizens that preserving whales is not an insult to traditional customs and practices, or a sign of Western cultural imperialism, but rather a sign of a culture's maturity.[400] ENGOs will need to make alliances with Japanese groups that can help ameliorate these ongoing cultural issues and seek alliances with like-minded politicians to challenge the strong bureaucratic desire to continue whaling.[401] Otherwise, the normative deadlock at the IWC will continue for the foreseeable future.

---

the food from their school lunch days. Blok, 'Contesting Global Norms: Politics of Identity in Japanese Pro-whaling Countermobilization', 50. Many Japanese believe that theirs is an ancient whaling culture. The fact that taking whales only became common post World War II due to a lack of protein in the national diet is ignored. Hirata, 'Why Japan Supports Whaling', 141.

[399] Oran R. Young, 'Fairness Matters: The Role of Equity in International Regimes' (paper presented at Environmental Justice: Global Ethics for the 21st Century, University of Melbourne, 1–3 October 1997), 34.

[400] Hirata, 'Why Japan Supports Whaling', 142.

[401] Ibid.: 149. Atsushi Ishii and Ayako Okubo put forth an intriguing argument that the main domestic actors in the Japanese fisheries bureaucracies (the Fisheries Agency, the Institute for Cetacean Research and the Japanese Whaling Association) do not wish to lift the moratorium, but rather are committed to continuing scientific whaling since they are too wedded to government largesse to risk any change. Ishii and Okubo, 'An Alternative Explanation of Japan's Whaling Diplomacy in the Post-moratorium Era', 55–88. These domestic forces are the driving force behind the current Japanese diplomatic stance and will need to be overcome by preservationist forces.

# 5. Let's be careful, it's a jungle out there: the International Tropical Timber Organization and sustainable forestry*

Death is one thing: an end to birth is something else[1]

## INTRODUCTION

Many people today worry about the destruction of our tropical forests and what this may entail for species diversity and climate change.[2] The ensuing global debate has crystallized to a great extent around the logging that is generally perceived as the main cause of deforestation.[3] On the other hand,

---

* A version of this chapter appears as 'The International Tropical Timber Organisation and Conservationist Forestry Norms: A Bridge Too Far', *Journal of South Pacific Law*, 13, no. 2 (2009).

1 Drs Michael E. Soule and Bruce A. Wilcox. Quoted in Norman Myers, 'The Future of Forests', in *The Fragile Environment: The Darwin College Lectures* ed. Laurie Friday and Ronald Laskey (Cambridge: Cambridge University Press, 1989), 29.

2 Jutta Brunnee, 'A Conceptual Framework for an International Forests Convention: Customary Law and Emerging Principles in Global Forests and International Law', in *Global Forests and International Law*, ed. Canadian Council of International Law (London: Kluwer Law International, 1996), 41. What constitutes a tropical forest remains contested. Marie-Claude Smouts, *Tropical Forests, International Jungle: The Underside of Global Ecopolitics* (New York: Palgrave Macmillan, 2003), 5. There is a tendency to treat tropical forests as 'monolithic' in nature, whereas in reality there are many different types of tropical forests ranging from rainforests in the wetter equatorial and tropical areas to semi-deciduous and deciduous forests. Duncan Poore, *Changing Landscapes: The Development of the International Tropical Timber Organization and its Influence on Tropical Forest Management* (London and Sterling, VA: Earthscan Publications, 2003), 12. It is defined, in fact, by 'opposition to dry, arid forests . . . and especially in contrast to the grassy, sparsely treed savannah'. Therefore, it needs to be understood that the social construction of what constitutes a 'tropical forest' in global discourse is a function of political ecology. It is not a precise scientific term, but rather 'a certain type of social, political, and economic relations that structure man's interactions with nature in a given environment'. Smouts, *Tropical Forests, International Jungle: The Underside of Global Ecopolitics*, 4, 9.

3 Ibid. For example, Roberto Repetto of the World Resources Institute (WRI)

many developing states have argued post-Stockholm that they are entitled to exploit all sovereign resources, including forests, as compensation for the colonial dependence forced on them in the nineteenth and early twentieth centuries.[4] These states set up the International Tropical Timber Organization (ITTO) as a commercial cartel to regulate the tropical timber industry.

International efforts to protect tropical forests have been a relatively recent phenomenon since forest management was considered an internal sovereign affair. The developing states have preferred to promote ITTO as the best organization to coordinate any debates about future sustainable development.[5] In the 1970s, the only global text even tangentially related to forests was the Ramsar Convention (adopted in 1971 and put into effect in 1975) that aimed to protect wetlands of global significance and their waterfowl.[6]

In the last few decades, an enormous body of scholarly and popular writing has championed the need for rainforest conservation.[7] Conservationists have tended to favour creating a system of protected areas, for example, nature reserves, through either a zoning idea where different regions are specified for particular activities, or by a system where multiple usage of all areas is allowed.[8] The concept of sustainable development has been incorporated into the debates on forests, and sustainable forest management (SFM) and generally conservationist ideals have become accepted terms in the global forestry discourse since the 1992 Rio Summit.[9] However, like the term sustainable

---

speaks for many critics when he argues that commercial logging is the main cause of global deforestation. Marcus Colchester, 'The International Tropical Timber Organization: Kill or Cure for the Rainforests?', in *The Earthscan Reader in Tropical Forestry*, ed. Simon Rietbergen (London: Earthscan Publications Ltd, 1993), 186.

4 A. Dan Tarlock, 'Exclusive Sovereignty Versus Sustainable Development of a Shared Resource: The Dilemma of Latin American Rainforest Management', *Texas International Law Journal* 32, no. 17 (1997): 42–3. See, for example, Permanent Sovereignty over Natural Resources Resolution 1803(XVII).

5 Ibid.: 38.

6 Smouts, *Tropical Forests, International Jungle: The Underside of Global Ecopolitics*, 28.

7 Adrian Forsyth and Kenneth Miyata, *Tropical Nature: Life and Death in the Rainforests of Central and South America* (New York: Simon and Schuster, 1984); Alan Grainger, 'The State of the World's Tropical Rainforests', *Ecologist* 10, no. 6 (1980); Robert Goodland, ed., *The Race to Save the Tropics: Ecology and Economics for a Sustainable Future* (Washington, DC: Island Press, 1990); Susan Head and Robert Heinzman, eds, *Lessons of the Rainforest* (San Francisco: Sierra Club Books for Children, 1990).

8 Smouts, *Tropical Forests, International Jungle: The Underside of Global Ecopolitics*, 172.

9 Ibid.: 15. SFM's defining feature has been a conservationist one. That is, of ensuring an unimpeded, continuing supply of timber for the foreseeable future. The value of a forest was primarily based on its function as a store of timber – not its bios-

development, SFM is an elastic term that enables stakeholders to import into the concept the content that suits their agenda. For this reason, it has been a success as a rhetorical device promoted by stakeholders. It leaves much to be desired as a practical application.[10]

Alternatively, the most common solution espoused in the North to save the tropical rainforests is the preservationist approach, that is, designating large swathes of forested land as forest reserves not to be logged. The argument is made that deforestation is proceeding at such a pace that it outstrips efforts to regenerate the forest and that it is critical to preserve the biodiversity of such forests.[11] This preservationist approach to tropical forests '. . . seeks to protect internationally recognized forest resources by setting standards of harvesting and control. Nations designate forest areas within their territory for inclusion in the international list of protected areas.'[12] As will be seen, such preservationist arguments have failed to gain any purchase at the global level, however, and indeed have rarely been argued due to a variety of factors, including vested interests opposed to anti-logging practices, preservationist-leaning ENGOs being denied access to the ITTO discourse and other non-environmental norms being privileged over preservationism.

Smouts agrees that preservationist approaches have become marginalized and argues that conservationism has become dominant in the global tropical timber discourse, without explaining why.[13] While conservationism has become dominant over preservationism as an alternative to exploitation within the tropical timber discourse, it is not true to say that conservationism has been able to supplant exploitation as the norm underpinning the regime. The reasons behind this failure of norm entrepreneurs to impose conservationist or preservationist mores and practices on the states involved in the tropical timber trade is the central focal point of this chapter. The general narrative is widely accepted that exploitation has prevailed over conservation in the tropical timber regime. This chapter seeks to track the story as to how this occurred and explain why conservation and preservation have failed to become widely accepted standards of behaviour in the management of tropical forests.

Both neoliberal institutionalism and constructivism have much to offer in

---

phere as a whole. Andrew Robert Cock, 'Tropical Forests in the Global State System', *International Affairs* 84, no. 2 (2008): 322.

10 Smouts, *Tropical Forests, International Jungle: The Underside of Global Ecopolitics*, 184.

11 Ibid.: 172.; Jacqueline Vaughn Switzer, *Environmental Politics: Domestic and Global Dimensions*, 4th edition (Belmont, CA: Thomson/Wadsworth, 2004), 279.

12 Emmanuel Kasimbazi, 'Sustainable Development in International Tropical Timber Agreements', *Journal of Energy & Natural Resources Law* 14, no. 2 (1996).

13 Smouts, *Tropical Forests, International Jungle: The Underside of Global Ecopolitics*, 173.

terms of understanding normative interaction within this regime. Neoliberal institutionalists understand deforestation as a collective action problem that requires a regime that provides the mutual assurance that conservationist practices will be implemented.[14] Humphreys is one who believes that an interest-based regime theory is adequate to explain the negotiation of forest soft law to date.[15] Certainly, on the face of it, neoliberalism would seem to have the easier task because states' interests in exploiting tropical timber can be shown to be paramount to date.

However, it is too glib to refer just to states' interests without examining what constitutes these interests. What interests are being served in a continuation of tropical forest exploitation? Whose interests are being served: producer states seeking export dollars or consumer states desiring a steady supply of tropical timber? There is a need to tease out the different interests at play. This chapter will examine the role played by certain producer and consumer states in safeguarding their own interests and the failure of the incentives offered to alter states' interests. Further, it will analyse how certain producer and consumer states have acted in concert, effectively forming unusually strong veto coalitions preventing normative change within the tropical forest regime.

Neoliberals must also come to grips with the vexed question of whether failed or weak states can actually enter into a regime agreement and be expected to keep to their agreement. Oran Young points out that regimes are unlikely to work if the state is subject to political and economic constraints or hampered by the fact that they are weak states.[16] Nor is normative change likely if states are weakened or limited by corrupt domestic power structures. The forestry literature is replete with examples of producer states that have been unable, because of domestic considerations, to prevent exploitation due to failures of leadership, greed or apathy. Neoliberals need to incorporate the concept of weak/failed states into their analysis to determine what impact such states have on normative evolution and regime integrity.

Lastly, there is a need to understand what institutional barriers implicit in the regime itself have stymied normative change. The regime itself appears at first glance to have been set up to prevent norm transformation, through the use of an intricate voting system that places the greatest power in the hands of those

---

14 Ibid.: 25.

15 David Humphreys, 'Life Protective or Carcinogenic Challenge? Global Forests Governance under Advanced Capitalism', *Global Environmental Politics* 3, no. 2 (2003): 43, n. 23.

16 Oran R. Young and George J. Demko, 'Improving the Effectiveness of International Environmental Governance Systems', in *Global Environmental Change and International Governance*, ed. Oran R. Young, George J. Demko and Kilaparti Ramakrishna (Hanover, NH: University Press of New England, 1996), 235.

with the most interest in exploiting tropical forests for short-term financial gain. This book will examine in detail the various institutional impediments and will offer suggestions as to how to overcome them in the future.

Constructivists would, at first glance, perceive the case study of tropical timber as a hard case. This is so since states' material interests appear clearly to hold sway. However, there is a need to unpack the idea of states' interests and examine the powerful role played by actors such as logging corporations and their impact on both state behaviour and, by extension, the ITTO. Holistic constructivism which does not focus solely on states' interests, but rather allows for the examination of the role of other actors, is an ideal lens through which to examine the non-state actors who have influenced the normative direction of the tropical timber regime.

Problematically, constructivists have tended to select case studies that demonstrate the sway of moral argument. However, it is no less important to understand why moral persuasion as an approach often fails. One reason why moral persuasion might fail is because the arguments advanced by norm entrepreneurs are weak and unconvincing and are not successfully linked to higher values as in the Antarctica and whaling case studies. A further reason might be that the environmental arguments adduced by norm advocates are overshadowed by different non-environmental normative arguments. To determine this matter, this chapter will ask of constructivists a counterfactual question as regards tropical timber.[17] If vested interests in timber exploitation or consumption are removed from the equation, would moral environmental norms necessarily win out? Or, to put it another way, is there an alternative explanation, where other norms or priorities are given greater weight by states and global actors, that could also explain why conservation or preservation has not yet been incorporated into the tropical timber regime? Another potential reason for norm failure within the tropical timber regime is if the communication context is distorted due to a lack of opportunity to present/air the arguments. Constructivism is premised on the need for an undistorted communicative discourse not tainted by avarice, misinformation or a determination not to engage in an honest dialogue. There is a need to examine empirically the data to determine if this is the case within the ITTO.

If there has been a communicative failure, how should ENGOs alter their approach to improve their persuasiveness within the ITTO? Or alternatively, should ENGOs be prepared to work strategically to achieve their goals rather

[17] As Checkel correctly points out, exploring counterfactuals can help sharpen an argument and perhaps in this case yield useful insights on the strengths and weaknesses of the constructivist approach. J.T. Checkel, 'Why Comply? Constructivism, Social Norms and the Study of International Institutions' (paper presented at the Annual Meeting, American Political Science Association, Atlanta, Georgia, 1999), 21.

than advance purely moral arguments, and at what cost to them? Should ENGOs be willing to abandon the ITTO if it is compromised, in order to find other global forums that would allow them greater opportunity to espouse their message? The failure of ENGOs to reframe the tropical timber debate also offers valuable lessons to researchers on the limits of moral persuasion as a means for social transformation, the possible need to combine strategic and communicative action, and the importance of all actors having recognized access to decision-making forums.

Constructivism as an approach does not deny that vested interests are important in understanding regime change or inertia. Certainly, the negotiations to create the ITTO and subsequent events reveal intense political disagreement and self-interested bargaining by particular states, determined to protect their own economic interests. By exploring the sway of economic power and moral argument, this chapter seeks to illuminate more fully the reasons why the tropical timber regime has been unable to change from being primarily a business cartel. Before examining the tropical timber regime, however, it is helpful to convey briefly a sense of the size, scope and dimension of the issue being examined.

## THE ENVIRONMENTAL ROLE OF TROPICAL FORESTS

Virtually all stakeholders agree that forests perform vital environmental functions, including the absorption of solar radiation, the production of oxygen, the stabilization of soils, the maintenance of an environment conducive to speciation, and the release back into the atmosphere of water vapour which creates further rainfall in other areas.[18] Tropical forests also act as global carbon sinks for carbon dioxide ($CO_2$). Forests absorb and hold a large part of humanity's fossil fuel consumption. The clearing and burning of forest cover releases the carbon sequestered within it, leading to elevated levels of carbon dioxide in the atmosphere.[19]

Tropical rainforests cover less than 2 per cent of the Earth's surface, yet contain between 40–50 per cent of all known life forms, perhaps as many as 10–50 million species of plants, insects and animals.[20] Only one in five

---

[18] Nicholas Guppy, 'International Governance and Regimes Dealing with Land Resources from the Perspective of the North', in *Global Environmental Change and International Governance*, ed. Oran R. Young, George J. Demko and Kilaparti Ramakrishna (Hanover, NH: University Press of New England, 1996), 138–9.

[19] Brunnee, 'A Conceptual Framework for an International Forests Convention: Customary Law and Emerging Principles in Global Forests and International Law', 46.

[20] Peter Dauvergne, *Loggers and Degradation in the Asia-Pacific: Corporations*

species inhabiting rainforests has even been identified and catalogued. These regions are also potentially immense silos of biological, medical and pharmaceutical resources that could aid millions if preserved. Thousands of animal species and up to 15 per cent of plant species there are threatened with not just exploitation but extinction.[21] Destroying tropical forests involves the destruction of potentially valuable genetic reservoirs that could provide humanity with new and improved foods, drugs and medicines.[22]

Twenty-three per cent of the world's rainforests are to be found in the states of Indonesia, Malaysia, Papua New Guinea, the Philippines and Thailand. The rainforests in Indonesia and Malaysia are generally regarded as having the greatest levels of biodiversity to be found.[23] For the purposes of this book, we will be referring to tropical forests found in three main locations. These comprise 70 states, 23 in the Americas, including Brazil, Colombia, Ecuador and Mexico, 16 in Asia, which has the highest rates of deforestation (particularly Indonesia, the Philippines and Malaysia) and 31 in Africa, which to date has been the least exploited region (but that is now changing) and encompasses Zaire, Cameroon, the Congo and Gabon.[24]

## TROPICAL FOREST DEFORESTATION

It is nigh on impossible to accurately reflect the rate of deforestation that has occurred. Such rates as are cited should be treated with scepticism since definitions of deforestation tend to vary, collected data are imprecise and subject

---

*and Environmental Management* (Cambridge: Cambridge University Press, 2001), 14; Rainforest Action Network, 'Money in the Rainforest', http://www.ran.org/info_center/factsheets/04b.html. For example, the La Selva reserve in Costa Rica, which is 13.2 square kilometres has 1800 vascular plant species, 394 breeding birds, 104 mammals, 76 reptiles, 46 amphibians, 42 fish and 143 butterflies. This is greater than the biotic reservoir of Great Britain. Myers, 'The Future of Forests', 27.

21 Brunnee, 'A Conceptual Framework for an International Forests Convention: Customary Law and Emerging Principles in Global Forests and International Law', 46.

22 Myers, 'The Future of Forests', 30–31. Forest habitat destruction has also been incriminated in the breakdown of indigenous societies such as the Penan in Sarawak. Lorraine M. Elliott, *The Global Politics of the Environment* (Basingstoke: Macmillan, 1998), 84. The World Rainforest Movement (WRM) estimated in 1990 that approximately 50 million indigenous people, plus a further 90 million forest dwellers, rely on forests for food, medicine, building materials and as a source of cultural and spiritual identity. World Rainforest Movement, 'Rainforest Destruction: Causes, Effects and False Solutions' (1990): 18.

23 Sing C. Chew, *World Ecological Degradation: Accumulation, Urbanization, and Deforestation 3000 B.C.–A.D. 2000* (Walnut Creek, CA: AltaMira Press, 2001), 148.

24 Smouts, *Tropical Forests, International Jungle: The Underside of Global Ecopolitics*, 5–6.

to different interpretations, and rates of deforestation can fluctuate wildly from year to year.[25] However, the data on deforestation can provide an overall picture, fuzzy though it may be, of the size and scope of the phenomenon. Certainly humans have always exploited the resources of tropical forests but again, as with whaling, the issue has emerged only when human populations and/or technologies have increased the scale and rate of exploitation to the point that tropical forests are threatened globally. At the dawn of the nineteenth century, it is estimated, there were about 3.5 billion hectares of forests in tropical states.[26] Throughout the nineteenth century economically viable forests were cut down for either fuel or building material to feed the burgeoning industrial economies.[27]

In the 1920s and 1930s, international journals devoted to forestry catalogued the increasing rate of destruction of tropical forests, but the issue was not at that time accorded a high priority by states, which assumed that forests were so large and plentiful that humans could draw resources from them for centuries before there would be a problem.[28] With the end of World War II and the rise of decolonization, forests were opened up to global industrial exploitation. Such practices suited both the state-building goals of the newly independent states as well as the burgeoning craving for tropical timber in Japan and the West.[29] The drive to exploit tropical forests began in earnest in the late 1950s and gained momentum in the 1960s, with forest being seen as having less value compared to cleared land's potential use for agriculture.[30]

---

25 Marcus Colchester, 'Colonizing the Rainforests: The Agents and Causes of Deforestation', in *The Struggle for Land and the Fate of the Forests*, ed. Marcus Colchester and Larry Lohmann (London: Zed Books, 1995), 2. Similar to the debate as to how to properly define a tropical forest, there is much debate about what constitutes deforestation. The FAO defines deforestation 'as the depletion of tree crown cover to less than 20% in developed countries and less than 10% in developing countries'. Dauvergne, *Loggers and Degradation in the Asia-Pacific: Corporations and Environmental Management*, 13. However, Dauvergne argues for a broader definition, whereby it is the complete loss of forest cover. Peter Dauvergne, *Shadows in the Forest: Japan and the Politics of Timber in Southeast Asia*, Politics, Science, and the Environment (Cambridge, MA: MIT Press, 1997), 1.

26 Smouts, *Tropical Forests, International Jungle: The Underside of Global Ecopolitics*, 1.

27 Janet N. Abramovitz and Ashley T. Mattoon, 'Reorienting the Forest Products Economy', in *State of the World 1999: A Worldwatch Institute Report on Progress Towards a Sustainable Society*, ed. Linda Starke (New York: W.W. Norton & Company, 1999), 61.

28 Switzer, *Environmental Politics: Domestic and Global Dimensions*, 277.

29 Cock, 'Tropical Forests in the Global State System', 332.

30 Poore, *Changing Landscapes: The Development of the International Tropical Timber Organization and its Influence on Tropical Forest Management*, 13.

It is estimated that between 1964 and 1984 half of every tree ever harvested by humans was cut down.[31] There is general agreement that depletion rates in the late 1970s ranged from 76 000 to 100 000 square kilometres, with a further 100 000 square kilometres being grossly disrupted.[32] By 1976, the scope of the problem was beginning to be understood by global international organizations. The Food and Agriculture Organization (FAO) publication *Unasylva*, published in 1976, concluded that the rate of tropical forest deforestation was 11 million hectares annually. It arrived at this figure by including all states in the tropical zone (65). It then gathered all available state annual rates of deforestation (13) and extrapolated across other states to achieve an average. The study was criticized as being deeply flawed, for both its methodology and its non-inclusion of critical states such as Brazil and Indonesia, but the report has become a yardstick, with its upper estimate of 15 million becoming lodged in the global consciousness.[33]

In 1980, a further study by the FAO estimated that, worldwide, deforestation was occurring at the rate of 114 000 square kilometres every year.[34] Deforestation figures compiled during the 1980s indicate that harvesting occurred at 16.9 million hectares per annum during the 1980s at an annual deforestation rate of 0.9 per cent, and since 1980 annual rates of deforestation have nearly doubled, from 0.58 to 1 per cent or approximately 17.1 million hectares per year.[35] By 1990, global deforestation was estimated to be 1715 million hectares approximately, with an estimated 38 per cent of this area considered to be tropical rainforest (656 million hectares).[36] While we can quibble about the precise rate, it is clear that tropical forest degradation is an ongoing, serious problem.[37]

---

31 United Nations Environment Programme, 'Environmental Data Report' (New York: Oxford University Press, 1990), 234.

32 Myers, 'The Future of Forests', 24–5.

33 Smouts, *Tropical Forests, International Jungle: The Underside of Global Ecopolitics*, 29.

34 Colchester, 'Colonizing the Rainforests: The Agents and Causes of Deforestation', 1.

35 Edward Barbier et al., 'Deforestation: The Role of the International Trade in Tropical Timber', in *The Causes of Tropical Deforestation: The Economic and Statistical Analysis of Factors Giving Rise to the Loss of the Tropical Forests*, ed. Katrina Brown and David W. Pearce (London: UCL Press Limited, 1994), 7; Brunnee, 'A Conceptual Framework for an International Forests Convention: Customary Law and Emerging Principles in Global Forests and International Law', 45.

36 Barbier et al., 'Deforestation: The Role of the International Trade in Tropical Timber', 5; Smouts, *Tropical Forests, International Jungle: The Underside of Global Ecopolitics*, 29.

37 The UN Economic and Social Commission for Asia and the Pacific concluded in 1990 that dramatic deforestation occurred in the region between 1950 and 1976

## CAUSES OF TROPICAL FOREST DEFORESTATION

Which actors and what factors have caused the rapid deforestation of tropical forests? Opinions vary, with many global development agencies and intergovernmental bodies blaming poverty, while many ENGOs attribute the problem to TNCs and the excessive consumption of developed states.[38] Both sides have a point and the interlocking problems make it impossible to discern one primary cause. The two principal organizations examining deforestation, the ITTO and the FAO, tend to blame agriculture and development policies, excessive fuelwood gathered, overgrazing, fires, over-exploitation of timber and poor harvest practices, in that order, for the depletion of forests.[39] Logging is considered to be merely a factor that 'aggravates changes in forest cover'.[40] Sing Chew argues that many of these factors are not so much causes as symptoms of other social, economic and political trends created by state policies, the global division of labour and capitalism, which are not taken into consideration within such reports.[41]

---

when approximately four million hectares were cleared annually. Chew, *World Ecological Degradation: Accumulation, Urbanization, and Deforestation 3000 B.C.–A.D. 2000*, 146. A report by the FAO, *The Tropical Forest Action Plan: Report of the Independent Review*, published in 1990, puts the global loss of tropical forests at 170 000 square kilometres annually, an increase of 54 per cent over the previous decade. The World Resources Institute, in its report, *World Resources 1990–91*, estimated the rate of deforestation as closer to 204 000 square kilometres. Colchester, 'Colonizing the Rainforests: The Agents and Causes of Deforestation', 1–2.

38 Colchester, 'Colonizing the Rainforests: The Agents and Causes of Deforestation'.

39 For example, the ITTO claimed in a 1993 report that the global timber trade is not a major source of tropical deforestation. The London Environmental Economics Centre, 'The Economic Linkages between the International Trade in Tropical Timber and the Sustainable Management of Tropical Forests' (London: International Tropical Timber Organization, 1993). Rather, the main problem cited is the conversion of forests to agricultural purposes and that most tropical timber is utilized domestically for fuelwood and other non-industrial uses. Barbier et al., 'Deforestation: The Role of the International Trade in Tropical Timber', 271; Chris Elliott and Richard Z. Donovan, 'Introduction', in *Certification of Forest Products: Issues and Perspectives*, ed. Virgilio M. Viana et al. (Washington, DC: Island Press, 1996), 3.

40 Smouts, *Tropical Forests, International Jungle: The Underside of Global Ecopolitics*, 105; Gareth Porter and Janet Welsh Brown, *Global Environmental Politics* (Boulder, CO: Westview Press, 1991), 97. The gathering of firewood is accorded the most blame since it is the main fuel source in tropical states and up to 80 per cent of wood taken is consumed as firewood. Smouts, *Tropical Forests, International Jungle: The Underside of Global Ecopolitics*, 88.

41 Chew, *World Ecological Degradation: Accumulation, Urbanization, and Deforestation 3000 B.C.–A.D. 2000*, 145.

However, ENGOs and other observers maintain that logging is the primary cause of forest loss and damage.[42] The World Resource Institute in 1997 reported in *The Last Frontier Forests: Ecosystems and Economies on the Edge* (Bryant et al., 1997) that logging was a moderate to high threat to 50 per cent of the remaining forest in Asia, 69 per cent in South America and 79 per cent in Africa.[43] In 1995, Nigel Dudley, Jean-Paul Jeanrenaud and Francis Sullivan, in *Bad Harvest: The International Tropical Timber Trade and the Degradation of the World's Forests*, argued that 'far from being a negligible cause, the timber trade is the primary cause of forest degradation and loss in many of the remaining natural forests'.[44]

Such forest exploitation has been carried out by governments or by corporations or individuals licensed by the state.[45] States have gone ahead with 'development' programmes that emphasize forest conversion regardless of the medium to short-term consequences, citing as rationale a higher moral duty to help lift their citizens out of poverty. Tarlock believes that the currently unsustainable levels of forest felling have their foundations in the 1960s when South and Central American states utilized foreign loans to 'develop' their forests for mineral extraction, cattle ranching or sowing export crops and such approaches have become the norm across the globe.[46]

To understand more fully the normative debate within the ITTO one must be cognizant of the concerns the producer states have had about the organization limiting their economic development to satisfy developed states' domestic popular opinion.[47] This fear influences the way developing states deal with the North and limits the ITTO's ability to implement environmental programmes. Northern environmental values are deemed antithetical to Southern development priorities. Indeed, the evidence suggests that the most important norm influencing the behaviour of producer states is the norm of development. Undoubtedly, government policy to pursue economic development has been one of the root causes of extensive deforestation in Lesser

---

42 Ibid.: 146.; Smouts, *Tropical Forests, International Jungle: The Underside of Global Ecopolitics*, 105.

43 Dauvergne, *Loggers and Degradation in the Asia-Pacific: Corporations and Environmental Management*, 15.

44 Kibel, *The Earth on Trial: Environmental Law on the International Stage*, 127–8.

45 Poore, *Changing Landscapes: The Development of the International Tropical Timber Organization and its Influence on Tropical Forest Management*, 24.

46 Tarlock, 'Exclusive Sovereignty Versus Sustainable Development of a Shared Resource: The Dilemma of Latin American Rainforest Management', 38.

47 Poore, *Changing Landscapes: The Development of the International Tropical Timber Organization and its Influence on Tropical Forest Management*, 107.

Developed Countries (LDCs).[48] For developing states, which are the bulk of the timber-producing states, the alleviation of poverty by government-sponsored development has been the overriding objective.[49]

The LDCs aspire to the same level of development enjoyed by many Northern states.[50] Developing states argue, with some justification, that developed states built their material wealth by extracting their own forests, and developing nations are utilizing the same approach.[51] From the perspective of Southern states, concerns about intergenerational equity are far less pressing than improving the welfare of current generations through development paid for by timber exports.[52] For many LDCs, the primary purpose of state-owned forests is to provide industries with raw material and in the long term, to provide potential exports.[53] However, it was not just the felling of trees for export revenues that created deforestation. Once timber extraction has begun, bulldozers and cranes move in and forestland opens up to the agricultural or urban development that is seen as essential to producer states' economic development.[54]

The ENGOs understand very well the link between state development policies and tropical deforestation and the restrictions it imposes on the ITTO. The WRM argue, in their Declaration of the World Rainforest Movement: An Emergency Call to Action for the Forests and their Peoples, that:

> Deforestation is the inevitable result of the current social and economic policies being carried out in the name of development. Such destructive projects and policies include; plantations, both for industrial forestry and for export crops; ranching

---

48 Harrison Ngau, Thomas Jalong Apoi and Chee Yoke Ling, 'Malaysian Timber: Exploitation for Whom?', in *Forest Resource Crisis in the Third World* (Penang: Sahabat Alam Malaysia, 1987), 45.

49 James Rush, *The Last Tree: Reclaiming the Environment in Tropical Asia* (Oxford: Westview Press, 1991), 30; Herb Thompson, 'The Ecological-economics of Non-sustainable Development: Logging Tropical Forests in Southeast Asia and the Pacific', in *The Political Ecology of Tropical Forests in Southeast Asia: Historical Perpectives*, ed. Lye Tuck-Po, Wil de Jong, and Abe Ken-ichi (Kyoto: Kyoto University Press, 2003), 202.

50 Gary C. Bryner, *From Promises to Performance: Achieving Global Environmental Goals* (New York: W.W. Norton & Company Inc., 1997), 260.

51 Thompson, 'The Ecological-Economics of Non-sustainable Development: Logging Tropical Forests in Southeast Asia and the Pacific', 201.

52 Bryner, *From Promises to Performance: Achieving Global Environmental Goals*, 262.

53 Anthony B. Anderson, 'Deforestation in Amazonia: Dynamics, Cause and Alternatives', in *The Earthscan Reader in Tropical Forestry*, ed. Simon Reitbergen (London: Earthscan Publications Ltd, 1993), 167; James J. Douglas, *A Re-appraisal of Forestry Development in Developing Countries* (Boston: Martinus Nijhoff Publishers, 1983), 134; Ngau, Apoi and Ling, 'Malaysian Timber: Exploitation for Whom?', 42.

54 Ngau, Apoi and Ling, 'Malaysian Timber: Exploitation for Whom?', 43.

schemes; dam projects; commercial logging; mining and industry; the dispossession of peasants and indigenous peoples; colonization schemes; highways into forested areas; pollution; tourism.[55]

However, it is not just domestic pressure to develop that has led to deforestation. Here holistic constructivism can direct attention to the role played by non-state actors in fostering an environment that privileges economic development over all other considerations. For example, pressure has been applied to developing states by institutions such as the World Bank, which has insisted on development projects and export-oriented economic policies.[56] High levels of foreign-owned debt have placed some LDCs in an invidious position that has forced them to agree to strictures placed on them by IOs such as the World Bank. Consequently, to meet crippling interest payments, LDCs are forced to ignore or cheat the tropical timber regime and exploit their forests at an ever-greater rate.[57] The debt crisis of the 1980s in particular exacerbated the political situation, leading to many developing states becoming dependent upon the revenue from timber exporting to repay debts owed to developed states.[58] The twin lash of both domestic and global pressure to develop only reinforced global tropical deforestation as a way to appease domestic and international constituencies. Without an understanding of this context, it is difficult to understand fully the actions of producer states within the ITTO.

The global tropical timber trade is a critical source of foreign exchange earnings for several states that traditionally have a poor export record.[59] Despite the attempts by the ITTO and the FAO to blame other factors, timber production has traditionally been, and is likely in the short term to remain, the primary resource usage of the forest.[60] The global trade in tropical timber is

---

55 World Rainforest Movement, *Rainforest Destruction: Causes, Effects and False Solutions* (Penang: World Rainforest Movement, 1990), Annex.

56 Peter Utting, *Trees, People and Power: Social Dimensions of Deforestation and Forest Protection in Central America* (London: Earthscan Publications Ltd, 1993), 37.

57 James Kahn and Judith McDonald, 'International Debt and Deforestation', in *The Causes of Tropical Deforestation: The Economic and Statistical Analysis of Factors Giving Rise to the Loss of the Tropical Forests*, ed. Katrina Brown and David W. Pearce (London: UCL Press Ltd, 1994), 66; Young and Demko, 'Improving the Effectiveness of International Environmental Governance Systems', 235–6.

58 Charles Secrett, 'How European Transnational Corporations and Government Control and Exploit 3rd World Resources', in *Forest Resource Crisis in the Third World* (Penang: Sahabat Alam Malaysia, 1987), 235.

59 Barbier et al., 'Deforestation: The Role of the International Trade in Tropical Timber', 277.

60 Smouts, *Tropical Forests, International Jungle: The Underside of Global Ecopolitics*, 105.

over a century old and has experienced both peaks and troughs. Jan Laarman estimates that after World War I exports in tropical timber rose throughout the 1920s, peaking in either 1929 or 1930. The Great Depression and World War II limited tropical timber exports, but after the war an uninterrupted export expansion occurred which dwarfed all previous export growth, with serious consequences for the tropical rainforests that supplied the timber. Exports rose from an annual average of 2.8 million cubic metres in 1946–50 to 66.6 million cubic metres by 1976–80, a factor increase of 24. We can observe further export growth in absolute terms during every five-year period until 1980.[61]

The reasons for this increase range from, on the demand side, the increase in income and population in states like the US and Japan that led in turn to an increased demand for tropical timber to, on the supply side, increased technological advances in mechanized logging and timber transportation, which have enabled the cutting of forests that hitherto were considered economically unfeasible.[62] Laarman estimates that from 1900 to 1980 almost 1.2 billion cubic metres of tropical hardwood were logged and exported.[63] The major tropical timber exporting nations in this period were Indonesia, Malaysia, Cote d'Ivoire, Brazil, Gabon and the Congo.[64]

In the latter half of the 1960s, global logging accelerated to the point that exploitation was so great that forest managers were unable to control it. Large swathes of forests were razed globally, particularly in Southeast Asia, with little effort to conserve forests for intergenerational needs.[65] Problematically, forests were only considered valuable for the timber and carbon, leading to a disincentive to promote sustainable practices.[66] There were some producer

---

61 Jan G. Laarman, 'Export of Tropical Hardwoods in the Twentieth Century', in *World Deforestation in the Twentieth Century*, ed. John F. Richards and Richard P. Tucker (Durham, NC: Duke University Press, 1988), 150.

62 Ibid.: 150–51.

63 Ibid.: 158.

64 Like the figures describing deforestation, it is nearly impossible to gauge the growth in tropical timber exportation since the figures are so unreliable. The FAO has made the most thorough attempt to obtain accurate figures but has conceded that even its own estimates must be treated cautiously due to problems in obtaining accurate statistics. The problem is compounded by definitional problems regarding the 'tropics', 'tropical countries', and a definitive answer to what constitutes a 'tropical wood'. Ibid.: 148. No doubt the figures are deliberately downplayed to hide the scale, nor can we account for illegal or domestic cutting with any certainty. FoE estimates that approximately half of the tropical timber for sale in the West is derived from illegal logging. Tim Boekhout van Solinge, 'Eco-crime: The Tropical Timber Trade', in *Organized Crime: Culture, Markets and Policies*, ed. D. Siegel and H. Nelen (New York: Springer, 2008), 98.

65 Poore, *Changing Landscapes: The Development of the International Tropical Timber Organization and its Influence on Tropical Forest Management*, 14.

66 Ibid.: 23.

states, like Brazil and Indonesia, whose governments foresaw long-term problems, and attempted unilaterally to ban the export of logs from their reserves in the 1970s and 1980s. Brazil imposed such a moratorium in the 1970s and Indonesia put up restrictions in 1980 and a total ban in 1985, neither of which lasted, due to pressure from organizations like the International Monetary Fund (IMF).[67] Ironically, these states have proven over the years to be two of the greatest resisters to enacting change within the ITTO. Despite these attempted control mechanisms, it is generally considered that the logging industry went through a boom during the 1980s and 1990s, with record exports and profits.[68]

By the end of the second millennium, the USA and Japan have become the two biggest consumer states of timber, with many of their companies having extensive logging operations in many parts of the globe. These included Siberia, Asia, Latin America and West Africa. While the USA still has comparatively greater reserves of forests, its voracious need for timber products has ensured that US corporations have exploited other states' forestry resources.[69] For nearly two decades, Japan has treated Southeast Asia as an extension of its own woodyard, importing 11 million cubic metres of unfinished logs from Southeast Asia on average during the 1980s until the early 1990s. The total volume of tropical timber imports into Japan was 29 per cent of the world's trade in 1986.[70] Hypocritically, Japan, while taking three-quarters of timber exports from Southeast Asia, could easily supply its entire hardwood timber needs from domestic forests. It has refused to do so while other states are willing to sell off their natural assets relatively cheaply.[71]

Both producer and consumer states have perceived it to be in their interests to continue the clearfelling of tropical forests to ensure that demand for tropical timber remains high and supply costs low.[72] Both producer and consumer states' governments are well represented as board members and shareholders among the transnational corporations (TNCs) who specialize in logging, with their corporate headquarters in the USA, Japan, Germany, France, Finland,

---

67 Smouts, *Tropical Forests, International Jungle: The Underside of Global Ecopolitics*, 109.

68 Wil de Jong, Lye Tuck-Po and Abe Ken-ichi, 'The Political Ecology of Tropical Forests in Southeast Asia: Historical Roots of Modern Problems', in *The Political Ecology of Tropical Forests in Southeast Asia*, ed. Wil de Jong, Lye Tuck-Po and Abe Ken-ichi (Melbourne: Trans Pacific Press, 2003), 1–2.

69 Chew, *World Ecological Degradation: Accumulation, Urbanization, and Deforestation 3000 B.C.–A.D. 2000*, 151.

70 Ibid.: 152.

71 Myers, 'The Future of Forests', 26.

72 Kibel, *The Earth on Trial: Environmental Law on the International Stage*, 128.

Sweden, Indonesia and Malaysia.[73] The developed world has also had its 'hand on the chainsaw' through its principal role in the international tropical timber trade, and the exploitation of forests by timber TNCs, and its voracious appetite for timber resources.[74]

## BUILDING AN INTERNATIONAL TROPICAL TIMBER REGIME?

With the problems of tropical forest destruction so well publicized globally for decades, there was an inevitable demand for a regime to protect the tropical forests. The genesis of the International Tropical Timber Agreement and its concomitant organization can be found not in individual states choosing to come together to overcome a mutual problem but rather from within the United Nations Conference on Trade and Development (UNCTAD). UNCTAD was dedicated to the ideal of restructuring historical patterns of global trade to enable lesser developed states to participate and derive greater benefits. It sought to pursue this goal through trade in tropical timber. The fact that states did not voluntarily come together to combat deforestation is significant and helps to understand the truculence and evasion shown by both producer and consumer states associated with the tropical timber regime.[75]

In November 1966, an UNCTAD/FAO Working Party on forest and timber products recommended that a tropical timber bureau be created. At a subsequent meeting in September 1968, the idea was revisited and again it was proposed that such an entity be established. At this time, the only preoccupation was that of trade and the bureau was meant to collect and exchange data on markets and on the uses of timber products.[76] The UNCTAD proposal languished for the next eight years due to stakeholder concerns that any such organization might be too bureaucratic, or alternatively, that it should have a wider brief than just tropical timber and should apply to all timber. The timber companies were especially concerned that such an entity would participate in commercial activities, possibly limiting their activities.[77]

---

73 'High Stakes: The Need to Control Transnational Logging Companies: A Malaysian Case Study – Part 2b: Politics, Law and the Logging Industry', World Rainforest Movement and Forests Monitor, http://www.forestsmonitor.org/reports/highstakes/part2b.htm.

74 Myers, 'The Future of Forests', 25.

75 Poore, *Changing Landscapes: The Development of the International Tropical Timber Organization and its Influence on Tropical Forest Management*, 27.

76 Ibid.

77 Ibid.: 29.

Following the Stockholm Conference in 1972, there was a flurry of global activity on the issue of tropical forest protection. In 1974, the IUCN held conferences on the topic of Guidelines for Tropical Forest Management in Caracas, Venezuela and Bandung, Indonesia. The conference recommendations were embodied in the Ecological Guidelines for Development in Tropical Rain Forests.[78] In July 1974, the idea to establish a tropical timber bureau was reinvigorated by the International Trade Centre (ITC), which commissioned a study to create such an entity for export-producing states. Although there is no direct evidence linking the renewed global interest in the issue of tropical timber protection to the desire to create a tropical timber organization, it can be reasonably stated that it helped create a more favourable climate for such an entity, even though the timber states were not driving the issue.[79]

The eventual report revealed that there was approval for such an organization among producer states, but that importing states should also be part of any accord. The authors thought the bureau's functions should be:

- to stimulate demand for, and further the use of tropical timber, including the lesser-known species and the products manufactured therefrom;
- to collect, collate and disseminate technical information on various tropical timbers warranting promotion and carry out appropriate market development programmes in light of the requirements of the import markets and the existing facilities for these types of work;
- to develop channels for, and maintain, the free exchange of market intelligence and technical knowledge between importing and producing companies.[80]

A further complicating factor to be borne in mind when examining the creation of the tropical timber regime was the price of commodities in the 1970s and the desire of producer states, mostly developing states, to extract a higher price for their resources. Following the success of the Organization of the Petroleum Exporting Countries (OPEC) cartel in 1973–74, many LDCs felt that cartels could enable states to control commodity prices and thus increase their power relative to developed states.[81] The issue of resource prices

---

[78] Ibid.: 14.

[79] Ibid.: 29.

[80] Ibid.: 29–30.

[81] Fred P. Gale, 'Discourse and Southeast Asian Deforestation: A Case Study of the International Tropical Timber Organization', in *The Political Ecology of Tropical Forests in Southeast Asia: Historical Perpectives*, ed. Wil de Jong, Lye Tuck-Po and Abe Ken-ichi (Melbourne: Trans Pacific Press, 2003), 238.

on the global market had been simmering since 1964, but UNCTAD had been unable to convince developed states of the necessity to improve the current order, which advantages the producer states in terms of their export revenues. Coupled with this changing global resource pricing order were new perceptions of appropriate resource usage and environmental protection (see previous chapters on Antarctica and whaling) and the end to a commodities boom cycle in 1972. UNCTAD and the G77 states believed that these factors could lead to developed states changing their attitudes towards commodity agreements and global regulation resulting in higher prices for raw materials, greater development and a decrease in global poverty.[82]

To promote this change in the global commodity order UNCTAD, led by Gamani Corea, the Sri Lankan Secretary-General of UNCTAD, created the Integrated Program for Commodities (IPC) to encourage international commodity organizations to be set up, focusing on resources such as tea and rubber.[83] From 1974 until 1979, the IPC sought to restructure the global resource order to enable LDCs to derive a greater percentage of wealth from commodity trading.[84] Tropical timber was a late addition to the set, but was one of the few IPC-led negotiations on resource issues to actually conclude negotiations and create a commodities agreement.[85] Thus, when examining the tropical timber regime, it must be borne in mind that it was not created to conserve/preserve tropical forests: rather, it was designed to facilitate the orderly extraction of tropical *timber*.[86] States' interests in this regime have always been perceived as tied to the issue of timber production and marketing, with forestry protection at best a secondary consideration.

Against this backdrop, and to promote UNCTAD's mission, negotiations for a tropical timber agreement (which eventually became the ITTA), began in

---

[82] Pamela S. Chasek, *Earth Negotiations: Analyzing Thirty Years of Environmental Diplomacy* (Tokyo and New York: United Nations University Press, 2001), 95–6.

[83] Gale, 'Discourse and Southeast Asian Deforestation: A Case Study of the International Tropical Timber Organization', 238.

[84] Chasek, *Earth Negotiations: Analyzing Thirty Years of Environmental Diplomacy*, 95.

[85] Gale, 'Discourse and Southeast Asian Deforestation: A Case Study of the International Tropical Timber Organization', 238. In many ways, tropical timber is not a commodity in the strictest sense, since it is difficult to characterize as one resource. Unlike jute, for example, it comes from a wide variety of tree species in many varied places in the world. This makes it difficult to treat it as a homogeneous resource. Colchester, 'The International Tropical Timber Organization: Kill or Cure for the Rainforests?', 188.

[86] Poore, *Changing Landscapes: The Development of the International Tropical Timber Organization and its Influence on Tropical Forest Management*, 30.

1976 with a series of preparatory meetings that were to last six years.[87] While states were not willing to drive the process, IOs were keen to pressure the states to achieve a regime that would better conserve tropical forests.[88] UNCTAD, which was still keen to create a regime under its aegis, organized the first of a series of Preparatory Meetings on Tropical Timber in May 1977.[89] At this point in time, states, whether producers or consumers, perceived no real benefit in participating in such a body, although producer states were still open to a tropical timber regime if it suited their desires for a continuing tropical timber trade.[90]

The First Preparatory Meeting in May 1977 on tropical timber dealt with questions of issue definition and the scale and the scope of problems in the tropical timber industry.[91] Consistent with their previous approach, delegates of both producer and consumer states were concerned to promote investment in the industry to ensure the long-term supply of tropical timber stocks. At the Second Meeting (24–8 October 1977), producer states outlined a set of recommendations designed to minimize market and price instability, again focusing on their interest in maximizing timber exports. Consumer states, with the same desire for a steady supply, were also amenable, and agreed to study the proposal and continued their examination, up to and including the Third Meeting (23–7 January 1978).[92]

Delegates to the Fourth Preparatory Meeting (31 July–4 August 1978) agreed that four issues would be included in a possible global agreement on the harvesting of tropical timber: reforestation and forest management, higher levels of processing within producing states, research and development, and

---

87 Kasimbazi, 'Sustainable Development in International Tropical Timber Agreements', 141.

88 Poore, *Changing Landscapes: The Development of the International Tropical Timber Organization and its Influence on Tropical Forest Management*, 14. For example, the FAO, at the Fourth Meeting of its Committee on Forest Development in the Tropics, held in November 1976, dedicated itself to evaluating 'the values of tropical moist forest ecosystems and the environmental consequences of their removal'. Poore, *Changing Landscapes: The Development of the International Tropical Timber Organization and its Influence on Tropical Forest Management*, 14.

89 Chasek, *Earth Negotiations: Analyzing Thirty Years of Environmental Diplomacy*, 96; Poore, *Changing Landscapes: The Development of the International Tropical Timber Organization and its Influence on Tropical Forest Management*, 31.

90 Poore, *Changing Landscapes: The Development of the International Tropical Timber Organization and its Influence on Tropical Forest Management*, 30–31.

91 Chasek, *Earth Negotiations: Analyzing Thirty Years of Environmental Diplomacy*, 96; Poore, *Changing Landscapes: The Development of the International Tropical Timber Organization and its Influence on Tropical Forest Management*, 32.

92 Chasek, *Earth Negotiations: Analyzing Thirty Years of Environmental Diplomacy*, 96–7.

market fluctuation. The participants also requested that the secretariats of the FAO and UNCTAD, working with any relevant body, create a draft document encompassing the above points.[93] The Fourth Meeting also marked a seminal moment, as it was the first time that environmental considerations in relation to tropical timber were discussed. Duncan Poore notes that this shift in focus was due to the dawning recognition, in the late 1970s, of a global consciousness of the high rates of deforestation globally, and the lack of reforestation projects to deal with the problem.[94] Despite these environmental concerns, there appears no evidence that states saw it as critical to their interests to deal with the problem of global deforestation at this time, preferring to focus on commodity trade issues.

The draft report was duly presented at the Fifth Meeting (22–6 October 1979), but the members were unable to complete their consideration of the text. Again, environmental issues were discussed peripherally, with much of the documentation on the issue focusing on reforestation and forest management.[95] The decision was taken to reconvene the following year and the following reports were annexed to the meeting report: the chair's draft recommendations, the producer states' draft conclusions and recommendations from the consumer states, submitted by the United States.[96] The consumer states were adamant that the key to any agreement from their perspective was the assurance of a continuous supply of tropical timber.[97]

At the second session of the Fifth Preparatory Meeting (7–18 July 1980), the Chair observed that the three draft agreements were substantially close enough to have allowed the FAO and UNCTAD secretariats to prepare five studies on three of the four elements that had been agreed could underpin any potential agreement. A further factor that had an impact on the negotiations was that of the parallel negotiations to create a Common Fund. During the break between the two sessions, negotiations had been concluded on the Common Fund. This removed one potential obstacle to the creation of a tropical timber agreement: the need for financial arrangements to assist commodity development.[98] Critically, however, a proposal to create a reforestation fund was rejected by the International Bank for Reconstruction and

---

93 Ibid.: 97.

94 Poore, *Changing Landscapes: The Development of the International Tropical Timber Organization and its Influence on Tropical Forest Management*, 33.

95 Ibid.

96 Chasek, *Earth Negotiations: Analyzing Thirty Years of Environmental Diplomacy*, 97–8.

97 Poore, *Changing Landscapes: The Development of the International Tropical Timber Organization and its Influence on Tropical Forest Management*, 33.

98 Chasek, *Earth Negotiations: Analyzing Thirty Years of Environmental Diplomacy*, 98.

Development (IBRD), a branch of the World Bank, which argued that such a fund was unnecessary as the IBRD would provide needed funds for forest regrowth and management. Poore considers this failure to access a secure source of untied funds to be a major flaw of the proposed organization, because it removed a potential source of influence in favour of conservationist aims (that is, funding could have been made conditional on conformity with certain conservation guidelines).[99]

The problematic solving of the over-arching financial issues opened the door for discussions to move from the general to the specific. The meeting concluded with the following recommendations:

- On the issue of research and development, the criteria for the selection of projects were approved and the task of developing a list of research and development projects was delegated to an intergovernmental group of experts.
- The group agreed that there was a need to improve market intelligence and requested the secretariats of the FAO and UNCTAD to create a report on the subject and delegate to an intergovernmental expert panel the task of creating proposals for the next meeting.
- The delegates recognized that financing would be essential to ensure reforestation projects would succeed and asked that the secretariats of UNCTAD, FAO and the World Bank prepare a paper on the issue for the Sixth Meeting.[100]

That Sixth Meeting occurred from 1–11 June 1982, when it was agreed that the preparatory phase was at an end and that the basic elements of an international tropical timber agreement were in place. Consensus was achieved and an instrument was created which had as its foundation the following summarized sections which emphasized the need for cooperative ventures if the regime was to succeed:

1. Individual research and development projects that had been drafted drawing on the 42 project profiles already examined (for example, wood utilization, forest development) would be selected by a designated producer/consumer body for implementation within the framework of a proposed agreement.

---

99 Poore, *Changing Landscapes: The Development of the International Tropical Timber Organization and its Influence on Tropical Forest Management*, 35.

100 Chasek, *Earth Negotiations: Analyzing Thirty Years of Environmental Diplomacy*, 98.

2. The various proposals, such as monitoring and evaluating data to improve market intelligence, should meet the threshold test for an international agreement.
3. Cooperation between producing and consuming states should cover issues such as technology transfers, training, the encouragement of investment and the creation of joint ventures. Such activities would be monitored by the new body created and would have a mandate to solve any problems in cooperation with any other competent entity.
4. Producer states and consumer states should cooperate to ensure a regular review of national and international support, with a view to encouraging increased technical assistance for national reforestation and forest management programmes. Further, there was a need to review the future requirements of international trade in industrial tropical timber products and identify and evaluate potential schemes to satisfy the need for industrial timber.[101]

The institutional requirements of such an arrangement were not considered at the meeting due to lack of time, so a further meeting was called from 29 November until 3 December. The Japanese delegation put forward its own draft articles for an international agreement based on previous agreements on rubber and jute, but no other state saw fit to do so.[102] At the end of discussions, the members agreed to create the International Tropical Timber Organization (ITTO).[103] The ITTO was designed as an autonomous entity with a mandate to administer the agreement and oversee its operation. The meeting also decided the organizational structure and organs of the ITTO. Two categories of members were set up, producers and consumers, but the exact definition of these categories was left open. Lastly, the delegates decided on a definition of the term 'tropical timber'.[104]

Poore argues that one can observe an evolution over the course of the Preparatory Meetings, from concerns over how best to improve tropical timber supplies and market intelligence to grappling with the vexed questions relating to conservation of forests. However, the issue of preserving such forests appears not to have been discussed, nor was it a consideration. Poore believes that ecological values were to gradually become embedded over the course of the discussions and eventually formed a bedrock part of

---

[101] Ibid.: 98–9.

[102] Ibid.: 99; Poore, *Changing Landscapes: The Development of the International Tropical Timber Organization and its Influence on Tropical Forest Management*, 35.

[103] Chasek, *Earth Negotiations: Analyzing Thirty Years of Environmental Diplomacy*, 99.

[104] Ibid.: 99–100.

the proposed ITTO.[105] However, he does not identify which actors/states held such beliefs, nor can it be ascertained under what conditions such environmental concerns would be manifest in practice. Certainly environmental issues were discussed, but the evidence suggests they were only ever secondary concerns. It is highly debatable, given the subsequent performance of the ITTO, that such ecological concerns were critical to states' interests, let alone internalized to the point where states considered such issues automatically.

A Conference on Tropical Timber was convened on 14 March 1983 in Geneva, Switzerland. By the end of the first session, 31 March 1983, delegates from 70 countries (36 producers and 34 consumers accounting for 98 per cent of the tropical timber trade) had agreed to 37 of the 43 Articles.[106] Problematic issues were the location of the headquarters of the new organization (Belgium, France, Greece, Japan, the Netherlands and the UK all vied to host the ITTO).[107] Also, the number of committees to be established proved to be a sticking point. The Chair offered three (Economic Information and Market Intelligence, Reforestation and Forest Management and Processing) while the consumer states argued that only two were necessary. A more important difference was over the definition of tropical timber for the purposes of the agreement, with producer states focusing on production and resource management, and consumer states wishing to privilege issues of trade.[108]

## THE ENGOs AND THE TROPICAL TIMBER REGIME

ENGOs across the globe, at many levels of government, sought to halt or decrease the rate of tropical forest deforestation. Again, as in the two previous case studies, there was no dominant normative entrepreneur calling for conservation or preservation of tropical forests, however. Rather, there were four

---

[105] Poore, *Changing Landscapes: The Development of the International Tropical Timber Organization and its Influence on Tropical Forest Management*, 34.

[106] Chasek, *Earth Negotiations: Analyzing Thirty Years of Environmental Diplomacy*, 100; Poore, *Changing Landscapes: The Development of the International Tropical Timber Organization and its Influence on Tropical Forest Management*, 36.

[107] Chasek, *Earth Negotiations: Analyzing Thirty Years of Environmental Diplomacy*, 100. Japan was eventually chosen as the site of the new organization, after it agreed to underwrite it. Japan also worked hard to secure the agreement of producer states, offering them preferential trading deals to agree to join the fledgling entity. These deals evolved into a 'network of influence' wielded by Japan and needs to be borne in mind whenever examining the history of the ITTO, since it has given Japan enormous power over the normative direction of the ITTO. Colchester, 'The International Tropical Timber Organization: Kill or Cure for the Rainforests?', 190.

[108] Chasek, *Earth Negotiations: Analyzing Thirty Years of Environmental Diplomacy*, 100.

ENGOs, which functioned as normative entrepreneurs at different times. The ENGOs which were most active during the 1987–94 period, when the ITTO was created and finding its footing, were the International Institute for Environment and Development (IIED), Survival International (SI), Friends of the Earth (FoE) and the WWF.[109]

It would be a mistake to presume that the environmental movement is a monolithic bloc when it comes to protecting tropical forests, as differing ENGOs espousing differing environmental norms are sometimes in competition with each other. The most radical ENGOs seek a preservationist outcome for tropical forests, as is the case with Greenpeace, a relative latecomer to the issue of tropical forestry, which argues that states should add more land to existing forest reserves. To achieve this goal it set up tropical forest units within its own organization, dedicated to lobbying governments.[110]

However Greenpeace, unlike in other global environmental regimes, was a limited actor in the ITTO. It had other campaign priorities at the time, such as Antarctica and whaling. As one of the more prominent international ENGOs, its failure to take a leadership role on this issue, combined with strong resistance from states determined to harvest and consume tropical timber, meant that preservation did not have a strong advocate within the ITTO. Other ENGOs, arguing a more hardline preservationist stance, found themselves excluded from the inner sanctum of the negotiations, and to date have been unable to influence the normative direction of the ITTO, which has confined itself to a debate between exploitation and conservation.[111] In general, preservationist-leaning ENGOs have not been able to link their arguments to higher values such as the beauty, uniqueness and fragility of the tropical forests, in a way that resonates meaningfully within producer states.

---

109 Fred P. Gale, 'The Mysterious Case of the Disappearing Environmentalists: The International Tropical Timber Organization', *Capitalism, Nature, Socialism* 7, no. 3 (1996): 109.

110 Switzer, *Environmental Politics: Domestic and Global Dimensions*, 278.

111 David Humphreys, 'Redefining the Issues: NGO Influence on International Forest Negotiations', *Global Environmental Politics* 4, no. 2 (2004): 56. At the first ITTO Meeting, ENGOs were granted observer status only, balanced out by allowing timber companies the same right. D. Humphreys, 'NGO Influence on International Policy on Forest Conservation and the Trade in Forest Products', in *NGO Diplomacy: The Influence of Nongovernmental Organisations in International Environmental Negotiations*, ed. Michele M. Betsill and Elisabeth Corell (Cambridge, MA: MIT Press, 2008), 163. Different ENGOs were accorded differing access depending on their stance on timber harvesting. For example, the WWF was seen as an 'insider' organization and some of its staff were seconded to state delegations for the UK, Denmark and Malaysia. This enabled unprecedented access to behind-closed-doors negotiations. Humphreys, 'Redefining the Issues: NGO Influence on International Forest Negotiations', 56.

The ENGOS that have argued for the conservation of tropical forests (traditional groups found principally in the United States, such as the WWF and FoE) are far more vocal within and without the ITTO. These organizations are willing, at least initially, to work with producer and consumer states, and their proposals call for improvements in efficiency, such as modernizing logging machinery, and management practices to make the process more sustainable.[112] The ENGOs willing to work within the system to achieve their objectives can be contrasted with those groups like Greenpeace which had grown accustomed to using outsider tactics to further their goals.[113]

This fracturing of the ENGO movement over goals, strategies and tactics is one key reason why the ENGOs have been unable to influence the ITTO's normative development. No consensus has existed on either the appropriate environmental norm to be advanced or the necessary strategies to achieve their goal of normative change. No clear leader has emerged to guide the ENGOs, as Greenpeace did in the whaling regime, nor have ENGOs been able to coalesce around a single idea to present a united front, as ASOC did within the ATS. This has severely limited the ENGOs' ability to act as norm advocates and is one of the chief reasons for the failure of the more radical environmental norms to take root in the tropical timber regime.

Despite their internal disagreements about how to approach the embryonic organization, the ENGOs initially were all hopeful that despite its apparent limitations, the ITTO could eventually become a force for environmental protection. The ENGOs supported the newborn ITTO for two reasons. First, the ENGOs saw it as a vehicle to potentially curb the excesses of the logging TNCs. Secondly, they were committed to the idea of sustainable logging and hoped such an aim could be achieved through the ITTO.[114] ENGOs were able to argue successfully at the Preparatory Meetings that the dominant frame of tropical timber should be reframed from a resource and development issue focused only on timber extraction to one of overall forest conservation. However, such concerns were reflected in the final treaty text wording as aspirational goals for the new organization.[115]

In many ways, the ITTO owes its existence to the ENGOs (and IOs like UNCTAD), for without their belief in its potential, it might never have materialized (given the continuing apparent lack of concern of tropical timber

---

112 Switzer, *Environmental Politics: Domestic and Global Dimensions*, 279.

113 Humphreys, 'Redefining the Issues: NGO Influence on International Forest Negotiations', 51.

114 Colchester, 'The International Tropical Timber Organization: Kill or Cure for the Rainforests?', 190.

115 Humphreys, 'NGO Influence on International Policy on Forest Conservation and the Trade in Forest Products', 163.

states). Despite the lack of enthusiasm for a completed regime, the UNCTAD Conference reconvened from 7–18 November 1983 in Geneva, where the decision to adopt the International Tropical Timber Agreement (ITTA) was taken by delegates. This occurred despite there being a number of outstanding issues, such as where the new organization should be situated.[116]

No explanation has been proffered in the literature as to why states agreed at this point to adopt the ITTA. According to a neoliberal account, producer and consumer states were prepared to cooperate and become involved in the ITTO to ensure that the smooth business cartel they had created ran smoothly. For consumer states, the ITTO would ensure a steady supply of timber products, while for producer states it would help ensure a steady stream of export dollars. Given the history of the tropical timber trade prior to the creation of the ITTA, this explanation fits the neoliberal desire for parsimony. However, the impetus to cooperate derived from economic interest rather than any desire to solve environmental issues.

From a constructivist perspective, the mere fact that there was widespread participation in the ITTO is important, since it is through dialogue, negotiation and cooperation that the bonds develop between member states that allow new norms to evolve.[117] From here, if states are willing to work towards that goal, the normative cycle can begin. Holistic constructivism, which acknowledges the role of non-state parties in shaping shared understandings, encourages an examination of whether ENGOs influenced the negotiations leading up to the creation of the ITTA. This assumes, however, that the ITTO is an organization that is able to facilitate dialogue and social learning between states and other actors by, for example, enhancing awareness of the need to address ecological problems such as deforestation.

However, there is little evidence to suggest an intention on the part of the states to foster social learning or trust between producer and consumer states and ENGOs. ENGOs might have hoped that the ITTO would foster social learning about the importance of conservationist practices, but the states were more preoccupied with furthering their economic interests. In particular, this was seen as an opportunity to bed down the business cartel which had been running up until that point. It is reasonable to surmise that developing states were interested in the ITTO in the hope that they might receive financial aid to bolster their forest policies, and so were willing to be involved in negotiations, but there is no evidence they were interested in improving conservationist practices as well.

---

116 Chasek, *Earth Negotiations: Analyzing Thirty Years of Environmental Diplomacy*, 100–101.

117 Peter Wood, 'Soft Law, Hard Law and the Development of an International Forest Convention', http://peterwood.ca/docs/Wood2004_ForestConvention.pdf.

Holistic constructivism allows for an examination of domestic preference formation within both producer and consumer states and its influence on the creation of the ITTO. Such an analysis provides a greater understanding of the resistance to the ITTO from both consumer and producer states and the size of the challenge confronting environmental norm advocates. In the consumer states, ENGOS worked to inform domestic populaces of the rising threat posed by deforestation. However, there is no evidence that domestic concern in consumer states over deforestation had any significant influence on the negotiating positions of consumer states. At best, such influence was only minor. In the producing states, ENGO influence was severely limited due to lack of resources, limited local networks, and sometimes authoritarian governments that disapproved of their activities. This meant ENGO attempts to influence attitudes towards creating a regime with a strong environmental component were even less successful.

Neoliberal analysis speaks of state interest, but rarely is the question asked as to what these interests are and who might be served by them. The constructivist approach espoused by those like Checkel at least allows for an examination of domestic considerations. These can shed useful light on the concept of state interest.[118] In the case of the producer states, for example, there was an assumption by governments that increasing the export of timber commodities would lift domestic income and raise the living conditions of all the people.[119] Developing states' elites understood that one pathway to quickly developing was to exploit their abundant forests, and this certainly did affect their perception of the ITTO as a potential brake on their operations.[120]

Developing state leaders were supported in this position by the majority of their constituents, who believed that rapid economic development must occur despite the environmental cost. This trend continues today. For example, in a recent survey in Brazil, 82 per cent of Brazilians agreed with the proposition that 'Brazil must use the resources of Amazonia to develop the country'.[121] Development discourse has also permeated the forestry debate. It started doing so in the 1960s and 1970s via the World Forestry Congresses and the work of international forestry experts such as Westoby, Chief of the Forests Economics

---

118 J.T. Checkel, 'International Norms and Domestic Politics: Bridging the Rationalist–Constructivist Divide', *European Journal of International Relations* 3, no. 4 (1997).

119 Dauvergne, *Loggers and Degradation in the Asia-Pacific: Corporations and Environmental Management*, 47.

120 Smouts, *Tropical Forests, International Jungle: The Underside of Global Ecopolitics*, 15.

121 Eric Raymond, 'Road Development in Northwestern Brazil: Economic Integration against Ethnic and Ecological Degradation', *International Affairs Review* 11, no. 1 (2002): 90.

Branch, Forest Products Division of the FAO.[122] Thus, by the time of the ITTO negotiations, the concept of exploiting forests for development was deeply entrenched at both the domestic level and within the various forestry IOs.

This has meant that ENGOs promoting environmental norms not only faced opposition from those actively exploiting forests, such as the political elites and timber companies, but also face populaces that believe that razing forests in the name of development is a public good which should be encouraged and continued. Furthermore, the idea of development has been a part of the global discourse on forests for several decades now and has been internalized by the main IOs. The ENGO campaigns to prevent the exploitation of forests do not seem to have taken into account the strength of this developmental norm at different levels, believing erroneously that influencing consumers within importing states would provide sufficient pressure to reorient the ITTO. Such a strategic mistake makes the job of the environmental norm entrepreneurs extremely difficult, particularly when it comes to convincing the domestic populaces of producer states that saving the forests is a public good.

There is another dimension to this issue too. Despite the public support for development, the historical record is clear that such activities tend to favour the ruling classes.[123] Thus, states' interests in development are primarily those of political and economic elites within producer societies. Poor rural and urban people or indigenous tribes enjoy very few of the benefits. However, they suffer a disproportionate part of the costs, both environmental and economic.[124] For example, in Malaysia, as more and more forestland has been opened up for exploitation, the impact on the rural population has been profound in terms of loss of traditional livelihoods.[125] The historical record also shows that the expectation that the development of states' forests will increase the welfare of a majority of people within LDCs has not been realized, despite the high environmental cost of razing tropical forests.[126] As will be seen later in the chapter, attempts by ENGOs and other actors to point this out to the ITTO have been blocked or have fallen on deaf ears.

---

[122] Fadzilah Majid Cooke, *The Challenge of Sustainable Forests: Forest Resource Policy in Malaysia, 1970–1995* (Honolulu: University of Hawai'i Press, 1999), 48.

[123] Raymond, 'Road Development in Northwestern Brazil: Economic Integration against Ethnic and Ecological Degradation', 94.

[124] Ngau, Apoi and Ling, 'Malaysian Timber: Exploitation for Whom?', 46; Raymond, 'Road Development in Northwestern Brazil: Economic Integration against Ethnic and Ecological Degradation', 94.

[125] Ngau, Apoi and Ling, 'Malaysian Timber: Exploitation for Whom?', 50.

[126] Thompson, 'The Ecological-economics of Non-sustainable Development: Logging Tropical Forests in Southeast Asia and the Pacific', 224.

Radoslav Dimitrov's work provides a possible explanation for the behaviour of both producer and consumer states and why they participated in the ITTA negotiations. For states, the 'normative logic of appropriateness' requires states to participate in regime negotiations.[127] He postulates that states need to be seen to be actively engaging with environmental problems. No state can afford the opprobrium directed at it for not being seen to be doing something about deforestation.[128] This was particularly true at the time of the creation of the ITTO, as the global ENGO movements of the 1970s worked hard to publicize the problem of global deforestation.[129] At this point, the global significance of tropical forests was becoming increasingly appreciated by developed state populations as part of an overall concern that was growing about global environmental problems such as resource supplies and the loss of global biodiversity.[130] While such growing ecological awareness was mostly limited to developed states, it is reasonable to surmise that both producer and consumer states felt pressure to be at least seen to be tackling this issue in a concrete way by attending negotiations and agreeing to a draft document. Such a strategy avoided reputational costs and potential shaming as poor environmental actors.[131]

Despite producer and consumer states having concluded a draft for ratification and signing, their continued indifference to the ITTA being passed meant that the earliest date for definitive entry into force, 1 October 1984, was not met. By early 1985, there was concern that the date for 'provisional entry into force' would pass without an agreement being ratified. While the consumer states willing to agree to the ITTA's provisions were nearly unanimous in their approval of the draft (only Spain and Italy did not sign and ratify at this stage), gaining the acquiescence of the producer states proved more problematic. By mid-February 1985, only six states (Liberia, Indonesia, Gabon, Honduras, Bolivia and Malaysia) had signed and only Indonesia and Malaysia had ratified the agreement. At least eight more instruments were required to be lodged, otherwise the Agreement could not enter into force.[132]

When in 1985 it appeared that the Agreement was in trouble, with no states ratifying the text by the agreed deadline, the IIED organized a conference in

---

[127] Radoslav S. Dimitrov, 'Hostage to Norms: States, Institutions and Global Forest Politics', *Global Environmental Politics* 5, no. 4 (2005): 3.

[128] Ibid.: 17.

[129] Switzer, *Environmental Politics: Domestic and Global Dimensions*, 277.

[130] de Jong, Tuck-Po and Ken-ichi, 'The Political Ecology of Tropical Forests in Southeast Asia: Historical Roots of Modern Problems', 2.

[131] Dimitrov, 'Hostage to Norms: States, Institutions and Global Forest Politics', 4.

[132] Poore, *Changing Landscapes: The Development of the International Tropical Timber Organization and its Influence on Tropical Forest Management*, 37.

March in London. This brought together key states (Japan, the UK, Malaysia, Indonesia, Brazil and the Netherlands), plus industry representatives, to promote the entity and to encourage ratification.[133] At the end of the seminar, after much debate, the conference participants agreed to a statement to be sent to all state participants.[134] The statement read in part:

> This seminar, convened to explore the implications of the Agreement for the relationship between the utilization and conservation of the tropical forest resource, confirmed that these need not be contradictory goals . . . The benefits derived from the trade, however, could greatly contribute to the management and conservation of the resource which in turn ensures the sustainability of economic and social development.
>
> Nevertheless, despite the consensus as to the potential value of the agreement. the seminar noted with grave concern that the requirements for entry into force have still not been met . . . The seminar urges everyone concerned to do all in their power to see that the Agreement enters into force . . . The seminar stresses that the ITTA can rightly be regarded by the whole international community as a major success for international cooperation and solidarity.[135]

Interestingly, and indicative of the thinking of states at this time, the seminar participants seemed to believe that the global logging trade played virtually no part in the rising rates of deforestation. Rather, an argument was outlined that the trade could only be a boon to conservationist activities in tropical forests. Despite this rather peculiar position, the ENGOs such as the IUCN, the IIED and the WWF were sufficiently enthused about the potential of an ITTA that they used their domestic state affiliates to encourage states to sign on to the agreement. Japan, in particular, was active in stressing the potential of such an agreement to South American states, especially the critical state of Brazil. To the surprise of the ENGOs, the conference was successful, and enough ratifications were deposited in New York by the 31 March deadline to enable UNCTAD to call the first meeting of the ITTO in June 1985.[136] This initial agreement came into force on 1 April 1985 for an initial period of five years. It was extended twice, for two-year periods.[137]

---

133 Gale, 'Discourse and Southeast Asian Deforestation: A Case Study of the International Tropical Timber Organization', 241.

134 Poore, *Changing Landscapes: The Development of the International Tropical Timber Organization and its Influence on Tropical Forest Management*, 37.

135 Ibid.: 38.

136 Gale, 'Discourse and Southeast Asian Deforestation: A Case Study of the International Tropical Timber Organization', 241; Poore, *Changing Landscapes: The Development of the International Tropical Timber Organization and its Influence on Tropical Forest Management*, 38.

137 Chasek, *Earth Negotiations: Analyzing Thirty Years of Environmental Diplomacy*, 100–101.

Why states were willing to sign on is still an open question. Certainly, the producer states saw merit in obtaining funding, but it is also likely that they realized that such an organization was inevitable and wished to ensure control of such an entity. Japan fought very hard for the new ITTO Secretariat to be situated at Yokohama, and with the lobbying aid of the WWF, IUCN and FoE-UK in consumer states, the proposal was eventually agreed to by all the negotiating states.[138] The main producer and consuming states also ensured that they maintained financial control of the fledgling entity. For example, in 1989 just over 50 per cent of the ITTO's annual budget was sourced from Japan, Brazil, Indonesia, Malaysia, the USA and Korea, all of which were heavily involved in the tropical timber trade.[139]

However, for all states, given the global awareness of the issue of tropical deforestation, there was pressure to be seen to be addressing this issue, and the ITTA allowed them the greatest latitude to continue 'business as usual', while arguing that they were aiming to conserve tropical forests. That is, despite agreeing to the ITTA, the member states, as will be seen in the rest of the chapter, continued to flout many of its provisions. Since there are no enforcement provisions in the agreement, states have continued their exploitative behaviour, seeking short-term gains that benefited the producer elites and the timber consumers of the importing states.

## THE INTERNATIONAL TROPICAL TIMBER AGREEMENT

Opinions regarding the purposes of the ITTA and the behaviour it was meant to engender remain divided to this day. Pamela Chasek believes that the ITTA is primarily a commodities agreement that, unusually, has no price regulation mechanisms or market intervention powers. Its aim is 'to promote sustainable development of tropical forests by encouraging and assisting the tropical timber industry and trade and thus conserve the resource base upon which they depend'.[140] Fred Gale argues that the ITTA is meant to be a conventional commodities agreement (for example, it contains mention of buffer stocks) and is designed to stabilize prices. However, by the time a draft was prepared, it was clear that tropical timber could not be regarded in such a light, due to the problematic nature of tropical timber extraction.[141] Ans Kolk agrees with

---

[138] Fred P. Gale, *The Tropical Timber Trade Regime*, International Political Economy Series (New York: St Martin's Press, 1998), 87.

[139] Ibid.: 85.

[140] Chasek, *Earth Negotiations: Analyzing Thirty Years of Environmental Diplomacy*, 102.

[141] Gale, 'The Mysterious Case of the Disappearing Environmentalists: The International Tropical Timber Organization', 106–07.

this conclusion, but for differing reasons, pointing out that while the ITTA was originally envisaged as being yet another commodity agreement, the attempted melding of conservation with the promotion of trade and increasing producer states' revenues made it an exceptional agreement.[142]

The ITTA as a document tried to balance these inherent contradictions when it 'attempted indirectly to conserve tropical forest resources by addressing uncertainty and fluctuation in the international market for tropical timber, with the idea that a more stable international market will allow states to choose when to harvest and sell their forest resources, rather than being driven to do so by market pressures or opportunities'.[143] Such an approach, however, ends up creating a cartel which is monopolistic in nature. This is more likely to lead to incentives to exploit rather than conserve tropical timber, since states' interests are met by focusing on ensuring a steady import/export trade in the short term for the benefit of the cartel members.

The Agreement defined tropical timber in Article 2(1) as comprising 'non-coniferous tropical wood for industrial uses, which grows between the Tropic of Cancer and the Tropic of Capricorn . . .'.[144] The objectives of the ITTA clearly reveal that its focus is on tropical timber utilization, with its agreed aims being:

- to create an effective framework ensuring cooperation and consultation between tropical timber consumer and producer states;
- to ensure the diversification and expansion of the global tropical timber trade and improve market conditions;
- to promote and augment forestry research and development with the aim of improving tropical forest management and the use of wood products;
- to encourage national forestry policies that encourage sustainability and conservationist practices of tropical forests and their resources.[145]

Again the language is of cooperation by the member states to promote the tropical timber trade, plus an understanding of the need to put in place sustainable practices to conserve tropical forests. However, this latter objective

---

142 Ans Kolk, *Forests in International Environmental Politics: International Organisations, NGOs and the Brazilian Amazon* (Utrecht, the Netherlands: International Books, 1996), 137.

143 Elizabeth R. DeSombre, *The Global Environment and World Politics*, International Relations for the 21st Century (London: Continuum, 2002), 149.

144 Beatrice Chaytor, 'The Development of Global Forest Policy: Overview of Legal and Institutional Frameworks' (International Institute for Environment and Development World Business Council for Sustainable Development, 2001), 16.

145 Chasek, *Earth Negotiations: Analyzing Thirty Years of Environmental Diplomacy*, 95.

appears to be undermined by the unspoken rationale that as far as the member states are concerned, 'tropical forests would only continue to exist if they were used for an economic purpose – the most important being the production of wood'.[146]

ENGOs, and IOs such as the WWF, the FoE, the IIED and the IUCN, were observers at the closing sessions of the negotiations and, due to their effective lobbying, were able to ensure that conservationist language was part of the Agreement's objectives.[147] Utilizing Finnemore and Sikkink's analysis, it is clear that, once again, the ENGOs were acting as the key normative entrepreneurs (and organizational platforms) for the norm of conservation. The primary documents of the negotiations and the secondary material reveal no real attempts by the ENGOs to argue for preservationist norms to be part of the Agreement. It is arguable that the ENGOs knew, given the opposition of producer and consumer states and timber companies, what they were up against and that their only hope was to start with the less ambitious aim of conserving areas and building on any success. The absence of traditional preservationist ENGOs such as Greenpeace enabled groups that traditionally espouse a conservationist ethos, such as the IUCN and the WWF, to have a greater influence on the proceedings.

The negotiating states agreed with the conservationist aims and, as mentioned earlier, Article 1(h) was inserted in the text with the following aim:

> to encourage the development of national policies aimed at sustainable utilization and conservation of tropical forests and their genetic resources, and at maintaining the ecological balance in the regions concerned.[148]

However, despite negotiating states agreeing to this conservationist aim, as was pointed out earlier, there is no evidence that their behaviour changed. Using the Finnemore and Sikkink analysis is problematic because it assumes that once a tipping point of states has been reached and a normative cascade has occurred in relation to the acceptance of the norm, then behaviour change should follow. However, Finnemore and Sikkink's analysis assumes that the parties are genuinely committed to the norm. This case study suggests that this cannot be assumed. In the case of tropical timber, any 'agreement' to put in place sustainable practices needs to be measured against what actually happens on the forest floor.

---

146 Poore, *Changing Landscapes: The Development of the International Tropical Timber Organization and its Influence on Tropical Forest Management*, 40.

147 Gale, 'Discourse and Southeast Asian Deforestation: A Case Study of the International Tropical Timber Organization', 241.

148 Humphreys, 'Redefining the Issues: NGO Influence on International Forest Negotiations', 54.

A closer examination of the operation of the Organization reveals that neither producer states nor consumer states have made conservation a priority over exploitation.[149] As David Humphreys notes:

> Neither the producers nor the consumers have contested the economic *exploitation* [my italics] of tropical forests for timber and for other forest products. Given this, and given also the conservation mandate of the ITTO, it is perhaps not surprising that the ITTO guidelines for the sustainable management of natural forests reflect inconsistencies between developmental and ecological objectives.[150]

The *Possible Action 33* document published in 1990 stated even more baldly the ITTO position on conservation versus trade when it declared that any environmental impact studies should 'assess compatibility of logging practices with declared *secondary* [my italics] objectives such as conservation and protection'.[151]

Over time, it has become clear that the conservationist clause of the ITTA is fundamentally at odds with the 'expansion and diversification' aim of the ITTA.[152] The ITTA as a whole is considered deficient by many commentators in that it does not take into consideration the issue of forest diversity essential to a sustainable forest ecosystem. Kasimbazi is particularly critical, arguing that the ITTA emphasis on conservation to the exclusion of preservation undermines the Agreement, since it has no ability to support the tropical forest biosphere.[153] However, the ITTO was founded on the idea that it was both politically and technically possible sustainably to extract timber from tropical forests while maintaining other values.[154]

The Preamble of the ITTA encapsulates this duality when it states that it recognizes the 'importance of, and the need for, proper and effective conservation

---

[149] Poore, *Changing Landscapes: The Development of the International Tropical Timber Organization and its Influence on Tropical Forest Management*, 43.

[150] D. Humphreys, 'Hegemonic Ideology and the International Tropical Timber Organization', in *The Environment and International Relations*, ed. John Vogler and Mark F. Imber (London: Routledge, 1996), 226.

[151] International Tropical Timber Organization, 'Technical Series 5: ITTO Technical Guidelines for the Sustainable Management of Tropical Resources' (Yokohama: 1990), 9.

[152] Friends of the Earth and World Rainforest Movement, 'The International Tropical Timber Agreement: Conserving the Forests or Chainsaw Charter? A Critical Review of the First Five Years' Operations of the International Tropical Timber Organization' (Friends of the Earth, 1992), 4.

[153] Kasimbazi, 'Sustainable Development in International Tropical Timber Agreements', 146.

[154] Poore, *Changing Landscapes: The Development of the International Tropical Timber Organization and its Influence on Tropical Forest Management*, 40.

and development of tropical timber forests with a view to ensuring their optimum utilization while maintaining the ecological balance of the regions concerned and of the biosphere'.[155] In many ways, the tension between the two goals of timber exploitation and maintaining the forests sustainably has led to the internal problems within the ITTO, as it tries to balance these competing interests and the stakeholders pushing their associated agendas.

The ITTO was not initially adverse to the input of outside organizations, whether they were IOs or ENGOs. Articles 14 and 27 of the ITTA encouraged the ITTO to use the facilities and skills of both national and international agencies and ENGOs in a collaborative effort on research and data collection.[156] However, the failure to allow such organizations, particularly ENGOs, a 'seat at the table' when it came to decision-making was to lead to institutional failure in achieving the objective to promote sustainable forestry.

Article 23 of the ITTA refers to projects to be undertaken by the ITTO and over time this has become a critical part of the work carried out by the organization.[157] Article 20 established a donor 'special account' to fund projects, but from the beginning was to prove inadequate to the scope of the task.[158] Moreover, the research projects undertaken by the ITTO have tended to focus on tropical *timber* to the detriment of tropical *forests*, with the conservation of forests being perceived as an incidental goal. Emmanuel Kasimbazi argues that such an approach leads inevitably to a diminution of ecological values and assets and the record of the ITTO bears this out.[159]

## THE INTERNATIONAL TROPICAL TIMBER ORGANIZATION

Under the ITTA the International Tropical Timber Organization is responsible for the administration of the regime.[160] The ITTO has played a critical part in

---

[155] 'International Tropical Timber Agreement 1983' (1983).

[156] Kasimbazi, 'Sustainable Development in International Tropical Timber Agreements', 144.

[157] One of the key functions of the ITTO has been, via its three Permanent Committees, the vetting of proposed and approved projects. Cases given approval include the building of databases, reforestation projects and a project to assess timber incentives. Humphreys, 'Hegemonic Ideology and the International Tropical Timber Organization', 223.

[158] Poore, *Changing Landscapes: The Development of the International Tropical Timber Organization and its Influence on Tropical Forest Management*, 40–41.

[159] Kasimbazi, 'Sustainable Development in International Tropical Timber Agreements', 144–5.

[160] Porter and Brown, *Global Environmental Politics*, 100.

proselytizing the idea of sustainable forest management. At the global level, it has provided a forum for debates about the relevant norm to underpin the organization.[161] Since its creation, the organization has progressively broadened its mandate and it now competes with the traditional forest organization, the FAO, in the field of forest-related information.[162]

The structure of the ITTO is a curious one. It privileges exploitation and as such is similar to some share arrangements within certain corporate structures, where two types of official members, made up of producing and consuming states, have a total of 1000 votes each.[163] The first 400 votes are reserved equally for producer states from Africa, Asia-Pacific and Latin America. A tranche of 300 votes is divided between states, determined by their relative share of tropical forests. The last 300 votes are apportioned according to the average of the values of each state's net exports of tropical timber during the previous three years (Article 10(2) ITTA 1983). While this apportioning gives all states with tropical forests a say, countries like Malaysia, Indonesia and Brazil, with extensive forests or a large proportion of export timber, have the most sway within the ITTO. This is because the greater the export volume of tropical timber, the more votes are assigned.[164]

Examining the inner workings of the ITTO, as personified in its voting structure, reveals further curiosities. The 'rules of the game', as constituted in the ITTO voting structure, are seriously flawed in that they do not allow countries with large swathes of tropical forests to be accorded due weight. Rather, the quicker a state destroys its forests, the more votes it gets, leading to the absurd situation where exploiting states carry disproportionate weight in council deliberations. This leads to the favouring of the interests of the exploiters.[165] Thus, from its inception, the voting mechanism utilized by the ITTO ensured that conservationist aims would be secondary to the putative need to promote the global timber trade.[166]

Consumer states are accorded ten votes each, with the remainder apportioned according to the average volume of their net imports of tropical timber

---

161 Gale, 'Discourse and Southeast Asian Deforestation: A Case Study of the International Tropical Timber Organization', 243.

162 Smouts, *Tropical Forests, International Jungle: The Underside of Global Ecopolitics*, 144.

163 Chaytor, 'The Development of Global Forest Policy: Overview of Legal and Institutional Frameworks', 17.

164 Gale, 'The Mysterious Case of the Disappearing Environmentalists: The International Tropical Timber Organization', 107–8.

165 Kasimbazi, 'Sustainable Development in International Tropical Timber Agreements', 154.

166 Colchester, 'The International Tropical Timber Organization: Kill or Cure for the Rainforests?', 189.

during the previous three-year period, starting four years prior to the allocation of votes (Article 10(5) ITTA 1983). This system penalizes states that import higher-value goods such as furniture, in favour of states such as Japan that import large quantities of unprocessed logs.[167] While the voting procedures of the ITTO can appear on the surface to be Byzantine, in practice most decisions are produced by consensus between the producer and the consumer blocs.[168] The ITTA restricts voting rights to states alone and merely declares that members should 'cooperate' with ENGOs to avoid duplication of efforts (Article 14(2) ITTA 1983). However, it does allow ENGOs to participate at Council Meetings as observers (Article 15 ITTA 1983). The ITTA also contains no procedures or programmes to allow for an increased ENGO presence over time.[169]

Furthermore, the ITTA does not confer on the International Tropical Timber Council (ITCC), the deliberative body set up within the ITTO, any specific powers or mandates such as submitting proposals to further conservationist ends.[170] The Council cannot propose protocols to implement reforestation schemes or designate areas as protected. The ITTA also confers no authority on the Council for the monitoring or enforcement of its provisions. It cannot even require member states to provide an Annual Report.[171]

Although producer states have more power on Council given the weighted voting system, there is nonetheless a dispute among commentators as to which side, producers or consumers, have the most power within the ITTO. Kolk believes that the voting structure vests power in the timber producer states, which have been dominant in negotiations, and that this has led to a diminution of the environmental objectives of the ITTA.[172] Of the producer states in voting situations, Brazil, while not a large player in the global timber market, often leads the producer states due to its well-organized and large delegation, and has had a disproportionate voice in the ITTO. Brazil has frequently sided

---

[167] Gale, 'The Mysterious Case of the Disappearing Environmentalists: The International Tropical Timber Organization', 108.

[168] Gale, 'Discourse and Southeast Asian Deforestation: A Case Study of the International Tropical Timber Organization', 240.

[169] David VanderZwaag and Douglas MacKinlay, 'Towards a Global Forest Convention: Getting out of the Woods and Barking up the Right Tree', in *Global Forests and International Environmental Law*, ed. Canadian Council of International Law (London: Kluwer Law International 1996), 12–14.

[170] Chaytor, 'The Development of Global Forest Policy: Overview of Legal and Institutional Frameworks', 17.

[171] International Tropical Timber Organization, 'About ITTO', http://www.itto.or.jp/live/PageDisplayHandler?pageId=225.

[172] Kolk, *Forests in International Environmental Politics: International Organisations, NGOs and the Brazilian Amazon*, 137.

with Malaysia in forum negotiations to achieve the objectives of preventing measures aimed at limiting timber production, and both have functioned as a highly effective veto coalition, leading other producer states in this regard – such as Indonesia – over the years.[173]

Porter and Brown believe that power resides more with the consumer states. They maintain, for example, that the ITTO is dominated by Japan, whose main consumer interest appears to be the maintenance of its tropical timber quotas at their current level (Japan held 380 out of 1000 consuming state votes when the ITTO was created in 1986). European Union member states also have a vested interest in continuing the flow of tropical hardwood to Europe, particularly for the manufacturing and sale of export furniture. The USA is the largest importer of finished tropical hardwood products and has been unwilling to take action against states like Malaysia and Indonesia, with which it has a close military and political relationship.[174] Nicholas Guppy is also critical of the role played by Japan in the ITTO. The goal of the ITTO was envisaged as one that would develop into a 'world forum', where the promotion of the trade of timber would be balanced by conserving forests in a sustainable manner. Guppy argues that this goal has not been realized, primarily because of the actions of Japan, which is the largest consumer of timber products. Because of its voracious timber appetite, Japan provides the largest share of funding to the ITTO and hosts the ITTO infrastructure. It therefore has been in a position to influence negatively attempts to introduce sustainable forestry.[175]

Undoubtedly, the global tropical timber market has been manipulated by the main consumer states, particularly Japan, to keep timber prices low for Japanese buyers.[176] Among the producer states, Brazil, Indonesia and Malaysia nonetheless form a powerful coalition to achieve their ends of continuing timber harvesting, and to access funding for new development schemes. The main consumer states – Japan, the USA and the European Union – all demand secure sources of tropical timber. So we can clearly observe two powerful veto coalitions converging to prevent challenges to their economic interests. This coming together of both producer and consumer states, dedicated to continuing timber exploitation, makes the promotion of conservationist norms within the ITTO a difficult and thankless task. Producer and

---

173 Smouts, *Tropical Forests, International Jungle: The Underside of Global Ecopolitics*, 146.

174 Porter and Brown, *Global Environmental Politics*, 100–101; Smouts, *Tropical Forests, International Jungle: The Underside of Global Ecopolitics*, 146.

175 Guppy, 'International Governance and Regimes Dealing with Land Resources from the Perspective of the North', 141.

176 Ibid.

consumer states have set up separate caucuses, starting from the first few ITTO meetings. This specifically excluded ENGOs. This denial of access makes it difficult for ENGOs to present their particular arguments, and prevents them from framing the debate in environmental rather than economic terms.[177]

## THE ENGO RESPONSE TO THE NEW ITTO

At the first ITTO Meeting in Yokohama in March 1987, over 31 ENGOs attended and were made to feel, at least initially, that they would have an integral part to play in the organization.[178] As stated previously, initially ENGOs were relatively positive about the organization, albeit wary of the difficult task ahead. This uneasiness with the ITTO structure is typified by Charles Secrett's missive, in an FoE newsletter, which argues that 'opportunities are there to materially improve the lot of tropical forests across the globe over the next few years', and points out how, given the forces at play within the organization, the ITTO at present appears:

> nothing so much as a nervous man trying to cross a very high wire in a thunderstorm – shaky, precariously balanced and at the mercy of elements beyond its control. It will need a lot of encouragement and support if it is to reach its objective.[179]

The WWF was an early supporter of the ITTO as well, and was willing to give it the benefit of the doubt. In a position paper, this particular ENGO argued that the ITTA had the potential to implement conservationist strategies on tropical forests because: 'It was the only commodity agreement which incorporated the concepts of the rational use and conservation of tropical forests'.[180]

However, this cautious optimism on the part of the ENGOs at the birth of the ITTO was soon to be replaced by despair and then by antipathy towards the ITTO for its perceived failures. The seeds of this sense were sown at the negotiations that created the ITTO and which set up the decision-making structure. ENGOs were initially successful in influencing the ITTA (1983)

---

177 Poore, *Changing Landscapes: The Development of the International Tropical Timber Organization and its Influence on Tropical Forest Management*, 45.

178 Ibid.: 44.

179 Charles Secrett, 'International Timber Trade Organises . . . And So Do NGOs,' *Friends of the Earth Newsletter* (1986): 14.

180 WWF, 'International Forest Conservation and the International Tropical Timber Agreement: WWF Position Paper 2' (Gland, Switzerland: WWF International, 1987), 10.

because they were part of the negotiations from a very early stage.[181] Under the new ITTA, ENGOs were allowed to participate only as observers. They did not have access to the inner sanctum where decisions were made. This limited the ability of ENGOs to influence the ITTO from within. This was problematic, particularly for those ENGOs that expounded a preservationist line.

As was noted previously, ENGOs such as the WWF, which were more conservationist in their philosophy, did gain minimal access to delegates to argue their case. However, most ENGOs found themselves increasingly marginalized, both during negotiations and at ITTC deliberations. Further, as soon as hard-line ENGOs proposed either conservationist or preservationist arguments from outside the ITTO they were met with fierce resistance. A coalition of producer and consumer states, in league with domestic timber industries, determined to ensure a steady supply of timber, overrode ENGO objections, and orchestrated their own version of the regime.[182]

Humphreys argues that the ENGO arguments that resonated most with ITTC members were those found within the dominant neoliberal arena and which did not threaten entrenched political and economic interests. This automatically ruled out preservationist arguments and outcomes (because logging suited the economic interests of both veto coalitions), and allowed for only some conservationist measures. The problem was finding some individual, group or state willing to advocate such positions. Humphrey contends that consumer states were pushing for a more conservationist agenda, but were not willing to openly go against producer states and the trade organizations.[183] Conservationist states such as Japan and the USA were not willing to jeopardize their own tropical timber supplies, so proposals floated by conservationists did not have any sanctions for non-compliance.

The rest of the chapter will examine the various ways the stakeholders within the ITTO have attempted to alter the normative structure of the ITTO towards a more conservationist position. It will also analyse the various veto coalitions and their strategies and tactics for maintaining exploitation as the paramount norm within the ITTO. Despite being locked out of the decision-making process, ENGOs and a small number of conservationist-leaning states have attempted to alter the regimes underlying the normative framework in a number of ways, including organizing:

---

181 Humphreys, 'Redefining the Issues: NGO Influence on International Forest Negotiations', 69.

182 Gale, 'The Mysterious Case of the Disappearing Environmentalists: The International Tropical Timber Organization', 116; Humphreys, 'Redefining the Issues: NGO Influence on International Forest Negotiations', 54.

183 Humphreys, 'Redefining the Issues: NGO Influence on International Forest Negotiations', 54–5.

- a debate over the term 'sustainable forest management' (SFM) and over the development of guidelines to manage tropical forests sustainably;
- an ITTO mission to Sarawak, as well as other states, to examine logging practices;[184]
- a push to have all timber sustainably produced by the year 2000;
- the development of Successor Agreements to the 1983 Agreement in both 1994 and 2005–6.

Examining each of these issues enables a clearer understanding of the moral and strategic campaigns undertaken by ENGOs and certain states, including their successes and failures, and enables a greater knowledge of the ITTO, its normative underpinnings and the reasons why it has been resistant to change.

## SUSTAINABLE FORESTRY MANAGEMENT

One of the goals the new ITTO set itself was the development of a common philosophy as to what constitutes sustainable forest management, in a negotiating context where producer and consumer states are considered equal. Given the disparate interests of the delegates to the ITTO, reaching agreement over such a common philosophy proved difficult.[185] The ITTC, in one of its first acts, attempted to clarify the exact balance between its stated goals of sustainable utilization and conservation, and to reduce the normative confusion over terminology. The hope was that definitional clarity would enable all stakeholders to advance a conservationist agenda. The new Executive Director awarded a contract to the IIED to investigate this disparity and report back, with recommendations to ITTO members for them to implement if so inclined.

---

184 Gale, 'The Mysterious Case of the Disappearing Environmentalists: The International Tropical Timber Organization', 105.

185 Smouts, *Tropical Forests, International Jungle: The Underside of Global Ecopolitics*, 147. For example, if one uses the Brundtland Report definition of sustainability and applies it to tropical timber harvesting, then any operation undertaken 'must be capable of repeat performances at the same level of output as the first'. Friends of the Earth, 'Special Briefing: Sustainability and the Trade in Tropical Rainforest Timber', Friends of the Earth, UK, www.foe.co.uk/pubsinfo/briefings/html/19971215150457.html. However, business and most states have preferred a narrower application, which in timber circles has been put in terms of 'sustainable yield', which has no place for the 'preservation of the biological integrity of the original forest ecosystem'. Friends of the Earth, 'Special Briefing: Sustainability and the Trade in Tropical Rainforest Timber'.

The IIED's Senior Advisor Duncan Poore, and others, thereupon wrote the report, *No Timber without Trees: Sustainability in the Tropical Forest*, on behalf of the Institute. They focused on the idea of what became known as sustainable forest management.[186] The report drew on state visits and interviews with knowledgeable stakeholders.[187] It was limited from the start, however, in that it focused merely on questions concerning timber output, rather than on forest management as a whole. Consequently, and unsurprisingly, the document concluded by characterizing SFM in terms limited to the 'management [of natural forests] for the sustainable production of timber', without any consideration of other potential uses of forests that did not involve timber extraction, such as biodiversity extraction.[188]

The report further revealed that the scale of the deforestation of the world's tropical forests was much higher than previously reported or indeed predicted. Poore et al. argued that, while there were many areas within various states' tropical forests that had some elements of sustainable management, they could not conclusively be judged to meet the current definition of providing even the sustainable production of timber.[189] The report concluded that the areas of tropical forests actually under sustainable yield management, as it related to timber production by the producer states of the ITTO in 1985, were only 800 000 hectares out of a total estimated area of 828 million hectares or approximately 1 per cent. No tropical forest was sustainably managed, with the exception of Queensland, Australia.[190]

---

186 Duncan Poore et al., *No Timber without Trees: Sustainability in the Tropical Forest* (London: Earthscan Publications Ltd, 1989), 1–27.

187 Ibid.: 26; Poore, *Changing Landscapes: The Development of the International Tropical Timber Organization and its Influence on Tropical Forest Management*, 49.

188 Poore et al., *No Timber without Trees: Sustainability in the Tropical Forest*, 191.

189 Ibid.

190 Ibid.: 196. However, the bona fides of the conclusion that Queensland's tropical forests were sustainably managed has been challenged. Dr Aila Keto of the Rainforest Conservation Society of Australia argues that the survey the Poore Report's conclusion was drawn from was scientifically flawed on two grounds. One, logging in Queensland was heavily subsidized by public monies, and secondly, the sample plots used to do the calculations were hopelessly unreliable, thus logging could not be considered sustainable. Colchester, 'The International Tropical Timber Organization: Kill or Cure for the Rainforests?', 192. It should also be borne in mind that while parts of the tropical forest in Queensland were being preserved via the mechanism of being granted World Heritage Status, Australia actually increased its import of tropical timber from other countries to make up the shortfall. For example, imports of industrial roundwood increased from 1000 square metres annually in the period 1980–88 and to 13 000 square metres in 1990. Edmund Redfield, 'North Queensland's Tropical Rainforests: The World Heritage Controversy', in *Sustainable Forestry Challenges for Developing Countries*, ed. Matti Palo and Gerardo Mery (Boston, MA: Kluwer Academic Publishers, 1996), 77, 89.

While most producer states had the stated aim of sustainably managing their forests, the reality was that sustainable systems were not being implemented in time to slow the overall decline in forests globally, even if one examines the issue in terms of the economic value of the forest's timber being extracted.[191] However, in a revolutionary announcement, the report declared that the goal of achieving a sustainable yield of timber was not the same as the goal of sustainable forestry management, contrary to the traditional approach taken by the FAO and European foresters.[192] This does mark at least a first tentative step away from exploitation to embracing conservationism on the forest floor.

At an International Seminar to consider the findings of the Poore Report on 12 November 1988 (just prior to the ITTC's Fifth Session), no delegate disputed the report's findings. Curiously, there is no record of any formal discussion of the report, though the Council did endorse the recommendations in their entirety. Certainly, given the lack of action by ITTC members subsequent to the report, it can be surmised that this was an example of states ignoring what was unpalatable and not even wishing to engage with the issues in discussion.

In Poore's eyes, however, there was now an understanding of the size of the task ahead, and the need to act immediately, but subsequent events would reveal that states were not prepared to act urgently.[193] The author hoped that the recommendations would lead to an effective action plan, to be implemented at the national level, to overcome the shortcomings his report identified. The actions identified were divided into four types: that of the promotion of necessary actions by affected stakeholders; scrutinizing critical issues for the proper course of action; the provision of highly publicized examples of appropriate action and facilitation of necessary actions by the ITTO.[194]

On the key issue of resolving the definitional confusion over the term sustainable management, the IIED and Poore were unsuccessful, in the face of enormous opposition, in having their position adopted by the ITTC. Due to the desire of different stakeholders for different interpretations that suited their own interests, the members refused to endorse a universal definition of sustainable management.[195] However, despite the definitional confusion, and

---

[191] Gale, 'Discourse and Southeast Asian Deforestation: A Case Study of the International Tropical Timber Organization', 244–5.

[192] Poore et al., *No Timber without Trees: Sustainability in the Tropical Forest*, 5.

[193] Poore, *Changing Landscapes: The Development of the International Tropical Timber Organization and its Influence on Tropical Forest Management*, 62.

[194] Ibid.: 60–61.

[195] Poore et al., *No Timber without Trees: Sustainability in the Tropical Forest*, 192.

the lack of an agreed definition, SFM has come to be widely utilized by all forest stakeholders. The term has been limited to merely sustained-yield forest management focusing on timber extraction, however.[196]

This focus on timber, to the detriment of other forest values, has in many ways led to the ITTO losing its way in its stated goal of sustainably managing the globe's tropical forests because it encourages states to see forests as a supply of logs (and logging inevitably leads to environmental degradation), rather than considering the forest as a whole and in non-economic terms. The implementation of SFM is usually left to the logging corporations and producer states that do not (yet) see sustainable management as being in their economic interests. They prefer to pay lip service to such a concept and, given the looseness of the definition, are therefore able rhetorically to state that they are committed to conservationist practices, regardless of the reality on the forest floor.[197]

Poore's report ignited a firestorm of controversy outside the ITTO. ENGOs were unhappy that the report confirmed their own suspicions that the producer states were not stewarding their forests well. The report enabled some ENGOs to quietly begin lobbying sympathetic states to change the status quo within the ITTO to enforce sustainable practices.[198] The WWF led a coalition of ENGOs that demanded that the ITTO impose a target date of 1995, by which time all tropical timber should be sustainably produced. The effort was partially successful, with the ITTO putting in place a plan for sustainable forest management, but the date was set at the year 2000 and it only applied to producer states.[199] This Objective 2000 will be examined in greater detail later in the chapter. Other ENGOs used the report as evidence of neglect, and responded by calling for a global boycott on tropical timber products. This call for a global ban did concern producer states and affiliated companies who were worried that such actions would curtail profits, but the ENGO campaign

---

196 Gale, *The Tropical Timber Trade Regime*, 102; David Humphreys, 'The Evolving Forests Regime', *Global Environmental Politics* 9 (1999): 251.

197 Smouts, *Tropical Forests, International Jungle: The Underside of Global Ecopolitics*, 218. For example, some state governments, particularly in Southeast Asia, are particularly prone to changing the estimate of timber-sustainable yields for political rather than ecological reasons, despite their avowed rhetoric, and their ostensible commitment to conservationist practices. Peter Dauvergne, 'The Environmental Challenge to Loggers in the Asia-Pacific: Corporate Practices in Informal Regimes on Governance', in *The Business of Global Environmental Governance*, ed. David L. Levy and Peter J. Newell (Cambridge, MA: MIT Press, 2004), 188.

198 Gale, 'Discourse and Southeast Asian Deforestation: A Case Study of the International Tropical Timber Organization', 245.

199 Humphreys, 'Redefining the Issues: NGO Influence on International Forest Negotiations', 55–6.

was only half-heartedly taken up within consumer states, which were no doubt worried about their own supply needs.[200]

## THE ITTO MISSION TO SARAWAK

The issue of unsustainable logging in Sarawak showed how difficult it was going to be for the fledgling ITTO to balance internal state socio-economic considerations against the conservation of precious forests.[201] A report by a Malaysian academic in 1992 examined the links between loggers and Sarawak politicians and their relatives in the district of Belaga. The report pointed out that from 1966 to 1992 all the forestry ministers for that region had shares in companies that had been awarded logging licences. For example, from 1970 to 1981, the Lembahah Mewah licence was 70 per cent owned by the daughters of Chief Minister Yaakub, with the other 30 per cent owned by the wife of State Assemblyman Laing. Similar 'arrangements' exist in many other regions in Malaysia, and other states, and continue to flourish.[202] These entrenched corrupt domestic interests make it hard both for governments and for outside actors to influence policy towards more sustainable practices.

Against this backdrop of historical institutional corruption, came calls from the rest of the world, and particularly from Bruno Manser, a human rights activist from Switzerland, to prevent such activities that were having an 'invidious' effect on the local indigenous peoples of Sarawak, the Penan. This led to the issue rising to the level of the ITTO.[203] The flashpoint was an action in 1987 by members of the Penan tribe, who instituted a road blockade in protest against the logging of their traditional lands. The Sarawak government reacted to this by placing the leader of the protest, Harrison Ngau, under house arrest, and enacting legislation that banned road blockades.[204]

---

200 Gale, 'Discourse and Southeast Asian Deforestation: A Case Study of the International Tropical Timber Organization', 245.

201 Poore, *Changing Landscapes: The Development of the International Tropical Timber Organization and its Influence on Tropical Forest Management*, 74.

202 'High Stakes: The Need to Control Transnational Logging Companies: A Malaysian Case Study – Part 2b: Politics, Law and the Logging Industry'.

203 Poore, *Changing Landscapes: The Development of the International Tropical Timber Organization and its Influence on Tropical Forest Management*, 65. Tragically, Bruno Manser disappeared in Sarawak in 2000, an apparent victim of foul play. He has been declared officially dead. 'Death of Rain Forest Defender Bruno Manser Declared', Ogiek People Website, http://www.ogiek.org/news/news-post-05-03-21.htm.

204 Gale, 'Discourse and Southeast Asian Deforestation: A Case Study of the International Tropical Timber Organization', 253.

In response, European ENGOs attempted to recast the debate as one of indigenous people's rights, as opposed to focusing on environmental issues. They intensified their public campaign for a ban on all tropical timber from Malaysia. The tropical timber industry became concerned that the negative publicity over the Penan protest, as proselytized by ENGOs in Germany, the UK and the Netherlands, would affect sales. The Malaysian government was also concerned about the way they were being perceived globally and undertook a mission to Europe to shore up their key import markets. The Penan had voluntarily agreed to be resettled in other villages, they argued, and the protest was merely the actions of a few disgruntled villagers. However, in March/April 1989 the USA sent its own mission to the Sarawak region. The mission's report was highly critical of the Sarawak government's treatment of the indigenous peoples and recommended that the USA should review its consumption of tropical hardwood and consider alternative sources.[205]

The European states also called for a mission to observe the problems in Sarawak. This caused alarm among producer states, particularly Malaysia, which were worried about a boycott campaign arising and affecting exports. With this threat in the offing, the ITTO Malaysian Executive Director, Freezailah, lobbied the Malaysian and Sarawak governments to allow the ITTO to establish an inquiry to implement sustainable forest practices. The Sarawak and Malaysian governments acquiesced in the face of this sustained pressure and agreed to a mission. This was formally announced by the Chief Minister of Sarawak at the May 1989 ITTO Meeting. This decision set off a round of mutual recriminations between the Malaysian and South American delegates, who were afraid that any such inquiry would establish a precedent that could in the future be applied to them, potentially damaging their economic interests.[206]

---

205 Ibid.

206 Ibid.: 254. As far as states like Peru were concerned, this action did not set a precedent since Peru was afraid that the ITTO might exercise its discretion to investigate other areas, potentially infringing on its national sovereignty. Poore, *Changing Landscapes: The Development of the International Tropical Timber Organization and its Influence on Tropical Forest Management*, 68. Brazil likewise considered the initiative to be *sui generis* and outside the scope of the ITTO. International Tropical Timber Organization, 'Draft Report of the International Tropical Timber Council, Eleventh Session' (Yokohama: International Tropical Timber Organization, 1991), 16–19. Malaysia responded to this implied criticism by saying that its invitation was an exercise within its discretion and should not be seen as creating a precedent for ITTO action. Poore, *Changing Landscapes: The Development of the International Tropical Timber Organization and its Influence on Tropical Forest Management*, 68. All three of these producer states appeared concerned that such missions could be called for by disgruntled factions in their states, and any adverse findings would embarrass them globally, so they were determined to limit such actions.

The ENGOs saw this as an opportunity to demonstrate the breadth of unsustainable logging that was occurring globally and hoped that it would be the starting point for a campaign against other states whose practices were less than ideal. Their fear was that such a trip would degenerate into a mere public relations exercise for the Sarawak and Malaysian governments. The first immediate issue of concern was the mission's terms of reference. ENGOs wanted it to include a reference to indigenous peoples' rights, but this idea was opposed by both the Malaysian and Sarawak governments. The matter was 'resolved' when it was agreed that the terms of reference would be a matter for only the mission members to decide, without any input by Malaysian officials. This compromise was acceptable to the ENGOs because the composition of the delegation was already known and included two individuals, the Earl of Cranbrook, the leader of the mission, and Duncan Poore of the IIED, who were trusted by the ENGOs to give full consideration to indigenous peoples' rights and to ecological issues. The other members of the mission were three delegates from consumer and producer states, a representative of the timber industry, and an intergovernmental member selected to reflect the makeup of the ITTO and the other stakeholders.[207]

The second issue of concern revolved around attempts by ENGOs to place a forest ecologist and a lawyer, with a background in issues of land tenure and customary land rights, as mission delegates. Attempts to achieve this goal were undertaken through a letter-writing campaign by Survival International (SI) aimed at the ITTO. Between 700 and 1000 letters were received, but the campaign was ultimately unsuccessful, as the ITTC was unwilling to expand the brief of the mission to include non-timber-related issues.[208] This narrowing of the terms of reference of the mission by the ITTO meant its investigative scope was confined to merely 'assessing the capacity of the forest to uphold a continuing and economically viable forestry and forest industry, maintaining at the same time, through appropriate management, the forests' soil and water quality as well as their biological diversity'.[209] The other major flaw was, despite indigenous rights being the catalyst for the mission, the investigators were unable, when determining 'sustainability', to consider broader questions of native claims based on customary rights. They were limited to matters of ecology and economics instead. In other words:

---

207 Poore, *Changing Landscapes: The Development of the International Tropical Timber Organization and its Influence on Tropical Forest Management*, 74.

208 Gale, 'The Mysterious Case of the Disappearing Environmentalists: The International Tropical Timber Organization', 112.

209 Cooke, *The Challenge of Sustainable Forests: Forest Resource Policy in Malaysia, 1970–1995*.

> the main focus of the work of the Mission was on the 'sustainability' of the forest resource in Sarawak. This was taken to mean the attainment and maintenance of a forest estate yielding a continuing and non-declining flow of benefits and products at levels each considered best by the people of Sarawak and at levels that can be supported in the future.[210]

The ITTO mission to Sarawak occurred from late 1989 until early 1990. In the end, the mission visited the Sarawak region three times, and had a base of operations in London, where groups with an interest in the proceedings could contact Cranbrook in confidence.[211] True to its mandate, the final report argued that on the vexed question of indigenous rights, it could not strictly comment on the matter, since it was not part of its brief from the ITTO. However, the mission did say that under the ITTO's broader remit it was responsible for the sustainable utilization of tropical forests. The report went on to argue that the simplest solution would be for timber companies to withdraw from the areas in dispute until any outstanding legal issues could be resolved. The mission participants refused to be drawn as to which side was correct, preferring a studied neutrality.[212]

Putting aside the question of the treatment of indigenous peoples, the mission's mandate was primarily to ascertain the success of SFM in Sarawak and to make recommendations for strengthening current practices where required. The critical part of its report, therefore, was the estimate of what Sarawak's Annual Allowable Cut (AAC) should be. Cranbrook was unable, however, to get agreement by the mission members as to what should be the appropriate estimate of the cut.[213] Some members were convinced the current

---

[210] International Tropical Timber Organization, 'The Promotion of Sustainable Forest Management: A Casestudy in Sarawak, Malaysia' (Bali, Indonesia: submitted to Eighth Session of the International Tropical Timber Council, 1990), 9.

[211] Gale, 'Discourse and Southeast Asian Deforestation: A Case Study of the International Tropical Timber Organization', 255. The mission was prepared to meet with all stakeholders, including government officials, timber companies, community leaders and members of the public. Special river transport was arranged for people from remote regions to meet with the mission. The delegates were afforded virtually complete freedom to investigate the situation. Poore, *Changing Landscapes: The Development of the International Tropical Timber Organization and its Influence on Tropical Forest Management*, 75.

[212] Poore, *Changing Landscapes: The Development of the International Tropical Timber Organization and its Influence on Tropical Forest Management*, 77–8.

[213] Gale, 'Discourse and Southeast Asian Deforestation: A Case Study of the International Tropical Timber Organization', 256. At that time, in 1989, the AAC was reported by the Sarawak government at 13 million cubic metres approximately. An exhaustive report by Castilleja of the US National Wildlife Federation, however, had put the sustainable cut at a mere 4–5 million cubic metres. Gale, 'Discourse and Southeast Asian Deforestation: A Case Study of the International Tropical Timber Organization', 256.

level could be considered sustainable, while members such as Poore contended that a massive reduction in the cut would be required before the forest could be considered sustainable, and neither side would budge.[214]

Cranbrook's solution to the ongoing impasse as to the AAC was to ask each faction to give him their best estimate and in Solomon-like fashion he divided the figure approximately down the middle, giving a total of 9.2 million cubic metres.[215] The report concluded that forest management in Sarawak was of a better standard than for most other timber-producing states, yet there were some areas that needed improvement, for example, in the management of ramen in the peat swamps.[216]

While the report's conclusions were relatively mild, barely enunciating what the concept of SFM should be in practice, it still met with a hostile reception from all stakeholders at the Ninth Session of the ITTC in Yokohama.[217] The Sarawak government and the timber producers were concerned that any drop in the cut would adversely affect their profits. Both the Malaysian and Sarawak government delegates argued that the report contained many factual errors and took issue with the proposed reduction, arguing that it took too negative a view of the consequences of harvesting. In the end, they accepted the broad recommendations. However, at subsequent meetings of the ITTO, the Sarawak delegate was constantly asked to justify (without ever providing a satisfactory explanation) why the cut rate was rising rather than falling, as mandated by the mission's recommendations.[218]

---

214 Gale, 'Discourse and Southeast Asian Deforestation: A Case Study of the International Tropical Timber Organization', 256.

215 Poore, *Changing Landscapes: The Development of the International Tropical Timber Organization and its Influence on Tropical Forest Management*, 90.

216 Ibid.: 88.

217 Gale, 'Discourse and Southeast Asian Deforestation: A Case Study of the International Tropical Timber Organization', 256; Poore, *Changing Landscapes: The Development of the International Tropical Timber Organization and its Influence on Tropical Forest Management*, 90.

218 Gale, 'Discourse and Southeast Asian Deforestation: A Case Study of the International Tropical Timber Organization', 256. Following the publication of the ITTO Sarawak report, Sarawak failed, for the next two years, to reduce its timber production. Cooke, *The Challenge of Sustainable Forests: Forest Resource Policy in Malaysia, 1970–1995*, 94; Gale, 'Discourse and Southeast Asian Deforestation: A Case Study of the International Tropical Timber Organization', 256. In 1990, the Chief Minister gave an undertaking that there would be a reduction in logging to the level recommended by the ITTO in the next 10–15 years. The following year, in March, the Chief Minister stated that Sarawak would reduce overall logging to 10 million cubic metres, but failed to provide a timetable. The Sarawak Timber Association was even more reticent in agreeing to a specific target, being only willing to declare in January 1991 that raw log production would be reduced to 9 million cubic metres in 1991, down

The ENGOs were also unhappy with the report. Three issues were of particular concern to ENGOs: the mission's treatment of the indigenous peoples question, the calculation of the tropical timber sustainable annual cut, and the narrow interpretation of tropical forest management practices. The ENGOs considered the report's recommendations to be weak, and thought the authors should have called for substantially reduced extraction rates to slow down the exploitation.[219] The ENGOs who attended the Ninth Meeting in Yokohama considered the ITTC's response to the report to be a defining moment in determining the body's commitment to sustainable forestry practices, and set out a programme to overcome the report's flaws.[220] The ENGOs' pleas were not heard and the state representatives to the ITTC voted overwhelmingly to accept the report without amendments, praising the report for the 'progress' achieved, with only the USA and Australia expressing reservations.[221] The ENGOs had a different take on the proceedings and their public pronouncement on the issue was filled with anger, arguing that the ITTO had failed its first real test and that it might not be the vehicle to achieve forest sustainability.[222]

Before the Sarawak mission, the tropical timber regime had been an abstract creation that had not called for any concrete sacrifices of any stakeholder's interests. The moment that there were proposed reforms that threatened to reduce potential profits, the fundamental divide between competing normative entrepreneurs was laid bare. This led to increasing ENGO disillusionment with the ITTO.[223] However, it appears that the ENGOs also made a tactical mistake in focusing on reframing the debate in terms of indigenous

from the promised 12 million. Cooke, *The Challenge of Sustainable Forests: Forest Resource Policy in Malaysia, 1970–1995*, 94.

219 Gale, 'The Mysterious Case of the Disappearing Environmentalists: The International Tropical Timber Organization', 113.

220 Ibid.: 114. The ENGO statement outlined five areas which were felt to be critical in addressing the deficiencies of the report: creating a mechanism for resolving conflicts over customary lands; setting strict standards for catchment management; increasing the size of protected zones; reducing the annual allowable cut by between 60 and 90 per cent; and freezing the development of projects by the Sarawak government until the first four conditions had been met. NGO Statement to the Ninth Session of the ITTC, Yokohama, 19 November 1990, reproduced in Gale, 'The Mysterious Case of the Disappearing Environmentalists: The International Tropical Timber Organization', 114.

221 Gale, 'The Mysterious Case of the Disappearing Environmentalists: The International Tropical Timber Organization', 115; Poore, *Changing Landscapes: The Development of the International Tropical Timber Organization and its Influence on Tropical Forest Management*, 96.

222 NGO Statement to the Final Plenary, Ninth Session of the ITTC, Yokohama, 23 November 1990, reprinted in Gale, 'The Mysterious Case of the Disappearing Environmentalists: The International Tropical Timber Organization', 115.

223 Ibid.: 116.

rights. This approach did not resonate significantly with member states or the global populace, at least to the extent necessary to overcome entrenched corruption, and powerful economic interests.

It has to be acknowledged that putting pressure on authoritarian states is difficult, particularly given that the Sarawak government is notoriously corrupt, and is governed by and for the elites of Malaysian society. Further, in tailoring their campaign around indigenous issues, ENGOs appear to have underestimated the commitment to economic development in Malaysia during this period. The Malaysian people's conception of their state was of a rapidly developing state which all should take pride in. Consequently, the issue of indigenous rights appears to have been given short shrift in the headlong rush to develop, despite the consequences for indigenous peoples.

ENGOs were unhappy with the first ITTO mission result, seeing it as a sell-out of their legitimate concerns. Further, they had come to realize that their presence on the ITTO was being used to give an imprimatur of legitimacy to its outcomes. They decided en masse to no longer attend ITTO meetings and to seek other global forums where their views would be more likely to be heeded.[224] This decision undermined the legitimacy of the organization, with only states with vested interests continuing to attend. It also limited its potential for normative transformation.

## SUSTAINABLE LABELLING

At approximately the same time as the Sarawak mission was taking place, efforts were being made to curb exploitationist timber culling by introducing a sustainable labelling system. At the Seventh Session of the ITTC at Yokohama, in November 1989, the British delegates proposed a labelling system to identify timber that was produced sustainably.[225] Similar to the strategy implemented by the ENGOs to stop whaling, the British delegate was actually a stalking horse for the ENGOs, with the proposal prepared by FoE and the Oxford Forestry Institute (OFI). It met with a hostile reception from timber producers, particularly Indonesia and Malaysia, who were worried that any such labelling would be detrimental to their economic interests and the proposal was downgraded to a study on how to provide incentives for sustain-

224 Gale 'Discourse and Southeast Asian Deforestation: A Case Study of the International Tropical Timber Organization', 257.

225 International Tropical Timber Organization, 'Pre-project Proposal, Incentives in Producer and Consumer Countries for the Promotion of Sustainably-Produced Tropical Timber' (1989).

able forestry management.[226] A report prepared by the Permanent Committee on Economic Information and Market Intelligence supported that view.[227]

The British took these criticisms on board and rewrote the document without the input of the FoE. Feeling aggrieved at the need to alter the report, the FoE promptly withdrew its support.[228] Even the watered-down document was not debated by the ITTC, but rather tagged as being an area needing further research.[229] At that time, the British shelved the idea of a labelling programme for the immediate future because it was not supported by a majority of the member states.[230] One observer to the above proceedings noted: 'The producers were privately alarmed that it would be difficult for them to provide such label [*sic*] for *any* timber that they marketed'.[231]

This did not mean the British delegation had given up, however, since they were determined to succeed in creating a sustainable labelling scheme. They enlisted the help of the OFI and the UK Timber Research and Development Association (TRADA) and revised their proposal to one that examined financial and non-financial proposals as regards sustainable forest management.[232] Their proposal was debated by the ITTC at the Tenth Session in 1991. The

---

226 Sandra Chan and Phillip Pattberg, 'Private Rule-making and the Politics of Accountability: Analyzing Global Forest Governance', *Global Environmental Politics* 8, no. 3 (2008): 111. The proposal was viewed with suspicion by producer states, which perceived it as 'a veiled attempt to . . . encourage the current campaign of boycott against the import of tropical timber products' carried out by some ENGOs. D. Humphreys, *Logjam: Deforestation and the Crisis of Global Governance* (London: Earthscan, 2006), 116.

227 Marcus Colchester and L. Lehmann, *The Tropical Forestry Action Plan: What Progress?* (Penang: World Rainforest Movement, 1990), 169; Poore, *Changing Landscapes: The Development of the International Tropical Timber Organization and Its Influence on Tropical Forest Management*, 69. ITTO document PCM(V)/D.1. 'Report to the International Tropical Timber Council, Fifth Session of the Permanent Committee on Economic and Market Intelligence', 3 November 1989, 6, reprinted in Humphreys, 'Hegemonic Ideology and the International Tropical Timber Organization', 224–45.

228 International Tropical Timber Organization, 'Pre-project Proposal, Incentives in Producer and Consumer Countries to Promote Sustainable Development of Tropical Forests' (1989).

229 Humphreys, 'Hegemonic Ideology and the International Tropical Timber Organization', 225.

230 Poore, *Changing Landscapes: The Development of the International Tropical Timber Organization and its Influence on Tropical Forest Management*, 70.

231 Chan and Pattberg, 'Private Rule-making and the Politics of Accountability: Analyzing Global Forest Governance', 111.

232 International Tropical Timber Organization, 'Pre-project Report on Incentives in Producer and Consumer Countries to Promote Sustainable Development of Tropical Forests' (1991).

Chair of the Roundtable neatly captured the essence of the problem when he stated there was a 'need to define an acceptable compromise between the environmental value of the forest and the economic value of trade in tropical timber'.[233]

Yet the ITTC was unwilling to acknowledge there was any tension in the Organization's goals, and instead asked delegates to try to achieve the year 2000 goal, examined more fully in the next section, of all imported and exported timber to be sustainable, supported by domestic trade liberalization policies.[234] The British tried one final time to present a report on the economic linkages between the tropical timber trade and sustainable forest management. They enlisted the help of the London Environmental Economics Centre to outline how environmental and social costs could be factored into the price. Again, however, this was ignored, and the chance to install a global sustainable labelling scheme, under the aegis of the ITTO, was lost.[235]

The ITTO itself admits that only 5 per cent of the globe's tropical forests are currently being certified as sustainably managed. There are two reasons for this, according to the ITTO's Executive Director Dr Sobral: first, almost all tropical states are developing countries, with competing demands for scarce resources, and forests are low on their priority lists. Secondly, tropical states have more complex economic, environmental and social requirements for sustainable management compared to non-tropical states.[236] Those of a more cynical bent might argue that it is not in producer states' interests to put in place such certification schemes, because their exploitationist practices might be exposed. Neither is such a scheme wanted by many consuming states because pressure could be brought to bear by actors like ENGOs to buy timber

---

[233] Humphreys, 'Hegemonic Ideology and the International Tropical Timber Organization', 225.

[234] International Tropical Timber Organization, 'ITTC (X)/16 Decision 3(X) Sustainable Tropical Forest Management and Trade in Tropical Timber' (International Tropical Timber Council, 1991), 1.

[235] London Environmental Economics Centre, 'Draft Final Report: ITTO Activity PCM(IX)/4 the Economic Linkages between the International Trade in Tropical Timber and the Sustainable Management of Tropical Forests' (1992). The drive to create such a labelling scheme did not die, however, but rather morphed into efforts to convince individual states to implement such programmes. Tropical timber states are currently developing national forest certification schemes, led by Malaysia's National Timber Certification Council and Indonesia's Ecolabelling Institute. The ITTO has been attempting to bolster such efforts by creating a framework of mutual recognition between the various national schemes. International Tropical Timber Organization, 'Annual Review and Assessment of the World Timber Situation' (2003), 1.

[236] International Tropical Timber Organization, 'News Release: Legality Shapes as New Certification Flashpoint', http://www.itto.or.jp/live/PageDisplayHandler?pageId=0213.

only from states with such a certification plan in place. This would considerably raise the price of tropical timber.

## THE ITTO AND THE YEAR 2000 OBJECTIVE

As noted earlier, the report, *No Timber without Trees*, in 1989 determined that virtually none of the globe's tropical forests were being managed according to sustainable principles, and that they would be logged into extinction unless immediate, remedial action was undertaken.[237] The ITTC responded in June 1991 by creating the 'Year 2000 Objective', which said that the ITTO should endeavour to ensure that the global tropical timber trade was sustainable by the end of the century.[238] Poore labelled this objective as possibly the most important policy step yet undertaken by the ITTO.[239]

To assist in the achievement of the goal, the organization created a fund for sustainable management of forests (the Bali Partnership Fund), with the aim of assisting member states to make the investments designed to increase the state capacity to implement a sustainable timber programme.[240] While both producer and consumer states were in favour of the general target, many members were against the adoption of specific targets, with the USA, for example, arguing that any '. . . target does not carry implications for our government's trade policy'.[241] Clearly, for many states, such an ambitious target was not going to be met without radical action. The desire to take such action was not readily apparent either. Subsequent events were to show such fears were well grounded. The Review of Progress towards the Year 2000 Objective found that there were signs of improvement but that much remained to be done.[242] It is clear that the funding commitments in the Bali Fund were neither clear nor powerful enough since they relied on voluntary contributions to effect the necessary change.[243]

---

[237] Poore et al., *No Timber without Trees: Sustainability in the Tropical Forest*, 196.

[238] 'ITTO Yokohama Action Plan 2002–2006', in *ITTO Policy Development Series No. 11* (International Tropical Timber Organization, 2002), iii.

[239] Poore, *Changing Landscapes: The Development of the International Tropical Timber Organization and its Influence on Tropical Forest Management*, 72.

[240] Chasek, *Earth Negotiations: Analyzing Thirty Years of Environmental Diplomacy*, 101.

[241] Poore, *Changing Landscapes: The Development of the International Tropical Timber Organization and its Influence on Tropical Forest Management*, 73.

[242] 'ITTO Yokohama Action Plan 2002–2006', iii.

[243] Chaytor, 'The Development of Global Forest Policy: Overview of Legal and Institutional Frameworks', 20.

The lack of discernible action led to increasing frustration on the part of ENGOs and this was manifest at the ITTC meetings. At the Tenth Session of the Council in Quito, Ecuador, in May 1991, Chris Elliott of the WWF spoke for many ENGOs when he complained that the meetings were degenerating into '. . . fruitless discussions, bargaining on projects concluded without transparency and the perceived lack of many delegates' commitment to the ITTA, 1983, the Action Plan and Target 2000'.[244] By the next Council Meeting in Yaounde in May 1992, disillusionment with the ITTO by ENGOs was near complete. Theo Anderson of the Ghanaian branch of FoE, speaking on behalf of the ENGOs, declared that '[t]oo much time was devoted to projects and not enough to policy'.[245]

## THE 1994 SUCCESSOR AGREEMENT NEGOTIATIONS

However, the negotiations to create a Successor Agreement did offer a chance to alter the direction of the ITTO and to put in place a stronger commitment to environmental norms. The renegotiations for a Successor Agreement began in 1993 and took over a year to finalize.[246] As noted by the President of the UN Conference, Wisber Loeis, in his address to the delegates, the mood amongst the delegates was particularly pessimistic as to the inherent schism in the ITTO.[247] The main point of contention was the scope of the agreement with some consumer states and timber companies that wished to retain the status quo (in this case, a commodities agreement covering only tropical timber). Producer states and ENGOs wanted the agreement to cover non-tropical timber, and provide that all timber should be sustainably produced by the year 2000. They also wanted to provide more funds for domestic forest projects.[248]

---

244 Poore, *Changing Landscapes: The Development of the International Tropical Timber Organization and its Influence on Tropical Forest Management*, 106.

245 Ibid.: 108.

246 The Conference was held in four parts at the Palais des Nations, Geneva, Switzerland: the first from 13 to 16 April 1993, the second from 21 to 25 June 1993, the third from 4 to 15 October 1993 and the fourth from 10 to 26 January 1994. The renegotiations were attended by representatives of 57 states, 55 as participants and two observers. International Tropical Timber Organization, 'International Tropical Timber Agreement', United Nations Conference on Trade and Development, http://www.itto.or.jp/live/PageDisplayHandler?pageId=201.

247 Kasimbazi, 'Sustainable Development in International Tropical Timber Agreements', 149.

248 Humphreys, 'Hegemonic Ideology and the International Tropical Timber Organization', 227–8; Kasimbazi, 'Sustainable Development in International Tropical Timber Agreements', 149.

The European delegates feared this result, not wanting the ITTO to become the paramount forest institution, as opposed to the FAO.[249] Many states seem to have only considered their own interests at the negotiations. The European Union wanted to reserve to itself the right to amend any reconstructed agreement. China took the position that it would not sign any agreement unless it was classified as a developing state, despite being a major consumer of tropical timber. On the other hand, some producer states threatened to withdraw from the negotiations altogether, citing that the 1983 International Tropical Timber Agreement allowed trade discrimination against tropical timber.[250]

ENGOs were present at the renegotiations, with the FoE, the WWF, the Rainforest Action Network, the Sierra Club and the World Conservation Union attending as observers. It was difficult for the latter to directly influence proceedings.[251] Their strategy was to argue, through some producer states, for a diminution of the operating scope of the Organization so that it would be limited to trade issues, collecting statistics and providing information on market transparency and pricing. The ENGOs' long-term goal was to ensure that all tropical and temperate timbers should eventually be harvested under a separate agreement; it was hoped to slow the increasing rate of tropical deforestation.[252]

At the first ITTA Meeting after the UNCED proceedings in June 1992, the factions and their positions became clearly discernible. Most consumer countries, led by the USA and supported by the European Union, the UK and Switzerland, were unwilling to broaden the scope of the ITTA to include temperate timber. Producer states wanted a new agreement to address their concerns, particularly over funding. The consumer states' bloc argued that any broadening of the agreement would change its fundamental structure, altering voting structures and membership. They pointed out that it would shift the balance of power from the South to the North and split the producer bloc. It was further claimed that such a move was unnecessary because the temperate timber industry was already transparent, and that the tropical timber states had

---

[249] Smouts, *Tropical Forests, International Jungle: The Underside of Global Ecopolitics*, 148.

[250] Kasimbazi, 'Sustainable Development in International Tropical Timber Agreements', 149.

[251] International Tropical Timber Organization, 'International Tropical Timber Agreement'.

[252] Humphreys, 'Hegemonic Ideology and the International Tropical Timber Organization', 226; Humphreys, 'NGO Influence on International Policy on Forest Conservation and the Trade in Forest Products', 165; Poore, *Changing Landscapes: The Development of the International Tropical Timber Organization and its Influence on Tropical Forest Management*, 118; Smouts, *Tropical Forests, International Jungle: The Underside of Global Ecopolitics*, 148.

already made significant progress in implementing sustainable development practices.[253]

Producer states and some ENGOs were incensed by these arguments, pointing out that there was a double standard at work, with developing states being forced to protect their rainforests, and consumer states being refused protection for their own temperate or boreal forests. The Brazilian representatives obtained a copy of the Dutch proposal to import only sustainably produced timber from 1995, which only heightened the tension.[254] In response, both factions produced separate working texts for consideration by the delegates at the Second Preparatory Meeting.[255]

The 'protect economic interests at all costs' approach by producer states and the major consumer states, and the lack of progress in negotiations, forced many ENGOs to re-evaluate their support for the ITTO. William E. Mankin of the Global Policy Project summed up the current situation:

> The future of ITTO [was] clouded with the last opportunity to give it a new lease of life was about to vanish . . . A decade of genesis and growth had still left ITTO in search of an identity, despite constructive criticism from various quarters . . . commitments to sustainability had produced few measurable results and ITTO and its members appeared to have been mere spectators to world debate and action on important trade-related issues.[256]

To overcome the criticism being levelled at consumer states by producer states and ENGOs, that little was being achieved, the USA and Australia proposed a non-binding side agreement. The agreement stipulated that consumer states would pledge to sustainably manage their own forests by the year 2000 (this was no hardship for the USA, which had already agreed to such a domestic target the year before). Over the objection of European states such as France, the UK and Germany, as well as the ENGOs, this consumer statement was agreed to.[257] As a non-binding agreement, it only declared that states that were already practising high levels of sustainable development would continue to do so, and that the others would commit to achieving the

---

253 Kolk, *Forests in International Environmental Politics: International Organisations, NGOs and the Brazilian Amazon*, 161.

254 Ibid.

255 Poore, *Changing Landscapes: The Development of the International Tropical Timber Organization and its Influence on Tropical Forest Management*, 119.

256 Ibid.: 125.

257 Kolk, *Forests in International Environmental Politics: International Organisations, NGOs and the Brazilian Amazon*, 161; Smouts, *Tropical Forests, International Jungle: The Underside of Global Ecopolitics*, 148.

Year 2000 Objective.[258] However, there was no agreement on the contentious issue of the transfer of funding to producer states, which retaliated by refusing to give a higher status to the year 2000 target.[259] Further, the ENGO idea of creating a separate agreement to cover all types of forests was not taken up. With the writing on the wall early, the WWF withdrew all state advisors from various delegations in an attempt to pressure and shame delegates into acquiescing. However, the protest proved futile in the face of a consumer state threat to discontinue funding initiatives to coerce producer states to acquiesce.[260]

Despite signing the Formal Agreement, the EU delegation to the 1994 renegotiations was unhappy with the outcome. While not blocking the Successor Agreement, they refused to append a signature until a more thorough examination was undertaken in the areas of procedure and substance.[261] Eventually, in 1997, the EU agreed to sign up to the new agreement.[262] This unusual step of not signing immediately probably reflects the EU's unhappiness at the negotiations not setting clear and meaningful targets in the target 2000 mandate and the sparing way the agreement was set out to limit measures to restrict or ban the global trade in timber and its by-products.[263] With the compromise agreed to, the Successor Agreement to the International Tropical Timber Agreement was adopted on 26 January 1994. It was opened for signature on 1 April 1994, entered into force on 1 January 1997 and is mostly similar to the previous Agreement.[264] Poore describes it as a victory for common sense, but it could just as easily be perceived as a continuation of the status

---

[258] 'Formal Statement by Consumer Members: International Tropical Timber Agreement 1994', http://www.itto.or.jp/live/Live_Server/144/ITTA1994e.doc. The Formal Statement was agreed to by Australia, Austria, Canada, China, the European Community, Finland, Japan, New Zealand, Norway, Republic of Korea, Russian Federation, Sweden, Switzerland and the United States of America. 'Formal Statement by Consumer Members: International Tropical Timber Agreement 1994'.

[259] Kolk, *Forests in International Environmental Politics: International Organisations, NGOs and the Brazilian Amazon*, 162.

[260] Humphreys, 'Redefining the Issues: NGO Influence on International Forest Negotiations', 56.

[261] 'European Union Statement, Annex 2: Statement in Explanation of Positions by Member Countries' (paper presented at the Fourth (Final) Part of the United Nations Conference for the Negotiation of a Successor Agreement to the International Tropical Timber Agreement, 1983, Geneva, Switzerland, 10–26 January 1994).

[262] Poore, *Changing Landscapes: The Development of the International Tropical Timber Organization and its Influence on Tropical Forest Management*, 165.

[263] VanderZwaag and MacKinlay, 'Towards a Global Forest Convention: Getting out of the Woods and Barking up the Right Tree', 16–17.

[264] Chasek, *Earth Negotiations: Analyzing Thirty Years of Environmental Diplomacy*, 101; Elliott, *The Global Politics of the Environment*, 85.

quo without fixing the problems that had become so apparent in the first ten years of the original ITTA.[265]

The Successor Agreement promoted a stronger emphasis on sustainability, at least in rhetoric, but remained confined to tropical forests. For our purposes, the key objectives of the 1994 ITTA are:

> (c) To contribute to the process of sustainable development;
> (d) To enhance the capacity of members to implement a strategy for achieving exports of tropical timber and timber products from sustainably managed sources by the year 2000;
> (e) To promote the expansion and diversification of international trade in tropical timber from *sustainable sources* [my emphasis] by improving the structural conditions in international markets, by taking into account, on the one hand, a long term increase in consumption and continuity of supplies, and, on the other, prices which reflect the costs of sustainable forest management and which are remunerative and equitable for members, and the improvement of market access.[266]

Again the language reflects the need for sustainable development, conserving forests, and valuing the forests for more than their timber. However, there appears to be no mechanism in the Successor Agreement to bring about such lofty objectives. The 1994 Successor Agreement remained, from an environmental perspective, limited, in that it only applied to tropical timber, new funding commitments were unclear and it remained primarily a commodities agreement. Further devaluing its environmental impact was that it still did not allow for any real public participation via ENGOs or the indigenous peoples affected by ITTO member-state activities.[267]

The 1994 ITTA entered into force in January 1997 for an initial five-year period but was extended twice for three-year terms.[268] The contentious voting structure that stymied environmental progress was retained in Article 10.[269] Article 15 of the Successor Agreement allowed the Council to invite NGOs or other organizations (referred to in Articles 14, 20 and 29 of the current agreement) interested in the issue, to attend Council Meetings as observers only.[270]

---

[265] Poore, *Changing Landscapes: The Development of the International Tropical Timber Organization and its Influence on Tropical Forest Management*, 125.

[266] International Tropical Timber Organization, 'International Tropical Timber Agreement'.

[267] Kasimbazi, 'Sustainable Development in International Tropical Timber Agreements', 150–51.

[268] Flejzor, 'Reforming the International Tropical Timber Agreement', 21.

[269] International Tropical Timber Organization, 'International Tropical Timber Agreement'.

[270] Ibid.

It stopped well short of making ENGOs true partners in the quest to make tropical forests sustainable, though. Article 21 established the aforementioned 'Bali Fund', with the aim of assisting producing members make the investments required to sustainably manage their tropical timber reserves as per objective 1(d).[271] It should be acknowledged that at least this put some flesh on the bare-bones idea of a reforestation fund mentioned in the original agreement.[272] Despite the 'carrot' of the fund potentially offering monies to producer states that did develop sustainable practices, the fund has been perceived as a failure due to underfunding by the consumer states.[273]

The negotiations left the ENGOs pessimistic that the ITTO could change. At the first ITTC Meeting post the renegotiations, in Cartagena in May 1994, the WWF, through Mr Gordon Shepherd, formally announced it was no longer attending the meetings, stating that:

> Negotiators had decided not to follow the WWF recommendations and this marked a parting of the ways. Therefore, the WWF would be reducing its participation in ITTO activities and considering reallocating resources to better options such as the Biodiversity Convention . . . The WWF found it difficult to see how the new ITTA, 1994 could make a useful contribution . . .[274]

By 1992, the ENGOs had lost any sense of the ITTO as a potential force for the environmental protection of tropical forests and had concluded that the ITTO was merely a cat's paw of the international tropical timber companies.[275] The ENGOs have virtually all withdrawn from the Organization as a consequence, choosing to no longer legitimate its actions. The ACF has not attended since 1990, Survival International and the Rainforest Action Network have been no-shows since 1991, and the WWF no longer attended from 1992 onwards. Only FoE and the Global Forest Policy Project have chosen to attend, up to and including the current Successor Agreement negotiations.[276]

The ENGOs have instead sought other global forums in which they can influence forestry practices. ENGOs (largely the WWF) have been involved in

---

271 Ibid.

272 Poore, *Changing Landscapes: The Development of the International Tropical Timber Organization and its Influence on Tropical Forest Management*, 127.

273 Flejzor, 'Reforming the International Tropical Timber Agreement', 21.

274 Poore, *Changing Landscapes: The Development of the International Tropical Timber Organization and its Influence on Tropical Forest Management*, 127.

275 Gale, 'The Mysterious Case of the Disappearing Environmentalists: The International Tropical Timber Organization', 104.

276 Humphreys, 'Hegemonic Ideology and the International Tropical Timber Organization', 227, 232, n. 37; Poore, *Changing Landscapes: The Development of the International Tropical Timber Organization and its Influence on Tropical Forest Management*, 159.

the creation of such entities as the Forest Stewardship Council (FSC), in March 1992, with the goal of establishing a non-governmental sustainable timber accreditation programme for all forests.[277] Its goal was to show that focusing on the supply chain aspect of tropical timber could lead to conservationist practices.[278] It functions to provide consumers with accurate information, by creating principles and criteria at a local level, on the source of forest products. The programme is predicated on the notion that consumer pressure can force more change than intergovernmental meetings and agreements, and it currently has no timber representatives on its Board of Management.[279] What is unique about the FSC is its governing structure. This mandates a devolved, chamber-based membership which encourages interaction. The decision-making body comprises the three main interest groups involved in tropical timber: the economic, the environmental and the social.[280] The FSC's lack of timber company representatives has led commentators like Poore to dismiss the organization, arguing that without timber organizations it lacks credibility.[281] Given its voluntary nature, less than 10 per cent of timber cut is currently certified under the scheme.[282]

To achieve their aims, ENGOs have also sought other IOs that they regard as less prone to 'agency capture' by the timber industry than the ITTO. Some schemes, such as the Tropical Forest Action Plan (TFAP), set up in 1983, predate the ITTO. It was designed to put in place a global moratorium on logging projects and give decision-making authority on forestry to an independent body in a state, with the aim of conserving forest resources.[283] Except

[277] Poore, *Changing Landscapes: The Development of the International Tropical Timber Organization and its Influence on Tropical Forest Management*, 148.

[278] D. Humphreys, 'Discourse as Ideology: Neoliberalism and the Limits of International Forest Policy', *Forest Policy and Economics* (2008): 3.

[279] Poore, *Changing Landscapes: The Development of the International Tropical Timber Organization and its Influence on Tropical Forest Management*, 148.

[280] Fred P. Gale, 'Public Accountability in Private Regulation: Contrasting Models of the Forest Stewardship Council (FSC) and Marine Stewardship Council' (paper presented at the Australasian Political Studies Association Conference, University of Adelaide, 2004), 15.

[281] Poore, *Changing Landscapes: The Development of the International Tropical Timber Organization and its Influence on Tropical Forest Management*, 148.

[282] Humphreys, 'Discourse as Ideology: Neoliberalism and the Limits of International Forest Policy', 3.

[283] Kasimbazi, 'Sustainable Development in International Tropical Timber Agreements', 155. ENGOs ensured that they were an integral part of the process of creating TFAP. The World Resources Institute and Environmental Liaison Centre set up regional workshops in Nairobi, Panama City and Bangkok to set out the ENGO position as regards forestry and to plan how to become full partners in implementing TFAP. A conference in Italy in July 1987, organized by the FAO, the World Bank, UNDP,

for Brazil and the Cote d'Ivoire, the ITTA has the same producer state members as the TFAP.[284] The TFAP is limited to coordinating development assistance and has no legal authority to conserve tropical forests. This lack of a conservationist norm underpinning the Plan has led to 'the funding of projects oriented towards conventional forestry such as commercial exploitation-projects' and has done nothing to address the root causes of deforestation, namely, poverty, foreign debts and fuel needs.[285] To date, ENGOs have been unsuccessful in influencing the managers of the Plan to adopt a more conservationist position.[286]

Other, more recent, IOs, such as the United Nations Forum on Forests (UNFF), were set up to 'promote the implementation of proposals for action for the management, conservation and sustainable development of all types of forests'.[287] The ENGOs, supporting this approach, now seem to have abandoned piecemeal improvement in differing forest types in favour of a unified approach encompassing all the world's forests. The attempt to create a global forest regime has only had a limited success, however, in producing a body of 'soft law', including various protocols. The regime is largely aspirational and lacks legal force. ENGOs perceive this as the most promising path to take, however.[288] The renegotiations to create the Successor Agreement come at a time when member states to the UN Forum on Forests (UNFF) are considering a potentially legally binding global forestry agreement.[289] If the ITTC is not careful and the new Successor Agreement 2006 makes no progress, then it

---

World Resources institute (WRI) and the Rockefeller Foundation, amended the TFAP to allow greater ENGO participation. VanderZwaag and MacKinlay, 'Towards a Global Forest Convention: Getting out of the Woods and Barking up the Right Tree', 8.

284 VanderZwaag and MacKinlay, 'Towards a Global Forest Convention: Getting out of the Woods and Barking up the Right Tree', 6.

285 Kasimbazi, 'Sustainable Development in International Tropical Timber Agreements', 155.

286 Porter and Brown, *Global Environmental Politics*, 99; Caroline Thomas, *The Environment in International Relations* (London: Royal Institute of International Affairs, 1992), 262.

287 'ITTO Yokohama Action Plan 2002–2006', 4. In October 2000, the Economic and Social Council of the United Nations (ECOSOC) created the United Nations Forum on Forests (UNFF) building on the work done by the Intergovernmental Panel on Forests (IPF) and its successor body the Intergovernmental Forum on Forests (IFF). 'ITTO Yokohama Action Plan 2002–2006', 4. ENGOs have virtually abandoned the ITTO for the IFF, branding sustainable forest management an illusion, in that it enables exploitative logging to continue, and the ITTO's conservation rhetoric as merely a smokescreen. Smouts, *Tropical Forests, International Jungle: The Underside of Global Ecopolitics*, 147.

288 Humphreys, 'Redefining the Issues: NGO Influence on International Forest Negotiations', 53.

289 Flejzor, 'Reforming the International Tropical Timber Agreement', 26.

may find itself outflanked and sidelined in favour of a more comprehensive regime.

## THE YEAR 2000 REPORT

The ITTO made such extravagant claims for itself when setting the Year 2000 Objective in the early 1990s (requiring member states' tropical forests to be sustainably managed by that date) that to some extent it created a rod for its own back as the date approached. It had to demonstrate that significant progress had been achieved or admit that the ENGOs' criticisms of its performance to date were accurate. Consequently, in late 1999, it commissioned a study, Decision 10(XXVI), to detail individual states' progress towards the sustainability goal, as well as its own performance as an organization.[290] Duncan Poore and Thang Hooi Chiew accepted the brief to assess this progress to date and gave their findings in the 'Review of Progress towards the Year 2000 Objective' in November 2000. Unfortunately, as Poore himself admits, the report was deeply flawed from the beginning, as none of the member states answered the key question about the Year 2000 Objective. This was '. . . how much of the timber exported came from sustainably managed resources, and what area of forest was under demonstrably sustainable management?'[291] While some progress was recorded by Poore and Chiew, the main ideal of sustainable forestry was still as much of a chimera as before.

The authors, hamstrung by the lack of engagement by member states with the report's progress, were forced to concede that the Year 2000 Objective was a process rather than a goal and that '. . . the process, in the view of the consultants, should be to move as swiftly as possible in the direction of that goal'.[292] The report also acknowledged that the symbiotic relationship the ITTO had initially enjoyed with the ENGOs had ceased '. . . because [the] ITTO did not and, by the nature of the fundamental changes it was trying to bring about, could not move as fast as the NGOs wished it to'.[293]

The report argued that there had been some successes by the ITTO in that its 1988 pre-project survey had alerted forest authorities, the trade and the public to the dire state of the official management of forests throughout the tropics. Further, the report maintained that scrutiny of forest activities had

---

290 Poore, *Changing Landscapes: The Development of the International Tropical Timber Organization and Its Influence on Tropical Forest Management*, 172.

291 Ibid.

292 Duncan Poore and Thang Hooi Chiew, 'Review of Progress Towards the Year 2000 Objective' (International Tropical Timber Council, 2000), 4.

293 Ibid.: 14–15.

effectively put states on notice that their actions were being monitored. The ITTO had created an action plan, put in place a series of guidelines on natural forest, on plantations, on biological diversity and on fire, as well as creating criteria and indicators and the idea of forest resource accounting. However, the report concluded that there had been many 'lost opportunities'. The first published version of the criteria and indicators had been a pallid document that was considered to have hindered rapid progress. Also the organization had not recognized the potential of certification schemes and had been reluctant to act on such a vital issue. Finally, the report concluded that the Year 2000 Objective was a critical ideal that had been allowed to meander to the detriment of the organization's perceived status as the premier tropical timber forum.[294]

The report's broad recommendations to continue aiding producer states to meet the criteria for SFM and to make the ITTO as efficient as possible in effecting this change did not lead to any formal decisions due to, as Poore puts it, 'a failure of procedures rather than will'.[295] However, the recommendations have not been put into practice to date. That suggests it was not so much a procedural error as a lack of desire on the part of the delegate states. Rather, the ITTC turned to what it knew best, the crafting of action plans to address the problems. The Yokohama Action Plan adopted in November 2000, which built on and replaced the previous Libre Action Plan, was meant to aid the ITTO in achieving its sustainable forest objective. It is a sharpening of focus compared to the previous plan, in that it reduces to six (as opposed to nine) the goals and adds a new action that aims '. . . to encourage and assist individual producing member countries to identify and address constraints in their implementation of sustainable forest management and the sustainable development of the forest industry'.[296]

Decision 2(XXIX) of the ITTC reaffirmed its desire to move as quickly as achievable to a scenario where tropical timber exports were sourced only from sustainably managed forests.[297] The plan's actions to achieve these goals include, among other things, to:

- support the effective enforcement of forest laws and regulations that ensure sustainable forest management and secure the production base;
- support networking and the exchange of information with relevant international organizations to maintain the integrity of the resource base, including protected area networks;

---

294 Ibid.: 15.

295 Poore, *Changing Landscapes: The Development of the International Tropical Timber Organization and its Influence on Tropical Forest Management*, 210, 13.

296 'ITTO Yokohama Action Plan 2002–2006', iii.

297 Ibid.: 4.

- promote the conservation, rehabilitation and sustainable management of threatened forest ecosystems . . . in collaboration with relevant organizations.[298]

Yet the report submitted by states to verify compliance with the Year 2000 Objective requirement was largely inaccurate, preventing the ITTO from properly assessing the problem, let alone engaging with it. For example, the 2000 Mission to Indonesia Report findings were virtually diametrically opposed to the official Indonesia Report submitted in compliance with its Year 2000 Objective requirements.[299] The ITTO has adopted a new Action Plan 2008–2011 to succeed the Yokohama Plan, but at the time of printing this was not yet available for analysis.[300]

## SUCCESSOR AGREEMENT TO THE INTERNATIONAL TROPICAL TIMBER AGREEMENT 2006

With the ten-year lifespan of the 1994 Successor Agreement over in 2004, UNCTAD again convened a Conference for the Negotiation of a Successor Agreement to the International Tropical Timber Agreement. The first session took place from 26 to 30 July 2004 in Geneva.[301] While all the major producer and consumer states chose to attend the renegotiations, of the ENGOs, only the IUCN and FoE (International), which were specially invited, chose to attend.[302] The meeting reflected a growing corporatization of the ITTO structures, with most delegates being timber trade advisors with an agenda to ensure the security of the global timber business.[303]

At the First Session, there was discussion about the role of SFM and the need for a long-term approach. Objective (b) of the new Successor Agreement was tentatively stated (sections in brackets indicate points not agreed to) as:

298 Ibid.: 11.

299 Poore, *Changing Landscapes: The Development of the International Tropical Timber Organization and its Influence on Tropical Forest Management*, 218.

300 International Tropical Timber Organization, 'Decision 4(XLIV) the ITTO Action Plan 2008–2011 Transitional Period', http://www.ito.or.jp.

301 'Working Document Resulting from the First Session' (paper presented at the Conference for the Negotiation of a Successor Agreement to the International Tropical Timber Agreement, Geneva, Switzerland, 26–30 July 2004).

302 Participants listed in ibid.

303 Humphreys, *Logjam: Deforestation and the Crisis of Global Governance*, 218.

> [To promote sustainable forest management] to enhance the [long term] capacity [and efforts] of members to implement a strategy for achieving exports of tropical timber and timber [and non-timber] products from sustainably managed forests [while conserving other forest values] [or sources].[304]

In the final draft to be ratified and signed by member states, the idea of sustainable development was linked to poverty alleviation, however, rather than put as a stand-alone goal to be worked towards.[305]

Once again, timber, as opposed to the forest as a whole, was the main focus of the regime as spelled out in the Preamble, section (e): 'Recognizing the importance of timber and related trades to the economies of timber producing countries'.[306] For the first time this section made explicit that timber is considered vital for producer states' economic interests. According to Flejzor, the negotiations also raised the poisoned chalice of expanding the ITTA to include all types of forests, but there was no sign of this in the agreed-to draft. Given the ITTO's performance to date, this may not be a bad thing.[307]

At the second part of the Conference in Geneva, held from 27 June to 1 July 2005, a new section was added to both the Preamble (c) and Article 1 of the Objectives relating to the exploitation of tropical forests.[308] The section has been retained in the final document as Section (d) of the Preamble and reads:

> Recognizing that States have in accordance with the Charter of the United Nations and the principles of international law, the sovereign right to exploit their own resources pursuant to their own environmental policies and have the responsibility to ensure that activities within their jurisdiction and control do not cause damage to the environment of other States or of areas beyond the limits of national jurisdiction, as defined in principle 1(a) of the Non-Legally Binding Authoritative Statement of Principles for a Global Consensus on the Management, Conservation, and Sustainable Development of all Types of Forests.[309]

The new section enshrines the basic principle of customary international law expressed in both Principle 21 of the Stockholm Declaration and the Rio Declaration on Forests that reaffirms the sovereign right of states to exploit

---

304 'Working Document Resulting from the First Session', 4.

305 'International Tropical Timber Agreement 2006', United Nations Conference on Trade and Development, http://www.itto.or.jp/live/PageDisplayHandler?pageId=201.

306 Ibid.

307 Flejzor, 'Reforming the International Tropical Timber Agreement', 20.

308 'Final Working Document Resulting from the Second Part of the Conference' (paper presented at the Conference for the Negotiation of a Successor Agreement to the International Tropical Timber Agreement, Geneva, Switzerland, 27 June–1 July 2005), 2.

309 'International Tropical Timber Agreement 2006'.

resources within their own national boundaries.[310] It further arguably enshrines exploitation as the governing norm of the regime and prevents global agents from interfering in the destruction of tropical forests that are internal to a state and that have no external ramifications. This could be regarded as only recognizing the actual situation on the forest floor. In many ways, it signals a retrograde step by the ITTO and a capitulation to the interests of producer states and timber companies. States are merely yet again encouraged to develop domestic policies to bring about 'conservation of timber producing forests . . . maintaining ecological balance, in the context of the tropical timber trade'.[311]

The final document provides no moves to change the decision-making structure of the ITTO. The distribution of votes remains the same as adopted in previous agreements, with 1000 votes accorded to both producer and consumer states depending on their timber-selling or buying activities.[312] Given this voting structure and the inability of ENGOs and conservationist-minded states like Britain to effect real change, the ITTC will remain deadlocked and unable to enact environmental measures which translate into action on the forest floor.

At the third part of the UNCTAD Conference, Norway, Switzerland and the USA proposed differing but complementary proposals for a global certification scheme for tropical timber, with the aim of:

> [Promoting the certification of tropical timber producing forests;] [and encouraging information sharing on and the use of voluntary mechanisms to promote such trade]; (Norway/Switzerland) [and encouraging information sharing on [private] [independent] voluntary market-based mechanisms]; (USA).[313]

---

310 Chaytor, 'The Development of Global Forest Policy: Overview of Legal and Institutional Frameworks', 5–6. Principle 21 of the Stockholm Declaration states that 'States have, in accordance with the Charter of the United Nations and the principle of international law, the sovereign right to exploit their own resources pursuant to their own environmental policies, and the responsibility to ensure that activities within their jurisdiction or control do not cause damage to the environment of other States or of areas beyond the limits of national jurisdiction'. United Nations, Conference on the Human Environment, Declaration of the United Nations Conference on the Human Environment, Principle 21, UN Doc. A/CONF. 48/14 (1972), reprinted in Tarlock, 'Exclusive Sovereignty versus Sustainable Development of a Shared Resource: The Dilemma of Latin American Rainforest Management', 42.

311 Preamble, (m), International Tropical Timber Organization, 'International Tropical Timber Agreement, 2006', United Nations Conference on Trade and Development, http://www.ito.or.jp.

312 Article 10, 'International Tropical Timber Agreement 2006'.

313 'Final Working Document Resulting from the Third Part of the Conference' (paper presented at the Conference for the Negotiation of a Successor Agreement to the International Tropical Timber Agreement, Geneva, Switzerland, 27 June–1 July 2005), 5.

The final document mentions briefly a tropical timber certification scheme, but only in terms of encouraging information to better understand voluntary schemes such as certification.[314] One of the key objectives (Article 1(n)) of the Successor Agreement will be:

> Strengthening the capacity of members to improve forest law enforcement and governance, and addressing illegal logging and related trade in tropical timber.[315]

The previous agreement only referred to this trade as 'undocumented'. While a step in the right direction, the difficulty of maintaining agreement on tackling the issue was exposed at the United Nations Forum on Forests Meeting (Sixth Session), held subsequent to ITTO negotiations where China, India and the Amazonian Pact states opposed the term 'illegal logging' as too provocative.[316]

The 2006 Successor Agreement was adopted in Geneva on 27 January 2006.[317] However, three years later, entry into force remains problematic, with only 18 states acceding to its entry.[318] If adoption occurs, we can expect to see no real environmental progress within the ITTO for the next decade and, given the lack of enthusiasm for real change, probably beyond.

## CONCLUSION

Applying Legro's test for norm robustness to conservationism as compared to exploitationist behaviour, we find a dismal situation for those promulgating environmentalist norms within the ITTO. In terms of norm specificity, conservation rates badly with the guidelines on sustainable forest practices, which are poorly articulated and not well understood. States, particularly producer states, have constantly sought to dilute even the weak environmental

---

314 Preamble, (o), 'International Tropical Timber Agreement 2006'.

315 'International Tropical Timber Agreement, 2006'.

316 Humphreys, *Logjam: Deforestation and the Crisis of Global Governance*, 162. The compromise wording states agreed to eventually was 'illegal practices according to national legislation and illegal international trade in forest products'. Humphreys, *Logjam: Deforestation and the Crisis of Global Governance*, 162.

317 Deborah S. Davenport et al., 'Summary of the Forty-fourth Session of the International Tropical Timber Council and Associated Sessions of the Four Committees: 3–8 November 2008', *Earth Negotiations Bulletin* 24, no. 81 (2008): 2; International Tropical Timber Organization, 'Decision 7(XLIV) Entry into Force of the International Tropical Timber Agreement, 2006', http://www.ito.or.jp.

318 International Tropical Timber Organization, 'U.S.$8.6 Million in New Funds for Tropical Forests', http://www.ito.or.jp/live/PageDisplayHandler?pageId=213.

constraints suggested by the ITTO. The prominent placing of the draft section in the 2006 Successor Agreement privileging exploitation is just one indicator of the relative strength of the party's acceptance of the norm of exploitation, compared to conservation and preservation. In fact, during the tenure of the ITTO, the global logging industry has actually expanded under the aegis of the ITTO, and consequently exploitationist practices have become further entrenched. It is virtually beyond dispute that global tropical forests are being exploited at an alarming rate and that the remaining areas of forest are rapidly shrinking to the point that if current trends continue, few states will have any sizeable forests left.[319]

In terms of the durability of the norm of conservation, there have been many violations of sustainable forest practices over the lifetime of the tropical timber regime. Conservation has not been widely accepted by the ITTO member states and, consequently, the parties' degree of concordance in relation to this norm is also low. As noted previously, according to the ITTO's own figures in 1988 less than 1 per cent of tropical forests (and even that figure is disputed) are being managed sustainably. The Poore and Chiew Year 2000 report reveals that in the following 12 years the situation had improved slightly. However, reading the report with a more jaundiced eye, it is clear that the improvements noted are in the administrative, legislative and regulatory arenas, and that the situation on the forest ground in terms of preventing over-logging has not improved.[320] A more independent study in 1999 by the IUCN found that in ten major forest states, less than a quarter of designated protected areas were managed effectively and most were not managed at all.[321] To compound the situation, it is also clear that any figures compiled by the ITTO are based on unreliable data supplied haphazardly by member states with a motive to hide the problem, so the extent of deforestation is still unknown.[322]

In terms of the consumption of tropical timber, there is no evidence that the trend for more and more tropical timber goods is subsiding. Indeed, the Asian development boom appears to be driving deforestation at an increased pace. To feed the need for tropical timber products in 1999, for example, producer states' exports of tropical logs were of the order of: Malaysia (17 per cent), Papua New Guinea (16 per cent), Gabon (14 per cent), Cameroon (9 per cent).[323] The largest importers were China (31 per cent), Japan (24 per cent),

---

319 Colchester, 'Colonizing the Rainforests: The Agents and Causes of Deforestation', 2.

320 Smouts, *Tropical Forests, International Jungle: The Underside of Global Ecopolitics*, 188.

321 Ibid.: 174.

322 Ibid.: 211.

323 Ibid.: 112.

India (9 per cent) and Taiwan (8 per cent). For sawn wood, the largest exporters in 1999 were Malaysia (49 per cent), Indonesia (9 per cent), with China (18 per cent) and Japan (16 per cent) being the main importers. Malaysia exports 54 per cent of wood veneer primarily to China (44 per cent) and Taiwan (14 per cent). Malaysia and Indonesia between them produced 60 per cent of the plywood on the export market, with China and Japan again being the largest consumers.[324] The ITTO's own figures show that in 2002 its producer states exported close to 13.1 million cubic metres of logs, with Malaysia providing one-third of the total, down from almost three-quarters in the early 1990s. In 2003, the figure had risen 2.3 per cent to 13.4 million cubic metres.[325] This trend shows no signs of abating in the near future, unless the mooted timber shortage, brought about by the cutting down of most tropical forests, becomes a reality.

The main problem is that conservationist ideals have been incorporated into the 'content' of forest polices without affecting actual practices on the ground.[326] States are willing to agree to 'motherhood statements' of the need to environmentally regulate and manage national forests without any intention of implementing the needed reforms. Consequently, according to the Legro test, we must rate the robustness of the conservationist norm as low, in that only a small minority of states appear to support conservationist practices in real terms. In terms of the preservationist norm, there is no evidence to suggest that it is even a consideration for the member-states, and if no such practices are applied to tropical timber, they cannot be measured using the Legro test.

From an environmental perspective, the ITTO regime was doomed from its conception. States never voluntarily came together to solve a collective action problem and create the tropical timber regime. Rather, the impetus came from UNCTAD and the ENGOs in the hope that such a regime would circumscribe exploitationist behaviour and provide a mechanism for states to 'learn' that their behaviour was wrong. However, an examination of the history of the ITTO to date reveals that environmental norms have not affected substantive policy conduct. They have only affected the *symbolic* behaviour of states.[327]

The evidence indicates that the global timber companies and producer states were concerned that the tropical timber regime would limit their timber-gathering activities, and actively sought to limit the ITTO's power. Unlike in

---

324 Ibid.: 112–13.

325 International Tropical Timber Organization, 'Annual Review and Assessment of the World Timber Situation', vi.

326 Dauvergne, *Loggers and Degradation in the Asia-Pacific: Corporations and Environmental Management*, 157.

327 Dimitrov, 'Hostage to Norms: States, Institutions and Global Forest Politics', 7.

the two previous case studies, ENGOs have not been able to highlight environmental interests over economic concerns.[328] Consumer states also wanted to ensure a steady supply of tropical timber, so neither the producer states nor the consumer bloc evinced the political will to bring about environmental normative change.[329] So why have states chosen to remain with the ITTO? Producer states have chosen to stay at the ITTO to gain access to the various funds on offer and to avoid being branded as international environmental pariahs and suffer the consequent 'reputational disadvantage'.[330] Consumer states have stayed within the ITTO to ensure their imports of tropical timber remain constant.

In the early days of the ITTO, there was optimism by many stakeholders, including the ENGOs, that the ITTO would enable real reform. However, lately it has come to be perceived as merely a lobbying group for timber interests.[331] The ITTA contains conservation clauses, but the ITTO, as a body, has chosen to favour trade over conservation, to the detriment of the forests.[332] Gale argues that this is because the ITTO has suffered a form of 'agency capture' and has come to be dominated by government and industry interests from a relatively small group of key producer and consumer states. On the producer side, Brazil, Malaysia and Indonesia, all with large timber company interests, dominate the ITTO, while the consumer states are dominated by Japan, the Netherlands, the UK and the USA.[333] Any attempt to understand the normative evolution of the ITTO must bear in mind this structure and this interplay of interests, since it is reflected in the decision-making framework of the organization.

A neoliberal analysis of the tropical timber regime shows clearly that vested economic interests, principally those of the TNCs and some producer and consumer states which have privileged tropical timber extraction to the detriment of other forest values, have proved remarkably successful in forestalling normative change. The logic of 'crony capitalism', with its emphasis on short-term profits for political elites at the expense of sustainable practices, has held sway. Although the arguments made by these stakeholders are rarely couched

---

328 Humphreys, 'NGO Influence on International Policy on Forest Conservation and the Trade in Forest Products', 166.

329 Young and Demko, 'Improving the Effectiveness of International Environmental Governance Systems', 234.

330 Wood, 'Soft Law, Hard Law and the Development of an International Forest Convention'.

331 Marcus Colchester, 'The International Tropical Timber Organization: Kill or Cure for the Rainforests?', *The Ecologist* 20, no. 5 (1990): 166.

332 Humphreys, 'The Evolving Forests Regime', 253.

333 Gale, 'Discourse and Southeast Asian Deforestation: A Case Study of the International Tropical Timber Organization', 243.

in terms of exploitation (with the exception of the 2006 Successor Agreement), it seems clear that such an approach is deemed crucial to their interests.

Neoliberals, applying a simple cost/benefit analysis, would say that for many states the abatement costs of stopping exploitationist practices were too high. Neither producer nor consumer states are interested in genuine dialogue, creating a 'super' veto coalition which prevents environmental normative change now and into the future. For producer states, the loss of export revenue would be too high a price to pay in the short term, while consumer states continue to crave a steady supply of tropical timber. Thus we can observe a situation similar to Putnam's analysis of a voluntary defection scenario: where states promise to support the ITTO's objective of SFM, but decide not to meet it. Proposals to limit tropical timber exports that are not sustainably produced have been stymied by a veto coalition of tropical forest states, led currently by Malaysia, which is currently the largest exporter of tropical timber at approximately 60 per cent of the total.[334]

The producer states, to date, consider goals like the Year 2000 Objective to be advisory rather than binding, and its fulfilment to depend on appropriate financial and technical assistance.[335] Attempts to create sustainable logging certificate schemes or restrict imports from states that do not utilize conservative logging techniques within the ITTO have foundered, with Malaysia leading producer states in blocking proposals to restrict such unsustainable trade. Consumer states such as Japan, where the ITTO is headquartered, have also been less than receptive to such proposals and since Japan is the biggest source of funding for the ITTO, and the major vote holder, it has generally succeeded in preventing such actions.[336]

The logic of rational choice applied to timber production does not lend itself to forest sustainability because it lends itself to the externalization of social and environmental costs. No matter what type of logging is used, however, whether clearfelling or selective cutting techniques, the collateral damage caused by logging is significant. Over 40 per cent of timber logged is left on the forest floor since it is considered too expensive to transport if it is not an easily saleable log. The low return on tropical timber leads to even greater logging. Studies have also shown that the higher the price of timber, the more companies log, even in areas they might have previously left alone.[337] This is despite the neoliberal economic assumption that the more

[334] Porter and Brown, *Global Environmental Politics*, 101.

[335] Smouts, *Tropical Forests, International Jungle: The Underside of Global Ecopolitics*, 148.

[336] Elliott, *The Global Politics of the Environment*, 85.

[337] Smouts, *Tropical Forests, International Jungle: The Underside of Global Ecopolitics*, 21.

valuable a commodity, the more care will be taken to ensure its long-term survival. States have used the rhetoric of sustainable development to claim that their practices are currently 'sustainable' or 'green', and to deflect criticism. See, for example, Sarawak's Chief Minister Taib in this regard.

In the case of tropical timber there is a large incentive to cheat, particularly when there are weak oversight provisions, both domestically and from the ITTO. At the state level, timber firms are generally willing to agree to regulations, secure in the knowledge that states are unwilling or unable to enforce them and that the only punishment is that of loss of reputation, such as naming and shaming, rather than economic loss.[338] Strategic bargains and compromises by logging interests and their socio-political allies also prevent genuine reform. Loggers have established informal networks with government officials and corporate elites that prevent change to the exploitationist behaviour between these stakeholders.[339]

From a neoliberal point of view, there are still many institutional barriers to environmental progress within the ITTO. The voting system prevents any significant change, with those doing the exploiting rewarded with control of the ITTO. There has also been a failure by producer states to secure adequate sources of untied monies to implement conservationist practices. The internal ITTO debate has been limited to discussions on improving sustainable logging rather than sustainable forests. The right of states to set their own environmental priorities has been upheld. The ITTO has been limited to making suggestions, with no real compliance mechanisms. This leaves the authorities with few means of pressuring non-complying states. Until these issues are tackled, it will be extremely difficult for the ITTO to change to the point where effective environmental norms underpin the regime.

Neoliberals can easily account for behaviour such as exploitation at the state level. However, because it tends to 'black box' states' interests, it cannot tell us much about whose interests are being met and whose are not. This is where holistic constructivism, with its emphasis on both global and domestic levels and non-state actors, holds an edge. Constructivism allows us to unpack the concept of interests and examine who benefits domestically, allowing for a more nuanced understanding of state interests.

In the case of tropical timber, politicians have business interests that require timber exploitation, and it can be readily shown that the elites in producer societies are the ones who benefit the most.[340] For the rural poor and indige-

---

338 Dauvergne, 'The Environmental Challenge to Loggers in the Asia-Pacific: Corporate Practices in Informal Regimes on Governance', 191.

339 Ibid.: 169.

340 For example, past Philippine President Ferdinand Marcos, Indonesian President Suharto, Solomon Islands Prime Minister Solomon Mamaloni and

nous peoples of producer states, the exploitation of tropical forests is certainly not in their interests, since it involves loss of livelihoods, an increase in crime, and the destruction of traditional ways of life. These insights are not new, and owe more of a debt to the Marxist 'exposé' of economic interests that lie behind legal superstructures.[341] Given this, what 'added (analytic) value' can constructivists provide?

To understand the tropical timber regime, we need to examine, as constructivism allows, not only material factors but also ideational factors. These include the significance of the norm of development. The evidence indicates that this norm is deeply embedded in the domestic culture of producer states, such that, even if corruption were stamped out, the majority of the domestic population would still support development based on the short-term exploitation of tropical forests. The political and economic costs of successful conservation policies are considered too high for most developing states' leaders, since the timber is valuable on the global market and the denuded land can be used for agricultural purposes by landless peasants, reducing domestic political pressures.[342] In short, development is considered far more important by LDC governments than environmental concerns.[343]

Clearly, environmental norms are unlikely to become incorporated into the ITTO or any forest regime till there is a shift in the social perceptions in developing countries and a realization that this type of development (deforestation) is counterproductive and only benefits the elites of producer societies. This is where ENGOs can play a valuable role in educating domestic populaces. They can link up with disadvantaged groups within producer states such as the rural poor and the indigenous peoples, and can provide critical monitoring and data collection services.[344]

In terms of the Finnemore and Sikkink analysis of normative change, it is clear that the environmental normative entrepreneurs, in this case the ENGOs and states like the Netherlands and the UK, have not succeeded in convincing

---

Sarawak Chief Minister Abdul Taib have all profited personally from logging in their states. When President Suharto was deposed in 1998, his family and their allies controlled timber licences comprising 4 million hectares. Dauvergne, *Loggers and Degradation in the Asia-Pacific: Corporations and Environmental Management*, 159.

341 Andrew Linklater, 'Marxism', in *Theories of International Relations*, 2nd edition, ed. Scott Burchill et al. (New York: Palgrave, 2001), 150.

342 Smouts, *Tropical Forests, International Jungle: The Underside of Global Ecopolitics*, 18.

343 L.M. Talbot, 'A Proposal for the World Bank's Policy and Strategy for Tropical Forests in Africa' (World Bank, AFTEN, 1990).

344 Young and Demko, 'Improving the Effectiveness of International Environmental Governance Systems', 233.

member states to reorient the normative purpose of the ITTO.[345] Further, Finnemore and Sikkink's approach is not especially helpful in explaining the failure of environmental arguments, since their concern has been to explain how norms succeed. As can be observed in this case study, the acceptance of conservationist or preservationist principles within a particular treaty does not necessarily mean that these norms themselves have been accepted. The Finnemore and Sikkink approach assumes that acceptance will necessarily lead to changes in behaviour. The case study suggests this is always an empirical question. A more critical constructivist approach, drawing on the Marxist critique, may better enable an analysis of normative failure.

The ITTO cannot be understood without examining the ITTO voting structure that has stymied normative change. The voting structure which constitutes the rules of the game prevents change because it rewards states that are exploiters, and disadvantages conservationist states. The quicker a producer state cuts down its forests, the more voting power it accrues, therefore rewarding its hegemonic position with greater hegemony. This also helps explain the ENGO decision to gravitate to the Forest Stewardship Council, whose voting and organizational structure allow greater input from ENGOs and offer a far better chance for meaningful dialogue and global environmental norm change.

Constructivism does allow an understanding of the strengths and weaknesses of the advocacy role played by ENGOs both within the ITTO and more broadly. Gale argues that ENGOs rejected the ITTO because they are '. . . unable to effectively influence the principles, norms, rules and decision-making procedures of the emerging international tropical timber trade regime'.[346] Humphreys takes issue with this position, maintaining that ENGOs have provided a challenge to the dominant ideology of economic neoliberalism. He is unsure exactly how strong that challenge has been, though.[347] It is clear from the evidence that the ENGOs are unable to challenge economic policies and have been unsuccessful in reframing the debate from one about sustainable timber production to one of sustainable forests or other higher values such as wilderness protection or environmental justice.

Given the institutional barriers to ENGO participation in the ITTO (which is limited to observer status and excludes access to key meetings), it is unlikely they could affect change, no matter what persuasive techniques were employed. ENGOs do not feel they are true stakeholders in the tropical timber

[345] Wood, 'Soft Law, Hard Law and the Development of an International Forest Convention'.

[346] Gale, 'The Mysterious Case of the Disappearing Environmentalists: The International Tropical Timber Organization', 105.

[347] Humphreys, 'Hegemonic Ideology and the International Tropical Timber Organization', 227.

regime and therefore are not wedded to ensuring it works.[348] Many ENGOs are concerned about the ITTO's poor conservation record and fear they were being used merely to legitimate decisions that are aiding the destruction of tropical forests, so they abandoned the ITTO.

Interestingly, some ENGOs have significantly changed their strategies to work creatively within the dominant neoliberal paradigm and to publicize the benefits of ecotourism and a viable forest ecosystem. This may well be a more effective strategy to break the normative impasse.[349] Such activities provide incentives to protect forests and provide ways for people, particularly local people, to make a living without damaging forest ecosystems.[350] While ENGOs have elected not to be part of the ITTO formally, they still intend to continue lobbying the ITTO as outside pressure groups, to bring about a normative and practical shift in the behaviour of states.[351]

The more radical groups on the environmental spectrum, such as Greenpeace, have proposed that the sale of tropical timber should be prohibited, or at the very least that the ITTO restrict the tropical timber harvest and trade.[352] The new strategies undertaken by the ENGOs indicate that they understand that their efforts to date regarding the ITTO have been a failure and that a new approach, which includes working in other forums not including the ITTO, is the way forward. However, as this chapter has demonstrated, time is running out to save tropical forests for future generations.

---

348 Young and Demko, 'Improving the Effectiveness of International Environmental Governance Systems', 238.

349 Food and Agriculture Organization, 'State of the World's Forests 2005' (Food and Agriculture Organization, 2005), 27.

350 Ibid.

351 Switzer, *Environmental Politics: Domestic and Global Dimensions*, 279.

352 Guppy, 'International Governance and Regimes Dealing with Land Resources from the Perspective of the North', 146–7; Switzer, *Environmental Politics: Domestic and Global Dimensions*, 278.

# Conclusion

When examining regimes, the importance and complexity of the normative element has too often been neglected.[1] This book has demonstrated that a focus on norm analysis can yield new insights into old problems. By better understanding how environmental norms come into existence and alter over time, more robust environmental regimes can be created to deal with seemingly intractable global environmental problems.

This book set out to answer two questions. First, which international relations approach, neoliberalism or constructivism, has the greater explanatory power with regard to the formation and evolution of the core environmental norms in environmental regimes? Secondly, are the two frameworks complementary or antithetical? Is a synthesis possible?

As stated in the introduction, neoliberalism has been the preferred analytical framework when examining global environmental regimes. However, the analysis undertaken in this book has revealed a number of deficiencies with the neoliberal approach in explaining norm development (or lack thereof). In contrast, constructivism, with its more contextual approach, provides a more satisfying and complex view of human motivation.

The two case studies of Antarctica and whaling clearly demonstrate that neoliberals are unable to coherently account for altruistic actions within their analysis. The two case studies reveal that Vogler is correct in his analysis that ideas such as wilderness values are 'largely inaccessible' to the neoliberal camp and constitute a major flaw in their ontology and epistemology.[2] The neoliberal conception of regime theory, with its emphasis on calculation, cannot adequately explain concepts such as 'uniqueness' or 'beauty' applied to the global environment in cases such as Antarctica and whales.[3]

Further, this failure by neoliberals to account for the 'moral element' is revealed by their inability to explain why states would act against their own

1 Andrew Hurrell, 'International Society and the Study of Regimes: A Reflective Approach', in *Regime Theory and International Relations*, ed. V. Rittberger (Oxford: Clarendon Press, 1993), 72.

2 John Vogler, 'Taking Institutions Seriously: How Regime Analysis Can Be Relevant to Multilateral Environmental Governance', *Global Environmental Politics* 3, no. 2 (2003): 27.

3 Ibid.: 37.

material interests, or why they would act without the prospect of any material gain. The neoliberal account of norm change is deficient in assuming that states obey norms merely because of the functional benefits they bring.[4] This book has shown that despite countervailing self-interest, states have been willing to promulgate and obey environmental norms. In the case of Antarctica, both France and Australia acted against their short-term strategic interests in failing to cooperate with other ATCPs and ratify CRAMRA. They risked becoming international pariahs, particularly within the Antarctic Treaty System, to ensure that mining would be banned for the foreseeable future in Antarctica.

The only explanation that neoliberals can advance to account for this behaviour is the extremely long-term benefits that can accrue to a state of an increased reputational advantage as 'moral' or more trustworthy. While this is perhaps a partial explanation of the actions of France and Australia, two problems with this characterization of interests are readily apparent. The first is that in the short term, other states might not trust moral renegade states to keep their word. Secondly, conceiving interests incorporating such a long-term calculation distorts the concept of interest beyond all workable recognition. It renders states' interests opaque to the researcher, since virtually all actions over such a large time scale can be considered to make up a state's 'reputation'.

In the case of whaling, it is difficult for neoliberals to explain cogently why states would choose to preserve whales, given the level of resistance by some traditional whaling states. Again, the idea that reputational advantage accrues to states advocating preservation of whales seems at best an incomplete explanation. Without an understanding that many people find the act of whaling morally repugnant and wished to save what they perceived as unique and intelligent creatures, there can be no complete explanation for the passing of the whaling moratorium.

Neoliberal theorists have been rightly criticized for reifying the state and placing it at the centre of their analysis, without considering the vital role played by non-state actors in regime origin and change.[5] Holistic constructivism, with its multi-level, multi-actor analysis, allows for a more complete understanding of successful norm change. The research confirms that ENGOs are now critical actors within global environmental regimes: they are members of state delegations, policy advisors, compliance monitors and providers of crucial scientific advice. They have been instrumental in applying pressure to

---

4 Hurrell, 'International Society and the Study of Regimes: A Reflective Approach', 56.

5 Vogler, 'Taking Institutions Seriously: How Regime Analysis Can Be Relevant to Multilateral Environmental Governance', 26.

politicians to live up to their commitments.[6] There can be no considered understanding of why preservationist norms are currently paramount within the Antarctic and whaling regime, without an analysis of the role played by ENGOs in publicizing, educating, organizing, preparing policy papers, and mounting persuasive arguments.

Further, holistic constructivism allows for an understanding of the often key role played by other non-state actors within global environmental regimes. IOs have played vital roles in creating environmental regimes, for example, UNCTAD helped establish the tropical timber regime. In the case of whaling, an examination of the inability of scientists to successfully promote conservationist norms in the 1960s and 1970s allows an understanding of how the failure strengthened the case of preservationist norm advocates. A more nuanced understanding of the tropical timber regime's failure to move beyond exploitationist practices is impossible without scrutiny of the role played by timber TNCs, in both felling forests and blocking normative change at the ITTO.

This is not to say that one should ignore the role played by states. They are still the main actors within global environmental regimes. The roles played by France and Australia in rejecting CRAMRA, and the United States of America and Australia in the whaling case study, were critical to the regimes adopting more environmental norms. The failure of any of the main producer and consumer states to promote environmental norms is one reason why the tropical timber regime's norms have not altered. Further, we must be mindful of Young's admonition not to treat ENGOs as an unalloyed good and states as the enemy.[7] The situation is more complex than a Manichean representation of good and bad. The case studies reveal that states have been both powerful advocates for normative change (the USA, Australia and France) as well as powerful norm vetoers (USA, Japan, Malaysia). An examination of the role played by states is therefore vital. However, the neoliberal exclusive focus on state interaction weakens their analysis and allows holistic constructivism to justifiably claim that their approach yields greater insights into regime change.[8]

---

6 Oran R. Young and George J. Demko, 'Improving the Effectiveness of International Environmental Governance Systems', in *Global Environmental Change and International Governance*, ed. Oran R. Young, George J. Demko and Kilaparti Ramakrishna (Hanover, NH: University Press of New England, 1996), 235.

7 Ibid.: 239.

8 Some neoliberals are now examining the role played by ENGOs and other non-state actors within their analysis (see, for example, Lorraine Elliott's *International Environmental Politics* (Basingstoke: Macmillan, 1998). However, as stated in the introduction, this book is critiquing an 'unreconstructed' neoliberal framework, typical of a mainstream neoliberal approach.

Further, the case studies reveal that a key neoliberal analytical weakness is their inability to account for the influence of domestic factors. Neoliberalism proffers no theory of preference formation, instead arguing that such preferences are formed exogenously.[9] Such a structurationist approach that 'black boxes' states' interests necessarily ignores crucial elements of any analysis, leaving the researcher with an incomplete picture.[10]

Holistic constructivism allows for a more complete picture of regime change by showing how domestic and systemic factors interact. Such an approach revealed in the Antarctic case study the domestic split between the French elites and the French populace which followed Jacques Cousteau's position on ratifying CRAMRA. It allows the researcher to unpack interests and examine the tropical timber trade and determine who is benefiting (elites) and who is losing (poor, indigenous peoples). Holistic constructivism also helps understand why rogue states continue whaling because of domestic cultural considerations, long after the economic imperative for whaling has gone.

The neoliberal approach (with the exception of researchers such as Putnam and Axlerod) has traditionally avoided the domestic level, citing reasons of theoretical parsimony. However, such an approach limits the neoliberal analysis in a profound way and opens the door to theoretical rivals such as constructivism. A desire for theoretical parsimony should not prevent researchers from exploring causation at any level and such an artificial limitation impedes the neoliberal research project.

Neoliberals argue that interests and, consequently, identity remain fixed for states. Constructivists do not deny the strength of the pursuit of both power and interests as components of state identity, but argue, with some justification, that identity is malleable. Constructivists regard the concept of identity as more fluid, and subject to change temporally, through interaction with other actors and as circumstances alter.[11] Not surprisingly, the results of the case

---

[9] Joseph Jupille, James A. Caporaso and Jeffrey T. Checkel, 'Integrating Institutions: Rationalism, Constructivism, and the Study of the European Union', *Comparative Political Studies* 36, no. 1/2 (2003): 12.

[10] Robert Putnam's two-level game theory examines domestic preference formation, but is not considered typical of neoliberal thought. Further, there is a new generation of liberal legal scholarship that is examining domestic preferences; see, for example, Andrew Moravcsik, 'Taking Preferences Seriously: A Liberal Theory of International Politics', *International Organization* 51, no. 4 (1997): 513. However, this liberal scholarship distinguishes itself from neoliberal institutionalism and, as yet, has not been incorporated by neoliberals in their theoretical frameworks.

[11] Charlotte Epstein's exemplary analysis on discourse theory and the anti-whaling movement also supports the key constructivist point that state identity is unfixed and fluid. Charlotte Epstein, *The Power of Words in International Relations: Birth of an Anti-whaling Discourse* (Cambridge, MA: MIT Press, 2008), 200.

studies are mixed on these issues. In the case of tropical timber, states' interests have remained relatively fixed. Producer states consider tropical forests for their export value to consumer states, who in turn desire a plentiful supply of tropical timber. While these outcomes confirm neoliberal predictions, constructivists are able to explain why alternative state identities were unable to emerge in this particular case study because of the strength of the norm of development.

However, in the global environmental regimes of Antarctica and whaling, constructivism provides a more cogent explanation than neoliberalism about how certain environmental ideas generated a new conception of states' interests for certain key states. It allows the researcher to better account for the motivations and actions of France and Australia within the Antarctic regime. According to a constructivist analysis, their identities altered over time from being active supporters of mining in Antarctica, to being promoters of a preservationist position. Over time, the concept of being a good environmental citizen became internalized to the point that it became part of their identities. Such internalization of a norm leads states to take on a particular set of environmental meanings, such as preservationism. States then both self-identify and identify other like-minded states, further strengthening particular environmental norms.[12]

Further, the constructivist fluid conception of state identity allows us to better understand the why the USA acceded to the introduction of the Madrid Protocol. Over decades within the ATS, the procedural norm of consensus was consolidated in ways that framed and disciplined acceptable behaviour for ATCPs. The USA, rather than jeopardize the decision-making framework of the ATS, chose to agree to ratify the Protocol rather than emerge as the only 'rogue state' preventing the will of the overwhelming majority.

The research also shows how, for a majority of states, preserving whales in virtually all circumstances (some states allow an exception for aboriginal whaling, but states like New Zealand will not even allow this) has become part of several states' identity (Australia, New Zealand, the UK). These states, once whaling nations themselves, changed their behaviour to the point that they became active norm proponents for the preserving of whales. Even notorious exploitative whaling states of the past (Japan, Norway and Iceland) are now obliged to formulate their arguments in conservationist rather than exploitationist language, and there are signs that these arguments are no longer merely rhetorical.

The constructivist framework, while providing a more nuanced analysis than a neoliberal approach, is not beyond criticism. The ideational approach of

---

12 Ibid.: 252.

constructivism has highlighted the power of persuasion to achieve goals. But does the evidence from the case studies support their contentions? Certainly, the case studies of Antarctica and whaling show that states (and non-state actors) will obey unenforceable rules if genuinely convinced of the rightness of the rules.

However, the case studies show that moral persuasion works sometimes, but rarely on its own. In both the Antarctic and whaling case studies, ENGO arguments on the fragility and beauty of Antarctica and the uniqueness and intelligence of whales carried great persuasiveness. This pegging of their arguments to higher values gave a 'moral authority' to their arguments that increased their persuasiveness and opened the door for norm change. However, these two case studies also point to the limits to persuasion as a stand-alone strategy. To achieve their goals, ENGOs used both persuasion and strategic means (such as entering into strategic alliances) to achieve their goals. Constructivists need to pay more attention to the interaction between communicative and strategic action in their analyses.

In the case of Antarctica, ENGOs prepared policy documents, had themselves seconded to state delegations and used fear as a tactic to achieve their goal of a world park (in many ways, the opposite of persuasion). They played on the ATCP's fears of the UN seizing control of the region on behalf of all states, as well as the concern by LDCs that technologically advanced states would have a greater edge in exploiting Antarctic mineral resources. In the case of whaling, ENGOs used the Seychelles as a stalking horse to gain entrance to the IWC and used it as a means of advancing its agenda. This tactic did enhance the ENGO's persuasiveness, in that it allowed them to directly debate with other IWC delegates. It also gave them voting rights and a means of gaining information and forming voting blocs dedicated to preserving whales.

However, there are also significant limits to the power of persuasion, as shown in the tropical timber case study. ENGOs and IOs were not able to reframe the issue of tropical forest protection to higher values such as wilderness. The entrenched interests of logging companies and producer and consumer states were able to resist the ENGOs' arguments about the need for wilderness protection or the negative impact deforestation practices are having on indigenous peoples, by excluding them from the key negotiating forum.

In all three case studies, the evidence suggests that persuasion alone is not enough to win or maintain support for an environmental norm. Rather, norm proponents looking to influence regime development in circumstances of distorted communication should consider persuasion as but one component of a 'toolkit' of approaches to achieve their goal. ENGOs, in particular, need to be aware of this and they need to continue reflecting on what has worked and what has not and build this into future campaigns.

In these three case studies, the lessons for environmentalists are that they cannot necessarily rely on altruistic arguments alone; they often need to utilize strategic methods as well when faced with powerful oppositional forces and/or when they are blocked from participating in regime negotiations. Moreover, if they are going to influence global environmental regimes, they need to work at the domestic level in key states to put pressure on the global negotiators of regimes to achieve their aims. If a forum is effectively 'deaf' to persuasion, such as in the case of the ITTO, ENGOs also need to be willing to abandon such forums for ones that may be more willing to listen.

In the past, constructivists have been accused of focusing on cases that suit their arguments. This inquiry has chosen one case study (the tropical timber regime) that reveals some critical limitations of constructivism which need to be addressed. First, the constructivist analysis of norm development is limited when it comes to norm failure in circumstances where entrenched interests hold sway. Secondly, the Finnemore and Sikkink model of norm development needs to be refined to account for situations of normative failure, rather than its current teleological assumption that norms will automatically progress towards internalization. Moreover, the ratification and signing of a treaty by states should not be uncritically taken to mean that the regime norms have been accepted and practised, as the tropical timber case demonstrates. Political actors could and often do give lip service to norms that serve as a camouflage rather than a genuine rationale for their behaviour.[13]

Constructivists, in their analysis, cannot take for granted the results of socialization on state preferences. Checkel is correct when he argues that constructivists need to examine the 'socialization of influential actors to new norms and beliefs, which in turn alter the underlying preferences of governments and thereby state behaviour'.[14] Constructivists need to devote more attention to the motivations of the actors, the context in which negotiations take place and an analysis over time to determine whether the standard of behaviour is being adhered to. Currently, constructivists are susceptible to the charge that constructivism is caught by the gap between what 'is' and what 'should be'.[15] For constructivists, the ongoing challenge for their

---

13 Radoslav S. Dimitrov, 'Hostage to Norms: States, Institutions and Global Forest Politics', *Global Environmental Politics* 5, no. 4 (2005): 19.

14 Andrew Moravcsik, 'Bringing Constructivist Integration Theory out of the Clouds: Has it Landed Yet?', *European Union Politics* 2, no. 2 (2001): 227.

15 Richard Price, 'Moral Limit and Possibility in World Politics', *International Organization* 62 (2008): 194. Price seeks to overcome this criticism by examining constructivist conceptions of the potential and limits of moral change.

research agenda is to utilize insights gleaned from empirical research to develop a more robust critical analysis of the concept of 'intersubjectivity'.[16]

Despite these limits, a constructivist analysis is still robust in that it can show that other non-environmental norms can serve as powerful factors (not just brute power or interests), adding a more nuanced understanding of global environmental regimes.

Both the neoliberal and constructivist approaches have shed significant light on the emergence and evolution of norms in environmental regimes and both are of use to the researcher of global environmental regimes. However, constructivism with its explanation of the social nature of the material world offers more insights and gives a more complete analysis of the social world.[17] Further, the case studies demonstrate that constructivists also appear to provide a more coherent answer for changing human behaviour towards the environment.[18] Even cases such as tropical timber, which is an easy case for an interest-based approach, can be shown to include a moral dimension (such as a commitment to the norm of development). By emphasizing the importance of ideas in defining and instantiating interests, as well as the impact certain non-state actors have had, constructivism puts interests into context. Constructivists might profit by returning to some of the insights generated by Marxist scholarship on the relationship between interests and ideology, but without falling into the trap of historical materialism – that all ideas are necessarily shaped by material interests.

## BRIDGE-BUILDING OR BRIDGE-BURNING?

The second question posed by this book asks whether, in the light of the case studies, the neoliberal and constructivist approaches should be considered as rivals or as complementary and, if so, whether a synthesis is possible. This latter consideration has long-term implications for the theoretical development of international relations.

For many researchers, particularly at the abstract level, the two approaches belong to two different universes. They argue that constructivist and rationalist theoretical assumptions are at opposite ends of the spectrum, with no hope

---

16 Antje Wiener, 'Constructivism: The Limits of Bridging Gaps', *Journal of International Relations and Development* 6, no. 3 (2003): 258.

17 J.T. Checkel, 'Social Constructivisms in Global and European Politics: A Review Essay', *Review of International Studies* 30 (2004): 230.

18 Vogler, 'Taking Institutions Seriously: How Regime Analysis Can Be Relevant to Multilateral Environmental Governance', 36.

of bridge-building between the two frameworks.[19] Jupille et al. maintain that the chasm between neoliberals and constructivists is enormous, particularly at the epistemological and ontological levels.[20] Maja Zehfuss argues that bridge-building between the two frameworks is not an option, since their methodological differences cannot be reconciled.[21]

For others, such as Vogler and Young (neoliberals) and Checkel and Zurn (constructivists), the search to bridge-build is itself a worthy goal. Efforts to understand each approach's scope conditions are valid and it is legitimate at both the meta-theoretical and case-study levels to focus on complementarities and points of contact of the two frameworks examined here.[22]

While there may be a divide that cannot be bridged, this need not preclude an inter-paradigm dialogue.[23] In practice, each approach has tended (to the detriment of international relations theory) to focus on a different set of explanatory variables. For neoliberals, it has been material interests and constraints while constructivists have examined issues of identity, ideas and norms.

The failure of scholars in each research programme to engage in a dialogue is hindering fruitful inquiry. The strength of each school's analyses should act as 'irritants' to the other, prompting further theoretical refinement.[24] The first step is to compare and contrast through the mechanism of what Jupille calls 'competitive testing'. Researchers need to evaluate claims not only against 'the evidence', but against other theories as well.[25] Empirical case studies should be framed to allow fair competition between competing frameworks. This book has followed this approach in testing the rival. To overcome the advantage of the 'first move', such as in chess, it was decided to combine the two theories examined here into a seamless analysis to facilitate comparison testing.[26]

---

19 Dianna Panke, 'The Differential Impact of Communicated Ideas: Bridging the Gap between Rationalism and Constructivism', *Hamburg Review of Social Sciences* 1, no. 3 (2006): 320.

20 Jupille, Caporaso and Checkel, 'Integrating Institutions: Rationalism, Constructivism, and the Study of the European Union', 15–16.

21 Maja Zehfuss, *Constructivism in International Relations: The Politics of Reality* (Cambridge: Cambridge University Press, 2002), 253–4.

22 Michael Zurn and Jeffrey T. Checkel, 'Getting Socialized to Build Bridges: Constructivism and Rationalism, Europe and the Nation State', *International Organization* 59 (2005): 1047, 1075.

23 Jupille, Caporaso and Checkel, 'Integrating Institutions: Rationalism, Constructivism, and the Study of the European Union', 16.

24 Elinor Ostrum, 'A Behavioural Approach to the Rational Choice Theory of Collective Action', *American Political Science Review* 92, no. 1 (1998): 6–10.

25 Jupille, Caporaso and Checkel, 'Integrating Institutions: Rationalism, Constructivism, and the Study of the European Union', 21.

26 Ibid.

It is possible to evaluate the two approaches in two different ways. One is to clarify the 'domains of application' of each approach. This approach identifies respective turfs or home domains where the theories are strongest and then seeks to bring them together into a larger analysis. However, theorists that test a single framework or merely delimit a 'domain of application' do a disservice to the complexity of the causal chain of these global environmental regimes.[27] Such an approach leads to a theoretically 'thin synthesis', whereby the combined theories are considered to yield a more comprehensive account of the case studies than either considered alone, but without any attempt at theoretical synthesis.[28]

A second approach is to incorporate one approach into another, if it can be shown that one theory can be logically derived from another. For example, if constructivists or neoliberals can explain cogently cultural variation, regime formation and development, preferences and normative change, then it would be theoretically superior to its competitor and may in fact subsume it as a broader, more complete explanation.[29] However, an examination of the three case studies suggests this is not possible. Neither theory has achieved so comprehensive an explanation of norm change within global environmental regimes as to be considered to have subsumed the other. Each approach yields differing insights into the role of global norms. The attempt to subsume all approaches under one umbrella theory does not necessarily advance research, if it ignores methodological incommensurability.[30]

Differing theoretical frameworks can also be considered complementary, even though they may be incommensurable.[31] Both constructivism and neoliberalism can yield complementary analyses of global interaction.[32] For example,

---

[27] J. Timmons Roberts, Bradley C. Parks and Alexis A. Vasquez, 'Who Ratifies Environmental Treaties and Why? Institutionalism, Structuralism and Participation by 192 Nations in 22 Treaties', *Global Environmental Politics* 4, no. 3 (2004): 24.

[28] Ibid.

[29] Ibid. Jupille, Caporaso and Checkel, 'Integrating Institutions: Rationalism, Constructivism, and the Study of the European Union', 23.

[30] J.T. Checkel, 'International Norms and Domestic Politics: Bridging the Rationalist–Constructivist Divide', *European Journal of International Relations* 3, no. 4 (1997): 488. For example, Duncan Snidal is one who believes that 'rational choice is a methodology incorporating general theoretical assumptions but that it is wide open in terms of specific substantive content', allowing for a rationalist model that incorporates constructivist insights, perhaps of preference formation, into a rationalist model. Duncan Snidal, 'Rational Choice and International Relations', in *Handbook of International Relations*, ed. Walter Carlsnaes, Thomas Risse and Beth Simmons (New York: Sage, 2002), 74.

[31] Jupille, Caporaso and Checkel, 'Integrating Institutions: Rationalism, Constructivism, and the Study of the European Union', 21.

[32] See Seeng Tan, 'Rescuing Constructivism from the Constructivists: A Critical

Chris Reus-Smit has argued that constructivism need not be considered a rival to neoliberal approaches, but rather there is potential for the two to complement each other.[33] However, he further states that limiting constructivism to answering questions of identity formation, leaving neoliberals to focus on strategic interaction, would lead to a 'thin' form of constructivism.[34] Such a lean conception of constructivism would not live up to its theoretical potential, leaving neoliberal thought dominating the field.

Rather, it is better to see if there is scope for rationalist and constructivist frameworks to be married together to form a more robust analytical model to examine empirical case studies. Some researchers argue that the ultimate goal should be to synthesize competing IR theories into one seamless analytical approach.[35] Checkel argues that analytical synthesis is critical if we are to understand why social actors comply with norms.[36]

To date, constructivists and neoliberals have been caught up in parsing meta-theoretical and ontological distinctions between the two approaches without seeking to construct mid-range theories, derive working hypotheses and critically test them.[37] This book sought to overcome such criticisms and started from the viewpoint that the two frameworks needed to be critically compared to see what insights could be yielded by both approaches. The end goals were to better understand normative development within global environmental regimes and to see whether the two approaches could be synthesized or were too epistemologically and ontologically different when applied to case studies.

There are a number of potential interstices where neoliberalism and constructivism develop points of theoretical contact. For both frameworks, the agent–structure conundrum is explicit and represents a potential exploration point where the two camps can come together.[38] At the abstract level, neoliberalism and constructivism do not necessarily come into conflict about

---

Reading of Constructivist Interventions in Southeast Asian Security', *The Pacific Review* 19, no. 2 (2006): 245; Zurn and Checkel, 'Getting Socialized to Build Bridges: Constructivism and Rationalism, Europe and the Nation State', 1075.

33 Christian Reus-Smit, 'Constructivism', in *Theories of International Relations*, 2nd edition, ed. S. Burchill et al. (New York: Palgrave, 2001), 223.

34 Ibid.

35 Jupille, Caporaso and Checkel, 'Integrating Institutions: Rationalism, Constructivism, and the Study of the European Union', 21.

36 J.T. Checkel, 'Why Comply? Constructivism, Social Norms and the Study of International Institutions' (paper presented at the Annual Meeting, American Political Science Association, Atlanta, Georgia, 1999), 30.

37 Moravcsik, 'Bringing Constructivist Integration Theory out of the Clouds: Has it Landed Yet?', 227.

38 Zurn and Checkel, 'Getting Socialized to Build Bridges: Constructivism and Rationalism, Europe and the Nation State', 1047.

what an actor wants. Contrary to the generally understood definition, 'utility' is a 'highly open-ended concept, and an actor's utility need be neither self-regarding nor materialistic. An actor's utility function may even contain altruistic or idealistic arguments.'[39] Neoliberals need to understand that any 'rational calculation' takes place within a social setting where underlying rules and norms, and the very meaning of rationality, are created, shaped and internalized.[40]

Consequently, it is possible to expand the idea of rational calculus to include altruistic positions such as wishing to preserve parts of the global environment. Thus, both neoliberals and constructivists can allow for calculations of the long-term interest in providing a safe environment, recognizing the intrinsic or existence value of species, and in preserving them for their fragile beauty. An examination of the concept of 'persuasion' is also not limited to altruistic arguments but may be extended to calculations of utility. There is no reason why persuasion cannot be included in the neoliberal analysis as one means by which actors fulfil their economic interests.

Further, there is no intrinsic reason why neoliberals cannot include an examination of domestic preference formation within their analytical framework. The work of neoliberals, such as Robert Putnam's 'two-level games' analysis, shows that such an approach can yield richer insights than a traditional neoliberal approach. Putnam's analysis also lends itself to a constructivist reading of *conceptual games* where 'not only leaders of states, but also other state and non-state actors bargain about who gets to impose meaning on material reality and thus to socially construct the situation in their own image'.[41]

Such an approach would broaden neoliberal analysis to include both the role of domestic preferences and non-state actors. But any move in this direction would require neoliberals to abandon their commitment to theoretical parsimony. However, this may not be such a bad thing. The quest for theoretical parsimony has limited neoliberalism, restricting the range of possible explanations for social behaviour. Expanding the framework of neoliberalism, and applying it to environmental case studies, would make an interesting future research project.

---

39 Jupille, Caporaso and Checkel, 'Integrating Institutions: Rationalism, Constructivism, and the Study of the European Union', 13.

40 Vogler, 'Taking Institutions Seriously: How Regime Analysis Can Be Relevant to Multilateral Environmental Governance', 38.

41 Emanuel Adler, 'Constructivism and International Relations', in *Handbook of International Relations*, ed. Walter Carlsnaes, Thomas Risse and Beth Simmons (New York: Sage, 2002), 110.

Reputation accruing to a state (and non-state actors) offers another site of potential bridge-building. The fact that states have to constantly interact with each other, and therefore preserve their reputations (for example, as 'moral' or good global environmental citizens), reinforces the constructivist argument that states are members of an international society. These members share mutual norms about appropriate behaviour (for example, keeping promises, following protocols, keeping agreements). Such norms help to define the role played by states as members of the global community.

This is not so far away from Andrew Hurrell's idea of incorporating the 'shadow of the future' into interest calculations. Such an approach broadens the concept of self-interest and reciprocity.[42] For Hurrell, if states can perceive themselves as having a long-term stake in the global community, 'then the idea of obligation and the normativity of rules can be given concrete form and can acquire a degree of distance from the immediate interests of the preferences of states'.[43] Global society is then potentially patterned on 'the existence of shared interests, of shared values, and of patterned expectations'.[44] Such a global community can internalize a common moral purpose such as conservation and preservation within itself.[45]

Much work remains to be done as regards a potential synthesis of neoliberalism and constructivism and it may prove patchy rather than comprehensive. Sadly, there is a danger that the neoliberal and constructivist schools are talking past each other, with neoliberals criticizing the constructivist approach as 'soft' and constructivists denouncing neoliberals for their preference for theoretical parsimony and abstract formal models. Both schools need to grapple with each other's conceptual and methodological underpinnings. This book has tested three case studies focusing on global environmental regimes, but there is a need for other researchers to test the two approaches in other issue-specific regimes to see what results are yielded.

This book started with the premise that neoliberalism, as the dominant framework in examining environmental regimes, has the most to say regarding global norm transformation. However, constructivism, with its ability to examine non-state actors, incorporation of interest calculations and the altruistic actions of actors, can also throw light on such transformations. There are no 'silver bullets' to solve complex environmental questions and situations but the ongoing debate between these two frameworks will continue to generate valuable insights for researchers, actors and the interested general public.

---

42 Hurrell, 'International Society and the Study of Regimes: A Reflective Approach', 59.

43 Ibid.: 60.

44 Ibid.

45 Ibid.: 62.

# Bibliography


Abbott, K.W., and D. Snidal (1998), 'Why States Act through Formal International Organisations', *Journal of Conflict Resolution*, **42** (1): 3–32.

Abramovitz, Janet N., and Ashley T. Mattoon (1999), 'Reorienting the Forest Products Economy', in *State of the World 1999: A Worldwatch Institute Report on Progress Towards a Sustainable Society*, ed. Linda Starke, New York: W.W. Norton & Company, pp. 60–77.

Adler, E., B. Crawford, and J. Donnelly (1991), 'Defining and Conceptualising Progress in International Relations', in *Progress in Postwar International Relations*, ed. Emanuel Adler and Beverly Crawford, New York: Columbia University Press, pp. 1–42.

Adler, Emanuel (2002), 'Constructivism and International Relations', in *Handbook of International Relations*, ed. Walter Carlsnaes, Thomas Risse and Beth Simmons, New York: Sage, pp. 95–118.

AFP (2004), 'Hunters Push to Harpoon Whaling Ban'. *The Australian*, 20 July.

African Timber Organization and International Tropical Timber Organization (2003), 'Principles, Criteria and Indicators for the Sustainable Management of African Tropical Forests', *ITTO Policy Development Series*, no. 14.

Alford, Peter (2005), 'Whaling Ban Faces Extinction as Japan Splashes Cash', *The Australian*, June 20.

Alford, Peter (2005), 'Japan's Whaling Friends a No-show', *The Australian*, 21 June.

Alford, Peter (2005), 'Whales Off the Menu'. *The Australian*, 22 June.

Alford, Peter (2005), 'Defeated Whalers Sense Tide Turning', *The Australian*, 25–26 June.

Alford, Peter (2005), 'Japan's Whalers Bite Off Too Much', *The Australian*, 8 November.

Anderson, Anthony B. (1993), 'Deforestation in Amazonia: Dynamics, Cause and Alternatives', in *The Earthscan Reader in Tropical Forestry*, ed. Simon Reitbergen, London: Earthscan Publications Ltd, pp. 165–84.

Andersen, Rolf Trolle (1991), 'Negotiating a New Regime: How CRAMRA Came into Existence', in *The Antarctic Treaty System in World Politics*, ed. Arnfinn Jorgensen-Dahl and Willy Ostreng, New York: St Martin's Press, pp. 94–109.

Anonymous (1983), 'Antarctic Mineral Regimes, Beeby's Slick Solution', *Eco*, **23** (1): 4.

Anonymous (2005), 'Death of Rain Forest Defender Bruno Manser Declared', Ogiek People Website, http://www.ogiek.org/news/news-post-05-03-21.htm, 21 July.

Antarctic Treaty Committee for Environmental Protection (2005), 'The Protocol on Environmental Protection to the Antarctic Treaty', http://www.cep.aq/default.asp?casid=5074, 24 April.

Antarctic Treaty Consultative Meeting (1977), 'Report of the Ninth Consultative Meeting', London.

Antarctic Treaty Consultative Meeting (1979), 'Report of the Tenth Consultative Meeting', Washington.

Antarctic Treaty Consultative Meeting (1981), 'Report of the Eleventh Consultative Meeting', Buenos Aires.

Antarctic Treaty Consultative Meeting (1989), 'Report of the Fifteenth Consultative Meeting', Paris.

Antarctic Treaty Consultative Meeting (1991), 'Final Report of the Eleventh Antarctic Treaty Special Consultative Meeting', Spain.

Aplin, G.J. (1995), *Global Environmental Crises: An Australian Perspective*, Melbourne: Oxford University Press.

Arend, Anthony Clark (1998), 'Do Legal Rules Matter? International Law and International Politics', *Virginia Journal of International Law*, **38**: 107–53.

Attfield, Robin (2003), 'Christianity', in *A Companion to Environmental Philosophy*, ed. Dale Jamieson, Oxford: Blackwell Publishing, pp. 96–110.

Axelrod, Robert M. (1997), *The Complexity of Cooperation: Agent-based Models of Competition and Collaboration*, Princeton Studies in Complexity, Princeton, NJ: Princeton University Press.

Axelrod, Robert and Robert O'Keohane (1985), 'Achieving Cooperation under Anarchy: Strategies and Institutions', *World Politics*, **38** (1): 226–54.

Bailey, Jennifer L. (2008), 'Arrested Development: The Fight to End Commercial Whaling as a Case of Failed Norm Change', *European Journal of International Relations*, **14** (2): 289–318.

Barbier, Edward, Joanne Burgess, Josh Bishop and Bruce Aylward (1994), 'Deforestation: The Role of the International Trade in Tropical Timber', in *The Causes of Tropical Deforestation: The Economic and Statistical Analysis of Factors Giving Rise to the Loss of the Tropical Forests*, ed. Katrina Brown and David W. Pearce, London: UCL Press Ltd, pp. 271–95.

Barnes, James N. (1988), 'Legal Aspects of Environmental Protection in Antarctica', in *The Antarctic Legal Regime*, ed. Christopher C. Joyner and Sudhir K. Chopra, Dordrecht: Martinus Nijhoff Publishers, pp. 241–68.

Barnett, M. (2002), 'Historical Sociology and Constructivism: An Estranged Past, a Federated Future?' in *Historical Sociology of International Relations*, ed. John M. Hobson and Stephen Hobden, Cambridge: Cambridge University Press, pp. 99–119.

Barnett, M.N. (1999), 'Culture, Strategy and Foreign Policy Change: Israel's Road to Oslo', *European Journal of International Relations*, **5**: 5–36.

Bartelson, Jens (1995), *A Genealogy of Sovereignty*, Cambridge Studies in International Relations, Cambridge and New York: Cambridge University Press.

Beeby, C.D. (1983), 'An Overview of the Problems which Should Be Addressed in the Preparation of a Regime Governing the Mineral Resources of Antarctica', in *Antarctic Resources Policy: Scientific, Legal and Political Issues*, ed. Francisco Orrego Vicuna, Cambridge: Cambridge University Press, pp. 191–8.

Bernstein, Steven F. (2001), *The Compromise of Liberal Environmentalism*, New York: Columbia University Press.

Betsill, Michele M., and Elisabeth Corell (2001), 'NGO Influence in International Environmental Negotiations: A Framework for Analysis', *Global Environmental Politics*, **1** (4): 65–85.

Birnie, Patricia W. (1985), *International Regulation of Whaling: From Conservation of Whaling to Conservation of Whales and Regulation of Whale-watching*, New York: Oceana Publications.

Birnie, Patricia W., and Alan E. Boyle (2002), *International Law and the Environment*, 2nd edition, Oxford: Oxford University Press.

Blok, Anders (2008), 'Contesting Global Norms: Politics of Identity in Japanese Pro-whaling Countermobilization', *Global Environmental Politics*, **8** (2): 39–66.

Boczek, Boleslaw A. (1984), 'The Soviet Union and the Antarctic Regime', *American Journal of International Law*, **78** (4): 834–58.

Boekhout van Solinge, Tim (2008), 'Eco-crime: The Tropical Timber Trade', in *Organized Crime: Culture, Markets and Policies*, ed. D. Siegel and H. Nelen, New York: Springer.

Boekle, Henning, Volker Rittberger and Wolfgang Wagner (1999), 'Norms and Foreign Policy: Constructivist Foreign Policy Theory', *Tubingen Working Papers*, 34a.

Boynton, Stephen S. (1994), '"Whaling Policy" of the United States Yesterday, Today and Tomorrow', Paper presented at the ISANA No. 11.

Braithwaite, J., and P. Drahos (2000), *Global Business Regulation*, Cambridge: Cambridge University Press.

Breitmeier, Helmut, and Volker Rittberger (2000), 'Environmental NGOs in an Emerging Global Civil Society', in *The Global Environment in the Twenty-first Century: Prospects for International Cooperation*, ed. Pamela S. Chasek, New York: United Nations University Press, pp. 130–63.

Brown, Peter (2000), *Ethics, Economics and International Relations: Transparent Sovereignty in the Commonwealth of Life*, Edinburgh: Edinburgh University Press.

Brunnee, Jutta (1996), 'A Conceptual Framework for an International Forests Convention: Customary Law and Emerging Principles in Global Forests and International Law', in *Global Forests and International Law*, ed. Canadian Council of International Law, London: Kluwer Law International, pp. 41–78.

Bryant, D., D. Nielsen and L. Tangley (1997), *The Last Frontier Forests: Ecosystems and Economies on the Edge*, Washington, DC: World Resources Institute.

Bryant, Peter J. (2005), 'Biodiversity and Conservation: A Hypertext Book', http://www.dbc.uci.edu/~sustain/bio65/Titlpage.htm, 25 October.

Bryant, Raymond L., and Sinead Bailey (1996), *Third World Political Ecology: An Introduction*, New York: Routledge.

Bryner, Gary C. (1997), *From Promises to Performance: Achieving Global Environmental Goals*, New York: W.W. Norton & Company Inc.

Buck, Susan J. (1998), *The Global Commons: An Introduction*, Washington, DC: Island Press.

Burchill, S. (2001), 'Liberalism', in *Theories of International Relations* (2nd edition), ed. S. Burchill, R. Devetak, A. Linklater, Matthew Paterson, Christian Reus-Smit and J. True, New York: Palgrave, pp. 29–69.

Burgess, John (1990), 'Comprehensive Environmental Protection of the Antarctic: New Approaches for New Times', in *The Future of Antarctica: Exploitation Versus Preservation*, ed. Grahame Cook, Manchester: Manchester University Press, pp. 53–67.

Bush, W.M. (1982), *Antarctica and International Law: A Collection of Inter-state and National Documents*, vols 1–3, London: Oceana Publications Inc.

Bush, W.M. (1992), *Antarctica and International Law: A Collection of Inter-state and National Documents*, London: Oceana Publications Inc.

Bush, W.M. (1994), *Antarctica and International Law: A Collection of Inter-state and National Documents*, London: Oceana Publications Inc.

Caldwell, Lynton K. (1990), *International Environmental Policy: Emergence and Dimensions*, 2nd edition, Duke Press Policy Studies, Durham, NC: Duke University Press.

Cardenas, Sonia (2004), 'Norm Collision: Explaining the Effects of International Human Rights Pressure on State Behavior', *International Studies Review*, **6**: 213–31.

Caron, David D. (1995), 'The International Whaling Commission and the North Atlantic Marine Mammal Commission: The Institutional Risks of Coercion in Consensual Structures', *The American Journal of International Law*, **89** (1): 154–74.

Carpenter, R. Charli (2003), '"Women and Children First": Gender, Norms, and Humanitarian Evacuation in the Balkans 1991–95', *International Organization*, **57**: 661–94.

Carter, Neil (2001), *The Politics of the Environment: Ideas, Activism, Policy*, New York: Cambridge University Press.

Casarini, Maria Pia (1996), 'Activities in Antarctica before the Conclusion of the Antarctic Treaty', in *International Law for Antarctica*, ed. Francesco Francioni and Tullio Scovazzi, London: Kluwer Law International, pp. 627–77.

Chan, Sandra, and Phillip Pattberg (2008), 'Private Rule-making and the Politics of Accountability: Analyzing Global Forest Governance', *Global Environmental Politics*, **8** (3): 103–21.

Chasek, Pamela S. (2001), *Earth Negotiations: Analyzing Thirty Years of Environmental Diplomacy*, Tokyo and New York: United Nations University Press.

Chaytor, Beatrice (2001), 'The Development of Global Forest Policy: Overview of Legal and Institutional Frameworks', International Institute for Environment and Development, World Business Council for Sustainable Development.

Checkel, J.T. (1997), 'International Norms and Domestic Politics: Bridging the Rationalist–Constructivist Divide', *European Journal of International Relations*, **3** (4): 473–95.

Checkel, J.T. (1998), 'Social Construction and Integration', *ARENA Working Papers*, WP 98/14.

Checkel, J.T. (1998), 'The Constructivist Turn in International Relations Theory', *World Politics*, **50** (2): 324–48.

Checkel, J.T. (1999), 'Why Comply? Constructivism, Social Norms and the Study of International Institutions', Paper presented at the Annual Meeting, American Political Science Association, Atlanta, Georgia.

Checkel, J.T. (1999), 'Norms, Institutions and National Identity in Contemporary Europe', *International Studies Quarterly*, **43**: 83–114.

Checkel, J.T. (2004), 'Social Constructivisms in Global and European Politics: A Review Essay', *Review of International Studies*, **30**: 229–44.

Chew, Sing C. (2001), *World Ecological Degradation: Accumulation, Urbanization, and Deforestation 3000 B.C.–A.D. 2000*, Walnut Creek, CA: AltaMira Press.

Clapham, Phillip J., Simon Childerhouse, Nicolas J.F. Gales, Lorenzo Rojas-Bracho, Michael F. Tillman and Robert L. Brownell Jr (2007), 'The Whaling Issue: Conservation, Confusion and Casuistry', *Marine Policy*, **31**: 314–19.

Clark, Margaret (1994), 'The Antarctic Environmental Protocol: NGOs in the Protection of Antarctica', in *Environmental NGOs in World Politics: Linking the Local and the Global*, ed. Thomas Princen and Matthias Finger, London: Routledge, pp. 160–85.

Cock, Andrew Robert (2008), 'Tropical Forests in the Global State System', *International Affairs*, **84** (2): 315–33.

Colchester, Marcus (1990), 'The International Tropical Timber Organization: Kill or Cure for the Rainforests?', *The Ecologist*, **20** (5): 163–73.

Colchester, Marcus (1993), 'The International Tropical Timber Organization: Kill or Cure for the Rainforests?', in *The Earthscan Reader in Tropical Forestry*, ed. Simon Rietbergen, London: Earthscan Publications Ltd, pp. 185–207.

Colchester, Marcus (1995), 'Colonizing the Rainforests: The Agents and Causes of Deforestation', in *The Struggle for Land and the Fate of the Forests*, ed. Marcus Colchester and Larry Lohmann, London: Zed Books, pp. 1–15.

Colchester, Marcus, and L. Lehmann (1990), *The Tropical Forestry Action Plan: What Progress?* Penang: World Rainforest Movement.

Colson, David A. (1986), 'The United States Position on Antarctica', *Cornell International Law Journal*, **19**: 291–300.

Committee for Environmental Protection (2004), 'Protocol on Environmental Protection to the Antarctic Treaty', www.cep.aq/apa/legal_docs/protocol.htm, 23 July.

Committee on Forest Development in the Tropics (1990), *The Tropical Forest Action Plan: Report of the Independent Review*, Rome: FAO.

Committee for Whaling Statistics (1931), 'International Whaling Statistics 1931', Oslo: Committee for Whaling Statistics.

Committee for Whaling Statistics (1935), 'International Whaling Statistics 1935', Oslo: Committee for Whaling Statistics.

Committee for Whaling Statistics (1936), 'International Whaling Statistics 1936', Oslo: Committee for Whaling Statistics.

Committee for Whaling Statistics (1950), 'International Whaling Statistics 1950', Oslo: Committee for Whaling Statistics.

Committee for Whaling Statistics (1953), 'International Whaling Statistics 1953', Oslo: Committee for Whaling Statistics.

Committee for Whaling Statistics (1959), 'International Whaling Statistics 1959', Oslo: Committee for Whaling Statistics.

Committee for Whaling Statistics (1960), 'International Whaling Statistics 1960', Oslo: Committee for Whaling Statistics.

Committee for Whaling Statistics (1965), 'International Whaling Statistics 1965', Oslo: Committee for Whaling Statistics.

Conference for the Normalization of the International Whaling Commission (2007), IWC/59/7 13–15 February, http://www.iwcoffice.org/_documents/, 12 July.

Cooke, Fadzilah Majid (1999), *The Challenge of Sustainable Forests: Forest Resource Policy in Malaysia, 1970–1995*, Honolulu: University of Hawaii Press.

Cordonnery, Laurence (1997), 'The Implementation of the Protocol on

Environmental Protection to the Antarctic Treaty: The Interplay between Law and Environmental Management', PhD thesis, University of Tasmania.

D'Amato, Anthony, and Sudhir K. Chopra (1991), 'Whales: Their Emerging Right to Life', *The American Journal of International Law*, **85**: 21–62.

Darby, Andrew (2004), 'Scientists Attack Whale Sanctuary', *The Age*, 13 July.

Darby, Andrew (2005), 'Whale Sighting', *The Age*, 28 April.

Darby, Andrew (2007), *Harpoon: Into the Heart of Whaling*, Crows Nest, NSW: Allen & Unwin.

Dauvergne, Peter (1997), *Shadows in the Forest: Japan and the Politics of Timber in Southeast Asia*, Politics, Science, and the Environment, Cambridge, MA: MIT Press.

Dauvergne, Peter (2001), *Loggers and Degradation in the Asia-Pacific: Corporations and Environmental Management*, Cambridge: Cambridge University Press.

Dauvergne, Peter (2004), 'The Environmental Challenge to Loggers in the Asia-Pacific: Corporate Practices in Informal Regimes on Governance', in *The Business of Global Environmental Governance*, ed. David L. Levy and Peter J. Newell, Cambridge, MA: MIT Press, pp. 169–96.

Davenport, Deborah S. (2005), 'An Alternative Explanation for the Failure of the UNCED Forest Negotiations', *Global Environmental Politics*, **5** (1): 105–30.

Davenport, Deborah S., Kate Louw, Jonathan Manley and Peter Wood (2008), 'Summary of the Forty-fourth Session of the International Tropical Timber Council and Associated Sessions of the Four Committees: 3–8 November 2008', *Earth Negotiations Bulletin*, **24** (81): 1–17.

Davies, Laurence (2007), 'The International Whaling Commission: Scientific Fact?', *Environmental Ethics*, **1**: 1–6.

de Jong, Wil, Lye Tuck-Po and Abe Ken-ichi (2003), 'The Political Ecology of Tropical Forests in Southeast Asia: Historical Roots of Modern Problems', in *The Political Ecology of Tropical Forests in Southeast Asia*, ed. Wil de Jong, Lye Tuck-Po and Abe Ken-ichi, Melbourne: Trans Pacific Press, pp. 1–28.

Denholm, Matthew (2005), 'Push to Harpoon Ban on Whaling', *The Australian*, 21 January.

DeSombre, Elizabeth R. (2002), *The Global Environment and World Politics*, International Relations for the 21st Century, London: Continuum.

Dietelhoff, Nicole, and Harald Muller (2005), 'Theoretical Paradise – Empirically Lost? Arguing with Habermas', *Review of International Studies*, **31**: 167–79.

Dimitrov, Radoslav S. (2005), 'Hostage to Norms: States, Institutions and Global Forest Politics', *Global Environmental Politics*, **5** (4): 1–24.

Dougherty, James E., and Robert L. Pfaltzgraff (1997), *Contending Theories of International Relations: A Comprehensive Survey*, 4th edition, New York: Longman.

Douglas, James J. (1983), *A Re-appraisal of Forestry Development in Developing Countries*, Boston, MA: Martinus Nijhoff Publishers.

Drewry, David J. (1994), 'Conflicts of Interest in the Use of Antarctica', in *Antarctic Science: Global Concerns*, ed. Gotthilf Hempel, Berlin, Germany: Springer-Verlag, pp. 12–30.

Dudley, Nigel, Jean-Paul Jeanrenaud and Francis Sullivan (1995) *Bad Harvest: The International Tropical Timber Trade and the Degradation of the World's Forests*, London: Earthscan.

Eckersley, Robyn (1992), *Environmentalism and Political Theory: Toward an Ecocentric Approach*, London: UCL Press.

Eckersley, Robyn (2001), 'Greening the Nation-state from Exclusive to Inclusive Sovereignty, Economy and Ecology', Paper presented at the European Consortium for Political Research Annual Joint Sessions, Grenoble, France, 6–11 April 2001.

Eckersley, Robyn (2003), 'Politics', in *A Companion to Environmental Philosophy*, ed. Dale Jamieson, Oxford: Blackwell Publishing, pp. 316–30.

Eckersley, Robyn (2004), 'Soft Law, Hard Politics, and the Climate Change Treaty', in *The Politics of International Law*, ed. Christian Reus-Smit, Cambridge: Cambridge University Press, pp. 80–105.

Eckersley, Robyn (2004), *The Green State: Rethinking Democracy and Sovereignty*, Cambridge, MA: MIT Press.

Editorial (1981), *SCAR Bulletin*, September, **69**: 98–100.

Einarsson, Niels (1993), 'All Animals Are Equal but Some Are Cetaceans: Conservation and Culture Conflict', in *Environmentalism: The View from Anthropology*, ed. Kay Milton, London: Routledge, pp. 73–84.

Ellickson, Robert C. (1989), 'A Hypothesis of Wealth-maximizing Norms: Evidence from the Whaling Industry', *Journal of Law, Economics, and Organization*, 1: 83–97.

Elliott, Chris, and Richard Z. Donovan (1996), 'Introduction', in *Certification of Forest Products: Issues and Perspectives*, ed. Virgilio M. Viana, Jamison Ervin, Richard Z. Donovan, Chris Elliott and Henry Gholz, Washington, DC: Island Press, pp. 1–10.

Elliott, Lorraine M. (1994), *International Environmental Politics: Protecting the Antarctic*, New York: St. Martin's Press.

Elliott, Lorraine M. (1998), *The Global Politics of the Environment*, Basingstoke: Macmillan.

Elliott, Lorraine M., and Australian National University (1993), *Protecting the Antarctic Environment: Australia and the Minerals Convention*, Australian Foreign Policy Papers, Canberra, ACT: Australian Foreign Policy

Publications Programme Dept. of International Relations Research School of Pacific Studies Australian National University.

Epstein, Charlotte (2006), 'The Making of Global Environmental Norms: Endangered Species Protection', *Global Environmental Politics*, **6** (2): 32–54.

Epstein, Charlotte (2008), *The Power of Words in International Relations: Birth of an Anti-whaling Discourse*, Cambridge, MA: MIT Press.

European Union (1994), 'European Union Statement, Annex 2: Statement in Explanation of Positions by Member Countries', Paper presented at the Fourth (Final) Part of the United Nations Conference for the Negotiation of a Successor Agreement to the International Tropical Timber Agreement, 1983, Geneva, Switzerland, 10–26 January.

Evteev, Sveneld (1991), 'Antarctica and Its Place in the Contemporary Environmental Movement', in *The Antarctic Treaty System in World Politics*, ed. Arnfinn Jorgensen-Dahl and Willy Ostreng, New York: St Martin's Press, pp. 147–52.

Falk, R.A. (1991), 'The Antarctic Treaty System: Are there Viable Alternatives?', in *The Antarctic Treaty System in World Politics*, ed. Arnfinn Jorgensen-Dahl and Willy Ostreng, Basingstoke: Macmillan, pp. 399–414.

Finnemore, M. (1996), *National Interests in International Society*, Ithaca, NY: Cornell University Press.

Finnemore, M. (1996), 'Culture and World Politics: Insights from Sociology's Institutionalism', *International Organization*, **50** (2): 325–47.

Finnemore, M., and Kathryn Sikkink (1996), 'International Norm Dynamics and Political Change', in *Exploration and Contestation in the Study of World Politics*, ed. P. Katzenstein, R. Keohane and Stephen D. Krasner, Cambridge, MA: MIT Press, pp. 247–78.

Finnemore, Martha, and Kathryn Sikkink (1998), 'International Norm Dynamics and Political Change', *International Organization*, **52** (4): 887–917.

Finnemore, M. and K. Sikkink (1999), 'International Norm Dynamics and Political Change', in *Exploration and Contestation in the Study of World Politics*, ed. P. Katzenstein, R. Keohane and S.D. Krasner, Cambridge, MA: MIT Press, pp. 247–78.

Firestone, Jeremy, and Jonathan Lilley (2005), 'Aboriginal Subsistence Whaling and the Right to Practice and Revitalize Cultural Traditions and Customs', *Journal of International Wildlife Law and Policy*, **8** (2): 177–219.

Flejzor, Lauren (2005), 'Reforming the International Tropical Timber Agreement', *Review of European Community and International Environmental Law*, **14** (1): 19–27.

Fletcher, Kristen M. (2001), 'The International Whaling Regime and U.S. Foreign Policy', in *The Environment, International Relations, and U.S. Foreign Policy*, ed. Paul G. Harris, Washington, DC: Georgetown University Press, pp. 217–37.

Flowers, R.J. (2002), 'International Norms and Domestic Policies in Japan: Identity, Legitimacy and Civilization', Ph.D., University of Minnesota.

Food and Agriculture Organization (2005), 'State of the World's Forests 2005', Food and Agriculture Organization.

Forsyth, Adrian, and Kenneth Miyata (1984), *Tropical Nature: Life and Death in the Rainforests of Central and South America*, New York: Simon and Schuster.

Fox, Warwick (1990), *Toward a Transpersonal Ecology: Developing New Foundations for Environmentalism*, 1st edition, Boston, MA: Shambhala.

Francioni, Francesco (1986), 'Legal Aspects of Mineral Exploitation in Antarctica', *Cornell International Law Journal*, **19**: 163–88.

Francioni, Francesco (1992), 'The Madrid Protocol on the Protection of the Antarctic Environment', in *International Environmental Law for Antarctica*, ed. Francesco Francioni, Milan: Giuffre Editore, pp. 1–30.

Francioni, Francesco (1993), 'The Madrid Protocol on the Protection of the Antarctic Environment', *Texas International Law Journal*, **28**: 47–72.

Freeman, Milton M.R. (1990), 'Political Issues with Regard to Contemporary Whaling', in *Who's Afraid of Compromise?*, ed. Simon Ward, Tokyo: Institute of Cetacean Research (ICR), pp. 1–7.

French, Duncan (1999), 'Sustainable Development and the 1991 Madrid Protocol to the 1959 Antarctic Treaty: The Primacy of Protection in a Particularly Sensitive Environment', *Journal of International Wildlife Law and Policy*, **2** (3): 291–332.

Friedheim, Robert L. (2001), 'Introduction: The IWC as a Contested Regime', in *Towards a Sustainable Whaling Regime*, ed. Robert L. Friedheim, Seattle: University of Washington Press, pp. 3–48.

Friends of the Earth (1997), 'Special Briefing: Sustainability and the Trade in Tropical Rainforest Timber', Friends of the Earth, UK, www.foe.co.uk/pubsinfo/briefings/html/19971215150457.html, 12 April 2004.

Friends of the Earth, and World Rainforest Movement (1992), 'The International Tropical Timber Agreement: Conserving the Forests or Chainsaw Charter? A Critical Review of the First Five Years' Operations of the International Tropical Timber Organization', Friends of the Earth.

Fuchs, V.E. (1983), 'Antarctica: Its History and Development', in *Antarctic Resources Policy: Scientific, Legal and Political Issues*, ed. Francisco Orrego Vicuna, Cambridge: Cambridge University Press, pp. 13–20.

Gale, Fred P. (1996), 'The Mysterious Case of the Disappearing Environmentalists: The International Tropical Timber Organization', *Capitalism, Nature, Socialism* **7** (3): 103–17.

Gale, Fred P. (1998), *The Tropical Timber Trade Regime*, International Political Economy Series, New York: St Martin's Press.

Gale, Fred P. (2003), 'Discourse and Southeast Asian Deforestation: A Case Study of the International Tropical Timber Organization', in *The Political Ecology of Tropical Forests in Southeast Asia: Historical Perpectives*, ed. Wil de Jong, Lye Tuck-Po and Abe Ken-ichi, Melbourne: Trans Pacific Press, pp. 236–64.

Gale, Fred P. (2004), 'Public Accountability in Private Regulation: Contrasting Models of the Forest Stewardship Council (FSC) and Marine Stewardship Council', Paper presented at the Australasian Political Studies Association Conference, University of Adelaide.

Gambell, Ray (1999), 'The International Whaling Commission and the Contemporary Whaling Debate', in *Conservation and Management of Marine Mammals*, ed. John R. Twiss Jr and Randall R. Reeves, Melbourne, Victoria: Melbourne University Press, pp. 179–98.

Gillespie, Alexander (2005), *Whaling Diplomacy: Defining Issues in International Environmental Law*, Cheltenham, UK and Northampton, MA, USA: Edward Elgar.

Godfrey-Smith, W. (1979), 'The Value of Wilderness', *Environmental Ethics*, **1**: 309–19.

Godfrey-Smith, W. (1980), 'The Rights of Non-humans and Intrinsic Values', in *Environmental Philosophy*, ed. D.S. Mannison, M.A. McRobbie and R. Routley, Canberra: Department of Philosophy, Research School of Social Science, Australian National University, pp. 30–47.

Goldmann, Kjell (2005), 'Appropriateness and Consequences: The Logic of Neo-institutionalism', *Governance: An International Journal of Policy, Administration and Institutions*, **18** (1): 35–52.

Goodland, Robert, ed. (1990) *The Race to Save the Tropics: Ecology and Economics for a Sustainable Future*, Washington, DC: Island Press.

Grainger, Alan (1980), 'The State of the World's Tropical Rainforests', *Ecologist*, **10** (6): 6–54.

Greenpeace Australia (1994), *Greenpeace Australia Magazine*, Spring. On file with the author.

Greenpeace Australia (1994), 'Whale Vote Leaves Japan out in the Cold (Publicity Material)', Greenpeace Australia. On file with the author.

Greenpeace International (1984), 'The Future of the Antarctic: Background for a Second UN Debate', Greenpeace International Working Paper.

Griesdorf, Michael Jeffrey (2008), 'Norms as a Rhetorical Competition: Soviet-American Confontations over Cuba, 1970–85', *Cold War History*, **8** (3): 299–326.

Guppy, Nicholas (1996), 'International Governance and Regimes Dealing with Land Resources from the Perspective of the North', in *Global*

*Environmental Change and International Governance*, ed. Oran R. Young, George J. Demko and Kilaparti Ramakrishna, Hanover, NH: University Press of New England, pp. 136–65.

Guzzini, Stefano (2000), 'A Reconstruction of Constructivism in International Relations', *European Journal of International Relations*, **6** (2): 147–82.

Haas, Peter M. (1990), *Saving the Mediterranean: The Politics of International Environmental Cooperation*, *The Political Economy of International Change*, New York: Columbia University Press.

Haas, Peter M., and Ernst Haas (2002), 'Pragmatic Constructivism and the Study of International Institutions', *Millennium: Journal of International Studies*, **31** (3): 573–601.

Haas, Peter M., Robert Owen Keohane and Marc A. Levy (1993), *Institutions for the Earth: Sources of Effective International Environmental Protection*, Cambridge, MA: MIT Press.

Hall, R.B. (1999), *National Collective Identity: Social Constructs and International Systems*, New York and Chichester: Columbia University Press.

Hasenclever, Andreas, Peter Mayer and Volker Rittberger (1997), *Theories of International Regimes*, Cambridge Studies in International Relations 55, New York: Cambridge University Press.

Hawke, R.J.L. (1989), 'Antarctica's Future – Speech by the Prime Minister to the 16th National Conference of the Australian Institute of International Affairs, 18 November 1989', *Department of Foreign Affairs and Trade: The Monthly Record*, **60** (11): 627–8.

Hawke, R.J.L. (1989), 'Our Country, Our Future: Statement on the Environment by the Prime Minister of Australia', Canberra: Australian Government Publishing Service, Canberra.

Hay, Peter (2002), *Main Currents in Western Environmental Thought*. Sydney: UNSW Press.

Head, Susan, and Robert Heinzman, eds. (1990), *Lessons of the Rainforest*. San Francisco: Sierra Club Books for Children.

Heller, Agnes (1987), *Beyond Justice*, Oxford: Blackwell.

Herr, Richard A., and Bruce W. Davis (1992), 'Antarctica and Non-state Actors: The Question of Legitimacy', *International Antarctic Regime Project, Fridtjof Nansens Institute*, **4**: 1–15.

High North Alliance (2005), 'High North Web: Whaling Today', http://www.highnorth.no/iwc2000/briefings/Whaling.htm, 16 May.

Hirata, Keiko (2004), 'Beached Whales: Examining Japan's Rejection of an International Norm', *Social Science Japan Journal*, **7** (2): 177–97.

Hirata, Keiko (2005), 'Why Japan Supports Whaling', *Journal of International Wildlife Law and Policy*, **8** (2): 129–49.

Hirsch, Moshe (2004), 'Compliance with International Norms in the Age of Globalization: Two Theoretical Perspectives', in *The Impact of*

*International Law on International Cooperation*, ed. Eyal Benvenisti and Moshe Hirsch, Cambridge: Cambridge University Press, pp. 166–93.

Hjelmar, Ulf (1996), *The Political Practice of Environmental Organizations*, Brookfield, VT.: Ashgate Publishing Company.

Hobson, John M. (2000), *The State and International Relations*, Themes in International Relations, Cambridge: Cambridge University Press.

Hodges, Brian Trevor (2000), 'The Cracking Façade of the International Whaling Commission as an Institution of International Law: Norwegian Small-type Whaling and the Aboriginal Subsistence Exemption', *Journal of Environmental Law and Litigation*, **15** (2): 295.

Hoffmann, M.J. (2006), 'Entrepreneurs and Norm Dynamics: An Agent-based Model on the Norm Life Cycle', University of Delaware, http://www.psych.upenn.edu/sacsec/abir/_private/Pamla/Hoffmann_norms.doc, 31 July.

Holt, Sidney J. (2007), 'Whaling: Will the Phoenix Rise Again?', *Marine Pollution Bulletin*, **54**: 1081–6.

Hopf, T. (1998), 'The Promise of Constructivism in International Relations Theory', *International Security*, **23** (1): 171–200.

Hovden, Eivend (1999), 'As if Nature Doesn't Matter: Ecology, Regime Theory and International Relations', *Environmental Politics*, **8** (2): 50–74.

Humphreys, David (1996), 'Hegemonic Ideology and the International Tropical Timber Organization', in *The Environment and International Relations*, ed. John Vogler and Mark F. Imber, London: Routledge, pp. 215–33.

Humphreys, David (1997), 'Environmental Accountability and Transnational Corporations', Paper presented at the International Academic Conference on Environmental Justice: Global Ethics for the 21st Century, University of Melbourne, Australia, 1–3 October.

Humphreys, David (1999), 'The Evolving Forests Regime', *Global Environmental Politics*, **9**: 251–4.

Humphreys, David (2003), 'Life Protective or Carcinogenic Challenge? Global Forests Governance under Advanced Capitalism', *Global Environmental Politics*, **3** (2): 40–55.

Humphreys, David (2004), 'Redefining the Issues: NGO Influence on International Forest Negotiations', *Global Environmental Politics*, **4** (2): 51–74.

Humphreys, David (2006), *Logjam: Deforestation and the Crisis of Global Governance*, London: Earthscan.

Humphreys, David (2008), 'NGO Influence on International Policy on Forest Conservation and the Trade in Forest Products', in *NGO Diplomacy: The Influence of Nongovernmental Organisations in International Environmental Negotiations*, ed. Michele M. Betsill and Elisabeth Corell, Cambridge, MA: MIT Press, pp. 149–206.

Humphreys, David (2009), 'Discourse as Ideology: Neoliberalism and the Limits of International Forest Policy', *Forest Policy and Economics*, doi:10.1016/j.forpol.2008.08.008.

Hurrell, Andrew (1993), 'International Society and the Study of Regimes: A Reflective Approach', in *Regime Theory and International Relations*, ed. V. Rittberger, Oxford: Clarendon Press, pp. 49–72.

Iliff, Mike (2007), 'The International Whaling Regime Post 2007', *Marine Policy*, **32**: 522–7.

Iliff, Mike (2008), 'Modernisation of the International Convention for the Regulation of Whaling', *Marine Policy*, **32**: 402–7.

Iliff, Mike (2008), 'Normalization of the International Whaling Commission', *Marine Policy*, **32**: 333–8.

International Tropical Timber Organization (1983), 'International Tropical Timber Agreement 1983', Environmental Treaties and Resource Indicators (ENTRI), available from http://sedac.ciesin.org/entri/texts/tropical.timber.1983.html, last accessed 12 April 2006.

International Tropical Timber Organization (1989), 'Pre-project Proposal, Incentives in Producer and Consumer Countries for the Promotion of Sustainably-produced Tropical Timber', Yokohama: ITTO.

International Tropical Timber Organization (1989), 'Pre-project Proposal, Incentives in Producer and Consumer Countries to Promote Sustainable Development of Tropical Forests', Yokohama: ITTO.

International Tropical Timber Organization (1990), 'Technical Series 5: ITTO Technical Guidelines for the Sustainable Management of Tropical Resources', Yokohama: ITTO.

International Tropical Timber Organization (1990), 'The Promotion of Sustainable Forest Management: A Casestudy in Sarawak, Malaysia', Bali, Indonesia: submitted to Eighth Session of the International Tropical Timber Council, Yokohama: ITTO.

International Tropical Timber Organization (1991), 'Pre-project Report on Incentives in Producer and Consumer Countries to Promote Sustainable Development of Tropical Forests', Yokohama: ITTO.

International Tropical Timber Organization (1991), 'Draft Report of the International Tropical Timber Council, Eleventh Session', Yokohama: ITTO.

International Tropical Timber Organization (1991), 'ITTC (X)/16 Decision 3(X) Sustainable Tropical Forest Management and Trade in Tropical Timber', Yokohama: ITTO.

International Tropical Timber Organization (1994), 'Formal Statement by Consumer Members: International Tropical Timber Agreement 1994', http://www.itto.or.jp/live/Live_Server/144/ITTA1994e.doc, 20 April.

International Tropical Timber Organization (2002), 'ITTO Yokohama Action

Plan 2002–2006', in *ITTO Policy Development Series*, No. 11, Yokohama: ITTO.

International Tropical Timber Organization (2003), 'Annual Review and Assessment of the World Timber Situation', Yokohama: ITTO.

International Tropical Timber Organization (2004), 'Working Document Resulting from the First Session', Paper presented at the Conference for the Negotiation of a Successor Agreement to the International Tropical Timber Agreement, Geneva, Switzerland, 26–30 July.

International Tropical Timber Organization (2005), 'International Tropical Timber Agreement', United Nations Conference on Trade and Development, http://www.itto.or.jp/live/PageDisplayHandler?pageId=201, 13 April.

International Tropical Timber Organization (2005), 'About ITTO', http://www.itto.or.jp/live/PageDisplayHandler?pageId=225, 17 June.

International Tropical Timber Organization (2005), 'Final Working Document Resulting from the Second Part of the Conference', Paper presented at the Conference for the Negotiation of a Successor Agreement to the International Tropical Timber Agreement, Geneva, Switzerland, 27 June–1 July.

International Tropical Timber Organization (2005), 'Final Working Document Resulting from the Third Part of the Conference', Paper presented at the Conference for the Negotiation of a Successor Agreement to the International Tropical Timber Agreement, Geneva, Switzerland, 27 June–1 July.

International Tropical Timber Organization (2007), 'International Tropical Timber Agreement 2006', United Nations Conference on Trade and Development, http://www.itto.or.jp/live/PageDisplayHandler?pageId=201, 30 October.

International Tropical Timber Organization (2007), 'International Tropical Timber Agreement, 2006', United Nations Conference on Trade and Development, http://www.ito.or.jp, 25 April.

International Tropical Timber Organization (2008), 'News Release: Legality Shapes as New Certification Flashpoint', http://www.itto.or.jp/live/PageDisplayHandler?pageId=0213, 23 December.

International Tropical Timber Organization (2009), 'Decision 4(XLIV) the ITTO Action Plan 2008–2011 Transitional Period', http://www.ito.or.jp, 20 January.

International Tropical Timber Organization (2009), 'Decision 7(XLIV) Entry into Force of the International Tropical Timber Agreement, 2006', http://www.ito.or.jp, 20 January.

International Tropical Timber Organization (2009), 'U.S.$8.6 Million in New Funds for Tropical Forests', http://www.ito.or.jp/live/PageDisplayHandler?pageId=213, 21 January.

International Whaling Commission (1950), 'First Report of the Commission', London: International Whaling Commission.
International Whaling Commission (1951), 'Second Report of the Commission', London: International Whaling Commission.
International Whaling Commission (1952), 'Third Report of the Commission', London: International Whaling Commission.
International Whaling Commission (1953), 'Fourth Report of the Commission', London: International Whaling Commission.
International Whaling Commission (1955), 'Sixth Report of the Commission', London: International Whaling Commission.
International Whaling Commission (1956), 'Seventh Report of the Commission', London: International Whaling Commission.
International Whaling Commission (1957), 'Eighth Report of the Commission', London: International Whaling Commission.
International Whaling Commission (1959), 'Tenth Report of the Commission', London: International Whaling Commission.
International Whaling Commission (1961), 'Twelfth Report of the Commission', London: International Whaling Commission.
International Whaling Commission (1965), 'Fifteenth Report of the Commission', London: International Whaling Commission.
International Whaling Commission (1966), 'Sixteenth Report of the Commission', London: International Whaling Commission.
International Whaling Commission (1969), 'Nineteenth Report of the Commission', London: International Whaling Commission.
International Whaling Commission (1972), 'Twenty-second Report of the Commission', London: International Whaling Commission.
International Whaling Commission (1973), 'Twenty-third Report of the Commission', London: International Whaling Commission.
International Whaling Commission (1974), 'Twenty-fourth Report of the Commission', London: International Whaling Commission.
International Whaling Commission (1975), 'Twenty-fifth Report of the Commission', London: International Whaling Commission.
International Whaling Commission (1976), 'Twenty-sixth Report of the Commission', London: International Whaling Commission.
International Whaling Commission (1979), 'Annual Report of the International Whaling Commission 29', London: International Whaling Commission.
International Whaling Commission (1980), 'Annual Report of the International Whaling Commission 30', London: International Whaling Commission.
International Whaling Commission (1981), 'Annual Report of the International Whaling Commission 31', London: International Whaling Commission.

International Whaling Commission (1982), 'Annual Report of the International Whaling Commission 32', Cambridge: International Whaling Commission.

International Whaling Commission (1982), 'Report of the International Whaling Commission (Special Issue 4): Aboriginal/Subsistence Whaling (with Special Reference to the Alaska and Greenland Fisheries)', Cambridge: International Whaling Commission.

International Whaling Commission (1983), 'Annual Report of the International Whaling Commission 33', Cambridge: International Whaling Commission.

International Whaling Commission (1984), 'Annual Report of the International Whaling Commission 34', Cambridge: International Whaling Commission.

International Whaling Commission (1985), 'Annual Report of the International Whaling Commission 35', Cambridge: International Whaling Commission.

International Whaling Commission (1986), 'Annual Report of the International Whaling Commission 36', Cambridge: International Whaling Commission.

International Whaling Commission (1987), 'Annual Report of the International Whaling Commission 37', Cambridge: International Whaling Commission.

International Whaling Commission (1988), 'Annual Report of the International Whaling Commission 38', Cambridge: International Whaling Commission.

International Whaling Commission (1989), 'Annual Report of the International Whaling Commission 39', Cambridge: International Whaling Commission.

International Whaling Commission (1990), 'Annual Report of the International Whaling Commission 40', Cambridge: International Whaling Commission.

International Whaling Commission (1991), 'Annual Report of the International Whaling Commission 41', Cambridge: International Whaling Commission.

International Whaling Commission (1992), 'Annual Report of the International Whaling Commission 42', Cambridge: International Whaling Commission.

International Whaling Commission (1993), 'Annual Report of the International Whaling Commission 43', Cambridge: International Whaling Commission.

International Whaling Commission (1994), 'Annual Report of the International Whaling Commission 44', Cambridge: International Whaling Commission.

International Whaling Commission (1995), 'Annual Report of the International Whaling Commission 45', Cambridge: International Whaling Commission.

International Whaling Commission (1996), 'Annual Report of the International Whaling Commission 46', Cambridge: International Whaling Commission.

International Whaling Commission (1997), 'Annual Report of the International Whaling Commission 47', Cambridge: International Whaling Commission.

International Whaling Commission (1998), 'Annual Report of the International Whaling Commission 48', Cambridge: International Whaling Commission.

International Whaling Commission (1999), 'Annual Report of the International Whaling Commission 49', Cambridge: International Whaling Commission.

International Whaling Commission (2000), 'Annual Report of the International Whaling Commission 50', Cambridge: International Whaling Commission.

International Whaling Commission (2001), 'Annual Report of the International Whaling Commission 51', Cambridge: International Whaling Commission.

International Whaling Commission (2002), 'Annual Report of the International Whaling Commission 52', Cambridge: International Whaling Commission.

International Whaling Commission (2003), 'Annual Report of the International Whaling Commission 53', Cambridge: International Whaling Commission.

International Whaling Commission (2004), 'Annual Report of the International Whaling Commission 54', Cambridge: International Whaling Commission.

International Whaling Commission (2005), 'Annual Report of the International Whaling Commission 55', Cambridge: International Whaling Commission.

International Whaling Commission (2007), 'Chair's Report of the 58th Annual Meeting', 16–20 June 2006, St Kitts and Nevis, http://www.iwcoffice.org/meetings/chair2006.htm, accessed 1 July 2009.

International Whaling Commission (2008), 'Chair's Report of the 59th Annual Meeting', 28–31 May, Anchorage, Alaska, http://www.iwcoffice.org/meetings/chair2007.htm, accessed 1 July 2009.

International Whaling Commission (2008), 'IWC Press Release, Day 2, Tuesday 24 June', http://www.iwcoffice.org/meetings/meeting2008.htm, 10 July.

International Whaling Commission (2008), 'IWC Press Release, Day 4,

Thursday 26 June', http://www.iwcoffice.org/meetings/meeting2008.htm, 10 July.

International Whaling Commission (2008), 'Chair's Report of the Intersessional Meeting on the Future of the IWC', Renaissance London Heathrow Hotel, UK, 6–8 March, 2008. C:\IWC60/60-7, http://www.iwcoffice.org/_documents/, 1 September.

International Whaling Commission (2008), 'Annotated Provisional Agenda, 60th Annual Meeting of the International Whaling Commission', Santiago, Chile, 23–7 June, C:\IWC60/60-2, http://www.iwcoffice.org/_documents/, 1 September.

International Whaling Commission (2009), 'Revised Draft Agenda, Conservation Committee, 60th Annual Meeting of the International Whaling Commission', IWC/60/CC1Rev., http://www.iwcoffice.org/_documents/, 1 September.

International Whaling Commission (2009), 'Revised Chair's Summary Report of the 60th Annual Meeting', Santiago, Chile, June, 2008, http://www.iwcoffice.org/_documents/, 1 January.

International Whaling Commission (2009), IWC Member Countries and Commissioners, http://iwcoffice.org/commission/members.htm, 12 January.

Ishii, Atsushi, and Ayako Okubo (2007), 'An Alternative Explanation of Japan's Whaling Diplomacy in the Post-moratorium Era', *Journal of International Wildlife Law and Policy*, **10** (1): 55–87.

Jackson, Robert H. (1990), *Quasi-States: Sovereignty, International Relations, and the Third World*, Cambridge Studies in International Relations 12, Cambridge: Cambridge University Press.

Jacobsson, Marie (2007), 'The Antarctic Treaty System: Legal and Environmental Issues – Future Challenges for the Antarctic Treaty System', in *Antarctica: Legal and Environmental Challenges for the Future*, ed. G. Triggs and A. Riddell, London: The British Institute of International Comparative Law, pp. 1–16.

Jakobsen, S. (1999), 'International Relations and Global Environmental Change: Review of the Burgeoning Literature on the Environment', *Cooperation and Conflict*, **34** (2): 205–36.

Jepperson, Ronald, Alexander Wendt and Peter Katzenstein (1996), 'Norms, Identity, and Culture in National Security', in *The Culture of National Security: Norms and Identity in World Politics*, ed. Peter Katzenstein, New York: Columbia University Press, pp. 33–75.

Jorgensen, Knud Erik (2001), 'Four Levels and a Discipline', in *Constructing International Relations: The Next Generation*, ed. Karin M. Fierke and Knud Erik Jorgensen, London: M.E. Sharpe, pp. 36–53.

Joyner, Christopher C. (1988), 'The Antarctic Legal Regime: An Introduction', in *The Antarctic Legal Regime*, ed. Christopher C. Joyner and Sudhir K. Chopra, Dordrecht: Martinus Nijhoff Publishers, pp. 1–8.

Joyner, Christopher C. (1988), 'The Evolving Minerals Regime for Antarctica', in *The Antarctic Legal Regime*, ed. Christopher C. Joyner and Sudhir K. Chopra, Dordrecht: Martinus Nijhoff Publishers, pp. 131–62.

Joyner, Christopher C. (1991), 'CRAMRA: The Ugly Duckling of the Antarctic Treaty System?', in *The Antarctic Treaty System in World Politics*, ed. Arnfinn Jorgensen-Dahl and Willy Ostreng, New York: St Martin's Press, pp. 161–85.

Joyner, Christopher C. (1992), *Antarctica and the Law of the Sea*, London: Martinus Nijhoff Publishers.

Joyner, Christopher C. (1998), *Governing the Frozen Commons: The Antarctic Regime and Environmental Protection*, Columbia, SC: University of South Carolina Press.

Joyner, Christopher C. (2000), 'The United States: Legislation and Practice in Implementing the Protocol', in *Implementing the Environmental Protection Regime for the Antarctic*, ed. Davor Vidas, Boston, MA: Kluwer Academic Publishers, pp. 417–38.

Jupille, Joseph, James A. Caporaso and Jeffrey T. Checkel (2003), 'Integrating Institutions: Rationalism, Constructivism, and the Study of the European Union', *Comparative Political Studies*, **36** (1/2): 7–40.

Kahn, James, and Judith McDonald (1994), 'International Debt and Deforestation', in *The Causes of Tropical Deforestation: The Economic and Statistical Analysis of Factors Giving Rise to the Loss of the Tropical Forests*, ed. Katrina Brown and David W. Pearce, London: UCL Press Ltd, pp. 57–67.

Kalland, Arne (1993), 'Whale Politics and Green Legitimacy: A Critique of the Anti-whaling Campaign', *Anthropology Today*, **9** (6): 3–7.

Kalland, Arne (1998), 'The Anti-whaling Campaigns and Japanese Responses', in *Japanese Position on Whaling and Anti-whaling Campaign*, Tokyo: The Institute of Cetacean Research.

Kamieniecki, S. (1993), *Environmental Politics in the International Arena: Movements, Parties, Organizations, and Policy*, New York: State University of New York Press.

Kasimbazi, Emmanuel (1996), 'Sustainable Development in International Tropical Timber Agreements', *Journal of Energy & Natural Resources Law*, **14** (2): 137–60.

Katzenstein, Peter (1996), *Cultural Norms and National Security: Norms and Identity in World Politics*, New York, NY: Columbia University Press.

Keck, Margaret E., and Kathryn Sikkink (1998), *Activists Beyond Borders: Advocacy Networks in International Politics*, Ithaca, NY: Cornell University Press.

Kellow, A. (2000), 'Norms, Interests and Environmental NGOs: The Limits of Cosmopolitanism', *Environmental Politics*, **9** (9): 1–22.

Keohane, Robert O. (1984), *After Hegemony: Cooperation and Discord in the World Political Economy*, Princeton, NJ: Princeton University Press.

Keohane, Robert O. (2001), 'Governance in a Partially Globalized World', *American Political Science Review*, **95** (1): 1–13.

Keohane, Robert O., and Joseph S. Nye (1989), *International Institutions and State Power: Essays in International Relations Theory*, Boulder, CO: Westview Press.

Keohane, Robert O., Joseph S. Nye and Stanley Hoffmann (1993), *After the Cold War: International Institutions and State Strategies in Europe, 1989–1991*, Cambridge, MA: Harvard University Press.

Kibel, Paul Stanton (1999), *The Earth on Trial: Environmental Law on the International Stage*, New York: Routledge.

Kimball, Lee (1988), 'The Role of Non-governmental Organizations in Antarctic Affairs', in *The Antarctic Legal Regime*, ed. Christopher C. Joyner and Sudhir K. Chopra, Dordrecht: Martinus Nijhoff Publishers, pp. 33–64.

Kindt, John Warren (1988), 'A Regime for Ice-covered Areas: The Antarctic and Issues Involving Resource Exploitation and the Environment', in *The Antarctic Legal Regime*, ed. Christopher C. Joyner and Sudhir K. Chopra, Dordrecht: Martinus Nijhoff Publishers, 187–218.

Klotz, Audie (1995), *Norms in International Relations: The Struggle against Apartheid*, Cornell Studies in Political Economy, Ithaca, NY: Cornell University Press.

Klotz, Audie (2001), 'Can We Speak a Common Constructivist Language', in *Constructing International Relations: The Next Generation*, ed. Karin M. Fierke and Knud Erik Jorgensen, London: M.E. Sharpe, pp. 223–35.

Kolk, Ans (1996), *Forests in International Environmental Politics: International Organisations, NGOs and the Brazilian Amazon*, Utrecht, the Netherlands: International Books.

Kozlowski, Rey, and Friedrich V. Kratochwil (1995), 'Understanding Change in International Politics: The Soviet Empire's Demise and the International System', in *International Relations Theory and the End of the Cold War*, ed. Richard Ned Lebow and Thomas Risse-Kappen, New York: Columbia University Press, pp. 127–66.

Krasner, Stephen D. (1983), *International Regimes*, Cornell Studies in Political Economy, Ithaca, NY: Cornell University Press.

Krasner, Stephen D. (1985), *Structural Conflict: The Third World against Global Liberalism*, Berkeley, CA: University of California Press.

Krasner, Stephen D. (1993), 'Global Communications and National Power: Life on the Pareto Frontier', in *Neorealism and Neoliberalism: The Contemporary Debate*, ed. D. Baldwin, New York: Columbia University Press, pp. 336–56.

Kratochwil, Friedrich V. (1984), 'Thrasymmachos Revisited: On the Relevance of Norms and the Study of Law for International Relations', *Journal of International Affairs*, **37** (2): 343–56.

Kratochwil, Friedrich V. (1989), *Rules, Norms and Decisions: On the Conditions of Practical and Legal Reasoning in International Relations and Domestic Affairs*, Cambridge: Cambridge University Press.

Kratochwil, Friedrich V. (2001), 'Constructivism as an Approach to Interdisciplinary Study', in *Constructing International Relations: The Next Generation*, ed. Karin M. Fierke and Knud Erik Jorgensen, London: M.E. Sharpe, pp. 13–35.

Laarman, Jan G. (1988), 'Export of Tropical Hardwoods in the Twentieth Century', in *World Deforestation in the Twentieth Century*, ed. John F. Richards and Richard P. Tucker, Durham, NC: Duke University Press, pp. 147–63.

Larminie, Geoffrey (1991), 'The Mineral Potential of Antarctica: The State of the Art', in *The Antarctic Treaty System in World Politics*, ed. Arnfinn Jorgensen-Dahl and Willy Ostreng, New York: St Martin's Press, pp. 79–93.

Legro, J.W. (1997), 'Which Norms Matter? Revisiting the "Failure" of Internationalism', *International Organization*, **51** (1): 31–63.

Levi, Werner (1965), 'The Relative Irrelevance of Moral Norms in International Politics', *Social Forces*, **44** (2): 226–33.

Linklater, Andrew (2001), 'Marxism', in *Theories of International Relations*, 2nd edition, ed. Scott Burchill, Richard Devetak, Andrew Linklater, Matthew Paterson, Christian Reus-Smit and Jacqui True, New York: Palgrave, pp. 119–44.

List, M., and V. Rittberger (1992), 'Regime Theory and International Environmental Management: Actors, Interests and Institutions', in *The International Politics of the Environment*, ed. Andrew Hurrell and Benedict Kingsbury, Oxford: Oxford University Press, pp. 85–109.

Litfin, K. (1993), 'Eco-regimes: Playing Tug of War with the Nation State', in *The State and Social Power in Global Environmental Politics*, ed. Ronnie D. Lipschutz and Ken Conca, New York: Columbia University Press, pp. 94–117.

London Environmental Economics Centre (1992), 'Draft Final Report: ITTO Activity PCM(IX)/4 the Economic Linkages between the International Trade in Tropical Timber and the Sustainable Management of Tropical Forests', London: London Environmental Economics Centre.

London Environmental Economics Centre (1993), 'The Economic Linkages between the International Trade in Tropical Timber and the Sustainable Management of Tropical Forests', London: International Tropical Timber Organization.

Lucas, Clay (2005), 'Evidence of Whale Vote Bribery', *The Age*, 18 July.

McHugh, J.L. (1974), 'The Role and History of the International Whaling Commission', in *The Whale Problem: A Status Report*, ed. W. Schevill, Cambridge, MA: Harvard University Press, pp. 305–35.

March, James G., and Johan P. Olsen (1998), 'The Institutional Dynamics of International Political Orders', *International Organization*, **52** (4): 943–69.

Maslow, Sebastian, and Ayako Nakamura (2008), 'Constructivism and Ecological Thought: A Critical Discussion on the Prospects for a "Greening" of IR Theory', *Interdisciplinary Information Sciences*, **14** (2): 133–44.

Mason, Michael (2008), 'The Governance of Transnational Environmental Harm: Addressing New Modes of Accountability/Responsibility', *Global Environmental Politics*, **8** (3): 8–24.

Meyer, Christoph O. (2005), 'Convergence Towards a European Strategic Culture? A Constructivist Framework for Explaining Changing Norms', *European Journal of International Relations*, **11** (4): 523–49.

Miller, Andrew R., and Nives Dolsak (2007), 'Issue Linkages in International Environmental Policy: The International Whaling Commission and Japanese Development Aid', *Global Environmental Politics*, **7** (1): 69–96.

Miller, Marian A.L. (1995), *The Third World in Global Environmental Politics*, Issues in Third World Politics, Boulder, CO: Lynne Rienner Publishers.

Mitchell, R.B., and T. Bernauer (1998), 'Empirical Research on International Environmental Policy: Designing Qualitative Case Studies', *Journal of Environment and Development*, **7** (1): 4–31.

Miyaoka, Isao (2004), *Legitimacy in International Society: Japan's Reaction to Global Wildlife Preservation*, New York: Palgrave Macmillan.

Moravcsik, Andrew (1997), 'Taking Preferences Seriously: A Liberal Theory of International Politics', *International Organization*, **51** (4): 513–53.

Moravcsik, Andrew (2001), 'Bringing Constructivist Integration Theory out of the Clouds: Has It Landed Yet?', *European Union Politics*, **2** (2): 226–49.

Morishita, Joji, and Dan Goodman (2005), 'Role and Problems of the Scientific Committee of the International Whaling Commission in Terms of Conservation and Sustainable Utilization of Stocks', *Global Environmental Research*, **9** (2): 157–66.

Mowat, Farley (1996), *Sea of Slaughter: A Chronicle of the Destruction of Animal Life in the North Atlantic*, Shelburne, VT.: Chapters Publishing Ltd.

Myers, Norman (1989), 'The Future of Forests', in *The Fragile Environment: The Darwin College Lectures*, ed. Laurie Friday and Ronald Laskey, Cambridge: Cambridge University Press, pp. 22–40.

Nelson, M.P. (2003), 'An Amalgamation of Wilderness Preservation Arguments', in *Environmental Ethics: An Anthology*, ed. A. Light and H. Rolston III, Malden, MA: Blackwell Publishing, pp. 413–36.

Ngau, Harrison, Thomas Jalong Apoi and Chee Yoke Ling (1987), 'Malaysian Timber: Exploitation for Whom?', in *Forest Resource Crisis in the Third World*, Penang: Sahabat Alam Malaysia.

Norton, B.G. (1986), 'Conservation and Preservation: A Conceptual Rehabilitation', *Environmental Ethics*, **8**: 195–220.

Norton, Bryan G. (2000), 'The Cultural Approach to Conservation Biology', in *Environmental Ethics: An Introduction with Readings*, ed. John Benson, London: Routledge, pp. 143–52.

Oberthur, Sebastian (1998/9) 'The International Convention for the Regulation of Whaling: From Over-exploitation to Total Preservation', in *Yearbook of International Co-operation on Environment and Development 1998/99*, ed. Olav Schram Stokke, London: Earthscan, pp. 29–37.

Oelschlager, Max (1993), *Idea of Wilderness: From Prehistory to the Age of Ecology*, new edition, New Haven, CN: Yale University Press.

Okereke, Chukwumerije (2008), 'Equity Norms in Global Environmental Governance', *Global Environmental Politics*, **8** (3): 25–50.

Ommanney, F.D. (1971), *Lost Leviathan*, London: Hutchinson.

Onuf, N. (1989), *The Idea of Wilderness*, Columbia: University of South Carolina Press.

O'Riordan, T. and A. Jordan (1995), 'The Precautionary Principle in Contemporary Environmental Politics', *Environmental Values*, **4**: 191–212.

Osherenko, Gail (2005), 'Environmental Justice and the International Whaling Commission: Moby-Dick Revisited', *Journal of International Wildlife Law and Policy*, **8** (2): 221–39.

Oslund, Karen (2004), 'Protecting Fat Mammals or Carnivorous Humans? Towards an Environmental History of Whales', *Historical Social Research*, **29** (3): 63–81.

Ostreng, Willy (1991), 'The Conflict and Alignment Pattern of Antarctic Politics: Is a New Order Needed?', in *The Antarctic Treaty System in World Politics*, ed. Arnfinn Jorgensen-Dahl and Willy Ostreng, New York: St Martin's Press, pp. 433–50.

Ostrum, Elinor (1998), 'A Behavioural Appraoch to the Rational Choice Theory of Collective Action', *American Political Science Review*, **92** (1): 1–22.

Oye, K. (1986), 'Explaining Cooperation under Anarchy: Hypotheses and Strategies', in *Cooperation under Anarchy*, ed. K. Oye, New Jersey: Princeton University Press, pp. 1–24.

Paehlke, R.C. (1997), 'Environmental Values and Public Policy', in *Environmental Policy in the 1990s: Reform or Reaction*, ed. N.J. Vig and M.E. Kraft, Washington, DC: Congressional Quarterly Inc., pp. 75–92.

Palazzo Jr., Jose Truda (1999), 'Whose Whales? Developing Countries and the Right to Use Whales by Non-Lethal Means', *Journal of Wildlife Law & Policy*, **2** (1): 69–78.

Panke, Dianna (2006), 'The Differential Impact of Communicated Ideas: Bridging the Gap between Rationalism and Constructivism', *Hamburg Review of Social Sciences*, **1** (3): 312–42.

Passmore, John (1980), *Man's Responsibility for Nature: Ecological Problems and Western Traditions*, London: Duckworth.

Paterson, Matthew (2000), *Understanding Global Environmental Politics: Domination, Accumulation, Resistance*, New York: St Martin's Press.

Payne, R.A. (2000), 'Habermas, Discourse, Norms, and the Prospect for Global Deliberation: Paper Prepared for Panel on Transparency and International Politics', Paper presented at the International Studies Association, Los Angeles, CA, 15–18 March.

Payne, R.A. (2001), 'Persuasion, Frames and Norm Construction', *European Journal of International Relations*, **7** (1): 37–61.

Percy, Sarah V. (2007), 'Mercenaries: Strong Norm, Weak Law', *International Organization*, **61**: 367–97.

Peterson, M.J. (1992), 'Whalers, Cetologists, Environmentalists, and the International Management of Whaling', in *Knowledge, Power, and International Policy Co-ordination*, ed. Peter M. Haas, Columbia, SC: University of South Carolina Press, pp. 147–86.

Phillips, Cassandra (1996), 'Conservation in Practice: Agreements, Regulations, Sanctuaries and Action Plans', in *The Conservation of Whales and Dolphins*, ed. Mark P. Simmonds and Judith D. Hutchinson, Chichester: John Wiley & Sons, pp. 447–65.

Pineschi, Laura (1996), 'The Madrid Protocol on the Protection of the Antarctic Environment and its Effectiveness', in *International Law for Antarctica*, ed. Francesco Francioni and Tullio Scovazzi, London: Kluwer Law International, pp. 261–92.

Plumwood, Val (1990), *Feminism and the Mastery of Nature*, London: Routledge.

Poore, Duncan (2003), *Changing Landscapes: The Development of the International Tropical Timber Organization and its Influence on Tropical Forest Management*, London and Sterling, VA: Earthscan Publications.

Poore, Duncan, and Thang Hooi Chiew (2000), 'Review of Progress Towards the Year 2000 Objective', International Tropical Timber Council.

Poore, Duncan, Peter Burgess, John Palmer, Simon Rietbergen and Timothy Synnott (1989), *No Timber without Trees: Sustainability in the Tropical Forest*, London: Earthscan Publication Ltd.

Porter, Gareth, and Janet Welsh Brown (1991), *Global Environmental Politics*. Boulder, CO: Westview Press.

Porter, Gareth and Janet Welsh Brown (1996), *Global Environmental Politics*, 2nd edition, Boulder, CO: Westview Press.

Porter, Gareth, Janet Welsh Brown and Pamela S. Chasek (2000), *Global*

*Environmental Politics*, 3rd edition, Dilemmas in World Politics, Boulder, CO: Westview Press.

Price, R. (1997), 'Moral Norms in World Politics', *Pacifica Review*, **9** (1): 45–72.

Price, R. (1998), 'Reversing the Gun Sights: Transnational Civil Society Targets Land Mines', *International Organization*, **52** (3): 613–44.

Price, R. (2008), 'Moral Limit and Possibility in World Politics', *International Organization*, **62**: 191–220.

Price, R., and Christian Reus-Smit (1998), 'Dangerous Liaisons? Critical International Theory and Constructivism', *European Journal of International Relations*, **4** (3): 259–94.

Puchala, D., and R. Hopkins (1983), 'International Regimes: Lessons from Inductive Analysis', in *International Regimes*, ed. Stephen D. Krasner, Ithaca, NY: Cornell University Press, pp. 61–91.

Putnam, Robert D. (1988), 'Diplomacy and Domestic Politics: The Logic of Two-level Games', *International Organization*, **42** (3), Summer: 427–60.

Rainforest Action Network (2005), 'Money in the Rainforest', http://www.ran.org/info_center/factsheets/04b.html, 28 February.

Raymond, Eric (2002), 'Road Development in Northwestern Brazil: Economic Integration against Ethnic and Ecological Degradation', *International Affairs Review*, **11** (1): 88–99.

Redfield, Edmund (1996), 'North Queensland's Tropical Rainforests: The World Heritage Controversy', in *Sustainable Forestry Challenges for Developing Countries*, ed. Matti Palo and Gerardo Mery, Boston, MA: Kluwer Academic Publishers, pp. 77–92.

Reeves, Randall R. (2002), 'The Origins and Character of "Aboriginal Subsistence" Whaling: A Global Review', *Mammal Review*, **32**: 71–106.

Reus-Smit, Christian (2001), 'Constructivism', in *Theories of International Relations*, 2nd edition, ed. S. Burchill, R. Devetak, A. Linklater, Matthew Paterson, Christian Reus-Smit and J. True, New York: Palgrave, pp. 209–30.

Reus-Smit, Christian (2002), 'Imagining Society: Constructivism and the English School', *British Journal of Politics and International Relations*, **4** (3): 487–509.

Reus-Smit, Christian (2004), 'The Politics of International Law', in *The Politics of International Law*, ed. Christian Reus-Smit, Cambridge: Cambridge University Press, pp. 14–44.

Rigg, Kelly (1990), 'Environmentalists' Perspectives on the Protection of Antarctica', in *The Future of Antarctica: Exploitation Versus Preservation*, ed. Grahame Cook, Manchester: Manchester University Press, pp. 68–80.

Rinaldi, Carlos (1991), 'Scar in the ATS: Conflict or Harmony?', in *The Antarctic Treaty System in World Politics*, ed. Arnfinn Jorgensen-Dahl and Willy Ostreng, New York: St Martin's Press, pp. 153–60.

Risse, Thomas (2000), '"Lets Argue!": Communicative Action in World Politics', *International Organization*, **54** (1): 1–39.

Risse, Thomas, and Kathryn Sikkink (1999), 'The Socialization of International Human Rights Norms into Domestic Practices: Introduction', in *The Power of Human Rights: International Norms and Domestic Change*, ed. T. Risse, S.C. Ropp and K. Sikkink, Cambridge: Cambridge University Press, pp. 1–38.

Risse, Thomas, and Cornelia Ulbert (2005), 'Deliberately Changing the Discourse: What Does Make Arguing Effective?', *Acta Politica* **40** (3): 351–67.

Risse, Thomas, Stephen Ropp, and Kathryn Sikkink (eds) (1999), *The Power of Human Rights: International Norms and Domestic Change*, Cambridge: Cambridge University Press.

Roberts, J. Timmons, Bradley C. Parks, and Alexis A. Vasquez (2004), 'Who Ratifies Environmental Treaties and Why? Institutionalism, Structuralism and Participation by 192 Nations in 22 Treaties', *Global Environmental Politics*, **4** (3): 22–64.

Rosamond, Ben (2001), 'Constructing Globalization', in *Constructing International Relations: The Next Generation*, ed. Karin M. Fierke and Knud Erik Jorgensen, London: M.E. Sharpe, pp. 201–22.

Rose, Gregory (1996), 'International Law and the Status of Cetaceans', in *The Conservation of Whales and Dolphins*, ed. Mark P. Simmonds and Judith D. Hutchinson, Chichester: John Wiley & Sons, pp. 23–53.

Rose, Gregory, and George Paleokrassis (1996), 'Compliance with International Environmental Obligations: A Casestudy of the International Whaling Commission', in *Improving Compliance with International Environmental Law*, ed. James Cameron, Jacob Werksman and Peter Roderick, London: Earthscan Publications Ltd, pp. 147–74.

Rothwell, Donald R. (1996), *The Polar Regions and the Development of International Law*, Cambridge Studies in International and Comparative Law 3, Cambridge: Cambridge University Press.

Rowland, J.R. (1988), 'The Treaty Regime and the Politics of the Consultative Parties', in *The Antarctic Legal Regime*, ed. Christopher C. Joyner and Sudhir K. Chopra, Dordrecht: Martinus Nijhoff Publishers, pp. 11–32.

Rowlands, Ian H. (1995), *The Politics of Global Atmospheric Change: Issues in Environmental Politics*, Manchester: Manchester University Press.

Rowlands, Ian H. (2001), 'Classical Theories of International Relations', in *International Relations and Global Climate Change*, ed. U. Luterbacher and D.F. Sprinz, Cambridge, MA: MIT Press, pp. 43–66.

Ruffle, Adrienne M. (2002), 'Resurrecting the International Whaling Commission: Suggestions to Strengthen the Conservation Effort', *Brooklyn Journal of International Law*, **27**: 639.

Ruggie, John Gerard (1998), *Constructing the World Polity: Essays on International Institutionalization, The New International Relations*, London and New York: Routledge.

Rush, James (1991), *The Last Tree: Reclaiming the Environment in Tropical Asia*, Oxford: Westview Press.

Sahurie, Emilio J. (1992), *The International Law of Antarctica*, The New Haven Studies in International Law and World Public Order, New Haven, CN: New Haven Press.

Sands, P.J. (1991), 'The Role of Non-governmental Organizations in Enforcing International Law', in *Control over Compliance with International Law*, ed. W.E. Butler, Norwell, MA: Kluwer Academic Publishing, pp. 61–7.

Schecter, M.G. (1998), *Historical Dictionary of International Organizations*, London: The Scarecrow Press Inc.

Sciso, Elena (1992), 'Are Mineral Resource Activities Still Compatible with the Protection of the Antarctic Environment', in *International Environmental Law for Antarctica*, ed. Francesco Francioni, Milan: Giuffre Editore, pp. 259–80.

Scott, Shirley V. (2008), 'Intergovernmental Organizations as Disseminators, Legitimators, and Disguisers of Hegemonic Policy Preferences: The United States, the International Whaling Commission, and the Introduction of a Moratorium on Commercial Whaling', *Leiden Journal of International Law*, **21**: 581–600.

Sebenius, J.K. (1992), 'Challenging Conventional Explanations of International Cooperation: Negotiation Analysis and the Case of Epistemic Communities', *International Organization*, **46** (1): 323–65.

Secrett, Charles (1986), 'International Timber Trade Organises . . . And So Do NGOs', *Friends of the Earth Newsletter*.

Secrett, Charles (1987), 'How European Transnational Corporations and Government Control and Exploit 3rd World Resources', in *Forest Resource Crisis in the Third World*, Penang: Sahabat Alam Malaysia, pp. 233–49.

Sessions, George (1992), 'Ecocentrism, Wilderness, and Global Ecosystem Protection', in *The Wilderness Condition: Essays on Environment and Civilization*, ed. Max Oelschlager, San Francisco: Island Press, pp. 90–130.

Shapley, Deborah (1985), *The Seventh Continent: Antarctica in a Resource Age*, Washington, DC: Johns Hopkins University Press.

Shue, H. (1995), 'Ethics, the Environment and the Changing International Order', *International Affairs*, **71** (3): 453–61.

Skodvin, Tora, and Steinar Andresen (2003), 'Nonstate Influence in the International Whaling Commission, 1970–1990', *Global Environmental Politics*, **3** (4): 61–86.

Skodvin, Tora, and Steinar Andresen (2006), 'Leadership Revisited', *Global Environmental Politics*, **6** (3): 13–27.

Smith, Mark J. (1998), *Ecologism: Towards Ecological Citizenship*, Concepts in the Social Sciences, Buckingham: Open University Press.

Smouts, Marie-Claude (2003), *Tropical Forests, International Jungle: The Underside of Global Ecopolitics*, New York: Palgrave Macmillan.

Snidal, Duncan (2002), 'Rational Choice and International Relations', in *Handbook of International Relations*, ed. Walter Carlsnaes, Thomas Risse and Beth Simmons, New York: Sage, pp. 73–94.

Stein, Arthur A. (1990), *Why Nations Cooperate: Circumstance and Choice in International Relations*, Ithaca, NY: Cornell University Press.

Stoett, Peter John (1997), *The International Politics of Whaling*, Vancouver, BC: UBC Press.

Stoett, Peter John (2005), 'Of Whales and People: Normative Theory, Symbolism, and the IWC', *Journal of International Wildlife Law and Policy*, **8** (2): 151–75.

Stokke, Olav Schram (1991), 'The Relevance of the Antarctic Treaty System as a Model for International Cooperation', in *The Antarctic Treaty System in World Politics*, ed. Arnfinn Jorgensen-Dahl and Willy Ostreng, New York: St Martin's Press, pp. 357–71.

Stroud, Chris (1996), 'The Ethics and Politics of Whaling', in *The Conservation of Whales and Dolphins*, ed. Mark P. Simmonds and Judith D. Hutchinson, Chichester: John Wiley & Sons, pp. 55–87.

Sucharitikul, S. (1996), 'State Responsibility and International Liability under International Law', *Loyola of Los Angeles International and Comparative Law Journal*, **18** (3): 821–39.

Susskind, Lawrence (1994), *Environmental Diplomacy: Negotiating More Effective Global Agreements*, New York: Oxford University Press.

Suter, Keith D. (1980), *World Law and the Last Wilderness*, Sydney: Friends of the Earth.

Suter, Keith D. (1991), *Antarctica: Private Property or Public Heritage?*, Leichhardt, NSW: Pluto Press Australia.

Switzer, Jacqueline Vaughn (2004), *Environmental Politics: Domestic and Global Dimensions*, 4th edition, Belmont, CA: Thomson/Wadsworth.

Talbot, L.M. (1990), 'A Proposal for the World Bank's Policy and Strategy for Tropical Forests in Africa', Washington, DC: World Bank, Africa Environment and Natural Resource Management (AFTEN).

Tan, See Seeng (2006), 'Rescuing Constructivism from the Constructivists: A Critical Reading of Constructivist Interventions in Southeast Asian Security', *The Pacific Review*, **19** (2): 239–60.

Tarlock, A. Dan (1997), 'Exclusive Sovereignty Versus Sustainable Development of a Shared Resource: The Dilemma of Latin American

Rainforest Management', *Texas International Law Journal*, **32** (17): 37–66.

Taylor, Paul W. (1989), *Respect for Nature: A Theory of Environmental Ethics*, Princeton, NJ: Princeton University Press.

Thomas, Caroline (1992), *The Environment in International Relations*, London: Royal Institute of International Affairs.

Thompson, Herb (2003), 'The Ecological-Economics of Non-sustainable Development: Logging Tropical Forests in Southeast Asia and the Pacific', in *The Political Ecology of Tropical Forests in Southeast Asia: Historical Perpectives*, ed. Lye Tuck-Po, Wil de Jong and Abe Ken-ichi, Kyoto: Kyoto University Press, pp. 200–235.

United Nations Environment Programme (1990), 'Environmental Data Report', New York: Oxford University Press.

United Nations General Assembly (1962), Permanent Sovereignty over Natural Resources Resolution 1803 (XVII) of 14 December.

United Nations General Assembly (1989), Question of Antarctica (Agenda Item 70), Forty-fourth Session, A/C.1/44/L.69, 20 November.

US Senate Sub-committee on Oceans and International Environment (1975), 'U.S. Policy with Respect to Mineral Exploration and Exploitation in the Antarctic', ed. US Senate Sub-committee on Oceans and International Environment of the Senate Committee on Foreign Relations: Congressional Record of Hearing, 94th Congress, 1st Session, 15th May.

US State Department (2002), 'U.S. State Department Handbook of the Antarctic Treaty System 2002', Washington, DC: US State Department.

Utting, Peter (1993), *Trees, People and Power: Social Dimensions of Deforestation and Forest Protection in Central America*, London: Earthscan Publications Ltds.

van der Essen, Alfred (1996), 'The Origin of the Antarctic System', in *International Law for Antarctica*, ed. Francesco Francioni and Tullio Scovazzi, London: Kluwer Law International, pp. 17–30.

VanderZwaag, David, and Douglas MacKinlay (1996), 'Towards a Global Forest Convention: Getting out of the Woods and Barking up the Right Tree', in *Global Forests and International Environmental Law*, ed. Canadian Council of International Law, London: Kluwer Law International, pp. 1–41.

Victor, David G. (2000), 'Whale Sausage: Why the Whaling Regime Does Not Need to Be Fixed', in *Toward a Sustainable Whaling Regime*, ed. Robert L. Friedheim, Seattle: University of Washington Press, pp. 292–310.

Vicuna, Francisco Orrego (1983), 'The Definition of a Regime on Antarctic Mineral Resourcs: Basic Options', in *Antarctic Resources Policy: Scientific, Legal and Political Issues*, ed. Francisco Orrego Vicuna, Cambridge: Cambridge University Press, pp. 199–215.

Vidas, Davor (2000), 'Entry into Force of the Environmental Protocol and

Implementation Issues: An Overview', in *Implementing the Environmental Protection Regime for the Antarctic*, ed. Davor Vidas, Boston, MA: Kluwer Academic Publishers, pp. 1–20.

Vogler, John (2000), *The Global Commons: Environmental and Technological Governance*, 2nd edition, Chichester: John Wiley.

Vogler, John (2003), 'Taking Institutions Seriously: How Regime Analysis Can Be Relevant to Multilateral Environmental Governance', *Global Environmental Politics*, **3** (2): 25–39.

Wapner, Paul Kevin (1995), 'Politics Beyond the State: Environmental Activism and World Civic Politics', *World Politics*, **47** (3) (April): 311–40.

Wapner, Paul Kevin (1996), *Environmental Activism and World Civic Politics*, Albany, NY: State University of New York Press.

Wapner, Paul Kevin (2000), 'The Normative Promise of Nonstate Actors: A Theoretical Account of Global Civil Society', in *Principled World Politics: The Challenge of Normative International Relations*, ed. Paul Kevin Wapner and Lester Edwin J. Ruiz, Oxford: Rowman & Littlefield Publishers Inc., pp. 261–74.

Wapner, Paul Kevin (2002), 'Horizontal Politics: Transnational Environmental Activism and Global Cultural Change', *Global Environmental Politics*, **2** (2): 37–62.

Weber, Cynthia (2001), *International Relations Theory: A Critical Introduction*, London: Routledge.

Wendt, Alexander (1987), 'The Agent–Structure Problem in International Relations Theory', *International Organization*, **41** (3): 335–70.

Wendt, Alexander (1992), 'Anarchy Is What States Make of It: The Social Construction of Power Politics', *International Organization*, **46** (2): 391–425.

Wendt, Alexander (1995), 'Constructing International Politics', *International Security*, **20** (1): 71–81.

Wendt, Alexander (1999), *Social Theory of International Politics*, Cambridge: Cambridge University Press.

Wertheimer, Alan (1996), *Exploitation*, Princeton, NJ: Princeton University Press.

Weyler, Rex (2004) *Greenpeace: An Insider's Account: How a Group of Journalists, Ecologists and Visionaries Changed the World*, London: Rodale.

Wiener, Antje (2003), 'Constructivism: The Limits of Bridging Gaps', *Journal of International Relations and Development*, **6** (3): 252–75.

Willan, Robert, David Macdonald and David Drewry (1990), 'The Mineral Resource Potential of Antarctica: Geological Realities', in *The Future of Antarctica: Exploitation Versus Preservation*, ed. Grahame Cook, Manchester: Manchester University Press, pp. 25–43.

Wood, Peter (2005), 'Soft Law, Hard Law and the Development of an International Forest Convention', http://peterwood.ca/docs/Wood2004_ForestConvention.pdf, 12 May.

World Council of Whalers (2005), 'WCW Profile', http://www.worldcouncilofwhalers.com/wcwprofile/history.htm, 23 December.

World Rainforest Movement (1990), *Rainforest Destruction: Causes, Effects and False Solutions*, Penang: World Rainforest Movement.

World Rainforest Movement and Forests Monitor (2005), 'High Stakes: The Need to Control Transnational Logging Companies: A Malaysian Case Study – Part 2b: Politics, Law and the Logging Industry', http://www.forestsmonitor.org/reports/highstakes/part2b.htm, 24 May.

World Wildlife Fund (1987), 'International Forest Conservation and the International Tropical Timber Agreement: WWF Position Paper 2', Gland, Switzerland: WWF International.

Young, Oran R. (1992), 'The Effectiveness of International Institutions: Hard Cases and Critical Variables', in *Governance without Governance: Change and Order in World Politics*, ed. J.N. Rosenau and E. Czempiel, New York: Cambridge University Press, pp. 160–94.

Young, Oran R. (1997), 'Fairness Matters: The Role of Equity in International Regimes', Paper presented at Environmental Justice: Global Ethics for the 21st Century, University of Melbourne, 1–3 October.

Young, Oran R. (1999), 'Hitting the Mark: Why Are Some International Environmental Agreements More Successful than Others?', *Environment*, **41** (8): 20–29.

Young, Oran R., and George J. Demko (1996), 'Improving the Effectiveness of International Environmental Governance Systems', in *Global Environmental Change and International Governance*, ed. Oran R. Young, George J. Demko and Kilaparti Ramakrishna, Hanover, NH: University Press of New England, pp. 229–47.

Young, Oran R. and Gail Osherenko (1993), *Polar Politics: Creating International Environmental Regimes*, Cornell Studies in Political Economy, Ithaca, NY: Cornell University Press.

Zacharias, Mark A., Leah R. Gerber and K. David Hyrenbach (2006), 'Review of the Southern Ocean Sanctuary: Marine Protected Areas in the Context of the International Whaling Commission Sanctuary Programme', *Journal of Cetacean Resource Management*, **8** (1): 1–12.

Zartman, William, I. (1997), 'Negotiation, Governance, and Regime Building', in *International Governance on Environmental Issues*, ed. Mats Rolen, Helen Sjoberg and Uno Svedin, Dordrecht: Kluwer Academic Publishers, pp. 57–68.

Zehfuss, Maja (2001), 'Constructivisms in International Relations: Wendt, Onuf, and Kratochwil', in *Constructing International Relations: The Next*

*Generation*, ed. Karin M. Fierke and Knud Erik Jorgensen, London: M.E. Sharpe, pp. 54–75.

Zehfuss, Maja (2002), *Constructivism in International Relations: The Politics of Reality*, Cambridge: Cambridge University Press.

Zelko, Frank (2004), '"Make It a Green Peace": The History of an International Environmental Organization', *GHI Bulletin*, **34** (Spring): 127–35.

Zurn, Michael, and Jeffrey T. Checkel (2005), 'Getting Socialized to Build Bridges: Constructivism and Rationalism, Europe and the Nation State', *International Organization*, **59**: 1045–79.

# Index